Due Diligence

Roodman pulls off the feat of examining microfinance from many angles without losing focus. The result is the most thoughtful book about the industry yet published—and consequently one of the most thought-provoking.

    STUART RUTHERFORD, *author of* The Poor and Their Money

This is a splendid book. It's original and very smart. It's an engaging read. Best of all, it displays a high order of intellectual honesty. None of this is any surprise to those of us who have followed Roodman's microfinance blog, which is the only one I never delete before reading.

    RICHARD ROSENBERG, *CGAP*

David Roodman does the kind of analysis the research world needs more of by bringing together quantitative studies, qualitative studies, and historical context into a rich, holistic, hype-free picture. It's not just the most thorough and balanced assessment of microfinance we've seen—it's a case study in how to do thorough and balanced assessment.

    HOLDEN KARNOFSKY and ELIE HASSENFELD, *founders, GiveWell*

Roodman's book astonished me. It is well researched, very well written, and perceptive. It could aid the microfinance industry in a shift from helping poor people cope with poverty to helping them move out of poverty.

    DEEPA NARAYAN, *Director of the World Bank's* Voices of the Poor *and* Moving Out of Poverty *series and former Senior Adviser on Poverty Reduction*

Microcredit perhaps never deserved the uncritical kudos it received between 1997 and 2006. Nor does it deserve the vilification since. David Roodman's voice is important and without prejudice. He comes up with several insights which will be useful for re-jigging the field.

    VIJAY MAHAJAN, *Chairman, BASIX, and chair of the executive committee, CGAP*

Due Diligence is a balanced, respectful, diagnostic effort to make microfinance a more powerful tool for social progress. For microfinance activists, Roodman has written a page turner. It is obligatory reading if you want to call yourself a microfinance leader.

    JONATHAN LEWIS, *founder and chair, MicroCredit Enterprises*

Due Diligence

An impertinent inquiry into microfinance

David Roodman

CENTER FOR GLOBAL DEVELOPMENT
Washington, D.C.

Library of Congress Cataloging-in-Publication data

Roodman, David Malin.
  Due diligence : an impertinent inquiry into microfinance / David Roodman.
    p. cm.
  Includes bibliographical references and index.
  ISBN 978-1-933286-48-8
  1. Microfinance—Evaluation. I. Title.

  HG178.3.R66 2011
  332—dc23   2011040139

2 3 4 5 6 7 8 9

Printed on acid-free paper

Typeset in Minion and Optima

Composition by Cynthia Stock
Silver Spring, Maryland

Printed by R. R. Donnelley
Harrisonburg, Virginia

Contents

Preface

Many big new ideas in global development elicit barely a ripple of interest beyond the community of practitioners, policy analysts, and researchers who are development professionals. Microfinance is different: it has burst beyond these confines, capturing the imagination of people from a huge variety of backgrounds, including many in the rich world who have little or no exposure to developing countries or other aspects of the development policy debate.

Since its inception in small experiments three decades ago—the Grameen Project in Bangladesh in the late 1970s, Acción International's trials in the Dominican Republic in the early 1980s—the business of providing formal financial services to poor people has blossomed into a global movement, and a global industry. It began with micro*credit*. But in time the word micro*finance* was coined to convey that other financial services, such as savings and insurance, could also be delivered economically and in bulk to the poor. In this respect, the success of the microfinance movement is indisputable and goes far beyond the estimated 150 million people, primarily in developing countries, who use it.

But in other respects, the success of microfinance is being questioned. Microfinance has succeeded as a movement by developing a reputation for stimulating microenterprise, empowering women, and lifting families out of poverty. Determining whether it is living up to that reputation is much harder than most people realize. In the last few years, high-quality randomized trials have begun to fill in the blanks, supporting some of the claims and challenging others. Meanwhile, the microfinance movement has been thrown on its heels by credit bubbles, government crackdowns, and a rising chorus of critics.

Into this controversy David Roodman has ventured with an analytical style that is at once open minded, as he hears out the arguments of the proponents and opponents, and intensely demanding of evidence and sound reasoning. This book provides a thorough review of microfinance: its history, its business logic, its impacts and prospects. And by assessing microfinance against three conceptions of development—that is, by asking what we mean when we question whether microfinance "works"—Roodman ends up providing a new way of evaluating a large class of development interventions. On this score, his work has implications well beyond the provision of small-scale financial services to the poor.

Roodman concludes that microfinance does not live up to its popular image. At the same time, though, 150 million people cannot all be wrong; financial services, like clean water, sanitation, and electricity, are essential components of the prosperous life. Though unlikely to end poverty, microfinance provides those services to the poor and it can be considered a success in the aid community. In what other sector has public and private aid helped build such businesses and business-like nonprofits at the bottom of the pyramid, which grow by meeting the market test every day? The principal challenge going forward is to help microfinance play to its strengths in delivering useful services in bulk while guarding against the dangers of ample credit.

This book is an invaluable contribution to understanding what may be the most celebrated development idea of our time. It is trailblazing too in the way it was written: Roodman authored the book in public, through an "open book blog," seeking feedback on drafts and questions from an international readership. I am aware of no other fusion of old and new media quite like this one. Read on to see the results.

NANCY BIRDSALL
President
Center for Global Development

Acknowledgments

The story behind this book begins just shy of ten years ago, when I spoke with Nancy Birdsall about what topics to tackle in my new job at the Center for Global Development, which she had just cofounded. Among other things, I mentioned microenterprise and microfinance. At the mention of the latter, her eyes lit up—for two reasons, I later learned. The first was her sense, while attending the historic 1997 Microcredit Summit, that rhetoric had galloped ahead of evidence; the second was the recent *Wall Street Journal* exposé by Michael Phillips and the late Daniel Pearl of repayment difficulties at the Grameen Bank. It was then that I decided to write a monograph on microfinance in the thoroughgoing, pedagogic mode of my last book, *The Natural Wealth of Nations*, written while I was at the Worldwatch Institute. But now that I had PhDs for colleagues—trained researchers with years of experience in economic development—I doubted the value of what I might do.

And yet, after some delays and distractions, I completed the book. Along the way, I gained confidence in what I had to offer, thanks in no small part to the *Microfinance Open Book Blog* CGD launched to share my writing process with the public. The journey has been important to me in several ways, helping me grow intellectually and build a sense of identity in my professional life. None of this would have been possible without Nancy's faith and support, her blend of understanding patience and constructive impatience. I will always be indebted to her. I also thank everyone who commented on the blog—my guess is they number in the hundreds—for engaging me in precisely the sort of debate that I sought and for keeping me honest. I thank Scott Gaul and Daniel Rozas, who actually reviewed posted chapter drafts. All the commenters gave me something precious for an author: a sense of audience.

Inevitably in such an expansive project, I crossed paths with many people, almost invariably to my benefit. In 2006 Uzma Qureshi joined me in authoring *Microfinance as Business*, a CGD report commissioned by Suellen Lazarus of ABN AMRO bank. That became the basis for chapter 5 of the present volume. Later, Suellen's son, Eben Lazarus, became an intern at CGD and would hand me reviews of that and the earlier chapters that showed remarkable maturity for a nineteen-year-old. My friend Anna Rain edited the early chapters with inspired rigor. At the end of the process, Deepa Narayan, Greg Chen, Stuart Rutherford, Elisabeth Rhyne, Jonathan Morduch, and Richard Rosenberg—all of whom I hold in great respect—patiently reviewed the full manuscript. They gave me the guidance I needed to bring it to maturity. Research assistant Julie Walz undertook the same labor, giving me an excellent reality check on how well the book worked (or didn't work) for lay readers. Her successor, Julia Clark, reviewed the typeset manuscript with a sharp eye. Paolo Abarcar worked diligently on the research for chapter 9.

Behind the scenes at CGD, publications manager John Osterman shepherded the complex book production process to completion. Lawrence MacDonald, vice president of communications and policy outreach, oversaw and advised on all aspects of the book and blog project as an exercise in communication. It was with him, under the essential tutelage of Dave Witzel, that I developed the concept of writing this book in the public eye, through the blog.

I am especially grateful to the MasterCard Foundation for supporting the completion and promotion of this book. To their contribution, as to all the others I have listed, the usual disclaimer applies: the views expressed in this volume are attributable to me alone. So I thank the foundation for what I will presume to call its wisdom in supporting this work, in the spirit of serious inquiry and constructive debate.

I am also grateful to the Consultative Group to Assist the Poor (CGAP) for its partnership with CGD and the MasterCard Foundation in promoting the ideas within this book. In particular, CGAP communications director Jeanette Thomas has done yeoman's labor fashioning this arrangement, carrying it through with hypercompetence.

As well, I thank a special proofreader, Jo Malin. Without her, the book would never had been written, for she is my mom. To Benjamin and Alexander, whose daddy has been working on microfinance for as long as they can remember: may you read this some day with an adult's eyes and understand me better. And to Mai: I love you.

Due Diligence

one

What's the Story?

To gauge the value of People's Banks at its fullest, one should go among the people whom they have benefited—the small tradesman, the peasant, the cottager, who has by their help purchased, rod by rod, a little holding which he surveys with pride. One should go, as I have done, stick in hand, walking from cottage to cottage, and hear these people describe the contrast between erewhile and now, and listen to them telling of their little troubles and embarrassments, and how the bank stepped in to relieve them. Many such a tale there is which could not fail to warm a philanthropist's heart.
—HENRY W. WOLFF, 1896[1]

People do not march on Washington because of pie charts.
—ANDY GOODMAN, 2006[2]

Most accounts of microfinance—the large-scale, businesslike provision of financial services to poor people—begin with a story. So I think it is fitting to start my inquiry into microfinance with two, about the most well-known kind of microfinance, microcredit, in which loans of $50–$1,000 are given to people typically earning no more than $2 per day. Both stories, I assume, are true. The first story is told by Muhammad Yunus, who won the Nobel Peace Prize along with the Grameen Bank he founded:

> Murshida was born into a poor family of eight children. Neither her father nor grandfather owned any farmland. At fifteen she was married to a man from a nearby village who worked as an unskilled laborer in a factory. The first few years of the marriage went relatively well, but things turned sour when Murshida began having children. Just as their family expenses went up, her husband started bringing home less and less money. Finally it became clear that he was a compulsive

1. Wolff (1896), 12.
2. Goodman (2006).

1

gambler. During the 1974 famine, he was given a company bonus of 1,800 taka. He lost it all gambling. When Murshida complained, her husband beat her. . . .

One day Murshida's husband came home after a week's absence and complained that there was not enough food for him. Murshida had cooked up something modest and had not eaten the entire day. Angry, her husband beat her and then left, saying he would return later in the morning. That day there was a thunderstorm, and as her husband had sold the roof of their house to pay gambling debts, Murshida and her three children were soaked. At that moment Murshida decided that something had to change. When her husband returned at midnight, Murshida confronted him.

"You have only brought a small quantity of flattened rice for your daughter," she remembers saying, "but nothing for me. Yet everyone in the village says you earn a lot of money." Her husband flew into a rage and beat her. Then he divorced her on the spot and told her to leave the house.

"What about the children?" Murshida asked.

"You can throw them into the river and let them drown, for all I care," he responded.

Murshida sent word to her brother, who offered to take her into his home. Once she had moved in, Murshida found some more work spinning on contract. She heard about the Grameen Bank when it came to her village. Initially, the village leaders opposed Grameen and tried to prevent it from opening centers. One Grameen worker discouraged Murshida from joining, thinking she would move back to her husband's village. But Murshida stopped another bank worker on the village path and begged him to give her money. "I told him I would swim across a river to attend Grameen Bank meetings if necessary. I told him that I wanted to follow him to wherever he was going to form a group, so I could join. I told him that he must give me money, otherwise I would not be able to survive with my children. He said I could not form a group right then, but that he would come to my home and form a group in a few days. And he really came!"

At first Murshida borrowed 1,000 taka [about $30] to purchase a goat and she paid off the loan in six months with the profits from selling the milk. She was left with a goat, a kid, and no debt. Encouraged, she borrowed 2,000 taka, bought raw cotton and a spinning wheel, and began manufacturing lady's scarves. She now sells her scarves wholesale for 100 taka with tassels and 50 taka without. Murshida's business has grown so much that during peak periods she employs as many as twenty-five women in her village to manufacture scarves. In addition, she has bought an acre of farmland with her profits, built a house with a Grameen Bank housing loan, and set up her brothers in businesses that include sari trading and raw cotton trading. Murshida has also emerged as a leader in her [borrowing group]. She was elected center chief several times.[3]

The second story comes from a documentary by Tom Heinemann called *The Micro Debt*:

Narrator: We . . . return to a little village in the northern part of Bangladesh. Here we met Razia and her daughter. Razia also has loans with Grameen Bank. She wanted to give her daughter an education.

Razia [in English subtitles]: I had cows, I had jewelry and I had the house. I sold everything to pay the debt off.

Heinemann: So you just told me that you had to sell your house. Can you show me your house?

Razia: Yes, I can.

Heinemann: Okay, let's go. . . . So, Razia, for how long [a] time did you have that house you had to sell?

Razia: For 15 years.

Heinemann: You built it yourself, your family?

Razia: Yes, we did. We bought the land and built the house ourselves. [Now] I have nothing left to sell, except the kitchen pots.

Heinemann: If you think back, do you sometimes feel that you should never have taken the first loan?

Razia: Then I would never have had to sell my house. I built the house without taking any loans.

Heinemann: And now it has become a neverending story to you, and your family.

Razia: That's right. I can't get out of it. I've tried everything but it failed up to now. I had no money to pay the installments. So I decided to sell the house. These [microfinance] organizations never stop. They really pressed me. They come and stay until they get their money. They press us to sell our belongings. So I sold the house to pay the debt. [*The camera zooms in on the long, sad face of Razia's teenage daughter. A single tear descends her cheek. One senses years of burden.*]

3. Yunus (2004), 199–201.

I offer these stories to demonstrate the power and limitations of narrative as knowledge. The stories of Murshida and Razia are individually moving. It is easy to imagine that if you encountered either alone, you would accept the implied lesson of microcredit as savior or snare. You would mentally assemble a general story of how microcredit changes people's lives, made convincing by the concrete instance and parallels with your own experiences and aspirations. A stack of statistical studies would not leave as strong an imprint. More than almost any other approach to helping the world's poor people, microfinance has this power to generate stories that resonate with potential supporters. Pierre Omidyar, the founder of eBay, saw a metaphor for his own success in microfinance, with its market-oriented leveraging of social networks to substitute for collateral. He became one of microfinance's biggest supporters, giving his alma mater, Tufts University, $100 million to invest in the field.[4]

While the two stories are powerful individually, their juxtaposition creates cognitive dissonance. Murshida's ascent offers us hope, while Razia's descent plays to our cynicism. I set up the contradiction to force some critical questions. When do small loans entrap, and when do they free? Is Razia's story the exception that proves the rule, or is Murshida's? Presumably Yunus and his staff sifted Murshida's from the biographies of thousands of Grameen members. Likewise, Heinemann may have sought the worst cases: glory in journalism follows the scoop. Can either story be trusted as representative? Indeed, can any story (or statistic) be representative?

Each client's experience with microfinance is unique. We constantly seek generalizations because we can understand the world only by simplifying it. But unlike in physics, where laws are pristine, almost all generalizations in the social realm are partly false—and how much so is often hard to tell. The truth turns out to be an elusive thing.

Until a couple years ago, the microfinance industry got on pretty well with stories and opportunistic use of academic studies. People generally thought microfinance was a proven weapon against poverty. But the last two years have dealt the industry a series of blows that have left insiders and outsiders increasingly muddled. In mid-2009 respected academics released the first two high-quality, randomized studies of the impact of microcredit on poverty. Neither found an effect over the approximately eighteen-month study periods on poverty indicators, such as household spending and the number of children going to school.[5] Simultaneously, New York University's

4. Connie Bruck, "Millions for Millions," *New Yorker*, October 30, 2006.

5. Banerjee and others (2009); Karlan and Zinman (2009).

Jonathan Morduch and I reported the fatal flaws of what *had* been the leading (non-randomized) studies, with their conclusion that microcredit reduced poverty.[6]

Outside the ivory towers, microcredit industries crashed in Bosnia, Morocco, Nicaragua, and Pakistan in 2008 and 2009. The causes variously included fast growth, global recession, debtor revolts, and political backlash.[7] And 2010 brought worse. In January, Nigeria's young microfinance banking industry tipped into crisis as institutions began defaulting. In October, amid reports of suicides and subprime-like overlending, the government of the state of Andhra Pradesh, India's microfinance hotbed, ambushed private microcreditors with a restrictive law. Weeks later, Heinemann's controversial documentary gave Bangladesh's prime minister, Sheikh Hasina, an opening to rekindle a vendetta against Muhammad Yunus. She all but called him a bloodsucking moneylender.[8]

Early in 2011, Vijay Mahajan—one of the most thoughtful and effective human beings in microfinance, the man who led the way to commercialization of microfinance in India, and one of India's fifty most powerful people according to *BusinessWeek*—embarked on a singularly humble act.[9] He went on a *Shodh Yatra*, a sixty-day soul- and truth-searching journey across India, looking to reconnect with poor people and learn from them anew. On his first day, he blogged about his purpose—and the depths of his uncertainty:

> "Here I am in the middle way, Having had twenty years, Twenty years largely wasted . . . The years of l'entre deux guerres [between two wars]". TS Eliot's lines come to mind and it metamorphoses into "Here I am at the end of the way, Having had thirty years, Thirty years largely wasted . . . The years of les guerres de l'interne [internal wars]." . . .
>
> Thirty years . . . largely wasted? Who can tell? Just emerging raw from the microfinance crisis. A field which . . . received a Nobel Prize for one of its pioneers, Dr Mohammed Yunus and was widely praised till a year ago is now widely condemned—by people like Bangladesh PM Sheikh Hasina, and the former Reserve Bank of India Governor Dr YV Reddy. What is real? The earlier assessment or the current one? What is real is what the people say.

---

6. Roodman and Morduch (2009).

7. Chen, Rasmussen, and Reille (2010).

8. "Fund Transfer Allegation against Prof Yunus Needs Inquiry: PM," *Financial Express* (Bangladesh), December 6, 2010.

9. "India's 50 Most Powerful People 2009," *BusinessWeek*, April 15, 2009 (j.mp/hX3TnS).

That is why this Shodh Yatra. Unable to match Gandhi, one can at least mimic him. . . . I will walk while in a village or a town, stopping by every once in a while to have a dialogue; and drive between habitations."[10]

In the pages to come, I will share the fruits of my own search for a full, balanced understanding of the impacts of microfinance. I wrote this book in public—something rarely done before—by sharing drafts, questions, and discoveries through an "open book" blog.[11] Working this way I garnered feedback on drafts, helpful leads, a sharper sense of audience, and a more personal voice. This book records my intellectual journey.

Here is the destination I reach: Murshida's story is not the whole story of microfinance. But neither is every borrower a Razia. The success of microfinance is real, if subtler than generally understood. Its strength lies not in lifting people out of poverty—industrialization and jobs do that better. Nor does its strength necessarily lie in empowering women. It lies, rather, in *leveraging modest subsidies to build financial institutions and industries that give millions of poor families more control over their finances.* Maybe that truth disappoints relative to the myth. But the good that microfinance can do is respectable by the standards of foreign aid and philanthropy, in which failures are common and successes hard-won. And whether microfinance lives up to the expectations of those too rich to need it is less important than whether microfinance does reasonable good at reasonable cost. As British academics Pankaj Jain and Mick Moore once wrote, "To properly appreciate the great achievements of the microcredit movement, one has to be more skeptical of its self-image than is normally considered polite or respectful."[12]

If your daughter shows a flair for guitar, you don't force her to paint instead. Just so, my evaluation leads to a prescription: help microfinance play to its strengths. Instead of using it to put capital in the hands of as many poor people as possible on the hope of launching them all into entrepreneurship and out of poverty, focus on mass-producing services to help people manage the uncertainties of being poor. To the extent practical, deemphasize pure credit, which amplifies risk, in favor of savings and insurance, which can cushion in times of trouble. Deemphasize subsidized credit to the poorest

10. Vijay Mahajan, "Day 1–January 30, 2011 Sevagram, Wardha," *vijaymahajan* blog, January 30, 2011 (j.mp/hypA9M).

11. See *Microfinance Open Book Blog* (blogs.cgdev.org/open_book).

12. Jain and Moore (2003), 29.

because dependence on limited subsidies throttles growth, and common sense says that the poorest are the most vulnerable to the downside of debt. Instead, build permanent, dynamic, customer-oriented institutions that cover most or all of their budgets with fees and interest.

For microfinance insiders, I side with the philosophy of the American network group Acción International and the German ProCredit group, a holding company of microfinance banks; I question the Microcredit Summit Campaign in its push to get microcredit to 175 million of the world's very poorest people by 2015.[13] For potential funders of microfinance, ranging from my mother to the Gates Foundation, I advise against directly financing microcredit portfolios. (I'm happy to report that neither does.) Instead, donate to organizations that have track records in institutional midwifery using adaptive blends of advice, training, and investment.

Finally, I express hope that modern communications technologies, such as mobile phones and card readers, will link poor people to the formal financial system in radically different ways, reducing the need for group microcredit.

Now that I have completed the journey, heard from blog commenters and peer reviewers along the way, and returned to edit this opening chapter, I realize I have something more to offer: a conviction that my journey is a destination, too. There is a lesson beyond *what* I learned, about *how* I learned. It is in the nature of modern society that talented people specialize. As a result, the global microfinance conversation is carried on by a wealth of experts, each approaching the subject from a narrow angle. But if you want to understand something as variegated as microfinance, you can't just think about it one way. You can't only listen to the economists running randomized trials, the anthropologists living in the villages, or the Wall Street financiers syndicating loans—though all have insight to share. You must be open-minded and patient enough to break down the walls between world views. Like Mahajan on his journey, you must visit many villages and listen to many voices.

In particular, I tweak a hot and good trend in development economics: conducting randomized experiments to find "what works." Leaders of this movement, such as Dean Karlan at Yale University and Massachusetts Institute of Technology's Abhijit Banerjee and Esther Duflo, have just popularized the trend with books enticingly subtitled: *How a New Economics Is Helping to Solve Global Poverty* and *A Radical Rethinking of the Way to Fight*

---

13. Reed (2011), 3. Nancy Birdsall, the president of the Center for Global Development, where I work, is a volunteer board member of Acción.

Global Poverty.[14] But as with microfinance in its reputational heyday, now that experimentation is ascendant, the public may overestimate its power. Consider: would a randomized study of the impact of mortgages on borrowing households in the United States in 2005–07 have told you everything you need to know about the mortgage industry's contributions to human welfare and national progress? No. For that, one also should study the dynamics of the industry that makes the loans and the households that take them. This book does that for microfinance.

I divided this final, frozen text into two main parts. The first part, chapters 2–5, approaches our subject obliquely, asking not what microfinance can do for the world, but how the world has shaped microfinance. I hope this sustained indirection does not try your patience. I think that before we impose upon microfinance the outsider's question, "What good does it do?" we ought to take it on its own terms. To start, chapter 2 talks about the financial challenges faced by the poor people whose patronage has allowed microfinance to thrive. In particular, it emphasizes that people who live on, say, $2 a day, *don't* live on $2 a day, but rather on $4 one day, $1 the day after, $0 the day after that. Their incomes are not just low but volatile. They suffer more often from injury and illness yet depend more on their physical vigor for their livelihoods. As a result, the global poor need financial services—ways to put aside money in good days and seasons and draw it down in bad—*more* than the global rich, a group I take to include the salaried classes of rich countries.[15]

Chapter 3 traces the history of what I call financial services for the masses, starting in ancient Athens. The rationales put forward for these services have varied over the centuries; constant are the evident demand for the services and the search for institutional forms to deliver them in bulk. Chapter 4 brings the history up to date and surveys the diversity of microfinance today. Chapter 5 takes an evolutionary perspective, asserting that the dominant characteristics of modern microfinance, such as the emphases on credit, women, and groups, dominate mainly because they confer survival advantage on microfinance institutions. They solve the tough business problem of mass-producing financial services for the poor without losing one's shirt. On the one hand, this thesis undercuts the assumption that microfinance is the way it is because that is what is best for the poor; on the other, it shows that it is much easier to propose alternative approaches, such as microsavings and mobile phone–based banking, than to execute them.

14. Karlan and Appel (2011); Banerjee and Duflo (2011).

15. Collins and others (2009).

Chapters 6–8, the heart of this book, directly confront the question of impact. Their structure came to me in 2008 during a tour in northern Bangladesh of credit groups run by BRAC, the largest nonprofit in the developing world. At the time, I was engrossed in the complex mathematics and computer programming that would help upend what were then the most influential studies claiming that microcredit reduces poverty. In Rangpur District, as in Cairo two months before (see chapter 6), I imagined the absurdity of pointing to the grids of numbers on my laptop screen and telling the women in the groups that taking microcredit *might not be such a good idea after all.* That forced me into a paradox. I believed in the importance of rigorous evaluation of microfinance and other programs. Yet the women knew their business better than I did. What, then, was the value of scientific studies of microfinance? Pondering all that I had read, I realized that several notions of success were at play in the grand global conversation about microfinance.[16] They were not incompatible, and each had validity. Each raised its own questions and tended to send one for answers to different kinds of evidence. In chapters 6–8, I address them one at a time. Really, they are different definitions of "development": as escape from poverty, as freedom, and as industry building. How the assessments against each standard would mesh into an overall assessment was hard to predict because it depended on the results of each. If rigorous studies of the impact on poverty showed that microcredit was the financial equivalent of cigarettes (addictive and harmful) or vaccines (a veritable silver bullet), the discussion would end there. As it happened, studies do not show either, which leads me to lean on alternative perspectives.

The first notion, development as escape from poverty, is explored in chapter 6. It asks, if microfinance is so worthy of acclaim and funding, shouldn't the benefits be measurable in the rise of a client's income, the quality of the roof over her head, and how many of her children are in school? As Susy Cheston of Women's Opportunity Fund and Larry Reed of Opportunity International put it in 1999, "Just knowing that we increased the debt of 100 million people will not tell us that we accomplished what we set out to do, even if we delivered that debt in a financially viable manner."[17] This definition of success relies for proof on academic researchers who are trained to collect and analyze data to study cause and effect. But their job turns out to be hard—more so, in fact, than many of them have realized. If someone shows you a rich microcredit borrower and a poor non-borrower, you can

16. Rhyne (2001) and Rutherford (2009a) were especially influential.
17. Cheston and Leed (1999), 6.

think of several stories to explain that pattern. Maybe, as we hope, microcredit made the rich one rich. On the other hand, the microfinance institution may have lent only to entrepreneurs who were already well-off. Or unlucky entrepreneurs may have tried credit and quit, dropping off the scientific radar. Perhaps microfinanciers only operate in more affluent provinces, ones linked by good roads to the cities. Or perhaps the pivotal choice is the borrower's: only households with good, going businesses dare take on the obligation of credit. No matter how fancy the statistical machinery brought to bear, it is extremely difficult to rule out such competing explanations. Indeed, I have found that fancy mathematics more often obscures than resolves the statistical challenges.[18] As a result, though microfinance groups have commissioned hundreds of assessments over the years, few convincingly rule out these other explanations for any positive association between borrowing and betterment.

As I wrote this book, the scholarship on microfinance broke with its past. Economists released results from the first tests of microfinance that were randomized in the manner of the best drug safety tests. By introducing a source of variation effectively uncorrelated with anything else in the universe—randomly offering some people microfinance and not others—these researchers are getting a firmer fix on impacts. I discuss these studies in chapter 6. So far, the tests of micro*credit* have conformed to the Stainless Steel Law of Evaluation coined by the late sociologist Peter Rossi: "the better designed the impact assessment of a social program, the more likely is the resulting estimate of net impact to be zero."[19] Although the story of microcredit stimulating microenterprise proves to be more than a myth, poverty did not fall on average in the studied populations.[20] The one randomized study of micro*savings*, however, *did* find it reducing average poverty, among female vendors in a rural Kenyan market.[21]

Thus, people wanting to understand the impacts of microfinance should mind the gap between upbeat rhetoric and rigorous evidence. But they should not fall into the trap of judging microfinance by such studies alone. As I did, they should turn for wisdom to alternative theories of how microfinance (or any other intervention) can contribute to development.

One of those has been most famously articulated by Amartya Sen, another native of Bengal territory who won a Nobel, his in economics. In chapter 7, I pursue the implications of his theory, as laid out in his book *Development as*

18. Roodman (2007a, 2009); Roodman and Morduch (2009).

19. Rossi (1987).

20. Banerjee and others (2009); Karlan and Zinman (2009).

21. Dupas and Robinson (2009).

Freedom. Sen argues that processes of economic, political, and social development are essentially about increasing freedom. By "freedom," he means not merely the libertarian's freedom from interference, but greater agency in one's life. High income, education, health, protected human rights, and democracy all give people more control over their circumstances. These freedoms reinforce one another, so that each is a means and an end. Sen buttresses this general theory with bits of compelling evidence. He notes, for example, that no democracy has suffered a major famine: freedom from tyranny begets freedom from want. He also cites findings that within India, better-educated women have fewer children; again, one kind of control over circumstances leads to another.[22] And he has suggested that microcredit increases freedom since it gives the poor a new way to navigate tricky financial currents.[23] By Sen's logic, expanded financial freedom in the form of better management of household finances can reasonably be expected to increase other freedoms in the long run, such as education and income. With safer ways to save, a family can more easily set aside money for school fees.

This idea should become obvious if you think about how *you* use financial services. Probably the most important financial services to you are the ones that help you hold things together in bad times and in good, in sickness and in health. Health insurance keeps a run-in with cancer from bankrupting your family. A retirement fund assures comfort in old age. Such services give you more control over your circumstances. The poor look to financial services to meet the same need for managing spending. For them it is not a matter of retiring to Palm Beach but putting food on the table (or floor) every day. Microcredit can help in a pinch; so can savings, insurance, and even money transfers, as when a rural Kenyan family calls in funds from a son working in the capital.

Viewing development as freedom leads to specific questions about microfinance. When does it give clients such as Murshida more autonomy within the household, village, or slum, what is sometimes called "empowerment"? How often does microfinance reduce freedom, as Razia seems to think it did for her? How can we tell which microcreditors operate in ways that limit the risk of the debt trap? Embedded in these questions is the puzzling one of when credit is usurious. The ancients never resolved it: Christianity used to ban interest, Islam still does, and whatever the doctrine, there have long been Christians and Muslims who charged interest by another name.

22. Sen (1999), 196–99, citing Murthi, Guio, and Drèze (1995).
23. Sen (1999), 39.

I conclude that while financial services can increase freedom, they do not automatically do so. Particularly ambiguous are the effects of credit because of its dual nature as a source of possibilities and a bond. From my review of studies by people who have spent weeks or months living among borrowers, the most famous form of microfinance, group microcredit, emerges in a surprisingly negative light—surprising, that is, for someone who was expecting a mix of good and bad news. Groups of women responsible for each other's loans can generate "peer support" in times of difficulty—or peer pressure to pay no matter what.

The third notion of success in microfinance, and the frame for chapter 8, emphasizes the transformational nature of economic development. The spectacular reductions in poverty in the United States in the nineteenth century and China in the twenty-first owe to processes of societal churning best labeled "industrialization" (despite its vaguely negative connotations).

Within economics, the interest in the dynamics of economic development goes back at least 100 years to Joseph Schumpeter, who popularized the term "creative destruction." In his view, the hero of economic development is the entrepreneur who pursues innovations that disrupt established ways of making and selling things. Development is a cascade of such economic revolutions, which save society from stagnation.[24] Disruptive innovations need not be high-tech. Just as Sears drove small American retailers out of business with its catalog, Walmart marginalized Sears with its aggressive cost cutting. Nor must the entrepreneurs work for a profit. According to this view, Yunus and the other visionary leaders of microfinance (some of whose stories are in chapter 4) emerge as heroes of development as industry building even though almost none has made a fortune in microfinance. The existence of major microfinance institutions—competing, innovating, employing thousands, serving millions in a ways once thought impossible—embodies the essence of development.

Notice that I do not claim that microfinance institutions are lifting their clients out of poverty or even turning them into Schumpeterian microheroes. Most microfinance clients pursue established activities, such as food processing and retail. But in the Schumpeterian view, the spread of microfinance is as obviously developmental as the spread of the mobile phone among the world's poor. In this respect, aid and philanthropy rarely have done so much for development as they have in supporting microfinance.

Accepting the definition of development as industry building and this preliminarily positive verdict, there is still room for critical inquiry. Consider

24. Schumpeter (1934).

the debacle in Andhra Pradesh that sent Mahajan on his *Shodh Yatra*. The way microcredit soared and crashed there is hardly a shining example of an industry enriching the economic fabric of nations. In India and beyond, the core analytical question is this: when is creative destruction more creative than destructive? The question does not admit sharp answers, only general principles. The microfinance industry contributes most to development when it links to its host economy in many ways, by not just making loans, but also taking savings from customers and some capital from local investors. When this happens, the forces abetting and checking the industry's growth are more likely to find a healthy balance.

Rather the opposite happened in India. Much of the capital, though domestic, came from banks pushed by government quotas to lend to "priority sectors" that serve its poor and disadvantaged citizens. Venture capitalists poured gasoline on this ample tinder in the form of equity, which was money that accepted the risk of losses in exchange for a fraction of ownership as well as the hope—indeed, pressure—for big, quick profits. Meanwhile, microfinance institutions were prohibited from deepening their relationships with customers by taking savings.[25] "Much better," mused blogger Felix Salmon, "that full-service banks grow organically out of local communities than monoline microlenders parachute in, flush with venture-capital funds, make a huge splash, and then implode."[26]

In the book's final chapter, I elaborate on lessons I've just laid out. I emphasize that those wanting to support microfinance should help it play to its strengths, which lie in leveraging modest subsidies to build financial institutions and industries that help millions of families manage poverty— and could help billions. A particularly promising path is microsavings, which comes out well in a randomized study, does not threaten freedom the way credit does, and, as just argued, enriches the contribution of a financial institution to the local economic fabric.

Busting the myths of microfinance has become a popular enterprise. I wonder now whether it is the *hype* that is overhyped. The case against microfinance as a proven anti-poverty tool needed to be made.[27] But I tend to lose patience with those who get excited about what microfinance does *not* do

25. Elisabeth Rhyne, "On Microfinance: Who's to Blame for the Crisis in Andhra Pradesh?" *Huffington Post*, November 2, 2010.

26. Felix Salmon, *The Lessons of Andhra Pradesh* blog, Reuters, November 18, 2010 (j.mp/ ge0zyQ).

27. Dichter said it before most others; Thomas Dichter, "Hype and Hope: The Worrisome State of the Microcredit Movement," Microfinance Gateway, March 24, 2006 (j.mp/dZRPZh).

while exhibiting less curiosity about what it *does* do. As a result, this book's contrarianism is aimed at the threats to microfinance's real strengths.

One of these threats has been the overenthusiastic flow of capital for the business, which was drummed up by all the mythologizing. Microfinance, or at least microcredit, needs less money, not more. A truth too easily ignored until the Andhra Pradesh crisis is that all markets in credit are susceptible to bouts of mania and depression. If companies try to sell too much credit, demand can seem to keep up with supply for years. Oversupply covers its own tracks as people use new loans to repay old loans. Put otherwise, microcredit is a prescription drug—useful in moderation, but dangerous in large doses.

Moderation is tough because it calls for cooperation among competitors: even when individual lenders exercise discipline in how much they lend to a person, an industry with several lenders can collectively prescribe an overdose. The microfinance industry will never perfectly balance prudence and expansion. But it can do better.

Overall, the greatest danger to the microfinance industry has been the hubris that came with success. The stories about the power of loans against poverty surpassed the evidence. That led to backlashes; and it made financing for microfinance dangerously enthusiastic, which led to bubbles. The dominant rhetoric about microfinance is not merely incorrect. It is a threat to the sustainability of microfinance itself.

two
How the Other Half Finances

The season of plenty should then provide for the season of want; and the gains of summer be laid by for the rigours of winter. But it must be obvious, how difficult it is, for even the sober labourer to save up his money, when it is at hand to supply the wants that occur in his family;—for those of intemperate habits, ready money is a very strong temptation to the indulgence of those pernicious propensities.

—Priscilla Wakefield, 1805[1]

If I had my way I would write the word "Insure" over the door of every cottage, and upon the blotting-book of every public man, because I am convinced that by sacrifices which are inconceivably small, which are all within the power of the very poorest man in regular work, families can be secured against catastrophes which otherwise would smash them up for ever.

—Winston Churchill, 1909[2]

Do you remember when you first heard about microcredit? Did it surprise you that one could help poor people by putting them in debt? The root of such surprise is the microfinance movement's successful replacement of the old story of lending to the poor—a story of usury—with a new one about microenterprise. After all, it seems, poor people can be masters of their fates, incipient entrepreneurs who lack only credit to bloom.

On the one hand, this upbeat story is rightly animated by the belief that people are no less ingenious or resourceful for being poor. On the other, it confines their creativity to one financial service and one use: credit and enterprise.

Living up to the spirit of respect embedded in microfinance requires minimizing preconceptions about how poor people do and ought to use financial services. Thus, I start my investigation of microfinance from the clients'

1. Wakefield (1805), 208.
2. Churchill (2007 [1909]), 146–47.

points of view. This perspective reveals that microcredit for microenterprise indeed has some value: lacking jobs, poor people more often work for themselves than do wealthier people. But microenterprise is just one use for credit and other financial services, and it is best thought of as subsistence, not a ladder out of poverty.

Broadly, poor people use financial services to meet the same needs as the rich do: transacting with others, investing for the future, building assets for security, and sustaining consumption of necessities. Embedded within most of these grand problems is a mundane one: accumulating small sums into large ones. Most financial services can be seen as helping people do that, partly by providing a safe place to put funds and partly by helping people impose discipline on themselves. And it turns out that because poor people live close to the jagged financial edge, they need this service *more* than rich people. As Priscilla Wakefield wrote in 1805, they need ways to set aside money on good days and in good seasons and draw it down in bad. Loans, savings accounts, insurance, and money transfers can all help them do that. Thus financial services are like clean water, sanitation, and electricity: they generally do not lift people out of poverty, but they improve life.

Unfortunately and inevitably, while rich people can usually find services tailored to their specific needs, those less fortunate must choose from options that are more expensive and less well matched to the needs at hand. As the seminal book *Portfolios of the Poor,* by Daryl Collins, Jonathan Morduch, Stuart Rutherford, and Orlanda Ruthven, has shown, poor people must patch together loans from friends, store credit, neighborhood savings clubs, and similar outlets to manage their finances as best they can.[3] Microfinance is about improving their options. This fuller, more realistic view is essential to understanding why microfinance can be a development success even if it isn't a reliable path out of poverty.

How Rich People Use Financial Services

Rich people can access a spectacular variety of financial services: checking and savings accounts, home mortgages, car loans, credit cards, mutual funds, and insurance for life, car, health, and home. It is hard for a New Yorker who samples a new restaurant each week to understand the life of a Guatemalan highlander subsisting on tortillas and beans; just so, it is hard for those who enjoy a wealth of financial services to empathize with a woman for whom saving means hiding money from her husband in the folds of her sari.

---

3. Collins and others (2009).

Table 2-1. *My Financial Services*

Service	Purpose
Savings account	Prepare for emergencies, such as job loss
Checking account	Transact safely over long distances or in large amounts
Wire transfer	Send and receive money internationally (rare)
PayPal account	Send money to friends; buy things online
Credit cards	Transact without cash; buy things I want before I have the money
Home mortgage	Live in a home I own before I can pay for it
Home equity line of credit	Same as above; and use cheap credit to improve house
Car loan	Own a car before I can pay for it
Student loan	Invest in my own skills for higher pay after graduation
Retirement savings	Prepare to support myself when I no longer work
College savings	Prepare to invest in children's education
Health insurance	Protect family against financial catastrophe in event of serious health problems; assure access to care
Homeowner's insurance	Protect family against financial catastrophe in event of serious harm to home
Automobile insurance	Protect family against financial catastrophe in event of serious harm to car, or liability for accident
Umbrella liability insurance	Protect family from liability suits in general
Life insurance	Protect family against financial catastrophe if I die
Disability insurance	Protect family against financial catastrophe if I am unable to work

Despite the gulf in experience, a rich person can gain insight into poor people's use of financial services by contemplating her own. Try this exercise. List all the financial services you use. For each, determine what it helps you do. Transact? Invest? Build a business? Spend money you have yet to earn? Then confront this question: if you had to give up all these services but one, which would you keep?

Table 2-1 is my list, which is fairly typical for middle-class American families.

If you show your list to a microfinance client (assuming it resembles mine), the luxury will become apparent—in the college education foreseen and the home valued in six figures, as well as in the low price and tailored suitability of the services. But if you articulate the needs that underlie your use of these services, you two might understand each other well. In my list, I discern four major reasons I use financial services. All come from universal needs:

1. To transact. The credit cards and checking account help me move sums too large to be safe in my wallet. They also help me remit amounts large and small over long distances. And they make it easy: My paycheck goes into the checking account automatically. The mortgage payment comes out just as smoothly. A swipe of a card pays for gas at the pump.

2. To invest. I borrowed to help pay my college tuition, and I save to do the same for my sons. Notably, like most people in rich countries, I have not used financial services to invest in my own business, for I have none. I prefer the stability of my job.

3. To build assets. Some people ascribe an investment purpose to the home mortgage, but in fact, on general principles, a mortgage-financed home is a terrible investment. It puts a lot of financial eggs in one basket, violating the principle of diversification. Using credit to buy a home—investing with leverage—multiplies the risk. And homes can be illiquid, meaning they are hard to sell. I bought my house for other reasons. With ownership comes security. By holding a title to my home, I need not worry about being forced out by a landlord who does view the building as an investment. And, as Peruvian economist Hernando de Soto has famously argued, title to a major asset also serves as collateral for credit.[4] I once borrowed against my house to fix the roof and could borrow again to help put my sons through college.

4. To sustain consumption. I was struck to discover that most of the services on my list secure my family's ability to obtain such necessities as food and clothing through thick and thin. The savings account is a safety net if I lose my job. Retirement savings should let me buy what I need after I stop working. Credit cards and the home loans let me make big purchases without starving. The insurance policies take the financial bite out of life's traumas.[5] Economists call this function *consumption smoothing.*

To respond to the challenge I posed earlier, if I was told I had to live with just one financial service, I would beg for two: life and health insurance. They protect my family from bankruptcy in the face of life's greatest tragedies.

We can learn a few more lessons from this exercise. First, risk is intimately intertwined with money. Insurance policies embrace risk head-on. But they are not unique in involving it because whenever one party commits to delivering money under certain circumstances at some future date, there is risk. Perhaps a borrower will not repay or a bank holding deposits will go under. Second, and related, many financial services *bind* even as they *serve*. The mortgage and other loans force me to set aside money each month. The retirement accounts add inertia to my financial regime since my employer

---

4. De Soto (2000).

5. Perhaps I should also have listed the government insurance programs my employer pays into on my behalf to aid me when I retire, or before then if I lose my job.

automatically makes the contributions out of my paychecks. In appropriate doses, this discipline is healthy; we all need help resisting the temptation to spend now.

Third, what financial services you can use depends on who you are. If I were a poor American, my financial service inventory would look different. I might not have the steady job that would make me an attractive risk for lenders. My compensation might not include a retirement plan. I might have trouble maintaining a minimum balance in a checking or savings account. To borrow a term from the Commission on Thrift, a coalition of U.S. non-profits, the "concierge services" of government-subsidized retirement and college savings accounts would probably disappear from my list of financial services.[6] So might most of the insurance and the checking account. In their place would appear check cashers and payday lenders extending credit at 400 percent per annum. Just as more drugs exist for male impotence than for malaria, the financial services available to the rich outshine those for the poor in quality, diversity, and cost.

This, too, is worth noting: my wife's inventory is identical to mine. But in many countries, law and custom come between women and formal finance.

Perhaps the most important lesson is about how financial services, like roads and piped water, undergird the comfortable life. Imagine living without financial services: no bank accounts, no bank loans, no credit cards, no insurance—just cash. The importance of financial services is belied by their intangibility. Their paramount benefit is the last one on my list of four, namely, helping people manage and maintain consumption, especially during catastrophes. In the vocabulary of the Nobel Laureate economist Amartya Sen, financial services give people more agency, more freedom. However, as Sen emphasizes, freedom begets freedom: those who already have more agency, thanks to being rich or male, say, can access more and better services.[7] Those who come to the financial service marketplace with fewer advantages leave with fewer.

The Financial Challenges of Poor People

"The rich are different from us," F. Scott Fitzgerald once observed. "Yes," retorted Ernest Hemingway, "they have more money."

---

6. Commission on Thrift (2008).
7. Sen (1999).

That exchange is actually a bit of Hemingway fiction, a put-down of his rival's fascination with the lives of the rich.[8] But it does capture a real question for us: is there much difference between being rich and being poor? Do the global rich and the global poor use financial services in essentially the same ways?

Broadly, rich and poor are no different: all need to transact, invest, build assets, and sustain consumption. But the financial circumstances of poor people are qualitatively, not just quantitatively, distinct. Poor households are not just microrich ones, and microentrepreneurs are not simply microversions of the iconic entrepreneurs who perpetually roil the capitalist economy.

Here is one difference: Poor families are more apt to send a member to the big city or to another country for work. That generates a need to transfer money over distance. Living in 1995–96 in a village in southern Bangladesh served by the Grameen Bank, graduate student Sanae Ito discovered that the surest way for residents to get out of poverty was to get out of the village. A family would save up or borrow to send a daughter or son or husband to the capital to work as a day laborer and send home money.[9] In Kenya, the wildly popular mobile phone–based money transfer service, M-PESA, got its start with the slogan "Send Money Home." The original target client (and there were millions) lived in Nairobi and needed safe ways to remit funds to his parents, wife, and children in the countryside.[10] Many villages in developing countries export workers even farther afield. Today, Bangladeshi villages are sending workers to the Middle East, thanks to a religious affinity. Bangladeshi men working on Kuwaiti construction sites (among others) are sending billions of dollars home.

Thus the global financial system is hugely valuable for linking dispersed families—if they can hook into it. BRAC Bank, a spin-off from the giant Bangladeshi nonprofit from which it gets its name, gives its low-income clients just that access through an arrangement with Western Union, turning its branches into money transfer points. In Kenya, M-PESA is working to bypass Western Union by extending its network internationally. Worldwide in 2010, $325 billion was remitted to developing countries, about three times the foreign aid from industrial democracies. For twenty-one receiving countries, the flow exceeded 10 percent of domestic economic output, which is a sign of how economically important the foreign earnings are for many poor families.[11]

8. Berg (1978), 304–05.
9. Ito (1999).
10. Mas and Radcliffe (2010), 9.
11. Mohapatra, Ratha, and Silwal (2010).

The differences do not end there. Even before migration became the economic option that it is today, poor households had fundamentally different financial needs than their rich counterparts. Poor people are short not just of money but also of control over their financial circumstances. Their incomes and spending needs are more variable and unpredictable and their lives more dangerous than is true for rich people. Perhaps the most important financial distinction between poor and rich—leaving aside the super-rich—is that by and large, rich people have salaries. My steady paycheck rivals all my insurance policies in bestowing financial security. It allows me to think long term, helping me invest in my children. And it makes me more creditworthy, helping me borrow to build up assets. Reviewing findings from household surveys done in thirteen developing countries, MIT economists Abhijit Banerjee and Esther Duflo found that what most distinguished people living above or below $2 a day was not education, health, or even wealth, but a steady job.[12] To put that another way, as I wrote in chapter 1, most people who live on $2 a day *don't* live on $2 a day: they make $4 one day, $1 the next, and $0 the day after that. Or perhaps their big earnings come once a season, at harvest time.[13]

No work has made this reality clearer to the world's salaried minority than *Portfolios of the Poor*. Following a suggestion some ten years ago by the University of Manchester's David Hulme, detailed financial transaction logs called financial diaries were assembled for a few hundred families in Bangladesh, India, and South Africa. Typically, a researcher visited a household biweekly for up to a year to update the logs, noting down every income and outflow, every instance of borrowing or saving.

Among the stories revealed in the diaries and the book is that of Pumza, who cooks and sells sheep intestines out of a stall in a Cape Town slum. After netting out her spending on firewood and raw intestines, Pumza made $95 a month on average during the eight months that researchers visited her. A $25 child support grant brought her monthly income to $120, which for Pumza and her four children worked out to $0.80 per person per day. Hidden within that average, however, was a great deal of daily and monthly unpredictability and volatility, shown in figure 2-1. The human body does not thrive on a diet that alternates between feast and famine: despite her volatile income, Pumza needed to feed the children every day.

12. Banerjee and Duflo (2008). The authors use purchasing power parities to convert to U.S. dollars.

13. See also Morduch (1995).

Figure 2-1. *Pumza's Revenues and Expenses, March–November 2004*

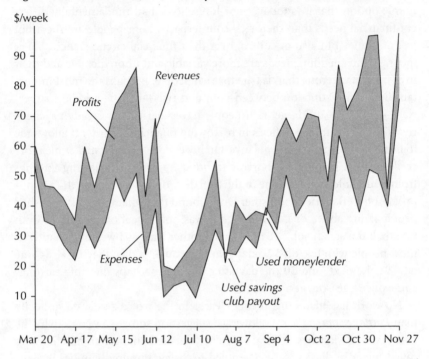

$/week

Source: Collins and others (2009), 41.
Note: Dollars are converted at the rate of $1 to 6.5 South African rand.

The collision between volatile income and constant needs creates an intense demand for financial services, ways to set aside money on good days or seasons and pull it out on bad. At least once when income fell below expenses, for example, Pumza went to a moneylender for a short-term loan at interest of 30 percent per month. Another time, she used a payout from a savings club she belonged to (see discussion of Rotating Savings and Credit Associations at the beginning of chapter 3). Interestingly, Pumza was also a provider of financial services, if an informal and hesitant one. To people she knew, she sometimes sold her wares on credit.[14]

As if income volatility weren't hard enough, poor people's spending needs also tend to be more unpredictable than rich people's, above all because of health problems. Disability and death are more frequent visitors at the doorsteps of poor people. And where a middle-class office worker can get by with

14. Collins and others (2009), 40–42.

a bad back, a poor laborer may have to stop working and earning when hurt. Together, the cost of medicine and doctors and the loss of income when a breadwinner takes sick can undo years of saving and asset building, plunging a family into destitution.

One day in 1989, recounts *Portfolios of the Poor*, a Bangladeshi rickshaw driver named Salil complained to his wife of a sore throat. He consulted a series of doctors. To pay them, he sold off his three rickshaws, the capital of his livelihood, one by one. The doctors did not help. Salil ended up in a hospital, was diagnosed with throat cancer, and died within days. Throughout the period his wife, bereft of income, borrowed to support the couple and their three small children. His widow and children became the poorest Bangladeshi household in the financial diary studies.[15]

Salil's story may be unusual only in degree. Fifty percent of the Bangladeshi households studied experienced illness during the periods of financial diary collection, as did 42 percent of Indian ones. Fully 81 percent of the households in South Africa, where AIDS is common, were financially affected by funerals outside the immediate family.[16] Also summarizing household surveys, Banerjee and Duflo found that depending on the country, 11–46 percent of households living on less than $1 a day (on average) had someone who had been bedridden or had needed a doctor within the last month.[17] A World Bank project to collect and analyze thousands of life stories in fifteen developing countries cited the second-most common cause of falling into poverty, after regional or national economic troubles, as "health/death shocks and natural disasters," at 19.4 percent of cases.[18]

One way families manage risk on the income side of the ledger is diversification. A survey of twenty-seven villages in West Bengal, India, found that households typically had three workers who among them practiced seven occupations. Banerjee and Duflo found that one-fifth of urban households in Peru living on less than $2 a day per person earn from more than one source, as do a quarter in Mexico, a third in Pakistan, and half in Côte d'Ivoire. In the countryside, it is common for a person to work his own land and the land of others. In the extremely poor Udaipur district in the Indian state of Rajasthan, almost everyone owns and farms some land, but 74 percent of those below $1 a day earn most of their money in day labor. Self-employment is

15. Collins and others (2009), 86–87.

16. Collins and others (2009), 68.

17. Banerjee and Duflo (2007), 149. The poverty line is $1 of household spending per member per day, converted to local currency using purchasing power parities.

18. Narayan, Pritchett, and Kapoor (2009), 21.

common, too, found among a quarter of similarly defined poor and rural households in Guatemala and a third in Indonesia and Pakistan.[19] Banerjee and Duflo explain the attraction of working for oneself:

> If you have few skills and little capital, and especially if you are a woman, being an entrepreneur is often easier than finding an employer with a job to offer. You buy some fruits and vegetables or some plastic toys at the wholesalers and start selling them on the street; you make some extra *dosa* [rice and bean pancake] mix and sell the *dosas* in front of your house; you collect cow dung and dry it to sell it as a fuel; you attend to one cow and collect the milk. These types of activities are exactly those in which the poor are involved.[20]

Subtle Truths about Microenterprise

Self-employment, then, is one natural response to being poor in a poor country. But thanks to the promotion of microcredit, microenterprise became something more in the public imagination: not just one reason the poor want financial services but *the* reason, not just a way to increase or diversify income but a way out of poverty.

While poor people do fend for themselves economically more than rich people do, accurate data on the extent and strength of microenterprise are hard to come by. The process in which a rich investor finances microcredit for a poor borrower can be seen as a chain with a reality at one end and an image at the other. The investor, say, a user of the online peer-to-peer microlending site Kiva, might lend money to one of the "entrepreneurs" listed on the site. The funds would go to Kiva, a local microcreditor, and then a borrower rather like the one pictured on the site.[21] That borrower might use the credit for microenterprise—or might not. Somewhere along the chain, the simple image and the complicated reality must come into tension. The more a fundraiser like Kiva promotes the image to raise funds, the more that point of collision is pushed toward the client. Microfinance institutions borrowing money from Kiva, for example, will understand that they should emphasize entrepreneurship in their own rhetoric. When collecting stories from clients, they will cue their clients in the same way. What

19. See Banerjee and Duflo (2007), 151, 152; "typical" figures are medians.

20. Banerjee and Duflo (2007), 162.

21. See David Roodman, "Kiva Is Not Quite What It Seems," *Microfinance Open Book Blog,* October 2, 2009 (j.mp/1yAS6n), included in the appendix.

clients really do with the credit, elusive under the best of circumstances, falls further below the radar.

When asked how they use a service, microfinance clients often give the answer they believe is wanted. They respond this way out of ordinary self-interest; to ignore self-interest is a luxury most poor people cannot afford. In Bangladesh, a borrower's husband told anthropologist Lamia Karim with a smile, "We took a cow loan. Fifty percent will be spent to pay off old debts, and another fifty percent will be invested in moneylending. If the manager comes to see our cow, we can easily borrow one from the neighbors."[22] But the fabrication is not always from whole cloth. Beatrice, the female half of an entrepreneurial couple in Zambia's Copperbelt, explained to British researcher James Copestake that, in Copestake's words, "the main difference the loans had made over the last year was in freeing their own capital for construction of their house." Formally, microcredit went into the business, but its main effect, because of the fungibility of money, was to bump the couple's own capital into additional personal uses.[23]

The Malaysia-based writer Helen Todd succeeded better than most researchers in piercing the fog, giving us a rare statistical view of what micro-credit allows poor people to do. Throughout 1992, she and her husband David Gibbons lived and studied in two villages in the Tangail district of Bangladesh, one of the first regions in which the Grameen credit program operated on a large scale. With a research team that included Bangladeshis, they tracked the financial and personal lives of sixty-two women, forty of whom borrowed from Grameen. The researchers record every loan payment, sale of rice paddy, and lease of land. Todd and her team complemented their quantitative data with "qualitative" evidence—records of hundreds of conversations and observations. Table 2-2 shows their tabulation of how the forty borrowers said they would use the credit so they could obtain loan approval and how they actually used it. All the stated purposes were invest-ments. Todd writes:

> According to the [Grameen] Bank records, 35 of our 40 member sample took loans in 1991/92 for either "[rice] paddy husking" alone or "paddy husking/cow fattening." As far as we could tell, only four women did any paddy husking for sale during the year and . . . only for limited periods. Two young women who lived in the same *bari* [home-stead lot] had taken their last few loans for "cow fattening." Although

22. Karim (2008), 16.
23. Copestake (2002), 746.

I was in and out of their *bari* for seven months of the year, I never saw hide nor hair of any cows.[24]

Todd's assessment revealed an interesting diversity of pragmatic uses. Nine of the forty took credit for what is usually thought of as microenterprise. Of these, four bought cows; another two invested in equipment or stock for back-breaking work grinding the oil out of mustard seeds; and three bought rickshaws, presumably for their husbands to use as a source of income. But more was going on. Two women used the loans to pay dowry, breaking a vow they took as Grameen members.[25] Others bought rice, which could be a kind of consumption smoothing, making sure there is enough to eat every day. One bought materials to improve her house, which we could call asset building. In fact a majority *did* use the credit for what could be called business activities, though not ones usually thought of as microenterprise: moneylending and the leasing or buying of rice land. Bank policy proscribed land leasing in particular, viewing the rents as usury extracted by landlords, a perspective that reflects the historical intertwining in South Asia of moneylending and land monopoly. But for many families, leasing land was a step up in security and freedom. Instead of working someone else's land for a daily wage, the husband could plant and manage the family's "own" field. Once during the research project, Grameen Bank founder Muhammad Yunus visited Todd and Gibbons, who briefed him on their findings. Todd wrote that they urged him to allow land leasing:

> Dr. Yunus listened but did not commit himself.
> "Let's go to the village," he said. . . .
> Professor Yunus questioned Kia [a borrower] about [a new] loan. "Do you want one?"
> "Yes, sir!"
> "What will you use it for?"
> I saw Kia hesitate for a moment. Then she looked the Managing Director in the eye.
> "I won't lie to you," she said. "I am going to lease in some land."[26]

Todd's data and stories suggest that people generally use loans to incrementally diversify and improve their control over their sources of income.

24. Todd (1996), 25.

25. The custom of dowry makes girls economically burdensome and boys lucrative, reinforcing discrimination against girls.

26. Todd (1996), 16–17.

Table 2-2. *Approved and Actual Use of Select Grameen Bank Loans, 1992*

Use	Number of loans		Amount of loans (taka)	
	Approved	Actual	Approved	Actual
Rice paddy husking	20		73,500	
Rice husking/cow fattening	8		46,000	
Cow fattening	7	4	42,500	19,300
Mustard-oil grinding	4	2	23,000	5,760
Grocery trade	1		5,000	
Mustard oil/sweets	1		5,500	
Land transactions		20		70,320
Loan repayment		16		24,720
Rice stocking		12		27,134
Lending		7		6,849
Rickshaw		3		6,137
Dowry/wedding		2		5,075
Housing materials		1		4,680
Other/unknown				25,025

Note: Loans were made to forty women. Those loans used for more than one purpose are listed more than one time. $1 = 40 taka.
Source: Todd (1996), 24.

This often does include what is called microenterprise. But the lines blur between microenterprise and agriculture, between investment, asset accumulation, and consumption. Few would consider stocking up on rice to be microenterprise. But how different is it from buying a cow? Both are ways to assure food supply. Yunus did not sanction land purchase and leasing when he initiated his microlending, but is buying an acre so different from buying a rickshaw? Both can be combined with the owner's labor to earn an income. Certainly, users of microcredit do not feel confined by such abstract distinctions. Even paying dowry, though it perpetuates an institution that makes women an economic burden, can be a smart investment if it transfers a daughter to a household where she will be better fed. When you look closely, "microenterprise" begins to look like one more resourceful survival strategy.

It is worth reflecting on how wealthy societies label people who work for themselves as a matter of survival. In the eighteenth and nineteenth centuries in the British Isles, such people were "industrious tradesmen."[27] Some

27. For example, Piesse (1841), 9.

on the Continent saw them through the lens of the labor–capital divide—as workers who could become small capitalists.[28] Today, rickshaws drivers and mustard grinders are often said to be running "microbusinesses." They are "microentrepreneurs." This fusion of a Silicon-era prefix with a capitalist projection appears to have originated with a volunteer for Acción International named Bruce Tippett in 1974, not long after "microprocessor" entered currency.[29] "Microentrepreneur" is apt in important respects because the people so labeled risk their tiny bits of capital, work for themselves, and reap the profits and loss of their operations.

But "microentrepreneurs" differ from the prototypical rich-world entrepreneur in important ways. Few tap capital markets, innovate, expand, or create jobs. They do not abandon steady employment to launch themselves into bold ventures. Rather, they are conservative in investing in themselves. Evidently, living on the edge curtails one's appetite for risk. An experiment in Sri Lanka showed that injecting modest additional capital into microenterprises let the owners earn average returns of 5 percent per month.[30] The same experiment in Mexico generated returns exceeding 20–33 percent per month.[31] Why poor people leave these potential winnings on the table by underinvesting in their own businesses is not clear. They may not recognize the opportunities to sew more saris or better stock their shelves. They may struggle to pull together the lump sums needed to invest. Or perhaps microbusinesses are like tech stocks: high return on average but also high risk. To reduce risk, poor people diversify across several businesses (as we saw), not investing too much in any one.

Whatever the reasons, poor entrepreneurs are not the agents of creative destruction whom economist Joseph Schumpeter saw as the heroes of economic development. They *undertake*—to revert to the root meaning of "entrepreneur"—in order to survive.[32] To this extent, labeling them "microentrepreneurs" romanticizes their plight and implies too much hope for their escape. This is why experts distinguish between "necessity entrepreneurs" and "opportunity entrepreneurs," and why Aloysius Fernandez, who

28. For example, Wolff (1896), 2, 10, 16, 19.

29. Tippett coined the term "microenterprise." Jeffrey Ashe, director of community finance, Oxfam America, Boston, Mass., interview with author, November 26, 2008. Seibel (2005) says he introduced "microfinance" in 1990.

30. De Mel, McKenzie, and Woodruff (2008a).

31. McKenzie and Woodruff (2008). Other studies have found similar conservatism among poor farmers in deciding, for example, whether to apply commercial fertilizer. See Morduch (1995), 105.

32. De Mel, McKenzie, and Woodruff (2008b).

founded the self-help group movement in India (see chapter 4), proposed the label "microsurvivors."[33]

A less fashionable view of poor entrepreneurs, historically associated with the International Labor Organization, is as victims of economic systems that fail to employ them. To put this more constructively, since the Industrial Revolution, explosive job creation has powered all national economic successes. Comprehensive economic development is hard to imagine without increases in jobs. In this view, the people of whom we speak have not benefited from such development. They are "people without jobs" or "self-employed" or "own-account workers" who heroically but tenuously survive their circumstances.[34]

Underlying both perspectives is the fact that poor people are engaged in just getting by. What matters is not that the world settle on one view or the other but that we come to understand how poor people put financial tools to work and how better tools can improve their lives. If you've ever tried to hammer a nail with a wrench, you know that the right tool makes all the difference.

How Poor People Use Financial Services

Perhaps no one is a better interpreter of how poor people manage money than Stuart Rutherford. A trim man with thin-rimmed glasses and a dusting of white hair, Rutherford loves nothing more than interviewing people about just this question. Trained as an architect, he became interested in the subject while investigating the effects of the earthquake in Managua, Nicaragua, just before Christmas 1972. As in Haiti in 2010, many slum dwellers lost their homes. Yet somehow they summoned the resources to rebuild rapidly, confounding many foreign aid officials.

In his book, *The Poor and Their Money*, Rutherford turns his gaze to India, focusing less than I have on the purposes for which the poor use financial services and more on the transactions involved. At base, he argues, poor people need financial services to turn small, regular savings into "usefully large sums" that can go toward most of the goals I discovered in my inventory: investment, gaining ownership of assets, and managing consumption.[35] The last, as we have seen, is essential. As one Bangladeshi told Rutherford, "I

---

33. Reynolds and others (2002), 13; Fernandez (2005).

34. International Labor Organization, Resolutions Concerning International Classification of Status in Employment Adopted by the 15th International Conference of Labor Statisticians, §§7, 10.3 (1993).

35. Rutherford (2009a).

don't really like having to deal with other people over money, but if you're poor, there's no alternative. We have to do it to survive."[36]

Rutherford emphasizes how credit, savings, and insurance help people build usefully large sums. Providers of these services can take small, regular payments from the client—loan payments, savings deposits, insurance premiums—and occasionally make large payouts. As a matter of money flow, the services differ only in when the large sums are paid out. In particular, borrowing and saving are not as opposite as they appear. Rutherford illustrates the kinship with two examples he and his research partner Sukhwinder Singh Arora found in the slums of Vijayawada, in southeastern India. The first example is of savings:

Jyothi is a middle-aged part-educated woman who makes her living as a peripatetic (mobile) deposit collector. Her clients are slum dwellers, mostly women. Jyothi has, over the years, built a good reputation as a safe pair of hands that can be trusted to take care of the savings of her clients.

This is how she works. She gives each of her clients a simple card, divided into 220 cells. . . . Her clients commit themselves to saving a certain amount of money, regularly, over time. For example, a client may agree to save five rupees (Rs 5) [about 10¢] a day for 200 days, completing one cell each day. . . . Having made this agreement it is Jyothi's duty to visit her client each day to collect the five rupees. . . .

When the contract is fulfilled—that is when the client has handed Rs 5 to Jyothi 220 times. . . the client takes her savings back. However, she does not get back the full amount, since Jyothi needs to be paid for the service she provides. These fees vary. . . but in Jyothi's case it is 20 out of the 220 cells—or Rs 100 out of the Rs 1,100 saved up by the client in our example.[37]

Notice that Jyothi does not pay interest on deposits as conventional banks do; she *charges*—at a rate that works out to 30 percent a year.[38] Rutherford

---

36. Collins and others (2009), 13.

37. Rutherford (2009a), 16–17.

38. As discussed later, steady repayments over the saving period make the *average* balance half the starting balance and approximately double the effective interest rate. Extrapolating from 220 days to 365 raises the rate further.

asked Jyothi's clients why they pay so much to save when stashing cash in a box is free:

> The first client I talked to . . . knew she had to have about Rs 800 in early July, or she would miss out on getting her children into school. Her husband, a day labourer, could not be relied on to come up with so much money at one time, and in any case he felt that looking after the children's education was *her* duty, not his. She knew she would not be able to save so large an amount at home—with so many more immediate demands on the scarce cash she wouldn't be able to maintain the discipline. I asked her if she understood that she was paying 30 per cent a year. . . . She said she knew she was paying a lot, but still thought it a bargain. . . . [D]wellers in a neighbouring slum, where there is no Jyothi at work, envied Jyothi's clients.[39]

Bankers would call Jyothi's service a "commitment savings account." By removing a bit of money from the house each day, Jyothi protects her clients from themselves—from temptation to spend everything on the needs of the moment—and from children, husbands, and parents pressing for cash. Jyothi facilitates thrift. Paradoxically, commitment savings ties the client's hands in a way that strengthens her control over money and her power in the family. Poor people do have other ways to save, such as in jewelry and livestock. But thieves can take rings, and pigs can die. And such assets are inconvenient: as one Indonesian pointed out, "When you have to pay the school fees, you cannot sell the cow's leg."[40]

In India, Rutherford also talked to clients of a moneylender, whose

> working method is simple. He gives loans to poor people without any security (or "collateral"), and then takes back his money in regular installments over the next few weeks or months. He charges for the service by deducting a percentage (in his case 15 per cent) of the value of the loan at the time of disbursal. One of his clients reported the deal to me as follows.
>
> "I run a very small shop" (it's a small timber box on stilts on the sidewalk inside which he squats and sells a few basic household goods) "and I need his service to help me maintain my stock of goods. I borrow Rs 1,000 from him, but he immediately deducts Rs 150, so I get

39. Rutherford (2009a), 18.
40. Robinson (2002), 264.

Rs 850 in my hand. He then visits me weekly and I repay the Rs 1,000 for ten weeks. As soon as I have finished he normally lets me repeat."

This client, Ramalu, showed me the scruffy bit of card that the moneylender had given him on which his weekly repayments are recorded. It was quite like the cards Jyothi hands out.[41]

The similarities with Jyothi's commitment savings service are striking. The moneylender, too, uses grids printed on cards to track payments. Both the savings and credit services operate cyclically, producing the same predictable rhythm of frequent, small pay-ins and infrequent, large payouts. Perhaps most importantly, both provide discipline. They help people set aside money each day or week and resist what must be strong temptations to spend or hand over it all. A study in Hyderabad, India, found that offering microcredit reduced household spending on "temptation goods," such as tea and cigarettes, and increased spending on durable goods, such as sewing machines.[42]

In general, financial services provide discipline in two ways: by reminding and binding. This distinction might seem odd. Isn't discipline synonymous with compulsion? Not quite. In an experiment run in Bolivia, Peru, and the Philippines, people with voluntary savings accounts saved 6 percent more on average if they received regular text message reminders.[43] Evidently, the reminders helped them summon self-discipline, and so the value of a loan repayment schedule, binding as it is, partly lies in regularly drawing clients' attention to the priority of setting money aside.

In reminding and binding, financial services meet a need that rich people experience less intensely: self-control is harder to summon when money is tighter and life is less predictable. In Nairobi, researchers Siwan Anderson and Jean-Marie Baland found that 84 percent of participants in local savings clubs known as ROSCAs were women.[44] And among women, the ones most likely to join were not those earning all the household's income or none of it, but those in between. Roughly speaking, sole breadwinners did not need the leverage (with respect to husbands) of a commitment savings arrangement; non-breadwinners had no income to leverage. And evidently, women needed the leverage with respect to their spouses more than men did.

41. Rutherford (2009a), 21.

42. Banerjee and others (2009).

43. Karlan and others (2010), 39.

44. Anderson and Baland (2002). The rotating savings and credit association (ROSCA) is the most prevalent form of informal group financial service. See chapter 3.

Economists Nava Ashraf, Dean Karlan, and Wesley Yin discovered the same need in the southern Philippine island of Mindanao. Working through a rural bank, they offered a new commitment savings account to randomly picked customers. Interestingly, though the commitment account locked up clients' money, it did not compensate for this inconvenience by paying more interest than the bank's ordinary savings account. Yet 28 percent of customers who got the offer took it. After one year, those offered had saved 81 percent more than those not. Of all those receiving the offer, the most likely to join were women who felt a strong tension between how they managed money in the moment and how they wished they would over the long term (as revealed by psychological tests).[45] Evidently they recognized their need for external discipline.

To the extent that financial services resemble one another—in providing the discipline to turn small, frequent pay-ins into large, occasional payouts—they can substitute for one another. One woman might save to buffer her family against the possibility of a husband taking sick. Another might avail herself of rudimentary health insurance, such as that sold by the microfinance group SHARE Microfin in India.[46] Another might borrow to pay clinic fees when needed. Of course, few poor people are in a position to choose from all these options. A survey in the Indian state of Karnataka found that 67 percent of households with someone who had suffered an expensive health problem in the last year tapped savings to help pay the bills, and 44 percent borrowed (and, as one can infer from those numbers, some did both).[47]

But financial services are neither perfect substitutes for each other nor freely substitutable. In Karnataka, only 0.3 percent of the households with health troubles drew on insurance, which is not surprising since almost none could buy any. Few could swap in this superior service to replace savings or credit. And credit and savings are opposite in crucial ways. For one, credit

45. Ashraf, Karlan, and Yin (2006). The average effect reported here is for those receiving the offer, not those taking it. The group receiving the offer is randomly defined and is the basis for meaningful comparisons. People in the subgroup taking the offer are self-selected and might have saved more anyway. "Tension" refers to the time consistency, or hyperbolic discounting, the researchers found. Asked to choose between hypothetically receiving 200 pesos today or 300 a month later, and then between 200 in six months or 300 seven months from now, those women offering conflicting answers—200 when the choice was today, 300 when it was deferred—were more likely to join than other women, and than men generally.

46. See sharemicrofin.com/services.html. The insurance is underwritten by the U.K. group MicroEnsure.

47. Duflo and others (2008). "Expensive" means costing more than 300 rupees. The average reported cost for such episodes was Rs 1,900, which is more than twice the average per capita consumption in the sample, Rs 708.

can cost more than savings. The core reason is that financial service providers are easier to hold accountable than their clients, some of whom can disappear overnight. Greater risk for the lender translates into greater cost for the borrower. In Vijayawada, for instance, Ramalu's moneylender charges far more than Jyothi the savings taker, rupee for rupee. After subtracting the Rs 150 fee, Ramalu's initial balance is Rs 850. He starts repaying immediately so that his *average* balance over the 10 weeks is half the Rs 850, or Rs 425, of which the Rs 150 is 35 percent. A rate of 35 percent for ten weeks compounds to a stunning 382 percent on an annual basis, more than ten times Jyothi's rate.

Another difference between credit and savings is in the risk imposed on clients. With savings (and insurance) the client runs the risk that the financial institution will collapse or steal her funds. Hyperinflation can effectively do the same thing. With credit, the danger is that bad luck or bad judgment will lead the borrower into repayment difficulties. Whatever mechanisms the lender uses to enforce collection—public shaming, peer pressure, the proverbial damage to kneecaps—will then come to bear.

Thus, various financial services can substitute for one another, but imperfectly. Because poor people often have scant services to choose from, they tend to use the services in ways that are not ideal. That a loan is taken in practice, for instance, does not mean that a loan is best in principle.

Conclusion

This review of the role of financial services in daily life and economic development generates a series of cautions for those who see microfinance—microcredit in particular—as an eliminator of poverty. Poor people need financial services for many things in addition to enterprise. Credit can serve many needs, but savings and insurance serve many needs more effectively when available. Microenterprise helps people survive poverty more than escape it. Next to the poverty-reducing power of industrialization, microfinance is a palliative.

Does that mean that the value of microfinance is sometimes exaggerated? Probably. Does that make it wasted charity? Not necessarily. Poor people need financial services even more than rich people do. For people navigating the unpredictable and unforgiving terrain of poverty, any additional room for maneuver, any additional control, can be extremely valuable. As Jonathan Morduch, a New York University economist and thoughtful observer of microfinance, told a writer for *The New Yorker*, "That is a valid critique, to a point. But get real. How long are you willing to wait for the revolution? I can't see any moral foundation for not trying to address the current deprivations of the world's poorest billions. If microfinance can help provide options in cost-effective ways, we should celebrate it."[48]

The practical question is how outsiders arriving under the umbrella of "microfinance" can best help the poor solve their financial problems. It is a tough task. While it is easy to argue that the poor ought to have access to, say, health insurance, it is much harder to deliver health insurance to large numbers of poor people in a financially viable manner. To gain insight into what realistically can be accomplished, we next turn to the past for lessons. The history of financial services for the masses is surprisingly long and rich. For centuries, intelligent, ambitious, and empathic men and women have toiled at this task. Microfinance is an heir to their labors.

48. Connie Bruck, "Millions for Millions," *New Yorker*, October 30, 2006.

three
Credit History

You've heard how microcredit was born. In a nation long shackled by British rule and wracked by famine, a brilliant man was seized with a desire to strike a blow against the poverty all about him. Defying common sense and the skepticism of his colleagues, he began lending tiny sums out of his own pocket to poor people, which they were to invest in tiny businesses. He demanded no collateral, only the vouchsafe of the borrowers' peers. The borrowers rewarded his faith with punctual repayment. In time, his experiment spawned a national movement that delivered millions of loans to poor men and women and broke the power of moneylenders.

The hero of this story is none other than Jonathan Swift, author of *Gulliver's Travels*. By the 1720s, Swift was an established man: a writer, a celebrated Irish patriot, and dean of St. Patrick's Cathedral in Dublin. About when he penned his satiric *Modest Proposal* that the poor sell their children to the rich as food, Swift began to aid Dubliners by lending them five or ten pounds at a time without interest. Each borrower needed two cosigners who would become liable for the debt if the borrower missed the required weekly repayments. Swift's godson and biographer, Thomas Sheridan, penned our primary account:

> As the sums thus weekly paid in, were lent out again to others at a particular day in each month, this quick circulation doubled the benefit arising from the original sum. In order to insure this sum from diminution, he laid it down as a rule that none could be partakers of it, who could not give good security for the regular repayment of it in the manner proposed: for it was a maxim with him, that any one known by his neighbours to be an honest, sober, and industrious man, would readily find such security; while the idle and dissolute would by this means be excluded. Nor did they who entered into such securities run any great risque; for if the borrower was not punctual in his

weekly payments, immediate notice of it was sent to them, who obliged him to be more punctual for the future. Thus did this fund continue undiminished to the last; and small as the spring was, yet, by continual flowing, it watered and enriched the humble vale through which it ran, still extending and widening its course. I have been well assured from different quarters, that many families in Dublin, now living in great credit, owed the foundation of their fortunes, to the sums first borrowed from this fund.[1]

Swift never expanded his lending beyond a side activity. But in the ensuing decades, charitable societies sprang up in Dublin to pool capital that could be lent to "industrious tradesmen" via the Swift system.[2] Among them was the Dublin Musical Society, which in 1747 began to donate proceeds from its performances to a loan fund. (The English rock band the Police would do the same during their 2008 reunion world tour, contributing to the microfinance group Unitus.) Originally just one of the Dublin society's good works, the credit project came to dominate. By 1768, the society had lent £2–4 at a time to each of 5,290 borrowers. The big break for the Swift system came in 1823, when the Irish Parliament approved an act to formalize, regulate, and encourage such loan funds, allowing them to charge interest and accept savings deposits.[3] The legislation gained favor partly because a famine had wreaked havoc on the economy the previous year and partly because credit was seen as cheaper than welfare. Freed to operate more commercially, the funds exploded in reach. By 1843, they disbursed half a million small credits a year, reaching a fifth of families on the island nation. Nearly all the borrowers were illiterate and a fifth were women, most unmarried.[4]

For anyone familiar with modern microcredit, the historical parallels in the Irish loan funds, in theory, practice, clientele, and organizational trajectory, are clear. Then, as now, the hope was that small amounts of capital would help self-employed people lift themselves by their own bootstraps. Desperation for a response to the twin evils of famine and usury drove the initial experiments. Creditors exploited "joint liability"—the backing of peers—to efficiently filter out unreliable people and press for repayment. Weekly payments, a short loan term, and aggressive pursuit of non-payers kept the system running smoothly. And then, as now, credit had a life of its

1. Sheridan (1787), 233–34.
2. Piesse (1841), 9.
3. Additional legislation followed in 1836 and 1838.
4. Hollis and Sweetman (1997, 1998a, 1998b); Hollis (2002).

own: it took over organizations and spread like wildfire, and critics compared it to the usury it sought to supplant. Of Swift, Samuel Johnson, the master of English letters, wrote, "A severe and punctilious temper is ill qualified for transactions with the poor. . . . A severe creditor has no popular character; what then was likely to be said of him who employs the catchpoll under the appearance of charity?"[5]

Nor are the Irish loan funds the only antecedents of today's microfinance. In books, manuscripts, and even stone tablets that have survived the ages are traces of a rich mosaic of arrangements that people have fashioned to help each other borrow, save, and insure. Yet so spectacular has been the growth and elaboration of microfinance since the 1970s that the movement has little sense of its own roots. In fact, modern microfinance did not arise *de novo* thirty-five years ago. The ideas within it are ancient, and their modern embodiments descend directly from older successes. Microfinance, you could say, comes from old money.

Whenever history is lost, wisdom may be lost. Priscilla Wakefield, an Englishwoman who founded historically important financial institutions for women and children circa 1800, professed herself willing to be forgotten. "The undertaking which affords most pleasure in the retrospection," she diarized, "is the successful establishment of a Female Benefit Club, a work that has engrossed a considerable portion of my time, which I do not lament as I trust that many will reap the benefit of it when I am no longer remembered."[6] But it would be better if she were not forgotten, nor the historical fabric of which she is part. Reviewing the history, we can answer questions relevant for today. What are the constants and variables in delivering financial services for the masses? What do they suggest about how best to do microfinance? Do some past successes point to current, overlooked opportunities?

And what does the past teach about the benefits of modern microfinance? In Swift's time, economists did not perform randomized studies of the impact of loans on industrious tradesmen, so we don't know exactly how much good he did. Still, there are some instructive patterns in the history. Repeatedly in the pages that follow, you will see that someone strikes a spark, an institutional form for helping people manage their money. Success has come less from inventing new methods than from combining old

5. Johnson (1781), 428. Johnson's own dictionary defines a "catchpoll" as a "bumbailiff," a sheriff's deputy who pursues debtors—which, as the etymology of "catchpoll" implies, is about as easy as catching chickens (Johnson 1755).

6. Diaries of Priscilla Wakefield, extract courtesy of Janine McVeagh, Rawene, Hokianga, New Zealand. See David Roodman, "Diary Entries from 1798 on First Savings Bank," *Microfinance Open Book Blog,* November 7, 2009 (j.mp/3Aw4HB).

ones, then tinkering, testing, publicizing, and propagating. The successful forms extend the financial system down the income scale, improving on the traditional arrangements, which are informal and often unreliable, available to poor people.

The history related here, if not written by the winners, dwells on them, the ones whose sparks lit lasting fires. Their successes proved the widespread desire among poor people for better ways to save, borrow, and insure. They demonstrated that many poor people are willing to pay for better services, which thus can be delivered on a commercial or near-commercial basis. And some of these providers, by selling simple savings services and insurance policies to millions, showed us ways to move beyond today's popular emphasis on credit.

Interestingly, while the demand from customers is a constant in history, the rationales in the minds of providers have varied: inculcation of thrift, liberation from usury, financing of small enterprises, reducing the burden of burial expenses, Christian fellowship, and even anti-Semitism. What these past successes do not establish is that financial services can be a reliable path out of poverty. Overall, history suggests that the real strength of microfinance, as of its forebears, is in bringing formal financial services to millions of people in minimally subsidized, businesslike ways.

A Preliminary: ROSCAs and ASCAs

Financial services need to ensure that when money or risk is transferred from one party to another, some basis for trust flows the opposite way. The bank that persuades you it is safe wins your deposits. The neighbor who is convinced that you are reliable may lend you money or cosign a loan from another.

The arrangements that humans have devised to conduct financial dealings on a foundation of trust can be roughly divided into two kinds, which differ in the stance of the provider with respect to the client. In *communal* or *group-oriented* provision, people join together for mutual support—lending to, saving with, and insuring each other. Typically they know one another and come from similar stations in life, and this social fabric of trust, interdependence, and peer pressure undergirds the financial linkages. All members are clients, and all members are providers.

In *individual* provision, one party delivers a service to another (or a group of others) often of lower standing or lesser economic power. Individual provision can take place commercially or charitably. In general, the parties forge trust from some combination of reputation, knowledge of the client, collateral, cosigners, and enforceable contracts.

The distinction between these two types of arrangements is not sharp; in fact, several examples we will encounter in the history have elements of both. Still, it helps frame the history.

Today, the most universal communal arrangement is what academics have labeled the Rotating Savings and Credit Association (ROSCA).[7] ROSCAs are found in slums and villages on every continent and go by many names. In India, they are commonly called chit funds, but also *kuri*, which harkens back to the use of cowry shells for money.[8] In a standard ROSCA, every member pays into a pot on a regular basis—for example, fifteen people could contribute weekly. Members take turns claiming the pot. For a woman who claims the pot early in this fifteen-week cycle, a ROSCA resembles a loan, since she receives a large payout and then must steadily pay back in. For those who come last, a ROSCA is more like a savings account. But if the cycle repeats enough, even this distinction may blur into an even rhythm of small pay-ins and occasional large payouts. ROSCAs have the virtue of simplicity: they are easy to understand; their operations are transparent; and no shared funds accumulate under someone's care, limiting the temptation to embezzle.[9] Perhaps precisely because ROSCAs require so little record-keeping, they hardly appear in the historical record.

If the advantage of ROSCAs is simplicity, the disadvantage is rigidity. It is the rare group of fifteen in which all members need to save or borrow exactly the same amount, and on such an inflexible, synchronized schedule. Because of this shortcoming, people have devised more complicated arrangements. Burial clubs, for example, accumulate contributions to cover funeral costs of members. Scholars today call all arrangements in which some funds collected are not immediately disbursed Accumulating Savings and Credit Associations (ASCAs). Unlike in ROSCAs, some funds are entrusted to the group's officers, producing an informal bank. This simple change unleashes a dizzying variety. The accumulated funds can be lent out to members or nonmembers on various terms, under various rules. Funds can be put in a bank. They can go into a pool for life insurance, as in burial societies. Different members can be allowed to contribute different amounts, earning proportionate dividends or interest. The rights to a given week's payout can be auctioned, the proceeds going into the general fund. ASCAs are more complex and burdensome to manage, and they create more opportunities for fraud. But many people have joined them through the ages for the added flexibility.

7. Bouman (1979) coined the term, adapting from Geertz's (1962) "rotating credit association."
8. Seibel (2005), 6.
9. Rutherford (2009a), 53–66; Armendáriz and Morduch (2010), 69–79.

Before the Industrial Revolution

Microfinance is conceived today as large-scale, businesslike provision of financial services to poor people. Defined this way, microfinance could not have developed in pre-modern times. It only works where even poor people are monetized—that is, where they have moved beyond barter or media of exchange other than money, such as wampum and rice. And it only works where large institutions, such as corporations and nonprofits, can be constructed and given legal identities that transcend the individuals within them. Thus microfinance by today's standard did not take off until the Industrial Revolution. Yet almost all the seeds were present beforehand, some for a very long time. In the story of Jonathan Swift, for example, we saw the devices of joint liability and weekly repayments as well as the impulses of philanthropy and self-help.

The world's oldest financial profession must be moneylending: in the mists of time, someone with a surplus of wealth lent it to someone with a deficit in exchange for the promise of repayment and a fee. Mathematically, the shuttling of money back and forth is reasonably symmetric. But the power relationship can be asymmetric: the borrower's difficulties put her in the weaker negotiating position. Often the relationship is so lopsided as to be exploitative, which is why moneylenders have been despised and even outlawed in religious teachings. Yet moneylenders have persisted because they meet a need. Some of the calumny heaped upon them has been a kind of scapegoating; sometimes it has been racist. Resentment of moneylending Jews is the obvious example but is not unique. Here is someone in colonial Burma blaming the country's economic woes on a class of moneylenders that originated in Chettinad, in what is now India's Tamil Nadu state:

> Chettiar banks are fiery dragons that parch every land that has the misfortune of coming under their wicked creeping. They are a hard-hearted lot what will ring out every drop of blood from the victims without compunction for the sake of their own interest. . . . [T]he swindling, cheating, deception and oppression of the Chettiars in the country, particularly among the ignorant folks, are well known and these are, to a large extent responsible for the present impoverishment in the land.[10]

Such sentiments stoked anti-Indian riots in the 1930s. After Japan invaded Burma in 1942, the Chettiars were forcibly expelled from the country.

---

10. Turnell (2009), 13.

No doubt the distastefulness of going to a moneylender is one reason people have long fashioned communal finance institutions. Homer told of the *eranos*, a communal meal in which all participants contributed a share of the food; that sense of mutual obligation carried over to a later meaning of *eranos*, a custom in which a person in need could ask each of his friends to lend him small sums. The borrower understood that his friends could one day reciprocate the imposition. From there, *eranos* loans seem to have taken more institutional forms in Athens. While the evidence is fragmentary enough to leave room for scholarly dispute, it hints that a single individual would borrow from a group—perhaps a businessman from his creditors and customers. Such debts had formal legal status, meaning that they could be pursued in court. An entry in the dictionary-thesaurus of the second-century Greek Julius Pollux implies that repayments were made in regular install-ments, rather than in a lump sum at the end of the term.[11]

Signs abound of communal financial arrangements since then. Ancient Greeks and Romans organized burial clubs, whose members shared a trade or deity of worship. In addition to relieving worries that funeral costs would compound the distress of bereaving families, the societies served as social bodies that would gather to dine, say, once a month.[12] "These meetings not only provided relief from the daily round of work," explains historian Robert Wilken, "they also provided friends and associates [with] mutual support, an opportunity for recognition and honor, a vehicle by which ordinary men could feel a sense of worth."[13] So common were they that some Greeks and Romans mistook early Christian groups for burial societies.[14] In Medieval Europe, guilds took on some of the functions of burial clubs. In England in the early 1600s, after the guilds disappeared, "friendly societies" began to form. The first were probably burial societies, although they diversified as they multiplied over the ensuing 300 years. Writings from nineteenth-century China contain references to "long-life loan companies" there. Similar institutions no doubt formed around the world.[15]

Another long-standing response to moneylenders has been to undercut them on a charitable basis, lending individually at low or no interest. The first recorded examples of such individual financial service with social purpose

---

11. Cohen (1992), 207–10; Pollux, *Onomasticon* 8, 144.

12. Brabrook (1898), 43–44.

13. Wilken (2003), 39.

14. Wilken (2003), 31–47.

15. "Friendly Societies," *Encyclopaedia Britannica*, 11th ed., vol. 11, 217–23; Brabrook (1898), 43–44.

date from about 1500. In 1462, the Franciscan friar Michele Carcano, having returned from the Holy Land to the town of Perugia on the Italian peninsula, made a fiery public speech against Jewish moneylenders and bankers. Those lenders interpreted their religious law as allowing them to charge interest to those outside their faith. Responding to Carcano, the town's Christian elite established a *monte di pietà*, a "mount of piety," to displace the Jewish financiers: a pawnshop financed with charitable capital. In time, *monti* sprouted up throughout Italy and much of Western Europe. Fortunately, their anti-Semitic bark proved worse than their bite: the Pope turned out to be an important patron of Jewish bankers in more than one sense, absolving of sin any town government that allowed Jewish banking to continue after the arrival of a *monte*.[16] Meanwhile, in England, bequests for charitable loan funds began appearing in the wills of the wealthy around 1500. The majority of the funds were dedicated to supporting young entrants into the benefactor's trade—weaving, haberdashery, and so on. But a significant minority were dedicated to the indigent, to "easse ther nede and payne," as instructed in the will of one John Terry, a former mayor of Norfolk.[17] Thus by the time of Jonathan Swift, lending was well established in English charity. Since Swift spent years in England, it seems unlikely that he formed the idea on his own.

A separate strand of evidence suggests that another ingredient in Swift's system, the use of cosigners for small loans, was also common in his milieu: as he began lending in the Irish capital to tradesmen with two cosigners, so did the Royal Bank of Scotland in the Scottish capital. In extending its credit, the two-year-old Edinburgh bank accepted as security the signatures of two or more "sureties" or "co-makers."[18] From today's perspective, the use of cosigners is interesting because joint liability formally undergirds most microloans. As Swift's biographer Sheridan explained, the arrangement put the cosigners to work on behalf of the lender. *They* had to judge whether the borrower was reliable, and *they* would go after him if he disappointed their trust.

Notably, while the Royal Bank of Scotland's lending practices appear in the history books as a novelty, the most innovative aspect was not that it used sureties. Indeed, the notion of surety itself is ancient. A passage of the Book of Proverbs that was probably written before the exodus warns, presumably out of bitter experience, "A man is without sense who gives a guarantee

---

16. Menning (1993); Toaff (2004).

17. Jordan (1959), 266–67; Jordan (1962), 142.

18. Lawson (1850), 421.

and surrenders himself to another as surety."[19] Rather, the loans were novel because they offered a flexible line of credit the client could tap and repay at times of his choosing. According to an account written a century later, "cash credit" began this way in 1729:

> A metropolitan shopkeeper . . . found himself at times in the posses-
> sion of more than a sufficient supply of ready money to carry on his
> trade, the overplus of which he consigned to the care of the neigh-
> bouring bank. But on other occasions, by reason of the length of the
> credits given to his customers, his money became so scarce that after
> exhausting his bank deposits, he still felt himself in difficulties. Several
> dilemmas of this kind having occurred . . . he was prompted to make
> a proposal of a novel nature to the bank; to the effect that, if it would
> accommodate him in straits with small loans, he would always shortly
> afterwards make up such debits, and that the parties should come to a
> balancing of accounts at periodical intervals. It seems this novel plan
> was acceded to. A cash credit, or liberty to draw to a certain extent,
> was instituted . . . and thus originated a system which has been of
> immense benefit to bankers and traders, and is now followed over the
> whole of Scotland.[20]

Cash credit became another financial innovation that took and spread—
in this case, across Scotland and then into England.[21] Just like flagship microcredit programs today, the joint-liability system boasted extraordinarily low
loss rates. One expert told a British parliamentary commission in 1826, "The
Bank of Scotland, I am sure, lost hardly anything in an amount of receipts
and payments of hundreds of millions: they may have lost a few hundred
pounds in a century."[22] And some observers saw the system as central to the
economic success of the people: Henry Wolff, a leading writer on cooperative
credit, recounted the following in 1896:

> A friend of mine was travelling in one of the northern counties of Scot-
> land, and there was pointed out to him a valley covered with beautiful
> farms. My friend was an Englishman, and his companion, who was a
> Scotchman, pointed down the valley and said, "That has all been done
> by the banks," intimating his strong opinion that but for the banking

19. Proverbs 11:15, *New English Bible*, 686, 675.
20. Chambers (1830), 344.
21. Wolff (1896), 65–66.
22. Lawson (1850), 421.

system of Scotland (the cash credit) the development of agriculture would be in its infancy compared to what it is now.[23]

Thus, Swift clearly drew on ambient ideas in arriving at his system for lending to the poor. His effort, though, appears to be the first on record that combined particular elements that are central to much of modern microcredit: a charitable motive; the requirement of a regular repayment schedule to make thrift habitual; and an approach that was individual in that the banker was clearly of higher standing than the banked, and yet was communal in leveraging bonds between signers and cosigners to assure repayment.

Swift's lending system and cash credit were not the only historically significant innovations that would take hold in the British Isles, soon to be the first territory convulsed by the Industrial Revolution. Mass production would begin to change the world and, along the way, the provision of financial services to poor people.

Takeoff in the British Isles

The economic transformation of Europe in the eighteenth and nineteenth centuries revolutionized every aspect of daily life, including financial services. At once, the transformation put new pressures on the poorest classes and created scope for innovations to relieve them. As for the pressures, mass production of such goods as cloth and flour threw traditional artisans out of work. Enclosure of once-common lands sent farmers into towns and cities, there to work in dangerous mines and factories in exchange for wages that were pittances against the swelling fortunes of the capitalist employers.

Then, in the early nineteenth century, advances in sanitation and hygiene lowered the death rate and unleashed the population explosion that so worried philosopher Thomas Malthus. The billowing ranks of the indigent led the British government to expand an Elizabethan welfare program called the Poor Laws. Rising costs of that policy and fear of unrest among the "lower orders" added urgency to the search for more constructive and long-lasting responses to poverty. The general thrust of the innovations developed over the nineteenth century was to supplant traditional, informal, communal systems with formal institutions providing individual services. And the innovations went well beyond credit, bringing modern savings and insurance to poor Brits for the first time. Today's microfinance movement has yet to match that achievement.

23. Wolff (1896), 66, quoting one Mr. Fowler.

One sign of the times: in 1797 a group of lords, bishops, members of parliament, and other respectable persons formed the Society for Bettering the Condition and Increasing the Comforts of the Poor, a rough equivalent for its day of the Center for Global Development (where I work). Funded by charity, the society collected data on what worked in the fight against poverty—"information respecting the circumstances and situation of the poor, and the most effectual means of meliorating their condition"—and spread ideas through "the circulation of *useful* and *practical* information, derived from experience, and stated *briefly* and *plainly*."[24] Its chief strategy was to set up a feed, a stream of content to which people subscribed, in the era's most powerful medium of dissemination, the printed book. Rather like a group blog, the articles in the society's periodical *Reports* hopped about randomly within a defined area. Topics in the first volume ranged from girls' education ("a school of industry for 60 girls") to diversification of rural livelihoods ("the advantage of a cottager keeping a pig").[25]

Evident in the pages of the *Reports*, which today can be browsed on Google Books, is that financial services were a concern, too. And the main vehicle for delivering them was the friendly society. In fact, the first article in the journal's first issue is "an account of a friendly society at Castle-Eden, in the country of Durham," which among other things made loans for buying cows. Explained the author, Rowland Burdon, esquire: "The great desideratum, with respect to the maintenance of the poor, has always appeared to me to be the encouragement of habits of economy, and of a system of periodical subscription towards their own subsistence."[26] Friendly societies, recall, were informal groups that provided burial and disability insurance, loans, and other such services to members. Members would typically contribute weekly or monthly. The societies varied in the often-complex formulas for dues and payouts as well as the services provided. Some societies made loans while others did not. Some were "collecting societies" that helped people save. These would "send volunteer officers about to collect, as a labour of love, the pence and twopences which workmen receive, and which, without collectors to carry them into safety, they so often manage to fritter away."[27] In 1905, a census of friendly societies would find 30,000, with 14 million members and £50 million on hand.[28] But friendly societies were also a constant source of

---

24. Bernard (1798), 265.

25. Glasse (1798), 140; Bouyer (1798), 204.

26. Burdon (1798), 10.

27. Wolff (1896), 31.

28. "Friendly Societies," *Encyclopaedia Britannica,* 11th ed., vol. 11, 217–23.

trouble. At the time of that report from Durham, actuarial science hardly had been invented, so dues were set by little more than sticking a finger in the wind. If dues were too low, collapse was inevitable as payouts exceeded pay-ins; people who had contributed for years could see all their thrift wasted. But especially if dues were too high (and even if not), the enticement to theft on the part of managers could be irresistible. Industrialization would bring another problem: migration. Farmers might contribute to a friendly society, then move to the city before they could benefit, again wasting years of thrift.[29] These vexations drew the British parliament into a century-long struggle to regulate friendly societies in the public interest, starting in 1793.[30] They also drew philanthropists, lawmakers, and businessmen into efforts to do better. One approach was for well-off people—such as Burdon—to sponsor friendly societies and thereby reassure common folk about their propriety and solvency.

Swift's charitable loan system was effectively an early project to improve on friendly societies. As recounted, though loan funds originated in the 1720s, before industrialization, they gained national significance in Ireland after the passage of a law in 1823 giving them legal standing. Within twenty years, they had reached a fifth of Irish families. But then twin disasters sent the Irish loan funds into a long decline. The great potato famine struck in 1846–48, killing a million people and sending an equal number overseas. And perhaps because conventional banks were threatened by the high rates the funds paid on deposits, new legislation lowered the cap on funds' lending rates from 13.6 to 8.8 percent a year, which squeezed their earnings.[31]

Another type of organization, legally classified as a friendly society, was the building society. Also called a cooperative savings and loan association, it helped members buy land and houses. Members' regular contributions built up a fund from which loans were made with interest; the profits were then divided among members. As mortgages, the loans were secured by col-lateral, the property whose purchase they financed. This aspect set building societies apart from most friendly societies, whose loans tended to rely on peer pressure and trust for security. By the same token, building societies probably formed among somewhat better-off people, those ready to join the propertied class. The earliest reference to a building society occurs in 1795, in the city of Birmingham.[32]

29. Dennett (1998), 5–8.
30. "Friendly Societies," *Encyclopaedia Britannica,* 11th ed., vol. 11, 220.
31. Hollis and Sweetman (1997, 1998a, 1998b); Hollis (2002).
32. "Building Societies," *Encyclopaedia Britannica,* 11th ed., vol. 4, 766.

The two most pivotal British innovations married the retail techniques of friendly societies with the strength of formal institutions. One of those was the savings bank. Some have traced the idea to writer Daniel Defoe. In addition to *Robinson Crusoe,* he wrote an *Essay upon Projects,* which in 1697 set forth many ideas for bettering society, including a "pension office" that would offer a similar form of insurance as a burial society would for old age and disability.[33] The earliest institution on this model may have been formed in the German city of Brunswick in 1765 to serve craftsmen and servants; it was more certainly followed by others in Hamburg, Berne, and Geneva.[34] These banks resembled savings banks to the extent that they took in money rather than lending it out, and did so on an individual rather than communal basis.[35]

Proper savings banks for ordinary folks, which allowed deposits to be taken in or out at any time, appeared in England around 1800. In 1797, philosopher Jeremy Bentham called for the formation of "frugality banks" to cultivate thrift among the poor. He criticized friendly societies on many grounds. They were liable to overestimate or underestimate the necessary contributions, as I explained earlier. They were prone to disagreement, dissolution, and embezzlement. They gathered at public houses, which often required members to spend and imbibe in exchange for meeting on the premises. "Choosing a tippling-house for a school of frugality, would be like choosing a brothel for a school of continence," Bentham observed.[36]

Within ten years, the equally influential Malthus concurred in an edition of his *Essay on the Principle of Population.* He pointed to savings banks as a way to encourage thrift and self-sacrifice among poor people, which would induce them to better their material lot, delay marriage, and have fewer children. Essential to success, he wrote, "the laborer should be able to draw out his money whenever he wanted it, and have the most perfect liberty of disposing of it in every respect as he pleased."[37] Sure that she could get her money out, he argued, she would more readily put it in.

As intellectuals inked ideas, others acted. In 1798, Priscilla Wakefield—a reader of Bentham, a granddaughter of the Barclay of Barclays bank, and the one heroine in this history—started a benefit club in Tottenham, north of London. It accepted tiny increments of savings from poor children.[38] She

33. Defoe (1697).

34. "Savings Banks," *Encyclopaedia Britannica,* 11th ed., vol. 24, 243.

35. Keyes (1876), 16.

36. Bentham (1843 [1797]), 410–23.

37. Malthus (1809 [1807]), 474–75.

38. Janine McVeagh, biographer of Wakefield, New Zealand, e-mail to author, November 10, 2009.

reported on it in the journal of the Society for Bettering the Condition and Increasing the Comforts of the Poor. Anticipating the previous chapter of this book by 210 years, she wrote, "It is well known to those who are conversant with the affairs of the labouring classes, that it is much easier for them to spare a small sum at stated periods, than to lay down what is sufficient . . . at once."[39] She expanded her banking to adults in 1801, with several wealthy individuals guaranteeing the safety of deposits. The benefit club took deposits as small as a shilling and paid 5 percent on complete pounds accumulated.[40] The first depositor in this, arguably the first savings bank, was "an orphan girl of fourteen, who placed two pounds in it, which she had earned in very small sums, and saved in the Benefit Club."[41] Wakefield's diaries reveal sentiments that would be familiar to later pioneers of financial services for poor people: the frustration of persuading others of a vision and the pride of proving it through practical success.[42]

Wakefield's idea took off in Scotland by 1815, thanks to parallel efforts of a minister, Henry Duncan, and the son of a banker in Edinburgh, a Mr. J. H. Forbes. Banks on Duncan's plan had elaborate rules for memberships, savings amounts, and interest rates, all contortions intended to make the banks qualify as friendly societies under the 1793 law. The Edinburgh model was more streamlined and eventually prevailed over Duncan's system, ironically thanks in part to Duncan's fervent advocacy for a new Scottish law to put savings banks on firm legal ground.[43] The Scottish savings banks paid interest, which they earned by putting their deposits in conventional banks. After spreading across Scotland, savings banks, like cash credit, moved south. The *Edinburgh Review* wrote in 1815:

> We are happy to understand that Savings Banks are spreading rapidly through Scotland; and we expect soon to hear the like good tidings from England, where such an institution is of still greater importance. It would be difficult, we fear, to convince either the people or their rulers, that such an event is of far more importance, and far more likely to increase the happiness and even the greatness of the nation, than the

39. Wakefield (1802), 145.

40. Horne (1947), 26.

41. Wakefield (1805), 210.

42. Diaries of Priscilla Wakefield, extract courtesy of Janine McVeagh, Rawene, Hokianga, New Zealand. See David Roodman, "Diary Entries from 1798 on First Savings Bank," *Microfinance Open Book Blog*, November 7, 2009 (j.mp/3Aw4HB).

43. Horne (1947), 39–70.

most brilliant sum of its arms, or the most stupendous improvements of its trade or its agriculture.—And yet we are persuaded that it is so.[44]

That was an impressive claim coming shortly after the British defeat of Napoleon at Waterloo.

Within the United Kingdom (including Northern Ireland), the number of savings banks climbed steadily, peaking at 645 in 1861, at which time they held 1.6 million accounts.[45] And savings banks went global almost as fast as microfinance today: by 1820, seeds had propagated and bloomed in Australia, France, Germany, the Netherlands, Switzerland, and the United States.[46] In Germany, municipal governments became particularly active as guarantors for savings banks (*sparkassen*); by 1900, they backed most of the 2,685 in operation.[47]

For the servants and laborers who used these banks, the prospect of saving to pay for a wedding, say, rather than borrowing for it must have been attractive because it eliminated the stress of debt. But if savings banks reduced the danger of debt entrapment, they put a new risk in its place: what if through fraud or incompetence, the bank made off with the hard-earned sums? Private savings banks therefore had their critics, too. One constructive remedy, first proposed in 1807 by a member of the British parliament and finally pushed through in 1861 by Chancellor of the Exchequer William Gladstone, was that the post office go into the savings business. By 1861, the post office did money transfers, handling millions of small orders a year. Its 2,000 branches gave it vast reach. And its official status would earn the trust of depositors.

The British postal savings system succeeded as envisioned. It reached 1 million accounts in 1869, 2 million in 1880, and 10 million in 1906. Many private savings banks shut down, though the survivors grew enough to stabilize the tally of accounts at such institutions. Gladstone, whose career included four stints as prime minister, would list the postal savings bank as one of his greatest achievements.[48] Today, savings banks are a global phenomenon, with roughly 250 million accounts in developing-country postal savings banks and more than 800 million in non–postal savings banks (see chapter 4). All those accounts descend from the work of Priscilla Wakefield—quite a legacy for a forgotten heroine.

---

44. "Publications on Parish or Savings Banks," *Edinburgh Review,* June–October 1815, 146.
45. Horne (1947), 388–89.
46. Horne (1947), 89–91; Keyes (1876); Tilly (1994), 305; Townsend (1878), 44.
47. Steinwand (2001), 54.
48. Horne (1947), 388–92.

Britain's second great achievement in financial services for the masses was establishing "industrial life assurance." While savings banks arose from a charitable impulse, the sellers of life insurance to working-class people were motivated by profit, if also a sense of mission. The Joint Stock Companies Act of 1844 made it much easier to create new companies and sell shares to the public—perhaps too easy. The financial industry saw dozens of start-ups in the 1840s, many short-lived and no more deserving of public trust than the worst friendly societies. Historian Laurie Dennett describes the scene:

> In the field of life assurance [unsound companies] seemed to succeed one another with exceptional rapidity. The *Post Magazine and Insurance Monitor* . . . , a weekly paper founded in 1840 to act as a reporter on the assurance industry and exposer of its abuses, certainly found numerous subjects for dissection. . . . The editor on one occasion referred to an entity "brought into existence under the facilities for forming such companies by the [Act] . . . whose robberies amounted to £60,000," another "composed of a low set of vagabonds, whose signatures as shareholders were procured at a pot-house for pints of beer," and finally, one which "at the end of three years, had only £14,512 left in every shape and form out of £45,081 received in solid cash. . . ." Charles Dickens' "Anglo-Bengalee Disinterested Loan and Life Insurance Company" had plenty of prototypes in life, as did its dissolute President, Tigg Montague, alias Montague Tigg.[49]

Yet from this pond scum, higher life evolved. In 1852 the British Industry Life Assurance Company and Family Friendly Society was founded. Its object was to combine for the first time the retail techniques of friendly societies, especially the practice of taking weekly payments, with the scientific rigor of modern life insurance, calibrating premiums to estimated probabilities of death at various ages. (Many friendly societies, in contrast, charged a person the same whether he was 20 or 40.) British Industry reported issuing an impressive 12,837 policies in its first half year, worth an average of less than £14 each.[50]

Little information has been preserved about how British Industry marketed so effectively to the masses; perhaps it sold through existing friendly societies. More is known about the company that would soon overtake it and then dominate. The Prudential Mutual Assurance, Investment, and Loan Association was founded in the same burst of corporate creativity, in 1848.

49. Dennett (1998), 8–9.
50. Dennett (1998), 39.

Initially its goals were to sell "ordinary assurance"—life insurance for the upper classes—and make loans to the same. (As a mutual association, all clients were required to buy shares.) But then a parliamentary study committee praised the success of British Industry in 1853 and intrigued Prudential. In 1856, the company's new director, the young Henry Harben, went after the industrial assurance market with all his ambition. Spending three days a week travelling the country on its rail network, talking to agents, and studying successes and failures, Harben refined and streamlined his business model.

Here, too, the history will feel familiar to modern microfinance managers. One key was selling policies and collecting payments door-to-door. Because poor people were illiterate, they could not be expected to read advertisements; because they were busy and lower class, perhaps ashamed of their ragged clothes, they could not be expected to find the time and courage to visit branch offices. Agents would be paid on commission. Selecting agents was critical: they needed energy, intelligence without condescension, and willingness to spend their days walking through crowded slums. Careful record-keeping was essential to prevent fraud among agents, as was aggressive prosecution to deter it. Prudential prided itself on rapid payment in the event of death but avoided the more transaction-intensive and fraud-prone disability insurance business. A final practice was covering whole families. Prudential at first resisted insuring children less than ten years old for fear it would reward infanticide, or be accused of such. But Harben changed his mind after he discovered that one of his most successful agents was breaking this rule. At a time when one in five infants died in the first year of life, Harben came to understand that parents were "anxious to insure their children, as in the event of death they found the funeral expenses press very hard upon them, and gladly welcomed the aid which a Society afforded." And parents who insured their children with Prudential were more likely to insure themselves as well.[51]

This system of operation turned Prudential into a juggernaut. By 1881 it had insured an eighth of the population of the United Kingdom; by 1886 a fifth; by 1891 a quarter; and by 1900 a third, or about 13 million people of all ages.[52]

Credit, savings, and insurance—probably never again will one small part of the world incubate so many innovations in financial services for the masses as the British Isles did in the nineteenth century. Oddly, the service types for which the contribution was greatest, savings banks and life insurance, have been overshadowed by credit in the modern microfinance

51. Dennett (1998), 12, 48–50. Quote from Dennett (1998), 48. Proneness to fraud from Hoffman (1900), 95.

52. Dennett (1998), 107–08.

movement. That points to underexploited opportunities today in microsavings and microinsurance.

Cooperation on the Continent

France, Germany, and other continental nations had analogs to friendly societies in the nineteenth century. They imported the building society and the savings bank from the British Isles. Industrial life insurance, too, crossed the English Channel. But the region also made an important contribution to the history of ideas in financial services: the credit cooperative. In the first half of the nineteenth century—the milieu that incubated the egalitarian revolutions of 1848 and the radical ideas of Karl Marx—a great deal of thinking and experimentation went into putting bits of capital in the hands of the laboring classes. Although the credit cooperative, too, had British roots, its manifestation in continental Europe was more intensely communal than anything that flourished in the British Isles, perhaps because farming villages in what is now Germany were themselves more tight-knit.

The intellectual father of the credit cooperative movement was a religious and prolific German writer named Victor Aimé Huber. Born in 1800, Huber attended a Swiss school from ages six to sixteen, during which time the Welsh industrialist Robert Owen once visited to talk about his experiments in cooperation. As manager and part owner of a factory in New Lanark, Scotland, Owen and his fellow investors, including Jeremy Bentham, had reduced the profit they extracted from the enterprise to leave funds for the company to spend "on the education of the children and the improvement of the workpeople at New Lanark and for the general improvement of the conditions of the persons employed in manufactures."[53] This emphasis on the moral responsibility of the capitalist made Owen a founder of socialism and foreshadowed Muhammad Yunus of Grameen Bank on the value of cause-driven "social businesses."[54] Others would extend Owen's ideas to starting cooperative stores, most famously in the English town of Rochdale in 1844. These made workers not just deserving beneficiaries of capitalist charity but capitalists themselves. Members of the Rochdale cooperative store contributed small amounts of their own money to build up the equity base. The store bought goods in bulk to lower the price, retailed them, then distributed any profits to members.[55]

53. Tucker (1922), 12.
54. Yunus (2010).
55. Tucker (1922), 12–14, 20.

Influenced by his early encounter with Owen and later travels in England, Huber came to the idea of a cooperative that would pool capital not to purchase goods, but to lend back to members. He began advocating it in writing by the late 1840s. The first practical realization came in Belgium in 1848, but it was in Germany that the idea really took. Donald Tucker, a perceptive historian of the cooperative movement, wrote in 1922 that it was perhaps "inevitable that Germany should become the cradle of the cooperative banking movement."[56] The population was large and dense; class lines were sharply drawn; people lived concentrated in villages of a hundred or more inhabitants. "Not only did Germans know to what social class they belonged, but outside of the great cities each German had also a definite place within a local group," Tucker wrote.[57] These dense and strong social structures were perhaps the dominant source of individual identity and status—in contrast to the individualist values of advanced consumer societies—and they provided a foundation for credit provision through groups of interdependent borrowers. Much the same might be said of Asian societies built on irrigated rice, including today's Bangladesh.

However inevitable, the rise of credit cooperatives in Germany had its visionary heroes. As usual in this history, they came from affluent backgrounds and sought energetically for practical remedies to the suffering they saw around them. The first was Franz Hermann Schulze-Delitzsch. In 1850, with memories fresh from the famine winter of 1846–47, he founded his first credit cooperative, in the town of his birth, Delitzsch. He copied the two-tiered English structure he apparently learned about through Huber, not unlike that friendly society in Durham: wealthy, honorary members contributed to a loan fund that lent to poorer members. But the thing fell apart: the loans were not repaid, and the rich members lost their money.[58]

As it happened, two friends of Schulze-Delitzsch founded a credit cooperative at the same time in nearby Eilenburg, which differed in excluding the benefactors from being shareholding members. They could lend to the cooperative, but they could not borrow from it, nor be held responsible for the debts of others, nor share in the profits. This arrangement gave the lower-class members maximum incentives to manage the funds for the long term. Overall, funds came from two sources: the poor members' own regular, modest contributions, which entitled them to democratic ownership and control of the cooperative, and the loans from benefactors, for which

56. Tucker (1922), 17.
57. Tucker (1922), 18.
58. Tucker (1922), 45–48.

all members accepted full liability. In theory, even if 90 percent of borrowers defaulted and disappeared and the remaining 10 percent never borrowed from the cooperative and owned tiny shares of it, the benefactors could go after that 10 percent for the full amounts of the original loans. Schulze-Delitzsch would later advocate this strong liability as necessary to attract outside capital, and many Germans accepted it. Out of the capital so obtained, the Eilenburg cooperative lent to individual members in the same way as Jonathan Swift and the Royal Bank of Scotland. Two neighbors typically cosigned with a borrower.[59]

By 1852, the Eilenburg cooperative had 586 members and had made 717 small loans. Two years later, it had borrowed from external supporters twenty-six times its own share capital. That degree of leverage Schulze-Delitzsch later judged too high, but it demonstrated the credibility the cooperative had quickly earned among benefactors.

Schulze-Delitzsch copied and promoted this model. The core innovation—drawing in benefactors only as creditors via the power of joint liability—became the germ of the global cooperative movement. "Your own selves and characters must create your credit," Schulze-Delitzsch wrote, "and your collective liability will require you to choose your associates carefully, and to insist that they maintain regular, sober and industrious habits, making them worthy of credit."[60]

In the mature Schulze-Delitzsch "people's bank," loans were usually made for three to six months—in theory only for investment in members' businesses. "Never borrow for consumption, as is frequently the case with wage-earners who render themselves liable to default," Schulze-Delitzsch admonished; no doubt some members did just that anyway (recall the discussion of fungibility in chapter 2).[61] At any rate, once fired by his initial success, Schulze-Delitzsch became an "economic missionary," the Muhammad Yunus of his era. "His striking personality, his convincing eloquence, his invincible faith in his own cause, and his truly contagious enthusiasm made him an almost ideal propagandist," according to Wolff, who himself was no slouch as an economic missionary.[62] People's banks proliferated across Germany and into other countries over the next several decades. Russia had 3,300 people's banks by 1913.[63]

59. Tucker (1922), 45–48.

60. Quote appears in Herrick and Ingalls (1914), 272–74.

61. Quote appears in Herrick and Ingalls (1914), 272.

62. Wolff (1896), 75.

63. Tucker (1922), 231.

Another German, Friedrich Wilhelm Raiffeisen, also left a strong imprint on credit cooperation. He, too, began experimenting in the 1850s but did not settle on a model until 1864, giving him ample time to learn from Schulze-Delitzsch. While Schulze-Delitzsch geared his cooperative to urban workers and shopkeepers, Raiffeisen worked with poorer farmers. From his point of view, the Schulze-Delitzsch requirement that members buy shares excluded truly poor people; and while the three- to six-month loan periods may have suited shopkeepers whose inventory turned over quickly, they were ill-matched to the rhythm of the harvest and the gestation of livestock. So Raiffeisen's cooperatives did not make people pay anything to join. All financing was borrowed from outsiders through the assurance of joint liability. Still, members were to deposit savings even as they repaid their loans, so that the cooperatives could eventually free themselves from outside credit. The terms of loans to members could extend to two years or more. A final difference, in conception: Raiffeisen founded his cooperatives on what he saw as fraternal love among Christians, with at least implied resentment of the typically Jewish moneylenders. An important purpose for him was moral uplift.[64]

Raiffeisen's "village banks," as they were sometimes called in English, spread slowly at first, not taking off until 1880. But by 1913, there were 16,927 rural village banks, compared to Schulze-Delitzsch's 980 people's banks in 1915.[65] Raiffeisen's variant also dominated in the spread of the cooperative movement to the rest of Europe, the Americas, and Asia.[66]

One hot controversy within the international credit cooperation movements was over the merits of the unlimited liability of members, with respect to the outside creditors, for the debts of other members. Several foreign adapters of the German systems rejected unlimited liability. For instance, in Italy, a Jewish banker named Luigi Luzatti started his *Banca Popolare* sitting at a table on a sidewalk in Milan in 1866. His people's banks were organized as cooperatively owned, limited-liability, joint-stock companies, meaning that members' responsibility for losses on lending operations were capped at whatever capital they paid in. In principle, this limitation on liability of shareholders made it easier to attract share capital but harder to attract creditors because in the event of default, the latter could only go after the bank, not its member-owners. In practice, Luzatti succeeded in not only launching his own bank but inspiring hundreds of others on the Italian peninsula. The change to limited liability also made his banks more like conventional ones,

64. Wolff (1896), 115–18.
65. Moody and Fite (1971), 9–13.
66. Steinwand (2001), 57.

with the persisting, crucial difference that joint liability allowed his banks to take character as collateral.[67]

The approach that spread in North America in the early twentieth century was also limited liability.[68] Meanwhile, cooperatives were introduced in Britain and Ireland but never took off.[69] Perhaps cultural differences lay at the root of these mutations and failures. People in more individualistic cultures may hesitate more to accept full liability for the debts of others. Or perhaps by the end of the century, Britons were wealthy enough that they could access credit without joint liability.

Despite disinterest in the Isles, in 1904, the British government in India enacted a law to support credit cooperatives as a means to quell unrest, following a recommendation of the Indian Famine Commission. The enabling law led to an explosion of activity. One important figure in the story is William Gourlay, a top British official in the state of Bengal, whose territory included modern-day Bangladesh. To prepare for his duties as registrar of credit cooperatives in Bengal, Gourlay visited and studied cooperatives in Europe for a month.[70] In 1906, he put the principles of cooperative credit in his own words, giving us a conceptual bridge from German innovations in the 1850s to the microcredit that would surface in the Bengal territory in the 1970s:

> In Germany [a system for providing services] has been found in Co-operative Credit Societies, and in India an attempt is being made to create a similar organization. This system aims at capitalizing the honesty of the villages. . . . We want, therefore, to teach the people to amalgamate this village credit and jointly borrow a sum sufficient to meet the needs of the whole village. The capitalist does not know which cultivator is good for [5 rupees] and which for [100 rupees]. It is the villagers alone who have all the information. . . .
>
> A man is not tempted to spend . . . more than he can afford when he has to run the gauntlet of public opinion, and the village will not lend him more than he can repay when they realize their joint responsibility.[71]

By 1946, just before independence, Indian cooperatives had a reported 9 million members.[72] But for all the apparent growth, the groups did not

---

67. Tucker (1992), 211–21.
68. Tucker (1992), 234.
69. Guinnane (1994) discusses the failure of credit cooperatives in Ireland.
70. Wolff (1927), 68.
71. Gourlay (1906), 217–18.
72. Armendáriz and Morduch (2010), 80.

always work as intended. Wolff, who had done much to bring about the 1904 act, in 1927 bemoaned the "dry rot" of high default rates and corrupt local administration.[73] In Burma, also part of British India, the system peaked at more than 4,000 cooperatives around 1925. But there, a government report worried that "societies were being registered too easily, . . . loans . . . were being made too easily [and] repayments have become slack." Sure enough, the Burmese system collapsed into a mound of bad debts just before the Depression. A 1929 investigative report, as summarized recently by Australian economist Sean Turnell, concluded that "'excessive leniency' was the order of the day. Worse, 'fictitious figures', 'paper adjustments' and the granting of new loans so that defaulters could pretend to repay old ones, were measures commonly resorted to. . . . [S]uch practices 'could not have persisted and reached the dimensions it did unless connived by everyone concerned.'"[74] In retrospect, the weakness of the Indian cooperative program grew out of the moral corruption of the colonial arrangement. Partly out of fear of unrest, the government worked harder to push subsidized credit than to hold the conveyors accountable for businesslike performance. (It would not be the last Indian government to behave this way: see chapter 4.) Meanwhile, buried resentment fomented, and cultural distance obscured, the subversion of the program's intent. Nevertheless, the idea that one could help poor people with joint-liability loans remained.

Small Loans for Profit in the United States

Americans were quick to copy European innovations. In 1816, the Massachusetts legislature chartered the first American savings bank, in Boston.[75] The first building society started up in Philadelphia in 1836.[76] Friendly (or "fraternal") societies formed over the nineteenth century under obscure names, such as "The Ancient Order of Hibernians" and "The Improved Order of Red Men."[77] Many were defined by the ethnicity of the immigrants they admitted.

In the mid-1870s, a man named John Dryden created the Prudential Insurance Company in Newark, New Jersey; the firm was entirely inspired by its British namesake. Dryden spent time with Henry Harben at the

73. Wolff (1927), 83. See also Rutherford (2009b), 27–28.

74. Turnell (2005), 17–19.

75. Keyes (1876), 38–40.

76. Dexter (1900), 41–69.

77. "Friendly Societies," *Encyclopaedia Britannica,* 11th ed., vol. 11, 217–23.

British Prudential studying the company's methods in detail.[78] His rival across the Hudson in New York, Metropolitan Life, had built a business selling insurance through German fraternal societies, with the societies doing the weekly premium collection. Eventually, Metropolitan, too, decided to copy the British Prudential system for direct retail. It made up for its slower start by importing hundreds of British Prudential agents. Soon it became the market leader.[79]

Early in the twentieth century, serious efforts were made to introduce two more models, one based on the European credit cooperatives, the other on the more individual approaches of the British Isles. The former grew steadily, and the institutions it spawned thrive to this day; the latter soared spectacularly and then disappeared just as fast—a pair of trajectories that once again point to how evolving national characteristics shape the uptake of financial services for the masses.

Americans encountered the credit cooperative several times in the nineteenth century but did not embrace it. In 1864, German-immigrant followers of Schulze-Delitzsch started a cooperative in New York City that was meant to provide credit, among other services. In Massachusetts, state senator Josiah Quincy introduced a bill in 1870 to give credit cooperatives legal standing after learning about them from his uncle, who had translated writings of Schulze-Delitzsch into English. Quincy's motion failed after it was decided that such organizations could be set up under current law. But they weren't, not until the next century.

In 1907, Gourlay accompanied Edward Filene, the Bostonian entrepreneur who invented the bargain basement, on a long tour through Bengal, which allowed Gourlay to inspect the new cooperative banks and show them to Filene.[80] Filene later visited President Theodore Roosevelt to advocate a similar system for the U.S.-controlled Philippines and followed up with copies of Gourlay's writings. But he did not yet propose it for the United States proper.[81]

Pivotal figures in the final, successful arrival of credit cooperative in North America were the Canadian Alphonse Desjardins and the American Pierre Jay, both of whom learned much about European cooperatives from the writings of Wolff. Desjardins was atypical of the visionary founders in this

78. Hoffman (1900), 57, 132, 285.

79. MetLife, "MetLife Begins" (www.metlife.com/about/corporate-profile/metlife-history/metlife-begins/index.html).

80. Filene (1907), 20–31.

81. Moody and Fite (1971), 16–17, 26–30.

history in that he grew up poor; he was typical in that he devoted years of his life to an obsession that many of his associates must have thought benighted. He founded his first joint-stock cooperative, a *caisse populaire,* outside of Quebec in 1901. Its first deposit was 10 cents. Within six years, it had made $200,000 in loans without losing a penny. By 1914, 150 *caisses populaires* had been started in Canada.

Meanwhile, Pierre Jay, a Massachusetts banking regulator who descended from the first U.S. Supreme Court Chief Justice John Jay, became hooked on cooperation after he stumbled on a book by Wolff in a public library in 1906. He soon learned of Desjardins's work, then collaborated with him to finally push enabling legislation through the Massachusetts legislature. In time, Filene joined and even led the U.S. credit cooperative cause. He was motivated by his desire as a Jew to put the lie to anti-Semitic slurs about usury and his own progressive passion—he gave his employees paid holidays, free medical care, and a savings and loan association. U.S. credit unions—so named to emphasize the formal democratic governance that becomes necessary when membership expands from dozens to hundreds—boasted 2.8 million participants by 1940.[82] Today in the United States, credit unions are found at many large employers, including the federal government, and have some 91 million members.[83] But perhaps because of America's affluence and individualism, the communal approach to lending never became as prevalent in the United States as it did in Germany. Credit unions may be jointly governed by their members, but they serve the members individually.

Another effort that seems to embody a more individualistic American style harkened back to Scottish cash credit. In 1910 a lawyer in Norfolk, Virginia, named Arthur Morris founded an unusual kind of for-profit bank. Under the Morris Plan of Industrial Banking, a person producing two sureties (or "comakers") could borrow a sum as small as $100 and repay it in weekly installments over the course of a year. The interest rate worked out to 17 percent per annum, making the Morris Plan an attractive alternative to loan sharks, who were seen as a social menace.[84] After Morris's enterprise had obviously succeeded, a former associate named David Stein sued, claiming that Morris's Plan was in fact Stein's. Ironically, by forcing evidence into the courtroom, the paternity dispute exposed the European roots of the plan. The judge ruled against Stein, concluding that even if one *could* patent such

82. Moody and Fite (1971), 18–52, 359.

83. WOCCU (2010).

84. Interest rate from Fisher (1929). Role of foundation from Carruthers, Guinnane, and Lee (2005).

financial services, the ideas predated Stein—here citing Wolff's writings sub-mitted into the record.[85] A pair of cosigners and weekly repayments were not new ideas.

The Morris Plan demonstrated again the explosive power that can be released by combining such established ingredients with management savvy. It also demonstrated the controversy inherent in for-profit lending to the poor. By 1931, Morris had built an empire: 109 banks in 142 cities making $220 million in loans per year. At one of the larger banks, comaker loans averaged $183 in 1925, rising to $271 in 1939. Dividing a representative fig-ure of $200 per loan into $220 million in total lending suggests that Morris banks served a million borrowers.[86] Industrial banks unaffiliated with but modeled on the Morris Plan also sprang up. The prefix "micro" not being in common use, people called it the "small loan business." Yet across the northern border, Desjardins decried the Morris banks as nothing "but a huge money-making concern devised to insure to the promoters a good business proposition, at the expense of the public."[87] For Desjardins turning a profit for outside investors, as distinct from member-owners, extinguished the soul of the small loan business.[88]

But Morris plowed ahead. His banks worked with retailers to provide installment credit, becoming for a time the country's largest source of con-sumer credit.[89] Morris's success helped provoke mainline commercial banks into direct competition. In 1928, after prodding from the Russell Sage Foun-dation, New York's attorney general succeeded in driving the loan sharks out of business. But people still needed credit, so the attorney general pleaded with leading banks to adopt the proven small loan business model. National City Bank of New York, the country's largest bank and the ancestor of Citi-group, heeded the call and started a midtown Manhattan office offering loans of $50–1,000 to salaried workers.[90] The move created a sensation: "500

85. Universal Savings Corporation v. Morris Plan Company of New York et al., *The Federal Reporter* 234, September–October 1916 (St. Paul: West Publishing, 382–86). The link between the European examples, especially Scottish cash credit, and the Morris Plan is not certain but seems very likely. In his history, Herzog (1928, 13) intimates the link; Stein claimed to have first developed the system in 1898, five years after the publication of Wolff's *People's Banks*, which Stein and Morris would almost certainly have read as they pondered how to bring credit to the masses.

86. Saulnier (1940), 87.

87. Moody and Fite (1971), 64.

88. Desjardins's remark could slip unnoticed into modern debating forums. Yunus, for exam-ple, has defined "microfinance" to exclude for-profit, investor-owned lending. See Clinton Global Initiative panel discussion, September 28, 2010 (j.mp/dWhuM9).

89. Mushinski and Phillips (2008).

90. Cleveland and Huertas (1985), 118–21.

Workers Seek City Bank's Loans," ran a *New York Times* headline after opening day.[91]

But in the years after World War II, Morris's Plan—if not the banks themselves—fell victim to the country's rising affluence. Today, most Americans no longer need to bind their peers into joint liability to obtain credit, so they don't.

Learning from History

Behind every paragraph of this history lie a thousand lost stories of individuals who pondered, experimented with, doubted, evangelized, or used particular financial services. Although much is forgotten, a handful of lessons can be learned from the stories that remain. What do they tell us about what to expect from financial services for the masses and how to support them?

First, rich and poor alike want good ways to save, borrow, and insure. They find ways to meet the need, however rudimentary, through cooperation, charity, or commerce.

Second, the demands of the poor often can be met on a large scale only with limited and low-quality services. German farmers probably wanted to borrow individually from cooperatives without being on the hook for their neighbors' debts, but that was not an option. British workers might have clamored to buy disability insurance to protect their incomes from all-too-common mining and factory accidents. But the insurers could not find a way to supply it in small denominations while breaking even.

Third, if the need for services is a constant, the ascribed purpose is not. Swift wanted his loans invested in productive uses. Wakefield wanted to teach savers thrift, so they would not dissipate their incomes in gin. Schultz-Delitzsch was galled by famine. Raiffeisen's vision was imbued with a dose of Christian fellowship. Gourlay saw the chief problem as helping people surmount major expenditures without falling into slavery to moneylending landowners. In medieval Italy, Carcano interpreted usury through anti-Semitism. Most of these figures saw some part of the truth and perhaps none saw all of it. In general, poor people shoulder many concerns and struggle creatively to manage with what they have. New financial services give them new options. The third lesson, then, is about the danger of ideology when it comes to understanding how those served use the services. If people across the ages have been that muddled about why they are supporting the poor, we should be skeptical of the storylines currently in fashion.

91. May 5, 1928.

Fourth, it is far more common to copy ideas in finance than to invent them. Most techniques of today's microfinance, such as sureties and high-frequency repayments, go back millennia. It is natural to see the heroes of microfinance as inventors. It is more accurate to appreciate that micro-finance success stories (like most invention successes, actually) involve observing, borrowing, thinking, creating, tinkering, testing, publicizing, and propagating—sometimes all by the same person, sometimes not. Perhaps the rarest heroes in the history of finance for the masses are those who actually brought it to the masses *en masse*, who found ways to operate on a large scale, thanks to vision, leadership, and management ability. Whether or not they sought profit, they were good business people, a perspective to which we will return in chapter 5.

A fifth lesson is about the role of government. Most of the historical suc-cess stories are of private initiatives. The British postal savings bank system and the German *sparkassen* are important exceptions, showing that some-times government agencies can be made to operate in business-like ways while bringing to bear their strengths in scale and reliability.[92] It appears that governments generally have done better by leaving room for private initia-tives than by pursuing public ones. The Irish loan funds, British friendly soci-eties, and Scottish savings banks thrived after laws formalized their status.[93] Morris succeeded in part because he prevailed on U.S. state governments to grant his unusual banks legal charters by stretching existing rules or enact-ing new ones.[94] Of course, sometimes the political winds blew against such financial institutions, leading the legislative hand to quash. Legal changes in Ireland brought down the movement there; in Germany, the "Iron Chancel-lor," Otto von Bismarck, fought less successfully to contain the grassroots cooperative movement, which he saw as threateningly independent.[95]

A sixth lesson is that small-scale financial services for poor people tend to arise in countries in the early stages of modernization, such as the British Isles around 1800 and Germany a few decades later. Such countries are not too poor and not too rich. It is hard to start credit cooperatives or savings banks in places so poor that the economy is not monetized, where there are no pools of philanthropy, or where there is no tradition of formal legal institutions.

92. Today, the Bank Rakyat Indonesia's *unit desas* system is an even better example of a public agency operating like a private one. See chapter 4.

93. "Friendly Societies," *Encyclopaedia Britannica*, 11th ed., vol. 11, 218–21; Hollis and Sweet-man (2001), 297–303; Horne (1947), 39–70.

94. Herzog (1928).

95. Hollis and Sweetman (2001), 303–05; Tucker (1922), 92.

On the other hand, economic success is the natural, happy enemy of financial services for the poor. Thus the generation of Americans who participated in the microfinance revolution beginning in the 1970s never crossed paths with "industrial banking." Similarly did affluence bring the ultimate end to the Irish loan system in the 1960s and force the credit unions and insurance companies to turn conventional and move upstream.[96] Today, Raiffeisen, Desjardins, Prudential, and Metropolitan Life are all household names in their respective countries—names, that is, of conventional institutions no longer delivering stripped-down services to the poor. This observation at once helps explain why so much of the history was forgotten and why developing countries have seen an upsurge in financial services for the masses. Roughly speaking, as developing countries emulate the economic history of today's rich nations, they are emulating its financial history, too. One might even say that the microfinance revolution was inevitable.

Finally, if history makes obvious that economic success affects the use of financial services, its verdict is muted on whether delivering financial services to the poor reduces their poverty. Thomas Dichter, a longtime evaluator of microfinance programs, has pointed out that no country that is today rich got that way through tiny loans for people with tiny incomes.[97] The robustly developed Irish loan funds of the 1840s were helpless against the onslaught of the Great Famine. Only broad industrialization consigned famine in Ireland to the history books. This does not mean that today's microfinance does no good—we just concluded that the need for such services is universal—but it does suggest that microfinance is rarely transformational. Fundamentally, the kind of economic transformation that ends poverty involves combining labor and capital in ways that do not happen within poor households.

It would be overly dire in reviewing microfinance's past to conclude that those who do not learn from history are doomed to repeat it. The new microfinance practitioners may have largely forgotten the history, but they have taken inspiration from the past more than they realize (as we will see in chapter 4). And they have repeated the successes at least as much as any failures. A fairer caution is that the historical amnesia has fostered a simplistic popular understanding of modern microfinance as a novel solution to poverty that bypasses government. More accurately, it is ancient in lineage; it often involves the government as regulator or administrator; it is more likely to be eclipsed by affluence than to cause it; and it meets a universal need for ways to manage money.

96. Hollis (2002), 13; Seibel (2005), 3–4.
97. Dichter (2007).

four
Background Check

When new ideas spring up out of precarious beginnings, the important details of who did what and why in those early stages are rarely recorded and easily forgotten: for winners, growth comes at a gallop, original records seem irrelevant, and young managers are unaware of the past; for losers, there is even less motivation or capacity to preserve records. History ignores the 99 seeds that fell on stony ground, or were washed out by a storm, and it forgets the insignificant details that decided the fate of one seed that succeeded.

—LUCY CONGER, PATRICIA INGA, AND RICHARD WEBB, 2009[1]

When biographer Thomas Sheridan likened Jonathan Swift's lending to a spring that "watered and enriched the humble vale through which it ran, still extending and widening its course," he probably did not foresee the spring tumbling on for two centuries, extending into the mighty rivers of South America, the deltas of South Asia, and the plains of Africa.[2] But so it did, intermingling with like streams from Priscilla Wakefield's Benefit Club and the German credit cooperatives. As we continue to follow the water's many courses, we arrive at the subject of this book, the financial services for the poor that took form in the 1970s and early 1980s. Though Muhammad Yunus's Grameen Bank most represents the movement, microfinance remains diverse as ever. Fingers branch apart and probe new courses, rejoin, and intermix. To prepare for the main work of this book, the chapter tells the stories of the latest generation of thinkers, tinkerers, and promoters who made the microfinance we observe today.

The modern microfinance movement links to history in a couple of ways. We glimpsed in the last chapter how, as the West grew rich, the popular ways of bringing financial services to the masses, including savings banks and credit cooperatives, moved upmarket. Modern microfinance derives from those

1. Conger, Inga, and Webb (2009), 5.
2. Sheridan (1787), 234.

same original forms, especially the cooperatives, and returns to the original spirit of reaching the poor by sacrificing flexibility to cut costs. Microfinance can also be seen as a reaction *against* a more recent phenomenon. Starting in the 1960s, many aid donors and developing-country governments subsidized loans targeted at poor farmers and other deserving groups. That strategy roundly failed as local elites hijacked the cheap credit for themselves. In contrast, microfinance succeeded by taking a more businesslike approach. The low subsidies embedded in microfinance, along with its inconvenience, helped it screen out the elite and reach the poor more effectively.

As in previous historical waves, microfinance arose in many places and many forms. Key breakthroughs took place in Bangladesh, Bolivia, the Dominican Republic, India, Indonesia, and Niger. Some of the more popular approaches connect to people in groups, others to individuals. Some proffer loans, others savings accounts or insurance policies. The institutions that manufacture these services vary, too, in size and form. Many are nonprofit. The Grameen Bank is for-profit but member owned. Other for-profits have outside investors.

One break with the past is that foreign aid agencies, notably of the United States and Germany, have funded and advised the tinkerers and promoters who developed ideas and spread them. The other novelty—a truly historic departure—is the focus on women. Many microfinance institutions report that 95 percent or more of their clients are female. The closest precedent I have seen is the Irish loan funds, which only got as high as 20 percent.[3]

As in the last chapter, I do not analyze what microfinance does or ought to do. Rather, I describe the varieties of microfinance that are popular today through short histories that bring the survey alive. Just as in the older history, the unifying theme in the modern history is that the winners—the ones whose models touched the lives of millions—succeeded by trial and error in devising ways to deliver useful services to poor people in bulk. That, more than scientifically demonstrated transformation of clients' lives, is the emergent virtue of microfinance.

Microfinance and Its Living Cousins

As we approach the present in our historical journey, we come to a puzzle. What happened to savings banks and credit cooperatives for poor people? Born out of the grinding poverty of the early English industrial revolution and the German famines of the 1840s, both models overspread the globe.

3. Hollis (2002).

In modern times, credit unions—cooperatives with formal legal status and democratic governance—were even tapped to fight poverty in developing countries. In the mid-1950s, the U.S. government funded the World Extension Department of the U.S. Credit Union National Association; the department's director proclaimed in 1959 that "credit unions have proven themselves adaptable to all economic levels anywhere in the world and have become a definite factor in the raising of the standards of living in developing countries."[4] With 4,000 credit unions in Latin America by 1969, 1,200 in Africa, and 26,000 in Asia and Europe, the movement appeared robust and promising.[5] Meanwhile, many developing countries had established private as well as postal savings banks that followed the British model. So why today does microfinance get all the attention? Why does it even exist?

The question is even more perplexing when you realize that in fact, credit cooperatives and savings banks are alive and well. At the end of 2009, 38,000 credit cooperatives operated in developing countries, claiming 67 million members.[6] And those figures exclude China, whose government sponsors some 30,000 rural cooperatives.[7] Savings banks are even more prevalent, stunningly so.

In 2004, Robert Peck Christen and Richard Rosenberg of CGAP, a microfinance research body in Washington, D.C., collected data on "alternative financial institutions" around the world, which they defined as ones attempting to reach a clientele normally unconnected to conventional commercial banks.[8] They included microfinance institutions (MFIs), credit cooperatives and unions, state-run agricultural banks, and postal savings banks. A year later, Stephen Peachey and Alan Roe of Oxford Policy Management added data on non-postal savings banks.[9] Table 4-1 summarizes the data—and comes with many caveats. The numbers are about ten years old because the exercise has never been repeated. Microfinance has grown a lot since then. The survey of credit cooperatives and unions was probably less complete than that underlying the much larger figures for 2009 just cited. For many of the institutions, we cannot tell how many of the loan accounts truly were active, as opposed to being de facto grants. Nor can we tell how many were

---

4. Moody and Fite (1971), 333.

5. Moody and Fite (1971), 317–21, 332–36.

6. WOCCU (2010).

7. Jennifer Isern and Li Zou, "Highlight on China, Part 1: A View of the Landscape," Microfinance Gateway, October 7, 2007 (j.mp/k25JJU).

8. CGAP (2004).

9. Peachey and Roe (2005).

held by "poor people," however defined—even at microfinance institutions. And because many people have more than one account, we don't know how many *people* these totals represent.

Nevertheless, the texture of the numbers is striking: microfinance institutions are but one major source of financial service for those outside the conventional financial system. State development banks, predominantly in India and China, provided more loans than MFIs, at 85.7 million accounts. Postal savings banks were estimated to hold 243 million savings accounts, the lion's share in China and India. And that total is tiny next to the 838 million accounts estimated for other kinds of savings banks—including private institutions and public ones run outside postal systems. It bears repeating that we know little about these accounts. One report suggests that many in Asia are dormant.[10]

Despite this rich "alternative finance" landscape, Yunus and other pioneers felt compelled to devise yet more forms. Evidently, the dominant approaches either were not reaching many poor people or were not serving them well. As chapter 3 noted, transplants of Western models did not always take as hoped in poor countries. Yes, the United Kingdom was a developing country by today's standards when it opened postal savings banks in 1861, and that would seem to bode well for postal banks in today's developing countries. But the United Kingdom was also the preeminent world power, had a long history as a nation-state, was run by a strong and competent government, and had achieved a per-capita income at least four times that of India or Bangladesh in 1973, the eve of the microcredit revolution.[11] The relative wealth of Britain probably meant a higher volume of mail (the financial foundation of the postal system), a denser postal network with branches closer to the average person, and a bureaucracy that was more accountable and aboveboard. In contrast, a 2006 report on postal savings in developing countries delicately noted corruption: "In some countries, mainly in Africa, . . . deposits have not been managed with transparency and are transformed into substantial unfunded liabilities."[12]

Another problem was that as western Europe and North America climbed out of poverty in the twentieth century, their savings banks and credit cooperatives became more formal, elaborately structured, and oriented to serving individuals rather than groups. Some evangelists for these models forgot their roots. For example, in rich countries today, credit unions cater to

10. World Bank and ING Bank (2006), 21.
11. Maddison (2003), 262.
12. World Bank and ING Bank (2006), 7.

Table 4-1. *Active Loan and Savings Accounts at Alternative Financial Institutions, circa 2000*

Million

	Micro-finance institutions	Co-ops and credit unions	Rural banks	State/agri-cultural/devel-opment banks	Postal savings banks	Other savings banks	Total	Share of total (%)
Loans								
Sub-Saharan Africa	3.8	0.8	0.0	0.3	0.0	0.0	5.1	3
Middle East/ North Africa	0.9	0.0	0.0	5.1	0.1	0.0	6.1	3
Eastern Europe/ Central Asia	0.4	0.1	0.0	0.8	0.0	8.9	10.3	6
Russia	0.1	0.0	0.0	0.0	0.0	3.5	3.6	2
South Asia	30.2	0.1	0.8	14.2	0.0	0.0	45.3	25
India	11.8	0.1	0.0	11.9	0.0	0.0	23.8	13
East Asia/Pacific	18.3	0.9	0.2	65.2	1.1	1.5	87.1	48
China	0.2	0.0	0.0	46.6	0.0	0.0	46.7	26
Latin America/ Caribbean	4.5	0.7	0.2	0.1	0.0	20.3	25.6	14
Total	58.0	2.6	1.1	85.7	1.2	30.7	179.4	100
Share of total (%)	32	1	1	48	1	17	100	
Savings accounts								
Sub-Saharan Africa	3.8	4.9	1.1	0.3	10.6	3.1	23.8	2
Middle East/North Africa	0.7	0.0	0.0	9.0	16.2	7.0	32.9	2
Eastern Europe/ Central Asia	0.2	5.7	0.0	20.0	14.8	283.8	324.4	21
Russia	0.0	0.1	0.0	0.0	0.0	229.0	229.1	15
South Asia	18.6	1.6	6.0	53.8	61.7	13.1	154.8	10
India	3.9	0.4	0.0	50.0	53.6	0.0	107.9	7
East Asia/Pacific	52.0	11.4	6.0	7.7	139.5	477.1	693.7	46
China	0.0	0.2	0.0	0.0	110.0	428.1	538.3	35
Latin America/ Caribbean	1.3	8.4	0.0	0.1	0.1	53.8	63.7	4
Total	76.5	32.1	13.2	90.9	242.8	837.7	1,293.2	100
Share of total (%)	5	2	1	7	19	65	100	

Source: Author's calculations, based on data from CGAP (2004), Peachey and Roe (2005), and Honohan (2008).

salaried people working for big organizations. They seem suited to their context, with 100 million members just in North America.[13] But credit unions involve and depend on much more legal structure than credit cooperatives. Once a credit group grows beyond 40 or 50 people, it becomes impossible for members to monitor all transactions through direct witness—much less to participate in all decisions through plenary meetings. The governance of the cooperatives must then become more complex, with officers and committees elected to track money and make loan decisions. To give members proper recourse against embezzlement, violation of rules, and capture of lending decisions by elites, cooperatives must become formal legal entities, and members must have access to law enforcement. But in poor countries, partly because of mass migration to cities, most people still work in the informal economy, where salaries are rare, the legal system is largely a threat (in the form of the tax man), and enterprises come and go like shadows.

The upmarket drift of the old traditions created an opening by the 1970s for a new movement—an opening whose true dimensions were not appreciated until it began to be filled. As in the previous century, private organizations led the way. Unlike in the previous century, this was not for lack of government attempts to lead.

Enter the Developmentistas

In the twentieth century, much more than in the nineteenth, financial services for poor people evolved under the auspices of strong states. Governments of developing countries, including India and Brazil, took an active role in planning and implementing economic development. Governments of rich countries granted and lent billions to help them. For the mid-century U.S. government, providing capital and technology to poor nations was a strategic prong in the grand battle with communism.[14] For Britain and France, foreign aid grew as well out of colonial administration, a way to maintain influence in former colonies.[15] Thus within the field of financial services, there was a strong thrust toward public-sector solutions.

In the earliest days of aid, the late 1940s and 1950s, the intangibility of finance and the dubious economics of delivering services to the poorest made banking for poor people a secondary concern. Officials tended to view the challenge of economic development as constructing what writer Catherine

---

13. WOCCU (2010).

14. For example, see Harry Truman's 1949 inaugural address.

15. On the interwar roots of British aid, see Barder (2005), 3–4.

Caufield called the "talismans of change": the roads and dams, power plants and canals that are the bulky building blocks of industrialization.[16] Roughly speaking, western Europe undertook this effort under the Marshall Plan, and the Western powers had emphasized it in "developing" their colonies. The trend-setting development institution, the World Bank, prided itself on its engineering and financial rigor. In effect, it took pride in filtering out countries so destitute as to be uncreditworthy and projects so soft-headed as to favor short-term welfare of poor people over productive investment in industrial capacity. After all, only industrial projects could generate the tax revenues needed to repay the loans.

But then poor people as objects of direct aid began a long rise on the priority lists of development institutions. The post–World War II economic recovery in industrialized countries gave their governments bigger budgets, with more room for compassion for those least fortunate. And as colonies in Asia and Africa gained independence, they became impoverished fronts in the Cold War. In 1960, following an Eisenhower administration proposal, the World Bank opened the International Development Association to lend money at almost no interest to the poorest nations.[17] Investing in the productivity of poor people—their health, education, and ability to grow food—had been hard to justify in the cold financial calculations accompanying traditional development loans with commercial interest rates. How exactly would vaccinating children help a government service a World Bank loan at 7 or 10 percent? But after rates fell below 1 percent and repayment terms stretched to forty years, education, health, and support for small farmers came to seem more aid-worthy. Over decades, investing in people could well increase economic growth and government revenue.

It was through agriculture that foreign aid first intersected in a big way with finance for poor people. One trigger was the specter of famine in India in the 1960s. The "developmentistas"—rich-country economic aid professionals—responded by calling for comprehensive government support for farmers. After Robert McNamara jumped ship from the U.S. Department of Defense and assumed the presidency of the World Bank in 1968, he expanded this line of work. His ambition: bring Lyndon Johnson's Great Society policy style to the entire developing world. Just a few years before, Norman Borlaug and other prominent agronomists had begun breeding varieties of wheat and rice that produced radically more food per hectare but also required modern inputs such as artificial fertilizer, pesticides, and irrigation. Poor farmers

16. Caufield (1996), 70–87.
17. Kapur, Lewis, and Webb (1997), 154–60.

could not invest in these "Green Revolution" technologies without credit, so meeting this need became a centerpiece of aid for agriculture.

The donors' push for credit to farmers coincided with the rise of state-led economic development philosophies in many countries, which appealed to leaders striving to consolidate their young nations or advance the equitable ideals of socialism. The state-led approach generally extended to finance; India was the foremost example. In 1969, a couple of decades after independence, it took control (but not ownership) of the country's banking system. Eight years later, it required any commercial bank opening a branch in an already-serviced area, such as a middle-class neighborhood, to open four in unbanked areas, such as remote villages. In so doing, the government elevated concerns about poverty and equity over traditional financial logic: presumably, many of the previously unbanked places were unbanked because they were unprofitable. The lending operations of these banks typically ran up losses, which were ultimately cross-subsidized by the banks' profitable operations or subsidized by the government. According to economists Robin Burgess and Rohini Pande, over the thirteen years the rule stayed in place, 30,000 rural towns and villages gained bank branches for the first time. It was the largest banking expansion in the world, ever.[18]

To dole out small loans to farmers, India and many other countries also set up dedicated public agricultural banks. Here, too, losses and subsidies were the rule. Doling out small loans to millions of small farmers was expensive and risky, which argued for charging them high interest rates to cover administration and default losses. But high rates would deter farmers from making the leap to a new way of growing food, especially if they perceived even a modest chance that the new way would lead to starvation and unpayable debts. So governments charged famers much less for the loans than it cost to deliver them. Over the decades, for example, Brazil, India, and Mexico each borrowed more than $2 billion from the World Bank to finance subsidized loans to farmers.[19] One consequence of subsidy was that programs were designed to give loans on the basis of need rather than ability to repay.

Subsidized credit had just one problem: it didn't work. As evidence of failings became impossible to ignore, a counterrevolution commenced within the aid world. Its beginning was, in the words of three World Bank historians, "smaller than a man's hand":[20] an article published in the *American Journal of Agricultural Economics* in 1971 by a junior economist at Ohio State University

---

18. Burgess and Pande (2005).

19. OED (1994). Figures are cumulative to 1994.

20. Kapur, Lewis, and Webb (1997), 436.

named Dale Adams.[21] Over the course of the 1970s, with backing from the U.S. Agency for International Development (USAID), Adams and a coterie of colleagues mounted an ultimately successful attack on subsidized, directed credit.[22]

Among the problems they pointed out was that top-level program managers in Washington or New Delhi could not control who actually received loans within villages. All too often, big landholders used connections and bribes to capture the cheap loans. Worse, because the employees at the government-controlled banks were rewarded more for getting loans out the door than protecting the bottom line, they relaxed about repayment. In other words, loans in practice were given neither on the basis of need nor responsible lending practices. One review of subsidized credit programs in Africa, Asia, and Latin America found that almost all had default rates between 40 and 95 percent.[23] Many of the loans were little more than disguised grants that only a fool would pay back. This laxity drained government coffers and destabilized lending institutions. Worse, it corroded the rest of the rural financial system, such as it was. No unsubsidized financial provider could compete with "credit" on such easy terms or, therefore, pay reasonable interest to depositors. In a Ph.D. dissertation, one anthropology student at the University of Hawaii described the pattern she witnessed in Indonesia:

There is always the danger that TPLs [government field workers], who are young, will form patron-client relationships with powerful village entrepreneurs or village officials. The entrepreneur or official, being an older and wealthier man, may come to dominate the TPL and try to dictate certain aspects of the implementation of a project. This is particularly evident in the selection of project participants. If the TPL has consciously or unconsciously relinquished control over the selection of participants, there is little hope that the owners of smaller and weaker enterprises will be included in the project. Experience shows that powerful entrepreneurs and village officials usually try to use credit and other resources distributed through development projects as personal patronage, steering them toward political allies, friends, and relatives.[24]

The student's name was Ann Dunham Sutoro. Haven't heard of her? During much of her fieldwork in the late 1970s, her son lived with her parents in Hawaii, attending high school. His name was Barack.

21. Adams (1971).
22. For example, Adams, Graham, and Von Pischke (1984).
23. Braverman and Guasch (1986), cited in Armendáriz and Morduch (2010), 11.
24. Dunham (2009 [1992]), 236.

In sum, the critics said, subsidized and directed credit damaged the financial systems when it ought to be doing the opposite. Adams and others called for interventions that operated in a more businesslike way, charging clients prices much closer to the cost of delivery, holding borrowers accountable for repayment, and holding banks and other financial entities responsible for their own bottom lines. Roughly, what was good for the financial business was good for the customers.

The rise of this "financial systems" view assisted microfinance in two ways. First, it directly influenced the key players. Notable among these were the German and American aid establishments, which contributed behind the scenes to blockbuster successes in India and Indonesia. (Obama's mama played a role in Indonesia.) Second, the new view created a receptive audience among donors for experimenters, including Muhammad Yunus, who were perhaps largely unaware of the Western debates and had independently found their own way toward businesslike methods.

The Making of Microfinance

Having constructed a backdrop—the deep history of the last chapter, the more recent developments in this one—it is time to describe today's microfinance scene. This section does so with a series of thumbnail histories. Before I start, I should head off two misimpressions. First, one might conclude that the pioneers highlighted were the first of their generation to aid the poor through financial services. Not so. Four years before Yunus made his first loan, for example, the U.S. nonprofit Acción International began lending to what it would label "microenterprises" in Recife, Brazil.[25] The Bangladeshi nonprofit BRAC—now the largest in the developing world—lent to the poor in Bangladesh before Yunus, too.[26] What distinguishes the efforts I spotlight is that they produced formulas for delivering these services in businesslike ways, minimizing subsidy and maximizing the scope for serving more people. These efforts *took off*.

The second potential misimpression comes from my focus on a handful of individuals. Many people unnamed also contributed. Still, I hope that by telling half a dozen origin "myths" rather than one, I will bring the history to life while conveying the diversity of a movement that indeed comprises the labor of thousands.

25. Tendler (1983).
26. Smillie (2009), 69.

Whatever the technique, the first thing to do in mapping a patch of territory is set the boundaries. Defining the boundaries of microfinance turns out to be surprisingly difficult. Breaking the word in two and taking its parts literally would equate it to "very small money management services." But the word is rarely taken to encompass loans from family or the sorts of informal credit and savings services Stuart Rutherford found in Vijayawada, India (discussed in chapter 2). Restricting the concept to services provided by *formal* institutions, ones with legal identities, helps bring it in line with what people usually mean by the word. But that does not suffice because it includes credit cooperatives, postal banks, other savings banks, and those agricultural banks that directed subsidized loans to farmers—none of which "microfinance" normally brings to mind. The derivation of "microfinance" and "microcredit" from the earlier "microenterprise credit" suggests that the purpose—investment in productive activities—is the key. But as we saw in chapter 2, the true reason for a poor person's borrowing or saving or insuring is often elusive, and any form of credit or savings can finance investment in microenterprise. Nor can we find recourse in stipulating the use of groups because some microfinance is individual (as we will soon see). Organization and ownership type do not seem to draw the line either: microfinance has been delivered by government-owned banks, nonprofits, for-profits owned by members, and for-profits owned by outside investors.[27] Perhaps because of all this ambiguity, in the 2004 statistical survey that inspired my table 4-1, Christen and Rosenberg defined microfinance in historical terms, no more precisely than "financial services designed for lower-income clients using the new delivery methodologies developed during the last twenty-five years."[28]

Maybe these definitions are unsatisfying because they are too classical, in the sense of classical physics. They view microfinance as existing independent of us, the observers. Quantum physics teaches that the act of observation changes what is observed, making subject and object inseparable. Just so, the answer to the meaning of microfinance lies partly in the fact that the methods social investors know most about are those working hardest to be known, the ones that seek external support. As a result of this selection process, microfinance is by and large that which connects rich-country donors and investors with poor-country clients.

Still, this characterization, too, is a bit of a dodge—not really a definition. What methods of providing financial services seek outside support and use it

---

27. Unusually, Yunus defines "microfinance" to exclude for-profit institutions owned by outside investors.

28. CGAP (2004), 1.

well? In general, the methods are provided by formal institutions; chit funds cannot submit grant proposals. The institutions tend to be nongovernmental because public agencies have less need for funds from the foreign public. And because these independent institutions operate under a "hard budget constraint"—unlike state banks, they cannot slough losses onto taxpayers— their operations tend to be businesslike: even if they receive subsidies, they strive to limit costs and charge enough to balance the books. As well, the institutions are characterized by their mission of serving poor people. Ones serving rich people are unlikely to solicit investors and donors with charitable motives. Finally, this mission combines with businesslike operation to favor large institutions that can manage other people's money with probity and mass-produce services in order to realize economies of scale. Microfinance, then, appears to encompass the *large-scale, businesslike provision of financial services to the poor.* Notice how this definition allows for the possibility (indeed, reality) of governments providing microfinance if in doing so they behave like nongovernmental organizations (NGOs) that must balance the books. And notice that the definition is agnostic about legal form: microfinance institutions can include NGOs, which are usually nonprofit, and for-profit companies, too.

Solidarity Group Lending

The most famous form of microfinance entails making loans to small groups of people, usually women. It arose separately in Bangladesh and in Latin America.

Bangladesh's Big Three. Our survey begins in 1976, in Bangladesh, with a young economist at the University of Chittagong. Educated at Vanderbilt University on a Fulbright, Muhammad Yunus was known in those years as an independent thinker and a brilliant teacher. One student told me that Yunus could explain profound mathematical theorems in ways that made the central ideas shine through.[29] He had an unconventional streak, too. "He had long hair, a VW bug, nicely tailored jackets, and colorful ties," says Asif Dowla, who studied under Yunus and then was effectively Grameen's first bookkeeper.[30] In 1971, Bangladeshis had won a bloody war of secession from Pakistan. The early years of Bangladesh's independence were a time of great suffering, new possibilities, and a near-vacuum of government. Yunus

29. Zahid Hussain, senior economist, World Bank, Dhaka, Bangladesh, interview with author, March 2, 2008.

30. Asif Dowla, professor, Department of Economics, St. Mary's College of Maryland, St. Mary's City, Md., interview with author, September 23, 2008. Dowla worked for the Ford Foundation–funded Rural Economics Program, which provided financial and administrative support to the Grameen Project.

became fed up with the incongruence between the Panglossian theories he taught inside the classroom, which spoke of optimal output and economic growth, and the starvation he saw outside. He began working in the nearby village of Jobra with his students to understand and address villagers' problems. After some trial and error with credit for farmers, he decided to try working with the poorest families, the ones who owned no land to grow rice. In his autobiography, *Banker to the Poor,* he tells how an encounter changed his life:

> We stopped at a run-down house with crumbling mud walls and a low thatched roof pocked with holes. We made our way through a crowd of scavenging chickens and beds of vegetables to the front of the house. A woman squatted on the dirt floor of the verandah, a half-finished bamboo stool gripped between her knees. Her fingers moved quickly, plaiting the stubborn strands of cane. She was totally absorbed in her work. . . .
>
> She was in her early twenties, thin, with dark skin and black eyes. She wore a red sari and had the tired eyes of a woman who labored every day from morning to night.
>
> "What is your name?" I asked.
>
> "Sufiyah Begum."
>
> "How old are you?"
>
> "Twenty-one." . . .
>
> "Do you own this bamboo?" I asked.
>
> "Yes."
>
> "How did you get it?"
>
> "I buy it."
>
> "How much does the bamboo cost you?"
>
> "Five taka." At the time this was about twenty-two cents.
>
> "Do you have five taka?"
>
> "No, I borrow it from the *paikars*."
>
> "The middlemen? What is your arrangement with them?"
>
> "I must sell my bamboo stools back to them at the end of the day as repayment for my loan."
>
> "How much do you sell a stool for?"
>
> "Five taka and fifty poysha."
>
> "So you make fifty poysha profit?" . . .
>
> Sufiyah Begum earned two cents a day. It was this knowledge that shocked me. In my university courses, I theorized about sums in the millions of dollars, but here before my eyes the problems of life and

death were posed in terms of pennies. . . . I was angry, angry at myself, angry at my economics department and the thousands of intelligent professors who had not tried to address this problem and solve it.[31]

Sufiyah Begum lived in bondage to the bamboo supplier, who allowed her just enough margin for her family to survive, and well less than she could have made buying bamboo with cash and selling stools at market price. But she had no cash. Buying bamboo on this "supplier credit" left her perpetually subject to monopolistic lending. A cheaper loan from an outsider might free her.

Yunus had a student survey Jobra for others in the same bind. She came back with a list of 42 people who could use a total of $27 in capital. Yunus tells how he took the money out of his pocket, handed it to her on the spot, and told her to lend it without any interest or fixed repayment schedule. Inspired by the experience, he next asked a local bank to lend to the villagers—to which it only agreed after Yunus personally guaranteed all the loans, in effect making him the borrower of record. Next, he persuaded a powerful friend at the state-run Bangladesh Agricultural Bank to let him open his own branch near Jobra, to operate as he saw fit. He called the new project "Grameen," meaning "of the village" or "rural." Yunus writes that he never intended to become a banker. Undeterred, he proceeded with vision, flexibility, conviction that the established banking system was wrong-headed, readiness to call on his personal connections in government, and tremendous energy as an advocate and salesman.

With his students, Yunus constructed the Grameen lending model. After much experimentation—including individual loans that were not paid back—they settled on a kind of group lending in which sets of borrowers choose each other, approach the lender together, and take responsibility for each other's debts.[32] Though Yunus does not mention it, some of his closest aides in those years make clear that extant credit cooperatives were one source of ideas—as both inspiration and foil. The cooperatives contained the interesting idea of joint liability, but they appeared ungainly at a typical size of twenty-five members and vulnerable to takeover by a village's richest residents. Yunus and his students settled on five as the right size for a Grameen group—the number of fingers on the hand, and the number of times a Muslim should pray each day.[33] Loans were repaid in weekly installments

31. Yunus (2004), 46–48.

32. Hulme (2008), 4.

33. Asif Dowla, professor, Department of Economics, St. Mary's College of Maryland, St. Mary's City, Md., interview with author, September 23, 2008.

over the course of a year. Within a group, the two neediest members would take loans first; then, while they were repaying, two more would start; then the leader of the five would borrow last.[34] After one loan was repaid, a larger one could be taken, in an ascending cycle. Borrowers also were required to make additional payments into a group savings account, which served as a kind of collateral and a buffer fund for times when borrowers could find no other way to meet installments. For efficiency, six or eight groups of five in a village would be clustered into "centers," which would meet weekly with a Grameen representative to do business. In time the centers became the primary grouping in the system (see chapter 5).

In 1979, having developed the model and demonstrated a high repayment rate, Yunus won the backing of Bangladesh's central bank to test it on a large scale in the Tangail district near the capital city, Dhaka. After learning and adapting during this pilot, Grameen went national and grew rapidly, thanks in part to funding from the Ford Foundation, the U.N. International Fund for Agricultural Development, and the governments of Bangladesh, the Netherlands, Norway, and Sweden.[35] In late 1983, Yunus obtained a unique banking charter from the military ruler of Bangladesh, and the Grameen Bank was born. Under Grameen's cooperative structure, each new member bought a share of the bank for 100 taka (a dollar or so). Formally, the borrowers owned most of the bank. In practice, until his politically motivated removal in 2011, Yunus enjoyed great autonomy, and most of the capital came from donors and retained profits. By the end of 2010, the bank reported, 8 million women and 300,000 men had become members.[36]

Within Bangladesh, Grameen inspired imitation and competition. In the 1980s, the Bangladeshi group BRAC integrated Grameen-style microcredit into its education, health, and grassroots development programs. As mentioned, BRAC had tinkered with credit before Yunus but had never hit on a formula that combined such high repayment rates, manageable costs, and scalability to millions of people.[37] Even after BRAC converted to Grameen-style credit, major differences remained. Where Yunus expresses faith in poor people's ability to find their own way once financed, BRAC founder Fazle Abed believes that microcredit helps more when combined with larger

---

34. Dowla and Barua (2006), 17–19.

35. Armendáriz and Morduch (2010), 12.

36. Grameen Bank, "Grameen Bank Monthly Update in Taka: December, 2010" (j.mp/n59fAe [January 9, 2011]); MIX (Microfinance Information eXchange) Market, "Grameen Bank Profile" (mixmarket.org/mfi/grameen-bank [January 4, 2011]).

37. Smillie (2009), 69.

programs for economic development. It is often futile, in the BRAC view, to give an illiterate widow with no land and a lifetime of wounds a small loan and expect her to blossom into an entrepreneur. Would-be microentrepreneurs need not just capital but also advice, supplies, and links to markets where they can sell their products.

One long-standing BRAC program integrates women into a vast poultry undertaking. Behind the scenes, BRAC set up at least half a dozen poultry farms nationwide, which produced more than a million chicks a year as of 2004. The women's job is to raise the hens. I met one of these women in the Rangpur district of Bangladesh in 2008. One of her grown sons had severe allergies that make it hard for him to work. She invested large sums in the education of another son who earned a master's degree, but a bus hit and killed him when he was biking. Much of her savings was effectively buried with him. BRAC gave her a series of loans, sold her chicks, feed, and vaccine, and bought the eggs her hens laid.[38]

In a neighboring village, I watched a monthly meeting of adolescent girls, part of a BRAC program that encourages the young women to borrow on behalf of their parents and even husbands. At meetings, the BRAC representative typically talks about AIDS, violence against women, and vegetable and livestock raising. For BRAC, the credit draws the girls into attendance, teaches thrift, and partly funds the work through interest receipts. Through programs such as these, BRAC's microcredit operations reached 5.5 million borrowers in 2010.[39]

Filling out the big three of Bangladeshi microfinance is ASA, an organization founded in the 1970s by Shafiqual Haque Choudhury. Choudhury and his associates began ASA to carry out a five-year plan for an armed national uprising against landlords and the government. The plan didn't work out. In 1991, ASA took up microcredit and soon morphed into one of the leanest microcredit operations in the world. Where BRAC bundled, ASA streamlined.[40] It led the way in dropping joint liability for loans and taking savings deposits, and it limited its offerings to a small set of standard products. Today, ASA offers its 4 million borrowers the purest microfinance.[41] In 2007, this formerly Maoist nonprofit topped the *Forbes* 50 list of microfinance institutions, thanks to its performance on such criteria as efficiency and profitability.[42]

38. Matin and Yasmin (2004), 90; see also Smillie (2009), 91–101.

39. MIX Market, "BRAC Profile" (mixmarket.org/mfi/brac [August 24, 2011]).

40. Rutherford (2009b), 97.

41. ASA (2010), 38.

42. Matthew Swibel, "The 50 Top Microfinance Institutions," *Forbes,* December 20, 2007.

The Bangladeshi big three bear strong imprints of their respective founders, who came into their prime as their nation came into existence. Despite the common history, each organization has a distinct character. Only Grameen is legally a bank, meaning that it can take deposits well in excess of its outstanding loans; and these are now its main source of funds for lending. ASA is also autonomous, financing itself by retaining profits from its efficient credit machine.[43] BRAC continues to take funding from outside donors to partly finance its non-credit programs.[44] For all, the system devised by Yunus and his students is still the core of the finance model, though all three have molded the original to suit their own strategies and respond to competitive pressures: as related in chapter 5, taking voluntary savings deposits is now common, and joint liability has been at least formally dropped.[45]

Acción in Central America. Group microcredit was apparently an invention whose time had come in the late 1970s; like cubism and non-Euclidean geometry, it was independently invented or at least brought to prominence more than once within a few years. Two U.S. institutions dating to the Kennedy administration helped to develop it in the Western Hemisphere: Acción International, which began as a sort of private counterpart of the U.S. Peace Corps; and USAID, which President Kennedy forged from disparate government programs.

In the 1960s and 1970s, USAID had tried various combinations of credit, technical advice, and equipment provision to support small businesses in poor countries. Frustrated with the perpetually weak results, it hired Acción in 1979 to scour the globe for methods that worked. Acción in turn tasked the young Jeffrey Ashe, who had worked with credit cooperatives in Ecuador as a Peace Corps volunteer and to this day exudes infectious enthusiasm for financial services that work. Sadly, back then, most examples his team found were emblematic of failed aid: "just awful—ill-conceived, expensive, paternalistic, top down. We'd see sewing machines covered in cobwebs," Ashe reported. But the team also found a few gems. These tended to focus on doing one thing well: providing finance. In Manila, the Philippines, a bank called the Money Shop made small loans out of stalls set up at the city's markets. In the main market of San Salvador, the capital of El Salvador, a credit cooperative called Fedecrédito lent to *grupos solidarios* ("solidarity

43. Stuart Rutherford, founder, *Safe*Save, Dhaka, Bangladesh, interview with author, March 2, 2008.

44. A separate legal entity, BRAC Bank, lends to small- and medium-sized enterprises.

45. Rutherford (2009b).

groups") of jointly liable clients. Just as in the fledgling Grameen Project, which the team also visited, the Fedecrédito groups had five members. To Acción and USAID, Ashe then proposed a lending program synthesized from these examples. Overcoming some institutional reluctance, Acción tried solidarity-group lending in Santo Domingo, capital of the Dominican Republic, among the *tricicleros,* who were named for the vehicles that they both pedaled and peddled from. It "took off like a shot," says Ashe. In that moment, Acción found its calling as a midwife for microfinance in the Americas. USAID, too, began a long involvement in the field.[46]

Of course, the two versions of solidarity lending on opposite sides of the planet were not identical. Acción's approach was indeed group-based: just as in the German cooperatives from which Fedecrédito descended, joint liability and individual self-interest combined to put members in the service of the lender, filtering unreliable borrowers and marshaling mutual pressure for payment. Acción's groups ranged from three to seven members, sometimes met monthly instead of weekly, and were not federated into centers. Elisabeth Rhyne, who was a senior vice president at Acción for many years, emphasizes that the organization's evolving philosophy was about more than joint liability:

> It included the idea of operating close to the ground, using local knowledge to select good clients. The product was a simple loan delivered quickly and easily, appealing broadly to people in the market, free from the weight of training requirements and restrictions on usage. The model also emphasized keeping costs low with a lean staff, plain offices, and efficiency. Finally, it included the idea that staff would have incentives to enforce on-time collections. In short, it was both a loan product and a delivery method.[47]

The first big break for this philosophy came in 1987 in Bolivia, where with funding from USAID and the cooperation of prominent Bolivians, Acción founded Prodem, a nonprofit solidarity lender. Prodem grew steadily; like Grameen, stirred imitation and competition; and eventually converted to a for-profit bank, called BancoSol, so that it could raise capital from investors. Chapter 8 tells more of that story.[48]

---

46. This account is based on Jeffrey Ashe, director of community finance, Oxfam America, Boston, Mass., interview with author, November 26, 2008; Rhyne (2001), 60–62.

47. Rhyne (2001), 62.

48. Rhyne (2001), 62.

Closest to the Roots: Village Banking and Self-Help Groups

The microcredit movement grew organically in the 1980s out of the early work in Bangladesh and small Latin states. Ideas spread through written reports and word of mouth. Foundations and aid agencies financed replications in Malaysia, India, and dozens of other countries. As more people joined the movement, they invented variations.

Village Banking. Among the most important innovators was John Hatch, an American who like Ashe had spent time in the Peace Corps working with credit cooperatives in Latin America—first as a volunteer in the mid-1960s in Colombia, then as an employee of the Corps in Peru. In the latter, he directed fifty-five volunteers working with farmer credit cooperatives. In 1970 and 1971, Hatch took a Fulbright grant to work as a hired agricultural laborer in Peru. He has written that the experience taught him "deep respect for the subsistence skills of the poor."[49] But he was much less impressed with the foreign aid–financed credit programs he saw up close, which often seemed to hurt more than help.[50]

In 1983, USAID asked Hatch to design a rapid-response program of aid to families in Bolivia beset by drought and hyperinflation. Hatch hit on a different form of microcredit:

> On a flight into La Paz, Bolivia—while consuming my second bourbon—God chose to drop into my relaxed mind a new idea for helping subsistence farmers and other severely poor families pull themselves out of poverty. The result of this epiphany was "village banking," which I instantly knew would become my life's purpose. I was 44 years old, recently divorced, with no savings, living in a tiny New York apartment, working as a semi-employed consultant, and painfully aware that not one of my 55 clients had ever adopted a single recommendation I had made. I was truly facing a dead-end.
>
> Who could have predicted that within 48 hours of my airborne epiphany, the Bolivian mission of [USAID] would award my consulting firm a grant of one million dollars to launch a nationwide test of village banking? Who could have predicted that over the next six months this project would reach 433 villages and benefit 17,000 families—the largest and fastest start-up in the history of microfinance?

49. Biography posted at Marriott School, Brigham Young University, Provo, Ut. (j.mp/dIJBJU [January 5, 2011]).

50. John Hatch, founder, FINCA, Santa Fe, N.M., interview with author, October 6, 2008.

Who could have predicted that the village banking methodology would eventually be adopted by hundreds of programs worldwide?[51]

The cooperatives he had worked with two decades before exercised a strong influence upon him; indeed, more than Hatch knew, his idea returned to the roots of credit cooperation. Even the name, "village banking," unwittingly recycled a nineteenth-century English term for Friedrich Raiffeisen's cooperatives (see chapter 3).[52]

For Hatch, solidarity groups were too laborious to assemble. In Hatch's plan, as in Raiffeisen's, cooperatives of some fifty villagers, not five or seven, would take block loans from an outsider benefactor, in this case USAID. (The group size would later fall to twenty-five.) The group, not an outside banker, would allocate the credit to members and keep the books. All could borrow immediately. Like the cooperatives of old, the banks would take savings while making loans, working in an informal, tight-knit setting in which members' own eyes, rather than those of a regulator, oversaw the keeper of the funds.[53] Hatch's village banking departed from the credit unions he had worked with in going downmarket: his system targeted poorer people and flew below the legal radar.

There followed in Bolivia what Rhyne calls "the closest program on record to the proverbial dropping money from the plane."[54] Shriveling crops and the evaporating value of cash threw aid workers into a manic race against time as they went from village to village starting banks and unloading sacks of pesos. The next year, Hatch started the U.S. nonprofit Foundation for International Community Assistance (now known as FINCA), which has made village banking another common form of microfinance. Through village banking, the Mexican lender Compartamos reached two million customers in 2011.[55]

Self-Help Groups. A cousin of village banking, the self-help group (SHG), has dominated microfinance in India. It, too, arose in the 1980s as a reaction to the way traditional credit cooperatives were operating and represents a partly unwitting return to their original spirit.

In 1959, after a failed Tibetan uprising against Chinese rule, the fourteenth Dalai Lama fled to India. Thousands of refugees followed him across the

51. Hatch (2010).

52. Wolff (1898).

53. Wolff (1898).

54. Rhyne (2001), 58–60.

55. Compartamos, "Banco Compartamos, S.A., Institución de Banca Múltiple, Surpasses 2 Million Client Milestone," press release, April 4, 2011 (j.mp/lhTLdH).

border into refugee camps where living conditions became deadly because of disease. The Dalai Lama asked Indian Prime Minister Jawaharlal Nehru for land for permanent settlement. The southern state of Mysore (now Karnataka) stepped forward first. Thus many Tibetans ended up some 1,500 miles from their native land. Like Oxfam, CARE, and many other private charities, one nonprofit that was founded to help the Tibetans outlived its baptismal humanitarian crisis, broadening its mission from meeting immediate needs, such as food and shelter, to longer-term goals, such as productive farming. The organization was called the Mysore Resettlement and Development Agency (MYRADA), and by the early 1980s, it was working with Indians as well as Tibetans, often by organizing them into groups in order to deliver training or credit.[56]

One problem MYRADA faced was that the cooperative societies it had organized, of the type inherited from British rule, were breaking down in just the way Henry Wolff had regretted in 1927, when he wrote about the "dry rot" of corrupt management: more-privileged people took them over and captured most of their benefits.[57] Aloysius Fernandez, who led MYRADA then and for decades after, picks up the thread:

> Between 1983 and 1985 several of the Co-operative Societies started by MYRADA with over 100 members broke up because of lack of confidence in the leadership and poor management systems. Members met MYRADA staff in small groups; they expressed their willingness to repay their loans to MYRADA, but not to the Co-operative Society, which was a large and heterogeneous group and dominated by one individual. We informed them that they had not taken the loans from MYRADA; hence the issue of repayment to MYRADA did not arise. We asked: "Why not repay to the small group of people assembled here?" They agreed. The large Co-operative broke down into several small groups and the group members repaid their loans to whichever group they chose to join.[58]

Feeling its way in the mid-1980s, MYRADA helped form hundreds of what it called self-help groups. For Fernandez, it was essential that the groups be no larger than about twenty members, and that they be homogeneous, arising naturally from the local social fabric. Members might be united by caste, creed, gender, profession, economic status, or kinship. (To emphasize this

56. Fernandez (1985), 1–2.
57. Wolff (1927), 83.
58. Fernandez (2005), 4.

feature, Fernandez would later call them "self-help affinity groups.") SHGs could engage in finance and, like BRAC groups, serve as conduits for other services, such as training in efficient irrigation. Where Yunus sought to build a big bank to serve the poor, Fernandez followed the Gandhian ideal of self-reliance. He wanted to help poor people produce their own financial services, informally and on a small scale. SHG rules encouraged all members to save regularly into a group fund, rather than obtain capital from an outside institution. Groups could then decide collectively on any lending to members.

Having grown out of the characteristically Indian philosophy of bottom-up development, it was perhaps inevitable that the successful SHG movement merged with the likewise characteristically Indian philosophy of top-down development. Earlier, I described the Indian government's history of driving banks to poor areas through mandates. This predisposed it to view SHGs as potential appendages to the formal financial system, a new way to channel credit to the poor. As it happened, that perspective was reinforced by advice emanating from Germany. In the early 1980s, thinkers connected to the Gesellschaft für Technische Zusammenarbeit (GTZ), an agency that specialized in technical advice and training, were joining the financial systems revolution started by Dale Adams, searching for alternatives to subsidized credit. Sensitized by their nation's history with cooperatives, they recognized that poor people all over the world operated small, autonomous, informal finance groups. Could GTZ help such groups link to established sources of capital like Raiffeisen's cooperatives had a century before, with a minimum of subsidy?[59]

In India, GTZ found a partner in the National Bank for Agricultural Development, a state institution whose job, ironically, was disbursing subsidized credit. It made its first grant to MYRADA after hearing the German aid professional Erhard Kropp speak in 1986 at a conference in Nanjing, China, of the Asian and Pacific Regional Agricultural Credit Association. There, he proposed that governments help encourage the creation of informal groups and guarantee them access, as groups, to bank accounts.[60] The German grant was to go toward organizing SHGs in this way. In 1989, the Indian government began funding other NGOs to do the same. Three years later, it piloted the SHG-Bank Linkage Program, which operates to this day.[61] With government funding, NGOs organize groups and train members in saving, lending, and accounting. The group then opens a savings account at a bank. Once the group has saved enough, the bank gives it a loan, typically four times as large as the

59. Seibel (2005), 6–7.
60. Seibel (2005), 9–10.
61. Fernandez (2005), 9–11.

savings balance, for which members are jointly liable. As in village banks and Raiffeisen's cooperatives, members apportion the credit among themselves.

Bank-linked SHGs proliferated beginning in the late 1990s, thanks in part to "priority-sector lending rules" that prodded commercial banks in India to devote 40 percent of their credit to deserving people and activities. By 2010, a cumulative 4.6 million SHGs had received bank loans. At a typical size of thirteen women per group, that suggests an astonishing 60 million women have access to loans through their SHGs.[62] However, many of the SHGs in the statistics may have gone defunct, and their members joined new groups, so this figure is probably high. Still, the Indian SHG–bank linkage system can be considered the largest microfinance program in the world, albeit with a degree of subsidy beyond that of other large microfinance programs.

Village Savings and Loan Associations. At the boundary between informal finance and "microfinance" are village savings and loan associations (VSLAs). These, too, are cooperative. Unlike most village banks and bank-linked SHGs, they generally eschew outside finance. At their best, they are self-sufficient, member-run, and therefore appropriate for the poorest of the poor.

In 1991, the U.S. charity CARE ran a small project in Niger to help women making and selling handicrafts. A Norwegian named Moira Eknes was put in charge. In time, Eknes discovered that the women knew more about handicrafts than she did, so she had nothing to teach them in that respect. What they lacked was capital. So Eknes studied the forms of community finance indigenous to the region and arrived at the idea of a group that would accumulate savings in a box with three locks, the keys held by three different people to prevent theft. The group could then lend money to its members or non-members. On the presumption of illiteracy, record-keeping would be oral. The biggest departure of the VSLA system from conventional microfinance in this example is that the supporting organization has no permanent local presence. It is there to train people to organize groups and provide some guidance to new groups.[63]

Many big international charities now organize VSLAs. They include CARE, Oxfam, Pact, Plan International, Catholic Relief Services, and World Vision. According to Hugh Allen, a leading VSLA proponent, the groups are multiplying fast. At least 4.5 million people in fifty-two countries have joined them, including 4 million in Africa. Most VSLAs are in the countryside, where the majority of the world's poorest live. They also operate in urban areas, such as the Kibera slum in Nairobi, Kenya, one of the largest in

62. Srinivasan (2010a), 2, 13.
63. Wilson (2010).

the world. The groups, Allen says, do not work well with more than about thirty people. Beyond that, the meetings become too long and the transactions become too numerous to remember, so they become opaque. With opacity come distrust, error, and theft.[64] Interestingly, when lending, VSLAs charge interest rates that in other contexts are decried as usurious: 2 percent per month is low and 10 percent is common.[65]

Like the differences between finches, the differences between VSLAs and better-known microfinance forms reflect adaptations for survival in different niches. The poorest cannot afford to pay, through interest, for the wages, computers, and buildings of microcreditors. And if people are poor enough, they will accept walking a mile and sitting under a tree for an hour in order to save $1.[66] From the microcreditors' point of view, a large stratum of people are so poor and their loans and savings needs are so small that they can only be served at great relative cost. Ashe—the man who helped launch solidarity-group lending in Latin America and who today leads Oxfam America's VSLA work—once described conventional microcredit to me from the point of view of a poor woman in rural Niger: "That is for rich people."[67]

Individual Microcredit and Microsavings

Microfinance is often equated in the public imagination with groups and loans. But there is more to it than that. The word "microfinance" was coined around 1990 precisely because the movement had expanded beyond group microcredit to include services other than loans. While group savings programs like VSLAs do exist, the main rationale for working in groups—joint liability—falls away in the switch from giving loans to taking deposits. Because most microsavings has been individual, savings and individual service appear together in this survey.

Indonesia. Like the Brits in India, the Dutch in Indonesia introduced German-style credit cooperation around the turn of the twentieth century. For reasons that are unclear, the similarities ended there. Where the Indian credit cooperative system apparently remained static and stagnant, the Indonesian one evolved and diversified into an array of "rural banks," "village banks," "market banks," and "people's banks." In general, these banks did

---

64. Hugh Allen, CEO, VSL Associates, Solingen, Germany, e-mail to author, April 16, 2011.

65. Wilson, Harper, and Griffith (2010), 5.

66. Hugh Allen, CEO, VSL Associates, Solingen, Germany, conversation with author, September 9, 2009.

67. Jeffrey Ashe, director of community finance, Oxfam America, Boston, Mass., interview with author, November 25, 2008.

savings as well as credit and could be owned by members and/or local and regional governments. They received government funding yet were left to die if they failed miserably on the market test. They generally did not use groups.[68] From this financial firmament sprang two particularly significant institutions in the 1970s, one private, Bank Dagang Bali (BDB), and one public, the Badan Kredit Kecamatan (BKK) program. Both would influence the development of an absolute giant of microfinance in the 1980s.

It appears that the private institution in this pair was the first large-scale, commercial microfinance institution in the current era—in the world. It was founded by a Balinese couple, Ms. Sri Adnyani Oka and Mr. I Gusti Made Oka. Around 1955, not long after they married, they took their small savings out of a bank account and began moneylending. Ms. Oka made and collected the loans, accepting gold as collateral, and her husband kept the books. To increase their capital, Mr. Oka borrowed $222 in 1956 from one of those cooperative banks descended from the colonial era. In order to borrow, Mr. Oka became a shareholder. His first shareholders' meeting changed his life.

> My wife and I already knew that when a person we trusted needed to borrow money, we could go to someone who had money and arrange the transaction. At the bank shareholders' meeting, I was surprised to learn that is exactly what banks do. I knew then that we could run a bank, that it could be profitable, and that it would help many people who were afraid of banks. From that time on, I was determined to obtain a bank license.[69]

The Okas realized their dream of graduating to formal banking a dozen years later. They opened a small "secondary market bank" in 1968, then the full-status Bank Dagang Bali in 1970, making it Bali's second private bank.[70]

BDB succeeded by knowing and going to its customers. Employees made regular rounds to clients' homes and market stalls by foot, bicycle, and motorcycle to collect savings and loan payments. These visits also helped BDB staff judge creditworthiness and build long-term relationships with clients—relationships that implicitly promised access to new loans if clients stayed current on old ones. As a licensed bank, BDB also took savings. By 1996, it grew to 15,645 loan and 363,859 savings accounts. While 92 percent of the loan balances that year exceeded $420, indicating a well-off clientele by the Indonesian standard, 94 percent of the passbook savings accounts

68. Robinson (2002), 94–99; Steinwand (2001).
69. Robinson (2002), 149.
70. Robinson (2002), 148–49.

were smaller, pointing to a poorer clientele for this service (though one perhaps a step above Grameen's target demographic). According to American
anthropologist Marguerite Robinson, many of the savers were entrepreneurs
who made or sold food, clothes, and other goods; they earned $2–6 a day, of
which they might save $1–2 on good days.[71]

In a shocking move, the Indonesian government closed BDB in 2004. The
Okas' daughter had married the son of another bank owner, and through that
relationship had flowed inappropriate loans.[72] Yet in Robinson's view, BDB
left a permanent legacy. Writing before the BDB's downfall, she explained
that the bank

> was not the first financial institution to provide microcredit profit-
> ably, nor was it the first institution to collect savings from the poor. In
> an important sense, however, BDB was where the microfinance revo-
> lution began. Today it is the longest-serving formal sector financial
> institution providing commercial microfinance (both savings services
> and loans) on a substantial scale in a developing country, having done
> so continuously and profitably since 1970—and without ever having
> received a subsidy.[73]

In 1970, the same year the Bank Dagang Bali opened, a public program
called Badan Kredit Kecamatan was launched in the province of Central Java.
Not unlike the Dutch long before, the provincial governor created these village banks to improve the lot of the poor and reduce unrest—only five years
earlier, communists had attempted a coup in Jakarta, Suharto had come to
power, and a million people had been massacred. True to its name, which
means "subdistrict credit organization," the BKK program set up 500 banking branches in subdistricts, local administrative units, throughout the province. To give the network finer articulation, each branch in turn dispatched
staff to rotate day by day among a dozen or so *pos desas* (village posts) within
its subdistrict. In a 1991 book, Richard Patten and Jay Rosengard, American
advisers to the program, described one *pos desa* at a busy market:

> In the middle of this cacophony of Javanese capitalism is a small
> wooden shack that looks like it won't withstand the next strong wind
> or major rainstorm. The floor is bare earth, the roof a zinc sheet. Air
> conditioning is a cross-breeze. On closer inspection, this appears to be

71. Robinson (2002), 150–61.
72. Bill Guerin, "New Worries for Indonesian Bank Sector," *Asia Times,* April 17, 2004.
73. Robinson (2002), 144.

a makeshift office: three young men in starched white shirts and dark blue trousers sit behind wooden tables, busily filling out forms, making bookkeeping entries, and handling cash transactions. Local vendors are seated on a few benches around the walls of this shack or are huddled at the front table. These petty traders, dressed in a mixture of traditional village garb and simple Western-style city clothes, carry on animated conversations in Javanese . . . while awaiting their turn. . . .

This is Pos Pasar Boja (Boja Market Post), one of sixteen *pos desas* . . . of the [Boja subdistrict]. Every Thursday, two or three employees from the BKK head office come to the market to conduct all normal BKK credit and savings operations: extend loans, accept loan payments, disburse savings, and receive savings deposits.[74]

The public BKK system differed from the private BDB in important respects. Its capital for lending came right from the public fisc, not the deposits of customers or the equity of investors. In fact, other than the "forced savings" (deposits required as partial collateral for loans), the BKKs could not take deposits until 1987. Individual BKKs functioned autonomously but according to common rules. This made the BKK program a laboratory for testing ways to blend public-sector support and mission with private-sector principles and discipline.

Yet another legacy of Dutch projects in credit cooperation is a national institution called the Bank Rakyat Indonesia (BRI). As BDB got its banking license and the governor of Central Java launched his BKKs, BRI began a massive credit program on quite opposite principles. It was classic subsidized credit, part of a larger effort to make Indonesia self-sufficient in rice. BRI set up 3,600 branches throughout the country, called *unit desas*, to dispense cheap credit for farmers for buying chemical fertilizer, pesticides, and seeds for high-yield rice varieties. The program developed typical ills: the richest farmers captured the credit, paying rates that were often negative after inflation, and hardly bothered to pay back. A military-style campaign to force repayment succeeded mainly in discouraging farmers from borrowing. By 1983, the loan portfolio was shrinking as defaults drained the government treasury.[75]

Hoping to break the downward spiral, the government sought advice from a Harvard-based team partly funded by the World Bank and USAID. The team studied Indonesia's experience with cooperatives and "people's

74. Patten and Rosengard (1991), 17–24.
75. Patten and Rosengard (1991), 166–94.

banks," as well as the recent successes of BDB and the BKKs. It recommended that BRI borrow heavily from these examples. The government took the advice and with remarkable speed created a Goliath of microfinance.[76] To imbue BRI with a business culture, each of those thousands of *unit desas* was required to generate a balance sheet as well as a profit and loss statement each month. To cut losses, many units were downsized or relocated to busy markets.[77] Today BRI services roughly 4.5 million loan accounts, none through groups, and an extraordinary 21 million savings accounts—about as many small accounts as in all of Bangladeshi microfinance.[78] The clientele is probably more affluent than is true for most group microcredit: about 21 percent of BRI's savings-only customers live below the poverty line, and just 9 percent of its borrowers do.[79] Still, by global standards, BRI's customers are poor and service to them worthy of the label "microfinance."

ProCredit in Bolivia and Beyond. If the Indonesian institutions demonstrated the potential of individual savings and lending for poor people, much credit for spreading individual services globally goes to a German company led by Claus-Peter Zeitinger. A hard-charging, chain-smoking bear of a man, Zeitinger is not a polished ambassador like Yunus, but he, too, knew how to influence the rich and powerful to get what he wanted. His commitment to good works—and some key working friendships—were forged when he was a young man, in the quasi-revolutionary year of 1968. After working for GTZ and other organizations in the 1970s, Zeitinger cofounded a consulting firm called Interdizciplinare Projekt Consult (IPC) in 1981. Two years later, GTZ got IPC into financial services by hiring it to apply the German *sparkassen* model (see chapter 3) in Peru.

IPC's job was to help establish what were known locally as *cajas municipales de ahorro y crédito* (CMACs), which like *sparkassen*, took guarantees from local governments to reassure depositors about the safety of their savings. In exchange for the guarantees, government representatives held positions on CMAC governing boards. In IPC's experience, CMACs worked when they were small and relatively self-sufficient. But when they received too much outside funding and grew too large, the temptation for collusion and corruption among local players grew strong while the ability of innocent members to detect it grew weak. Such failures forged a philosophy at IPC that a financial institution had to create the right incentives for all involved

76. Patten and Rosengard (1991), 163, 364–409.

77. Maurer (2004), 96.

78. MIX Market, "BRI Data" (mixmarket.org/mfi/bri/data [January 16, 2011]).

79. Johnston and Morduch (2007), 29.

to be effective. According to their thinking, an outsider setting up the institution should hold shares in it to give the outsider a serious stake in the institution's success. Subsidies should be minimized to expose shareholders to the consequences of poor performance. Borrowers should be held individually accountable for their debts. And loan officers should be paid in part based on the performance of the loan portfolios they built and managed.[80]

Zeitinger and IPC colleagues set up a separate entity called ProCredit Holding to deliver microfinance according to IPC's philosophy. In 1992, it entered Bolivia, already Latin America's microfinance hotbed because of Prodem, the nonprofit lender mentioned earlier in this chapter. ProCredit's Bolivian affiliate, ProCrédito, rebelled against local convention by lending to the poor individually rather than through groups. Zeitinger had argued that people don't like being on the hook for others' debts and would rather borrow amounts tailored to their needs than be shackled to the rigid cycle of a group loan schedule. But ProCrédito had to compensate for the loss of the two services the group guarantee provided: filtering and enforcement. To filter out the uncreditworthy, ProCrédito loan officers, like their counterparts in Indonesia, had to understand their clients' businesses and cash flows and be wise to their local reputations. To enforce repayment, ProCrédito took collateral—but not the government-registered property that conventional banks demanded. ProCrédito accepted looms, washing machines—things that were a hassle to collect and sell but meant a great deal to the borrower.[81]

ProCrédito succeeded in Bolivia and in 1995 followed Prodem in transforming into a for-profit company (see chapter 8). Today, ProCredit Holding owns banks in twenty-one countries including Colombia, Bosnia, and the Democratic Republic of Congo. It ended 2010 with €3.6 billion in outstanding loans and €3.2 billion in savings deposits.[82] The group's motto, "Banks for 'Ordinary People,'" embodies Zeitinger's doubts about the value and practicality of credit for the *poorest*.

Placed next to group lending, individual lending looks conventional. Indeed, no line sharply divides individual microlending from mainstream small-business lending. As in conventional lending, loan officers assess clients' current and potential earnings rather than leaving such judgments to the borrower's peers. Still, individual microfinance differs in spirit from its upscale sibling. Where mainstream lenders rely heavily on collateral,

80. J. D. von Pischke, chairman, Frontier Finance International, Washington, D.C., interview with author, October 15, 2008.

81. Rhyne (2001), 91–94.

82. ProCredit Holding (2011), 4.

individual microcreditors lean more on assessments of character and business operations. Gabriel Solórzano, president of the recently dissolved Nicaraguan microfinance group BANEX, which also took collateral on the ProCredit model, once told me that his company didn't "want a used, rusty refrigerator. We lose two-thirds of the value when we seize collateral." BANEX took such collateral chiefly to threaten borrowers with the distress and embarrassment of having a truck arrive at their domicile to remove the item. He once said that BANEX extended not "asset-based credit" but "integrity-based credit."[83] Zeitinger echoes him, calling ProCredit's loans "information-based credit."[84]

Microinsurance

This survey of microfinance, like the movement itself, focuses on credit first, savings second—and insurance only third. Yet chapter 2 argued for the paramount importance of risk management in households rich and poor. As I wrote, health and life insurance are the financial services I am most loath to lose. The need to manage risk is even greater for the poor. Their earnings are unpredictable and volatile. And for them, an illness in the family can cause expenses to spike and income to plunge; the only way out of the pincers may be to sell the assets on which livelihoods depend—tools, land, even children. While loans and savings accounts can help people navigate these waters, insurance would seemingly serve best. So why doesn't microinsurance get more ink?

It turns out that it is tough to sell appropriate, adequate insurance to poor people without losing a lot of money. The next chapter details the reasons. For now, suffice it to say that the economics of selling tiny insurance policies calls for low administrative costs and high sales volumes; yet insurance is generally more complex than credit and savings, making it harder for sellers to administer and buyers to understand. For instance, many people are dubious at the prospect of paying insurance premiums month after month and getting nothing in return.

Of course, there are many kinds of insurance, and some are more workable at micro scale than others. Easiest and most common is credit life insurance, which covers the outstanding balance on a loan if the borrower dies.[85]

83. Gabriel Solórzano, president, FINDESA (later BANEX), Nicaragua, interview with author and Uzma Qureshi, April 27, 2006.

84. Claus-Peter Zeitinger, chairman, ProCredit Holding, presentation at Pangea Artisan Market & Café, International Finance Corporation, Washington, D.C., June 19, 2006.

85. Roth, McCord, and Liber (2007), 29.

Tacking this on to a loan is cheap and lets borrowers sleep easier at night, knowing that if they die, they will not burden their families with debt.

Many microcreditors offer their borrowers additional life insurance, which promises to go beyond cancelling debts to covering funeral expenses or making payouts to survivors. Mexico's leading microcreditor, Compartamos, is also one of its largest life insurers, measured in lives covered. Its standard microcredit product includes free insurance for the outstanding loan balance and a $1,250 death benefit. All 2 million current borrowers have that policy. They can buy additional policies covering $1,250 each for $13 per year, and another 800,000 such policies are currently active.[86] In an interesting twist on the typical credit life insurance, Bolivia's BancoSol offers what might be called savings life insurance: sold to depositors, its payouts are based on the average savings balance over the last three or six months. This nicely combines the virtues of insurance with an incentive to save.[87]

More complex are health and crop insurance. The latter especially has been tried for decades. Brazil, India, Mexico, and other governments have sold farmers multiple-risk crop insurance, which indemnifies them against damage from pests, drought, floods, and other threats that together make poor farmers the most risk-prone people on earth. But this subsidized crop insurance has succeeded little better than subsidized credit, with which it went hand in hand in the 1960s and 1970s. In an authoritative and diplomatic review, agricultural economists Peter Hazell, Carlos Pomareda, and Alberto Valdés conclude that "multiple-risk crop insurance has proved disappointing, and it has fulfilled few of its supposed objectives."[88] New York University economist Jonathan Morduch is blunter: "Experts that I have canvassed have difficulty naming even one truly successful small-scale crop insurance program anywhere (i.e., one that serves the poor, makes profits, and meaningfully reduces the largest risks)."[89] Thus the big challenge in microinsurance has been going beyond credit life insurance.

Several initiatives have grown large enough to make this imaginable, but on inspection most prove ambiguous. One is the Self-Employed Women's Association (SEWA), which also appears in the history of women's banking later in this chapter.

86. Banco Compartamos, "Seguro de Vida (Life Insurance)" (j.mp/hYRhq8 [March 2, 2011]); Carlos Danel Cendoya, executive vice president, Banco Compartamos, e-mail to author, March 1, 2011.

87. BancoSol, "Micro Insurance: Sol Seguro" (j.mp/hP2XmD [February 22, 2011]).

88. Hazell, Pomareda, and Valdés (1986), 294.

89. Morduch (2006), 339. See also Hazell (1992).

In 1992 SEWA started an insurance arm, Vimo SEWA. Like SEWA Bank, Vimo SEWA strives to deliver services similar to what the middle class enjoys rather than the rigid, stripped-down insurance analog of solidarity-group lending. The firm offers life, accident, health, and property insurance to poor women in India, and it counted 119,477 policyholders in 2010—substantial, but down from 214,181 three years earlier.[90] Vimo SEWA's history is one of trial and error without clear-cut success or failure. In the property insurance line, it first retailed another company's insurance, then switched to selling its own, absorbing risks and processing claims itself to improve service. But the Gujarat earthquake of 2001 loosed an avalanche of claims that showed the danger for a small insurer of going it alone. Vimo SEWA resumed partnering with large insurers. Meanwhile, the dramatic payouts to insured earthquake victims led to a quick tripling of membership—which then partly reversed in the earthquake-free years that followed as new customers grew disappointed over receiving no payouts themselves. In 2001, Vimo SEWA planned to reach financial self-sufficiency within seven years. Four years later, a case study concluded that financial independence still lay seven years off. Funding from the German aid agency GTZ and SEWA proper has kept Vimo SEWA afloat.[91]

Such difficulties suggest that microinsurance does need to be streamlined in a way roughly analogous to group credit in order to cut costs, if at the expense of quality. One simplified approach that has generated much excitement is that of "index insurance" for farmers. As with so much in microfinance, the idea goes back farther than most realize, to an Indian scholar named J. S. Chakravarti during World War I.[92] The idea then arose independently in the West. In 1947, a young man named Harold Halcrow who had grown up farming in North Dakota was studying for a Ph.D. in economics at the University of Chicago. He was concerned that crop insurance programs like those Franklin Roosevelt had introduced fifteen years before were fraught with "adverse selection" and "moral hazard"—that is, farmers who were most likely to suffer losses took the insurance most, running up costs; and by covering losses, insurance actually offered a disincentive for prudent husbandry. Halcrow hit upon an alternative. Instead of insuring all wheat farmers for all losses, the government should base payouts on an area index, such as a county's average wheat production or rainfall per acre. If the county's wheat production or rainfall was below preset thresholds in a given

---

90. Vimo SEWA, "Background" (j.mp/i7bZvW [January 23, 2011]). Figures include spouses and children covered by life insurance policies.

91. Garand (2005), 5–10.

92. Chakravarti (1920), cited in Mishra (1997), 307.

year, all farmers who bought the insurance in that county would get payouts at the same rate per acre, regardless of actual losses.[93]

Index-based insurance is subpar in the sense that variations in climate and growing conditions within a county would cause more damage to some farmers than would be covered, while others would escape harm and still get payouts. Insurers call this mismatch "basis risk." But if local microclimates are not too variable (as they tend to be in mountainous areas), index-based payouts might correspond reasonably with actual losses.[94] And collecting the necessary data would be cheap and nearly fraud-proof. The system would also vitiate the bugaboos of adverse selection and moral hazard. Since every farmer in a country would represent the same bet to the insurer—all would be paid or not according to the same formula—the insurer would not find itself insuring only the farmers liable to make the biggest claims. And since the insurance would not automatically compensate for individual farmers' carelessness, it would not, in Shakespeare's words, "dull the edge of husbandry."[95] Halcrow's dissertation committee members, including future Nobel Laureates Theodore Schultz and Milton Friedman, saw much to like and persuaded him to publish and pursue his proposal. But it went nowhere for forty years.[96]

Then in 1989, an agricultural economist of a younger generation came to Washington, D.C., to direct research for the congressionally mandated Commission for the Improvement of the Federal Crop Insurance Program. Pondering how to revamp the now-venerable and perpetually loss-making program, Jerry Skees became the third person in history to invent index-based crop insurance. He then discovered Halcrow's work (and later, Chakravarti's). This time around, the idea was tested. Acting on the commission's recommendation, Congress created the Group Risk Plan in 1992, which insured against county-level crop yield drops. At Skees's invitation, the 81-year-old Halcrow attended the program's official launch.

In 1998 Skees consulted for the World Bank, collaborating on a proposal for index-based rainfall cover for farmers in northwest Nicaragua. Rainfall measuring stations would be spaced across the region; if precipitation at a station failed to attain a set minimum, nearby policyholders would receive payments whether or not their crops had dried out. Calibrating to rainfall

93. Skees (2007), 1–2; Jerry Skees, professor, Department of Agricultural Economics, University of Kentucky, Lexington, Ky., interview with author, May 4, 2009.

94. On microclimates and basis risk in Nicaragua, see Morduch (2001), 3.

95. *Hamlet*, in G. Blakemore, ed., *The Riverside Shakespeare* (Boston: Houghton Mifflin, 1974), 1.3.77.

96. Halcrow (1949); Jerry Skees, professor, Department of Agricultural Economics, University of Kentucky, Lexington, Ky., interview with author, May 4, 2009.

seemed practical since historical data essential for the insurer in computing odds were available. Focusing on rain also would make a single policy useful to growers of many crops, as well as to shopkeepers and other non-farmers whose fortunes depended on the local agricultural economy. Unfortunately, the Nicaraguan government paid the proposal little attention. Perhaps insuring against low rainfall seemed ludicrous after Hurricane Mitch, which had smashed through the country the previous fall, dropping a meter of rain in places and killing thousands.[97]

Still, Skees and his collaborators had sowed the seeds of an idea. One would sprout back in India. There, the World Bank partnered in 2003 with ICICI Lombard and BASIX, an Indian company that provides financial and technical services to farmers, to pilot rainfall insurance. ICICI Lombard underwrote the insurance, while BASIX retailed it to growers of peanuts and castor beans in the state of Andhra Pradesh, leveraging its credibility in villages where it already worked.[98] By 2005, the program reached 6,700 farmers in six states, and other programs brought the national index insurance total to 100,000 policies.[99] The biggest disappointment has been low uptake. One study of the pilot found that only 5–10 percent of households that could buy the insurance did, and many bought far less than needed to fully cover their crops.[100] Apparently, as Vimo SEWA found, people with tight cash flows are skeptical of buying a product that might pay them nothing in return. At least with a savings account, you get your money back.

Progress in insuring the people and their crops should be fervently supported, wished for, and welcomed. Yet if history and the success of microcredit are any guide, it is the simplest forms of microinsurance, notably life insurance, that will reach the most poor people. Since credit and savings are likely to dominate the financial service portfolios of the poor, this book is mostly about those simpler services.

Crosscurrents

We have traveled along four branches of microfinance—solidarity lending, village banking, individual microbanking, and microinsurance—in each branch following the flow of time. For a fuller understanding of the

97. Jerry Skees, professor, Department of Agricultural Economics, University of Kentucky, Lexington, Ky., interview with author, May 4, 2009; Skees, Hazell, and Miranda (1999).

98. Manuamorn (2007).

99. World Bank (2005), 99.

100. Cole and others (2009).

contemporary landscape, I now take leave of time's arrow to explore some crosscutting themes in thought and practice. Associated with each is a long-standing, passionate debate about how best to do microfinance. My purpose here is less to analyze the arguments than to document the diversity.

Gender

Modern microfinance stands out against the historical record in its emphasis on serving women. But it did not start out that way. John Hatch targeted his first village banks primarily at male household heads.[101] Barely 20 percent of Grameen borrowers in the experimental first three years were female.[102] Every *triciclero* in Acción's solidarity group pilot was a man.[103]

Yet microfinance was a creature of its time, and in its time came a global wave of feminism. By the late 1970s, practitioners of economic development were primed by the tide of ideas to view poor women as disadvantaged by their gender as well as their economic status, therefore doubly deserving of aid. Indeed, even before the delivery methods that led to the microfinance takeoff were perfected, some groups were working to bank poor women. One early leader was Ela Bhatt, who founded SEWA in the city of Ahmedabad, in India's Gujarat state. Here is what happened, as told by journalist Elisabeth Bumiller:

[Mohandas] Gandhi's first fast . . . was in Ahmedabad in 1918, on behalf of the striking workers who labored in the city's textile mills. Out of that fast grew the Textile Labor Association, or TLA, the oldest and largest trade union of textile workers in India. A generation later, a young Brahmin woman from a well-to-do Gujarati family could find no better place to nurture her Gandhian ideals than in a job with the TLA, which did extensive welfare work among its membership. By 1968, Ela had taken over the women's division of the union, a job that historically entailed social work among the members' wives.

Ela would soon demolish the assumption that what these women needed was charity from well-meaning people like herself. In 1971, she met with a group of "head loaders"—women who carry cloth on their heads between Ahmedabad's wholesale and retail markets—who complained that the cloth merchants routinely cheated them. Ela helped

101. John Hatch, founder, FINCA, Santa Fe, N.M., interview with author, October 6, 2008.

102. Grameen Bank, "Historical Data Series in USD" (j.mp/e6wwqS [November 28, 2008]).

103. Jeffrey Ashe, director of community finance, Oxfam America, Boston, Mass., interview with author, November 25, 2008. Acción's first credit program, in Recife, Brazil, was 85 percent male (Tendler [1983], 105).

them form a group to collectively demand better pay, then wrote an article about their plight for one of the local newspapers. When the merchants countered with an article of their own, insisting they were paying the women fairly, Ela printed the merchants' claims on cards and distributed them to the women.

Out of that effort grew the SEWA, which today has organized women into 70 different trade cooperatives, from fish vending to cattle raising to weaving to hand-rolling the small Indian cigarettes called bidis.[104]

From the start, Bhatt saw financial services as central to economic emancipation: in 1974, SEWA started a bank for self-employed women. As a bank it could take savings as well as lend. Because SEWA Bank won the ideological fight it picked—proving that poor women were bankable—it is hard for us today to appreciate just how radical the bank was in its early days. The bank continues to this day, with 26,000 loan accounts (none through groups) and 348,000 savings accounts.[105]

In 1974, when BRAC was two years old, it, too, began searching for ways to reach women. An English journalist reported:

> It was in northeastern Sylhet, where the Bangladesh Rural Advancement Committee works, that I saw the seed of the quiet revolution starting in village women's lives. At the meeting houses BRAC has built, the wives, young and old, are learning to read and write. Forbidden from doing marketing, they now at least can keep the accounts.
>
> At community centres, I saw destitute widows, war victims, and wives of the landless, the poorest farmers and fishermen, learning skills like sewing, mat-making, and vegetable growing that will give them some security. "Most of the men were very surprised at the idea at the beginning, but few object now," said a young BRAC field worker.
>
> In one fishing village, the women have even become the bankers, saving over $2,000 and lending it to their men to buy better equipment. It started in the simplest way—they collected a handful of rice a week from each family, stored it, and sold it in the market. About 50 villages in the area have thriving women's cooperatives, investing in new power-pumps or seed, and winning respect for their members.[106]

104. Elisabeth Bumiller, "The Jewel in the Town," *Washington Post,* March 26, 1995.

105. MIX Market, "SEWA Bank Data" (mixmarket.org/mfi/sewa-bank/data [January 24, 2011]).

106. Quoted in Chen (1983), 4–5. The journalist and source are not identified. The $2,000 sum seems implausibly large given how much the dollar was worth in 1973 and how poor most Bangladeshis were then.

In August 1975, an American named Martha Chen began working for BRAC to improve and expand its programs for women, helping them find new economic activities to engage in individually or collectively. A daughter of missionaries, Chen had grown up in India. Later, with her husband, she had worked with Fazle Abed to found the predecessor to BRAC.[107] As with other early BRAC programs, one model for this project was the credit cooperative, which showed the value of forming groups, taking savings, and making loans. Over the course of a year, her team organized 6,000 women into 250 cooperatives to perform activities from silk spinning to fish farming. For her team, financial services were never ends in themselves, merely means to supporting such livelihoods. So in BRAC's early work with women, credit played only an incidental role.[108]

But after Yunus demonstrated the power of mass-producing credit, it was only a matter of time before Grameen's ideas about making loans and BRAC's ideas about reaching women blended in Bangladesh and beyond. BRAC began mass-producing credit on the Grameen model. At Grameen, lending to women went unmentioned in the 1983 Ordinance that created the bank but became an official priority in 1985.[109] Today, about 97 percent of Grameen borrowers are female (see figure 4-1) and 92 percent of BRAC borrowers are female.[110] Worldwide, the figure for the typical lender that works exclusively through groups is 99.6 percent; that for village banks is 86.6 percent. The share for individual microlenders is a comparatively low 46 percent; but even gender parity goes against history.[111]

The full reasons for microfinance's shift to women are difficult to sort out. Without doubt, the rise of feminism helps explain why modern microfinance favors women more than its forebears. So does a body of scholarly evidence roughly confirming the stereotype that women invest extra resources in their children while men spend them on beer.[112] But pragmatism was at work, too: women turned out to pay back more reliably than men in group-based microcredit. For example, after several repayment crises among its predominantly male clientele, during 1981–83 Grameen doubled its female fraction

---

107. Smillie (2009), 19–20. The Chens' son Greg, of CGAP, peer-reviewed a draft of this book.

108. Chen (1983), 6.

109. Grameen Bank Ordinance No. XLVI of 1983 (j.mp/nNoO2A).

110. Grameen Bank, "Historical Data Series in USD" (j.mp/e6wwqS [November 28, 2008]); MIX Market, "BRAC Data" (mixmarket.org/mfi/brac/data [February 25, 2011]).

111. MIX (2010). Figures are end-2009 medians among institutions reporting to the *Micro-Banking Bulletin*.

112. Armendáriz and Morduch (2010), 224.

Figure 4-1. *Grameen Bank Members by Gender, 1976–2010*

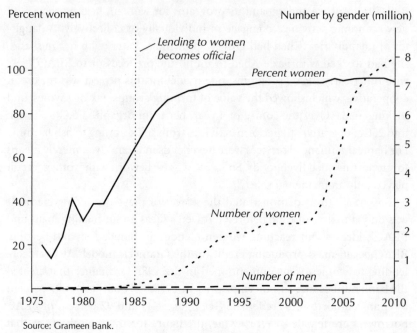

Source: Grameen Bank.

to 40 percent.[113] Evidently peer pressure worked better on women than men in Bangladeshi villages. That women are more susceptible to this pressure may be a sign that credit *disempowers* them. Or it may merely corroborate the view that women use finance more responsibly. At the heart of this ambiguity is the paradox that women like Jyothi's savings clients (in chapter 2) may gain financial autonomy in the home precisely by binding themselves financially in public. Chapters 5 and 7 return to these themes.

Savings versus Credit

Chapter 2 showed how people can view borrowing and saving as more similar than different. Although the two services allocate risk and obligation oppositely, whatever credit can do, savings can, too. Both can finance investment, pay for consumption, and help a family through health crises. This is why all but the poorest households can and want to save. Indeed, "most people, including the poor, want to have savings nearly all the time

113. Todd (1996), 20; Grameen Bank, "Historical Data Series in USD" (j.mp/e6wwqS [November 28, 2008]).

and to be in debt less frequently," says Malcolm Harper, former chairman of BASIX.[114] The most common informal saving methods—cash under the mattress, jewelry, livestock, Rotating Savings and Credit Associations (ROSCAs, defined in chapter 3)—carry considerable risks. Jewelry can be stolen. Cash can be lost through inflation or fire. When disasters such as floods and earthquakes strike, livestock can lose their value if everyone tries to sell them at the same time.

Despite the need for better ways to save, credit has dominated in microfinance. In the classic Grameen groups, members saved even as they borrowed, but in an involuntary way. They were required to put part of a new loan's proceeds into an emergency fund to guard against defaults and contribute regularly to a group fund, which members could only access when they departed. And though Hatch foresaw that members' own savings would eventually supplant that of sponsors, FINCA continues to pump millions into village banks, tilting them toward credit.[115]

The dominance of credit has been neither complete nor uncontested. Recall BRI's 4.5 million loan accounts and 21 million savings accounts, the latter generally held by poorer people. Stuart Rutherford, the British microfinance expert, worked hard to prove the practicality of microsavings in the emblematic nation of microcredit. In the mid-1990s, he became convinced that microcredit in Bangladesh was stuck in a rut. In addition to being inflexible, opaque, and authoritarian (with male loan officers running weekly meetings of groups of female borrowers), it did not offer individualized blends of credit and savings. So Rutherford started *Safe*Save, which caters to dwellers in Dhaka's slums, dense warrens of one-room houses of bamboo, tin, and thatch. *Safe*Save holds no group meetings. Rather, as with some nineteenth-century British "collecting societies" (see chapter 3), a bank officer visits clients at home daily, allowing them to save a penny at a time if they want, and collecting loan payments on a flexible basis. Program officers use handhelds to record transactions into a computer system designed to prevent fraud.[116]

With just 14,550 clients and an average savings balance of $40, *Safe*Save is not a Bangladeshi finance giant, but it may have influenced one of them.[117] A major plank of the "Grameen II" package of reforms adopted around 2001

114. Harper and Vogel (2005), 5.

115. John Hatch, founder, FINCA, Santa Fe, N.M., interview with author, October 6, 2008.

116. Stuart Rutherford, founder, *Safe*Save, Dhaka, Bangladesh, interview with author, March 2, 2008.

117. *Safe*Save (safesave.org/performance.html [January 28, 2011]).

was to make the Grameen Bank into an institution worthy of that name: a good place to put money. Grameen introduced new kinds of individual savings accounts and raised interest rates on existing ones. In a startling development, the bank saw its savings "portfolio" surpass its loan portfolio at the end of 2004. The icon of microcredit was doing more savings than credit.[118] Established microbanks in Latin America, including BancoSol in Bolivia and MiBanco in Peru, have also moved strongly into savings. BancoSol now holds 130,000 loan accounts and 323,000 savings accounts.[119]

It seems that there are two good ways to provide savings services. One is intimate and informal, such as in small, functioning cooperatives, village banks, and ROSCAs. The other is large-scale and formal, through government-run public banks or government-regulated private ones. There is little middle ground—*Safe*Save squeezes through a loophole in Bangladeshi law—because legally chartered entities such as nonprofit groups must almost always meet high regulatory standards before they can be entrusted with other people's money. A small NGO, on the other hand, can go about lending money rather easily. And for the provider, lending earns income more reliably than taking deposits. As a result, most self-identified microfinance institutions do more credit than savings.[120]

Pure Finance versus Bundling Services

Few would deny that poor people need more than financial services to better their lot. Health, education, infrastructure, physical security, political freedom, and other things matter, too. In the convening power of group microfinance, many organizations have spied an opportunity to provide nonfinancial services as part of the package at little extra cost, to do "credit plus." One example is Pro Mujer, a microfinance institution that delivers a package of microfinance and basic health services to women in five Latin nations. Pro Mujer's Carmen Velasco and Saiko Chiba explain the company's philosophy: "We conceive that Human Development is given not only through access to financial resources but also [through] an integrated group of basic services that will allow poor people and poor social groups to improve their quality of life and insert themselves in the economic cycle of their country."[121] California-based Freedom from Hunger supports affiliates on three continents

---

118. Grameen Bank, "Historical Data Series in BDT" (j.mp/pVks8w [January 4, 2011]).

119. MIX Market, "BancoSol Profile" (mixmarket.org/mfi/bancosol [May 11, 2011]).

120. MIX Market, "Microfinance at a Glance" (mixmarket.org [November 27, 2008]).

121. Velasco and Chiba (2006), 4.

administering the Credit with Education program: at weekly village bank meetings, officers teach clients "basics of health, nutrition, birth timing and spacing, and small business skills."[122] Vijay Mahajan, the director of India's BASIX, has remarked that "if you look at [our] income statements, 80 percent of it is still financial services because that's the fuel which makes it all go. But unless you add on these other things, you're just burning the fuel without really getting much result."[123] A decade ago, BASIX commissioned research that concluded that about as many of its microcredit clients were slipping behind as getting ahead. In reaction, Mahajan overhauled BASIX to more fully address the needs of its clients—not the generic challenges of health, education, sanitation, and so on, but the concrete obstacles to, say, raising a water buffalo for milk. If you want to invest in a buffalo, BASIX will lend you the money, and it will vaccinate and deworm the animal and check its health every two weeks for another $10 a year.[124]

Some argue that microfinance institutions do best when they stick to their knitting. Rich people don't want *their* bankers telling them what to feed their kids. And even if poor women value such education—and they well may, for lack of alternative sources—the benefits of weekly training on a limited set of topics may decline after a year or so. The question also arises of whether one organization can do two different things well. Acción affiliates, including BancoSol in Bolivia and Compartamos in Mexico, have succeeded by delivering financial services only, striving for constant gains in efficiency and quality and, ultimately, permanent extension of the financial system to poor people. As Elisabeth Rhyne wrote in reference to the "credit plus" partners of Pro Mujer and Freedom from Hunger in Bolivia, "The tool of microfinance . . . sits somewhat uncomfortably atop the objectives and motivations of these institutions, creating ongoing tension within them. It fits most solidly with institutions whose objective was always fundamentally financial."[125] A virtue of providing one service is that it is subject to a clear market test: people can take it or leave it. Once a well-intentioned donor begins bundling, the risk rises that the added services are so many unneeded sewing machines, doomed to gather cobwebs. Or worse, if the lender uses profits from credit to subsidize the added services, as BRAC does, both lender and borrower may find themselves propelled into inappropriate loans.

122. MkNelly and Dunford (1998), 6.

123. CGAP, "Microfinance Now: Vijay Mahajan," October 2009 (j.mp/e2uhgS).

124. Naren Karunakaran, "How to Fix Flaws in the Present Microfinance Model," *Economic Times*, November 12, 2010.

125. Rhyne (2001), 101.

The success of purists like BancoSol and credit plus providers like Pro Mujer lends credence to both sides of the debate. Given that fixed packages of services designed by outsiders to help poor people so often fail, much can be said for financial purism. But if specific, bundled interventions can be shown to work, they deserve support. A study done through Freedom from Hunger's Peru affiliate, for instance, found that borrowers assigned to receive business training along with their credit earned higher and more stable incomes. They also repaid their loans more reliably, perhaps because the training attracted them into attending more of the weekly meetings.[126]

From Charity to Profit

As a project meant to help poor people, microcredit is unusual in asking the beneficiaries to cover most or all of the costs. Hence its capacity for explosive growth. Because of repeated success on a market test, what began as a non-profit movement has trended toward commercialization and profit—not en masse but on average. As a result, microfinance institutions today exhibit a variety of institutional forms and levels of profitability. Among institutions providing data to the Microfinance Information eXchange (MIX), 407 were nonprofits with a combined 27.9 million loans outstanding in 2009; 384, with 34.9 million loans, were "non-bank financial institutions," which are generally for-profit companies limited to lending; and 81, with 24.4 million loans, were full banks.[127] Among all the institutions reporting to the MIX, the majority stated that they had a profit between 0 and 30 percent during 2007–09 (see figure 4-2). Subsidized finance, such as grants and low-interest loans, improves the income statements of many of these institutions; were these removed, apparent profitability would fall to the extent costs were not passed on to clients. Still, the point stands that microfinance institutions are as diverse in profitability as in legal orientation toward profit-making.

Beneath these dry statistical differences lie a pair of passionate disagreements about how best to serve the poor with microfinance. The first, which Jonathan Morduch once called the microfinance schism, is whether subsidizing microfinance is appropriate, especially to reach the poorest with the smallest loans.[128] If microcredit is a powerful weapon against poverty, then even the poorest deserve it. If reaching the poorest costs more than they should be asked to pay in interest, then donors should pay the difference. On the other hand, if microfinance is "merely" a useful service, which

126. Karlan and Valdivia (2007).

127. Author's calculations based on the MIX (mixmarket.org).

128. Morduch (2000).

Figure 4-2. *Microfinance Institutions, by Average Profit or Loss Rate during 2007–09*

Share of MFIs in each bracket (percent)

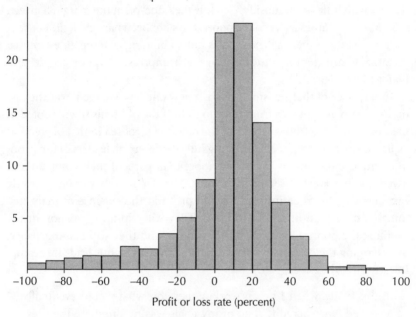

Profit or loss rate (percent)

Source: Author's calculations, based on the Microfinance Information eXchange.
Note: For clarity, the figure excludes ninety-nine microfinance institutions with profit rates less than 100 percent or greater than 100 percent.

leavens but does not end poverty, as I argue, then the case for subsidization loses its punch. Rather, it makes more sense to help microfinance play to its strengths as a businesslike way to serve millions of people who are poor by global standards, if not the poorest. In fact, as told in chapter 8, many in the microfinance world would go farther than breaking even. Microfinance institutions ought not to be merely businesslike nonprofits, they argue, but real businesses, with profits, capital, and investors. Michael Chu, who once ran Acción, has written that "humanity has found only one way to deliver consistently and simultaneously the four attributes of scale, permanence, efficacy and efficiency, and it is through private enterprise. This is the result not of any single firm—individual enterprises are born, prosper and die—but of the emergence of an entire industry. And industries are born out of the union of two factors: an economic activity and above-average returns."[129]

129. Michael Chu, "Profit and Poverty: Why It Matters," *Forbes*, December 20, 2007.

Today, the microfinance schism is mostly forgotten. Exemplars such as Pro Mujer and Grameen seem to reach quite poor people by the standards of their countries—as indicated by average loans of $400 and $250, respectively—with little or no subsidy.[130] While the trade-off at the margin between self-sufficiency and service to the poorest has not been banished, the consensus appears to be that the trade-off is not so binding as to be an existential threat. Self-sufficient institutions can reach impressively poor people, and that is to be celebrated.

In the place of that schism, though, a new one has emerged over the justice of channeling profits from poor to rich. If the old schism was rooted in the caricature of credit as salvation, the new one is rooted in that of credit as exploitation. Some argue that in going fully commercial, leaders of for-profit microfinance institutions are selling more than parts of their companies to investors; they are also selling their souls. The charge is that to hit quarterly earnings targets, these institutions will profit at the expense of their customers rather than in service to them. They will slip into "mission drift," avoiding the poorest, least profitable people. And they will commit usury, overcharging the customers they keep. Muhammad Yunus leads this camp. In early 2011, he wrote,

> In the 1970s, when I began working here on what would eventually be called "microcredit," one of my goals was to eliminate the presence of loan sharks who grow rich by preying on the poor. In 1983, I founded Grameen Bank to provide small loans that people, especially poor women, could use to bring themselves out of poverty. At that time, I never imagined that one day microcredit would give rise to its own breed of loan sharks.[131]

Yunus's barb was clearly aimed at for-profit companies doing Grameen-style microcredit in India, above all SKS Microfinance, founded by Indian-American Vikram Akula. In 2010, Yunus clarified in a debate with Akula that he does not oppose profit. He draws the line at sending the profits to outside owners. The Grameen Bank, he pointed out, was 96 percent owned by its members, making it a giant, for-profit cooperative. In recent years, the bank has paid out dividends of 30 taka per annum on the shares each member bought for 100 taka.[132]

130. MIX Market, "Pro Mujer Data" (j.mp/gUzcV5 [February 23, 2011]); MIX Market, "Grameen Bank" (j.mp/h4wzbB [February 23, 2011]).

131. Muhammad Yunus, "Sacrificing Microcredit for Megaprofits," *New York Times*, January 14.

132. Grameen Bank (2010), 25.

But Grameen was never a storybook credit cooperative: members contributed little to the working capital and the management.[133] Foreign donors
gave much more than members; and while members filled the majority of
the board seats, they demonstrated little independence from the founder.
Yunus was right that Grameen was not beholden to outside investors, and
that this may well have made it a more trustworthy, mission-driven institution. But the singularity of the Grameen Bank, particularly its ability to
attract substantial donations in its early years, makes it a hard act to follow. Most microfinance institutions have needed investment from outsiders
if they want to grow large. As a result, the number of for-profit, investor-
owned microfinance institutions will probably keep rising.

Conclusion

Clearly the microfinance phenomenon is a movement. It is a historical
development united by the shared ideal of bringing financial services to
the world's poor. Yet, it is divided—or at least diversified—by differences
of opinion about how best to do so in various contexts. The unifying ideal
predates the microfinance movement, which is why the methods dubbed
"microfinance" are merely a subset of the strategies deployed today to bring
financial services to poor people, along with savings banks and credit cooperatives. Because microfinance is the approach most apt to seek the aid of
outsiders, it is worth assessing with particular care, which is what the rest
of this book does.

I opened this book by pointing out the powers and limits of storytelling.
This chapter exploited that power in order to breathe life into a survey of
contemporary microfinance. After all, understanding where things come
from helps us understand where they are headed. The common thread in
this history is the potential for microfinance to catch on in a big way when
practical formulas are found for delivering on a cost-covering basis. Superficially, the fact that microfinance can operate in a businesslike fashion and
reach many people tells us nothing about how it affects those people. But I
would argue that the propensity for businesslike operation and growth is a
core strength of microfinance.

Having spread the map of the microfinance world before us, it is
time to scrutinize it, to ask the impertinent (and vague) question, "Does

---

133. At this writing, the member-majority's loyalty to Yunus has made it suddenly powerful,
the main obstacle to government control of the bank.

microfinance work?" Here, we hit the limits of narrative. So now we will mostly leave storytelling behind and shift into analytical mode. In chapters 6–8 we will review what is known about how microfinance contributes to economic and social development. But first, in chapter 5, we will approach that question through a back door, by exploiting one of the most powerful scientific paradigms ever: natural selection.

five
Business Plan

A system of finance which might prove a commercial success would not necessarily prove an economic success, but the system which promises to be an economic success must be based on commercial principles.

—WILLIAM R. GOURLAY, ON "CO-OPERATIVE CREDIT IN BENGAL," 1906[1]

Microfinance is manufactured by macro-sized organizations. In 2009, thirteen microfinance institutions (MFIs) in Bangladesh, India, Indonesia, and Mexico had more than a million borrowers, giving them 48 percent of all microcredit loans worldwide. Worldwide, 122 lenders—or 11 percent of the total—had more than 100,000 customers and accounted for fully 79 percent of outstanding microloans (see table 5-1). To cut the data another way, the "average microcredit client" was served by a lender with 2.2 million borrowers, a national market share of 22 percent, 9,000 employees, $730 million in assets, and operating profits equal to 16 percent of revenue.[2]

Most of the largest 122 MFIs hardly existed twenty years ago and so must have arrived at their position through sustained growth. Though many received grants and capital at lower prices than is available to conventional organizations of similar risk, the lenders are large enough that subsidies are a modest fraction of overall revenue. In other words, the providers of most microfinance are successful businesses. They have found ways to control

This chapter is based on Roodman and Qureshi (2006).

1. Gourlay (1906), 216–17.

2. Author's calculations, based on MIX (2011). Microfinance Information eXchange (MIX) data are voluntarily reported by self-identified MFIs. Probably many small ones do not report. (Reed [2011, 3] counts 3,589 compared to 1,104 in table 5-1.) Nonprofit MFIs reinvest any earnings in their operations or pass them back to funders. Note that these figures measure different concepts than the averages at the bottom of table 5-1: they are averages over MFIs, weighting by number of borrowers. For example, the simple, unweighted average of the number of staff members at an MFI is 444, but the weighted average is 9,000. In words, because most clients patronize big MFIs, the average client is served by an MFI with 9,000 staff.

Table 5-1. *Characteristics of Microfinance Institutions (MFIs), by Size, 2009*

MFI size (number of borrowers)	MFIs[a]		Borrowers		Staff members/ MFI	Assets/ MFI (million $)	Profit (% of revenue)
	Number	Share of total (%)	Number	Share of total (%)			
< 100,000	**982**	**89**	**17,072,429**	**21**	**396**	**57.2**	**+1**
< 100	21	2	1,315	0.002	6	0.2	−67
100–1,000	121	11	52,941	0.06	14	2	−44
1,000–10,000	401	36	1,829,750	2	64	7	−14
10,000–100,000	439	40	15,188,423	18	312	48	+3
> 100,000	**122**	**11**	**67,524,505**	**79**	**14,559**	**1,271**	**+20**
100,000–1 million	109	10	26,800,777	32	1,426	193	+15
> 1 million	13	1	40,723,728	48	13,133	1,078	+23

Source: Author's calculations, based on data from Microfinance Information eXchange (February 12, 2011).

Note: Profit margins averaged across MFIs weighting by number of borrowers. Excludes some large institutions that are heavily subsidized or up-market on the credit side: Banco Caja Social Colombia, Banco Popular do Brasil, Kenya Post Office Savings Bank, Khushhali Bank of Pakistan, Postal Savings Bank of China, and Vietnam Bank for Social Policies.

costs, build volume, keep repayment high, and prevent internal fraud, all while operating in countries with weak infrastructure and governance.

The task of this book is to impose an outsider's question on microfinance: What is its social bottom line, its contribution to development? But before tackling the question directly (starting in the next chapter), this chapter approaches the question indirectly. Most descriptions of microfinance put the client front and center. The intermediating MFI is rendered transparent. Here, I adjust the lens so that the client blurs and the MFI comes into focus. I observe microfinance institutions the way Darwin did finches, looking for links between how they operate and whether they survive and thrive. No doubt most MFI leaders, staff, and investors care deeply about the ultimate impact on borrowers and communities. But viewing MFIs more crassly—as practical solutions to challenging business problems—turns out to be enlightening.

On the one hand, this exercise buttresses skepticism about the most famous claims for microfinance. For example, if the common emphasis on credit over savings is a business practicality, that seeds judicious doubt that credit is what the poor most need. Likewise, if women are favored as clients because they are more reliable, we should be less confident that targeting women is better for them and their families. On the other hand, viewing microfinance as business fosters appreciation for the achievement of the microfinance movement in creating durable institutions to mass-produce useful services for poor people.

The central business problem for MFIs is keeping costs near or below revenues. That observation makes sense: organizations need to at least break even to persist and grow. But it is also vacuous, like saying that organisms must survive in order to pass on their genes. The concrete challenges for MFIs include attracting an adequate customer base to realize economies of scale, retaining those customers, keeping loan repayment rates high, preventing fraud, complying with regulations, and avoiding organizational stagnation. This chapter highlights specific ways that MFIs meet such challenges, emphasizing credit because it is the most prevalent service.[3]

The big picture that emerges is of an interaction between human ingenuity, chance, and winnowing. Microfinance leaders have found a suite of techniques in product design and management that meet the business challenges they face. Most they consciously designed. Others were stumbled upon. And in any particular case, most were copied from another MFI. Regardless, because the techniques worked, organizations using them moved to the forefront of the microfinance movement through a process of "natural" selection.

The need to succeed as a business can explain much of how microfinance is done today, including the emphases on women, groups, and loans. The survival imperative also helps explain less-noted aspects: the greater success in highly urbanized or densely populated areas; the wealthier, more heavily male clientele for individual loans compared to group loans; and the requirements that people deposit saving as they repay loans. Fundamentally, because the amounts transacted in microfinance are small, administrative costs must be cut to the bone, which forces sacrifices in quality. As a result, microfinance is a business of mass production of low-quality services. Fortunately, however, competition and experimentation have gradually reduced costs and improved quality. The practice of forced savings, for example, is becoming less common in mature markets and voluntary savings more common. In microfinance, evolution never stops.

The Dominance of Credit over Savings and Insurance

We have seen in previous chapters that a stand-alone savings account can substitute for credit in many uses—one can save or borrow for a sewing

---

3. On scale economies, see Gonzalez (2007), 39, who finds them up to 2,000 customers per MFI, though not beyond.

machine—and that poor people often prefer to save out of a healthy fear of debt. And we have seen that in some situations, insurance is superior to savings and credit. Ideally then, everyone should have opportunities to save and insure along with opportunities to borrow. Yet the microfinance movement has emphasized credit. The Microcredit Summit Campaign is working "to ensure that 175 million of the world's poorest families, especially the women of those families, are receiving credit for self-employment and other financial and business services by the end of 2015."[4] Muhammad Yunus has called access to credit a human right.[5]

The Lure of Lending

Why has the movement favored credit? The answer seems to be principally out of practicality. Appropriately, regulators erect fewer barriers to lending than to collecting deposits and insurance premiums. A small nonprofit ought not, and in most places cannot, easily become a bank or insurer. In general, institutions legally entrusted with other people's money are supervised by the government to assure that they are managing that money with propriety and prudence. Consumers generally view matters the same way, hesitating to save and insure with lightweight start-ups.

In addition to this prudential consideration, credit has advantages from a business point of view. For lenders, the regularity and uniformity of loan repayment schedules speed weekly meetings and stabilize and perhaps increase revenue by disciplining clients to repay more regularly than they would save. Crucially, it is easier to charge enough to cover costs when doing small loans. After all, if an MFI needs to charge 30 percent a year to break even on a microloan, then seemingly it needs to charge about the same on a savings account. While Jyothi's clients in Vijawada, India, have come to accept paying interest on savings (see chapter 2), many people will pull their money out of a bank once the interest on savings goes negative.[6]

Another factor in favor of credit is that it is more attractive to many social investors than less capital-intensive savings and insurance programs: with the same effort, an investor looking to disburse large amounts in the least amount of staff time could place $10 million in a lending project or $1 million in a savings project. And in a sense, credit makes the intermediating institution disappear in the minds of donors so that clients alone fill the visual field. In 2007, *New York Times* columnist Nicholas Kristof wrote about

---

4. Reed (2011), 3.

5. Muhammad Yunus, "What Is Microcredit?" June 2011 (j.mp/lri1Gl).

6. Rutherford (2009a), 16–17.

his experience meeting a baker in Kabul to whom he had lent money through Kiva. From members of parliament able to move millions to people with $100 to spare, most find it more appealing to follow in his footsteps than to invest that money purely in the training, equipment, and reserves needed to start a microbank.[7] These activities do not stir the same feelings of connection as the image of a smiling baker.

Overall, the path of least financial resistance for many microfinance institutions is to pitch this image and borrow in bulk to finance small loans. Malcolm Harper, the longtime chairman of the Indian MFI BASIX, has reflected that as a source of capital, "client savings are not cheap, in spite of the low interest rates we pay, because the mobilisation and transaction costs are high. It is much cheaper to take bulk loans from the national or global financial system. It is more profitable to put poor people into debt than it is to take care of their savings."[8]

The Scope for Savings

Still, this point should not be overdrawn: many microfinance players have broken against the historical dominance of credit over savings. As a funder, the Gates Foundation is a huge and notable exception to the preference for credit; it has committed hundreds of millions to savings and insurance. Among microfinance institutions, the Bank Rakyat Indonesia and the Grameen Bank hold millions of voluntary savings accounts. At Bolivia's BancoSol, a pathbreaker in Latin America, savings accounts now outnumber loans nearly three to one.[9] Among six Bolivian MFIs at the end of 2003, including BancoSol, 86 percent of savings accounts held less than $500 dollars, averaging just $43, suggesting that the majority of the savers are poor. The pattern is similar in Peru, another mature microfinance market.[10]

If a detailed study of deposit-taking MFIs in Uganda and the Dominican Republic is any guide, the ones in Bolivia and Peru are probably losing money on those small accounts.[11] The same study, however, found several incentives for MFIs accepting small savings accounts as loss leaders. Many of the accounts get bigger and more profitable over time. MFIs may not want to invest the effort in predicting which customers' small accounts are likely

7. Nicholas D. Kristof, "You, Too, Can Be a Banker to the Poor," *New York Times,* March 27, 2007.

8. Malcolm Harper, chairman, BASIX, DevFinance online discussion group, August 20, 2009.

9. MIX Market, "BancoSol Profile" (mixmarket.org/mfi/bancosol [March 16, 2011]).

10. Maisch, Soria, and Westley (2006), 6–7. The pattern was also similar in England in 1830; see Fishlow (1961), 32.

11. Westley and Palomas (2010).

to grow, calculating that it is more efficient to take all. In this case, the big accounts effectively subsidize the small ones. And people who save at an MFI are more likely to return for other services, such as loans. While microsavings is tougher than microcredit, the business case for savings can be made, especially for mature institutions able to take the long view.

The Impediments to Insurance

The business perspective also explains why despite the evident value of insurance to poor people, microinsurance remains a fledgling thirty years after microcredit took off. An insurance policy can be thought of as a savings account with one change: while both entail repeated small pay-ins and an occasional large payout, an insurance payout occurs after some specified event, such as a death—or not at all. Thus insurance raises the same prudential concerns for regulators as deposit-taking. And the conceptual switch from savings to insurance raises additional business challenges. For one, regulators need to make sure that what insurers charge and what they promise are roughly in balance so the insurers neither grossly overcharge, accumulating large surpluses, nor undercharge, rendering them insolvent in the hour of greatest need.

Other problems bedevil insurance, almost all of which derive from the relatively complex nature of the service. One of these is "adverse selection": insurance buyers know better than the sellers about the risks they face, and the people who know they are most likely to need insurance are the ones most likely to buy it. In defense against the invisibly ill, for example, health insurers in the United States usually price individual policies exorbitantly. The standard solution to adverse selection is to deliver insurance through groups that are formed on the basis of criteria broadly disconnected from the risks that trigger insurance payouts. In selling group health policies to large employers, for example, American insurers charge less because the employees as a group are closer to the general population in their proneness to illness and injury (and pregnancy). Another classic problem is "moral hazard": insurance insulates people from some consequences of their own actions, which can make them reckless or wasteful. Why irrigate the field if the insurer takes the hit for parched crops? Why not get that medically useless kidney ultrasound if it costs the patient nothing and profits the doctor? Co-payments (an example of "co-insurance") aim to minimize this problem by sharing costs between the insurer and the insured.

Then there are problems of distrust, denial, complexity, and misunderstanding:

—Distrust: Unless the insurer has a rock-solid reputation, potential customers will view *it* as a risk.

—Denial: In general, human beings try not to think too much about the bad things that could happen to them—or they at least underestimate the risks and underinvest in insurance.

—Complexity: Whatever event triggers insurance payments must be economical to observe. Checking that a drug was medically necessary and actually dispensed or that a rice paddy far from the nearest paved road really was flooded can be expensive—worthwhile for a claim of $10,000 but not for one of $100.

—Misunderstanding: Insurance can strike people as a bad deal. Why purchase a policy that might never return a penny when you could save the money for an overly rainy day? Money in an insurance policy is locked up in that one purpose, defending against just one kind of risk. Money in a savings account can be used for anything. Recall the study cited in chapter 4 of index rainfall insurance in India: a product that solves many of the problems listed above and makes eminent sense from the point of view of risk reduction nevertheless sat on the metaphorical shelves to a disappointing extent.[12] The logic of insurance stands up to this kind of thinking; people can be taught it—but perhaps at a cost that is prohibitive relative to the small sums in microinsurance. It is no wonder, then, that only three in 100 people in the 100 poorest countries have formal life, health, or property insurance.[13]

Facing this complex of challenges, those hoping to bring the benefits of insurance to more people have worked along several lines of development. The first has been to look to solidarity groups and village banks as the analog of employers in U.S. health insurance—in other words, as assemblages of people not adversely selected to run up insurance costs. Second, they have emphasized life insurance. As Daniel Defoe wrote in 1697, death is hard to fake (although death certificates can be forged and missing bodies explained away).[14] And life insurance is relatively free of moral hazard because no insurance payout can compensate for the human costs of loss of life. These two considerations explain why credit life insurance—insurance packaged with a microloan that covers the outstanding debt if the borrower dies—is the most common form of microinsurance to date. The chapter 3 example of Prudential in nineteenth-century Britain, the first large-scale enterprise

12. Cole and others (2009).
13. Roth, McCord, and Liber (2007).
14. Defoe (1697).

selling insurance to the poor, further suggests that if the microinsurance business grows, life insurance will lead the way.

An Evolutionary Theory for the Taxonomy of Microcredit

In chapter 4 I described three types of microcredit that have become globally popular: solidarity groups, village banking and self-help groups, and individual lending. I emphasized the organic way in which these methodologies arose. But that the three dominant methods have survived suggests that they are more than accidents of history, that an order underlies the historical happenstances.

The microcredit methods that have been deployed on a large scale can be seen as arrayed along a spectrum. At one end, loans are small, more costly to provide relative to loan size, and made practical only by shifting certain costs onto borrowers. At the other end, loans are larger, more expensive to administer yet cheaper as a percentage of the amount lent, and more convenient for the customer.

This continuum is discernible in table 5-2, which breaks out statistics on loan sizes and expenses of MFIs by lending method. In reading the table, keep in mind that all but a core of dedicated poverty-focused solidarity lenders have moved into the mixed individual–solidarity category (making individual and group loans), so those in the "solidarity" category are unrepresentative. The second data column shows that village banking and solidarity group loans are much smaller than individual ones. More accurately, the typical loan size for solidarity lending is probably between those listed for solidarity lenders and mixed ones—and above that for village banking.[15] The fourth column of the table, in percentages of national GDP per capita, also suggests that village banking reaches at least as deep as solidarity lending into the ranks of the poor.

The table confirms that lenders' expenses decrease with loan size but not as fast. As a result, smaller loans cost more to deliver, per dollar. For example, median total expenses for individual lenders, who made the biggest loans in the table, were 19.2 percent of assets, the lowest percentage in the table.[16] In general, such expenses can be divided into three categories. The first two vary

15. This is the case in an analysis by Cull, Demirgüç-Kunt, and Morduch (2007), F115.

16. The median is the fiftieth percentile; assets are a financial variable in which the value of outstanding loans predominates.

Table 5-2. *Characteristics of Microfinance Institutions (MFIs), End-2009*
Medians

Lender type	Number of MFIs in sample	Credit per borrower $	Credit per borrower % of GDP/ capita	Expenses (% of assets) Financial	Expenses (% of assets) Loan loss provision	Expenses (% of assets) Operating	Expenses (% of assets) Total[a]	Operating expenses/ loan ($)	Loans/ loan officer
Individual lending	364	1,415	45.0	5.3	1.4	10.8	19.2	203	238
Mixed individual–solidarity lending	426	455	26.9	4.7	1.7	16.3	24.4	112	237
Solidarity lending	97	145	13.8	4.8	0.8	14.9	22.1	28	284
Village banking	85	238	12.7	4.9	1.2	16.8	23.9	90	306

Source: MIX (2010).

Note: Assets include, and are typically dominated by, the outstanding loans to clients. Financial expenses include interest and fees in obtaining funds to lend. Loan loss provision is set-asides to cover costs of client defaults.

a. Previous columns do not sum to totals because median totals differ from total medians.

little across lenders: financial (interest on money borrowed to fuel lending) and default (which appears in accounting through loan loss set-asides). The last, largest, and most variable is operating costs, which include everything from rent to wages. Village banking has the highest operating costs relative to the small amounts lent, at 16.8 percent of assets. The figure for solidarity lenders is 14.9 percent, and that for individual lenders is just 10.8 percent. But the "operating expenses/loan" column in the table demonstrates that group lenders spend less per loan. The final column shows that they achieve this economy in part by generating more loans per employee: some 300 each, compared to 238 for individual lending.

Group lending methods achieve these high volumes in particular ways. Recall that in solidarity lending, borrowers join in sets of three to seven, most commonly five. Usually the pattern of disbursements and repayments is regimented. Typically payments begin immediately after disbursement, are due weekly, and are constant over the life of the loan. In classical Grameen credit, recall from chapter 4, entry into the regimen is staggered within a group: first two borrowers take their loans and begin to repay, then two more, then the fifth. After a borrower pays off one loan, she becomes eligible for a larger one if all group members are in good standing. In Asia, six or eight solidarity groups are federated into a larger unit called the "center," which is the congregation that gathers with the credit officer to transact all business.

At least as originally conceived, village banks bring together a dozen people or so, give them a single loan, then delegate authority to them for lending to individual members. Members elect officers to conduct the village bank's affairs. In practice, village banking loan officers often involve themselves in lending decisions. As a result, many village banks come more to resemble solidarity-group centers. Usually loan sizes are allowed to differ among individual members. But all loans generally carry the same repayment and interest rate terms, and borrowers are generally offered a loan ladder, a sequence of three to five loan cycles with a maximum amount for each cycle.

A microcredit officer's daily labor—what generates most operating costs—consists of a few tasks: marketing, sales, underwriting new loans, monitoring use and repayment of borrowed funds, and enforcing repayment. MFIs lending to individuals handle these jobs directly. But group lending shifts several of these responsibilities onto borrowers. Responding to the incentives of joint liability, clients help with underwriting by choosing peers they deem reliable, monitor their activities, and pressure them to keep up on debt service. The delegation is most complete in village banking as originally conceived because the MFI just makes a loan to the group. In general, the delegation makes group lending cheaper per loan, which advances the frontier of practicality in lending small sums to poor people.

The various forms of group lending share a feature whose role in the efficient operation of MFIs is rarely explained: compulsory public meetings every one or two weeks. As the Grameen Bank gained fame in the late 1980s, future Nobel Laureate Joseph Stiglitz and other economists latched onto the five-member solidarity group as a structure of theoretical interest. They modeled how joint liability obviates the need for group lenders to get to know their clients.[17] But more than formal joint liability, social pressure appears to be the real glue of group lending. This pressure does not bear down solely in the privacy of people's homes as they negotiate the formation and conduct of their groups of five. Rather, its real application is orchestrated by the loan officer in a large, public meeting of several dozen participants. "It is staff pressure that triggers peer pressure," reports Imran Matin, who is now a Deputy Executive Director at BRAC.[18] If a woman shows up for a meeting unable to pay, she risks bringing shame on herself and her family—not to mention the ire of other women inconvenienced by the disruption of the

17. For example, Stiglitz (1990) and Ghatak (1999).
18. Matin (1997b), 266.

meeting's routines. The presiding MFI loan officer may hector her, delay new loans to her peers that day, or otherwise force the group to sit for extra hours until someone makes a side deal to cover the unfortunate woman's payment.[19] Nor are village banks free of such pressures: Pro Mujer "does not end its village bank meetings until all loan delinquencies are cleared up," wrote Glenn Westley of the Inter-American Development Bank in 2004. "Village bank members are expected to extend a loan to any member with a payment shortfall. Many program dropouts complain of these long meetings and of coming to hate meetings."[20]

Microfinance practitioner and researcher Stuart Rutherford calls this pressure "meeting-day joint liability." He explains, "The pressure falls especially strongly—and especially effectively—on members who are known to have cash, or the prospect of cash, that day. Thus, members due to get a loan disbursed that day, or members who have brought large [savings] deposits ... often feel themselves morally obliged to lend short-term to members with repayment difficulties."[21] The practice described earlier of staggering the loan cycles assures that usually someone is close to getting a new loan.

Rigorous research has confirmed this anecdotal evidence that informal group dynamics exercise more power than formal liability. In an experiment run with the Green Bank in Caraga, the Philippines, economists Xavier Giné and Dean Karlan found that after borrowers in randomly chosen, ongoing solidarity groups were notified that joint liability had been dropped, repayment rates and other indicators of portfolio health showed no change in the following three years—except that centers without formal joint liability attracted more new clients.[22] The preeminence of meeting-based peer pressure explains why the Bangladeshi microfinance giants have gradually dropped formal joint liability but not public meetings (see the last section of this chapter).

Presumably poor people like the peer pressure of group lending no more than rich people would. As Malcolm Harper writes, "Group-based microfinance delivery systems are temporary low-quality expedients, like shared toilets, primary school classes of 60 children, or clinics without doctors. These are the best that can be provided at the present time for some people in some places, but they are recognized as fundamentally unsatisfactory."[23] Individual lending is unattractive for lenders at the low end of the income scale because it

19. Jain (1996), 83; Matin (1997a), 456; Montgomery (1996), 296–97; Rutherford (2009b), 135.

20. Westley (2004), 22.

21. Rutherford (2004), 30. Also see Matin (1997a), 456–57.

22. Giné and Karlan (2008).

23. Harper (2007a), 36.

is too expensive, while group lending is unattractive to borrowers at the high end because it is too burdensome. As a result, village and solidarity banking serve the poorest while individual lending goes to the less poor. This pattern is universal in service businesses: the less you are willing or able to pay, the less you are catered to. But the situation is not unchangeable. There is good reason to hope and work for improved financial services for even the poorest, thanks in part to such technologies as mobile phones, discussed in chapter 9.

Additional Adaptations

An evolutionary perspective helps explain more than just the dominance of credit and the three-way typology within it. Like the fronds of a fern, the finer details of microfinance practice are also honed by selection. This section describes features that shape the microfinance experience for poor people and thus connect to the question of how microfinance affects their lives. The business imperative can explain why group credit has focused on women; why microfinance has thrived in dense places, such as the deltas of Bangladesh and the *favelas* of Latin America, while struggling in much of Africa; why the very poorest do not partake of microcredit; and why it is rarely used for farming.

It might seem rude to impose this Darwinian perspective on an activity meant to help poor people—to suggest, for instance, that group credit favors women for the narrow commercial reason that it helps MFIs operate cheaply. But just as in natural selection, the processes that generate variation and those that prune it can be entirely separate. People who invented or borrowed the idea of lending to women may have done so out of noble motives. But the approach would not have spread if it did not make business sense.[24]

Frequent Transactions and Short Loan Terms

Borrowers use microcredit for everything from weddings to school fees to business investment that won't see returns for a year. Yet most microloans require frequent, regular payments that start immediately after disbursement and continue for at most a year. The ancient Athenian *eranos* groups appear to have required frequent payments, as did Jonathan Swift (see chapter 3).

Clearly these loan terms are pragmatic. Just as with holders of thirty-year home mortgages, allowing microcredit borrowers to defer too much payment would invite disaster. For group credit, meeting frequently also strengthens

24. Armendáriz and Morduch (2010), 137–68.

the essential social glue.[25] But the demand for immediate repayment has profound consequences for who uses microcredit and how they use it. Two kinds of borrowers can be relied on to generate the demanded payment stream: those who intend to invest the loan in a high-turnover business, which usually means high-volume retail or craft work; and those who already earn income from sources other than the investment project they finance with the loan. Microcredit payment plans, however, are poorly matched to such investments as calves and crops whose returns may not come for months. Households can still finance a few cows with small loans if they can tap steady, preexisting income streams.[26] To this extent, though, microcredit lies beyond the reach of the poorest people, including many women without husbands.[27] In fact, most of the world's poorest people are farmers, and some of the most important investments they can make are in the seeds, fertilizer, and labor needed to raise crops. So ill-suited is standard microcredit to crop-raising that the two generally do not intersect.[28]

Dynamic Incentives

Typically an MFI will start small with new clients. It will initially lend less than might be needed, observe repayment, reward promptness with a larger loan, and repeat, in an ascending cycle. Group lenders in particular follow loan ladders that specify a maximum loan size for each loan cycle. This "progressive lending" creates what economists call "dynamic incentives": what a client does today affects her options tomorrow.[29] Lenders create dynamic incentives whenever they offer better loan terms down the road as a reward for on-time repayment today.

These incentives can be powerful. In an experiment in South Africa, Karlan and fellow economist Jonathan Zinman found that offering a borrower a lower interest rate on his next consumer loan had a huge impact on repayment of the current one.[30] Analyst Daniel Rozas has shown that when microcreditors go bankrupt, their chief assets—their portfolios of outstanding loans—lose almost all their value. When people think that new loans will no longer be in the offing, they stop repaying current ones.[31]

25. Feigenberg, Field, and Pande (2010).

26. Jain and Moore (2003), 15.

27. Ito (1999), 108–37.

28. Harper (2007b).

29. Armendáriz and Morduch (2010), 140–47.

30. Karlan and Zinman (2008b).

31. Rozas (2009).

Progressive lending, like frequent payments, is practical. By gingerly test-ing the waters with a new client, it winnows out risky customers before they can do much harm to an MFI's balance sheet. But progressive lending also shapes the clients' experience of microcredit. For a borrower who is strug-gling to fully repay a loan, the last few weeks of the loan cycle are the most stressful. Yet they are exactly when the new, larger loan looms close. This cre-ates a powerful incentive for the borrower to go to a second lender—a family member, a peer borrower, another MFI, or a moneylender—for a bridge loan to be repaid as soon as the new, larger loan comes through from the primary MFI. Progressive lending can thus feed a cycle of debt, concealing, deferring, and exacerbating the ultimate confrontation with trouble. This is why the dynamic incentive of a larger loan must be paired with mechanisms of restraint, such as frequent repayments and group liability.

Compulsory Savings

A common element in solidarity groups and village banking is compulsory or "forced" savings. Some forced savings are taken directly out of the loan amount before disbursal; as of 2003, for example, the Bolivian village bank-ing MFI Crédito con Educacíon Rural withheld 10–20 percent of a loan up front. In contrast, FINCA Nicaragua took forced savings equal to 32 percent of the loan amount incrementally, like loan payments, at successive group meetings.[32] Some MFIs allow clients to withdraw forced savings when they are done paying off the associated loan, others not until the client leaves the program altogether.

This counterintuitive combination of saving and borrowing accelerates loan repayment so that toward the end of a loan cycle, the MFI is actually in debt to its clients. The effects are several. Clients know they have a buffer stock to draw on when they just can't come up with a loan installment. MFIs are less exposed should a village bank or a solidarity group collapse. Throughout the 1990s, for example, when the Grameen Bank was firmly credit oriented, members' sav-ings exceeded 40 percent of their borrowings from it.[33] And the threat of losing savings can deter default in the first place. Similarly, creating the possibility that one person's forced savings will be used to cover another's missed pay-ments strengthens meeting-day joint liability. Finally, forced savings increases the cost of credit in a way that lenders understand better than borrowers: it lowers the average net credit balance over the loan cycle without reducing the interest charged. In 2009, the Nigerian MFI Life Above Poverty Organization

32. Westley (2004), 49.

33. Grameen Bank, "Historical Data Series in USD" (j.mp/cGEN0o [May 13, 2011]).

(LAPO) lowered its interest rate from 3 percent to 2.5 percent per month. At the same time it doubled its forced savings requirements to 20 percent of the opening loan balance up front plus 20 Nigerian *naira* per week. Together, these changes made what looked like a rate cut into an effective increase in the effective annual interest rate, from 114.3 percent to 125.9 percent.[34]

MFIs sometimes describe forced savings as a way to inculcate thrift. But the practical value has as much to do with building up a shock-absorbing cartilage between MFI and client. MFIs also can teach the habit and discipline of regular saving by offering voluntary time deposit accounts (analogous to certificates of deposit), or commitment savings accounts (see chapter 2). These are less common.

Credit Life Insurance

Some lenders require borrowers to buy credit life insurance, which, recall, covers their debt to the lender upon death. For instance, LAPO has borrowers pay 2 percent of the loan as a "risk premium."[35] Like forced savings, forced insurance cushions the joint where lender and borrower connect. It helps borrowers by reducing risk. In group settings, it protects members from having to choose between running after a deceased's grieving family or covering a loss themselves. For the MFIs, it lowers the risk from death of a borrower.

Credit life insurance is also another opportunity to raise the effective cost of credit. In fact, LAPO's 2 percent fee seems high when you consider that the break-even price of credit life insurance as a percentage of the loan balance, leaving aside administration costs, equals half the percentage of borrowers who can be expected to die during the loan repayment period. For example, if an MFI lends $100 each to 100 women and one (i.e., one percent) can be expected to die—on average, halfway though repayment, when her outstanding balance is $50—then the average loss would be about $50, or 0.5 percent of the $10,000 lent. A half-percent fee would cover insurance costs. If LAPO were selling the credit life insurance on a break-even basis, the 2 percent fee on LAPO's eight-month loans would imply a death rate of 4 percent per eight months, or 6 percent per year. That is extremely high in a country with an annual death rate of 1.6 percent—or it is a hidden way to raise the effective interest rate.[36]

---

34. Planet Rating (2009), 6. The rates of 2.5 and 3 percent are themselves arguably nontransparent: they are flat rates, expressed relative to the opening balance rather than to the actual, declining balance. See the section on transparency in chapter 7.

35. Planet Rating (2009), 6.

36. CIA, "The World Factbook: Nigeria" (j.mp/o1dsWi [July 5, 2011]).

Lending to Women

The face of microfinance is usually a woman's. Some MFIs, like Pro Mujer in Mexico and SKS in India, lend exclusively to women.[37] But while 99.6 percent of the borrowers of pure solidarity group lenders and 86.6 percent of those of village banks are female, going by medians from the 2009 *Micro-Banking Bulletin* survey, only 46 percent of borrowers of the median individual lender are.[38] Why the gender gap between individual and group lenders? Conceivably, individual lenders care less about helping women. More likely, the reason is practical. The larger loans of individual lenders go more for enterprises big enough to operate outside the home, and in most places men still dominate in the sphere of commerce.

As described in chapter 4, most of the early group microcredit programs started out targeting men but shifted to women. Here, too, practicality appears to have figured at least as much as the desire to help women and the children they care for. When John Hatch and his team were launching village banking in Bolivia, they switched to women for two reasons. First, it seemed that the men invested in farming, which did not generate returns quickly enough to service weekly loans. "The women know how to do turnover. They buy, make, and sell within a week. Men don't even think of doing that," says Hatch. Second, women worked together better in groups. "Women were more empathic. They worked better together. If you get more than five men together, they start fighting to see who is the alpha male."[39]

The story seems similar in Bangladesh, the milieu where microcredit has been best studied. After thirteen months of field work there, anthropologist Aminur Rahman of the University of Manitoba stressed in his writings that women were more sensitive to the reputations of their families, perhaps precisely because of their relative lack of power. As a result, they repaid more reliably. A loan officer explained to him, "In the field it is hard to work with male members. They do not come to meetings, they are arrogant, they argue with the bank workers and sometimes even threaten and scare the bank workers." Women, he was told, are more vulnerable and submissive, less mobile, and thus easier to track down if they do not pay.[40]

37. MIX Market, "Percent of Borrowers Who Are Female, All MFIs" (j.mp/ojaPIG [August 29, 2011]).

38. MIX (2010).

39. John Hatch, founder, FINCA, Santa Fe, NM, interview with author, October 6, 2008.

40. Rahman (1999a).

One woman put it to Rahman this way:

When a woman fails to make her installment on time, she experiences humiliation through verbal aggression from fellow members and bank workers in the loan center. Such humiliation of women in a public place gives males in the household and in the lineage a bad reputation (*durnam*). In an extreme case peers may take the defaulter to the bank office. For a man, if he is locked inside the bank building for several days it would mean almost nothing to other people in the village. But if this happens to a woman then it will bring *durnam* to her household, lineage and village. People in other villages will also gossip about it.[41]

MFIs also may gain leverage because of the attractiveness of public meetings for women otherwise barred from public spaces, such as markets.[42] None of this means that microfinance does not help women. That women are repaying year after year hints that they use the money responsibly and productively. That women have been gathering week after week to conduct business in group meetings has changed norms about women's use of public space in many countries. The next two chapters explore these themes in depth. But MFIs' preference for working with and through women strongly suggests that they do so in part because it helps them solve a business problem. Rutherford, perhaps the keenest observer of microfinance in Bangladesh, calls the reliability of women "a stroke of great good fortune" because targeting women appealed to Western funders.[43] "It is not a philosophical thing; it is very practical," says Carlos Labarthe, Executive President of Compartamos, nearly 98 percent of whose clients are female.[44] And thanks to evolutionary selection, the business logic can operate even when MFI managers see themselves as targeting women purely for the sake of the women.

Streamlining for Mass Production

An unfortunate side effect of frequent transactions is a high administrative burden. To control costs, MFIs must streamline and routinize the exchange of money between staff and clients. Microfinance must be mass produced.

One way to economize staff time is to limit field-officer travel. In urban slums where it is possible to stroll by hundreds of homes in an hour, field

41. Rahman (1999a), 70.
42. Goetz and Sen Gupta (1996).
43. Rutherford (2009b), 102.
44. Connie Bruck, "Millions for Millions," *New Yorker,* October 30, 2006; MIX Market, "Percent of Borrowers Who Are Female, All MFIs" (j.mp/ojaPIG [August 29, 2011]).

workers can go door to door, just as Prudential's agents did two centuries ago in the United Kingdom. In Dhaka, the dense capital of Bangladesh, collectors working for *Safe*Save visit up to 200 clients a day.[45] Field workers for individual lenders in urban Latin America also typically spend much of their time visiting clients where they live and work. But in less-dense areas, most MFIs have the clients come partway to the loan officers at group meetings. Thus, in addition to making banking a public event, the meetings facilitate mass production. "The main purpose and function of the groups and centers was to [enable] routine repetition of identical behavior by all . . . members, week after week, 52 times a year, which made it a 'cultural habit' for each individual member to follow Bank norms," wrote Pankaj Jain of Grameen operations in the 1990s.[46] A group field worker can bicycle into a village, process a large number of transactions, and move on to several more in the same day.

Another way to keep transaction processing efficient is to limit the diversity of product offerings. This is one reason loans tend to have inflexible and uniform repayment schedules and why associated products, such as forced savings and credit life insurance, tend to be formulaic, too. It also explains why MFIs have found it difficult to offer voluntary savings accounts that give the client control over the timing and size of transactions.

No MFI has pursued efficiency with as much zeal and to such dramatic effect as SKS Microfinance in India. Vikram Akula founded SKS in the late 1990s after several years observing microfinance programs in India and Bangladesh. Between 1998 and 2009 SKS typically doubled or tripled its customer base every year, growing from 19 borrowers to 5.8 million.[47] In his book, *A Fistful of Rice*, Akula describes the inefficiency he reacted against:

> Because the loan repayments were in different amounts, each loan officer had to keep careful track of who paid how much, counting out crumpled bills and sorting through handfuls of coins, then writing the varying numbers down in a ledger. He'd then record the amounts in a receipt for each borrower, again writing everything by hand, on the spot, as there weren't standard preset amounts. The process wasn't

45. *Safe*Save (safesave.org/people-staff.htm). For more on *Safe*Save, see chapter 4's section on savings versus credit.

46. Jain (1996), 83.

47. MIX Market, "MFIs—Trends" (j.mp/p3dYqj [August 15, 2011]). Note that credit markets can overshoot, as appears to have happened in India—an issue to which I will return in chapter 8.

automated at all—not in the field, and not back at . . . headquarters, where information from the ledgers was painstakingly hand-copied into other ledgers, and stored in giant stacks of books.[48]

In time, Akula realized there was a better way:

It started with a bottle of Coca-Cola. One dust-choked afternoon in rural India, I bought a Coke at a roadside stand. As I gratefully gulped it down, I found myself thinking: how did that company manage to scale globally at such a rapid pace? A few years earlier, you couldn't buy a Coke anywhere in India.

But in 1993, the Coca-Cola Company returned to India and expanded at a breathtaking pace, and soon you could find that familiar red logo in the remotest corners of the country. . . .

All of a sudden, it came to me. A Coke is a Coke is a Coke, no matter where you buy it. . . . Why couldn't we create similar products, loan and insurance products for the poor that were standardized across the board, no matter where we offered them, and to whom?

The answer was, we could. And so we did.

We had already taken the first step, by offering loans only in preset amounts. . . .

The next step was to eliminate coins. . . .

I became obsessed with the idea of cutting meeting times down to the absolute minimum required. My model for this was McDonald's: at any McDonald's in the world, a customer can walk in and get food served within minutes. I had even seen little timers by the cashiers showing "average time to serve," with forty-five to sixty seconds being a typical average. The transactions at our borrowers' meetings were certainly no more complex than those at McDonald's, so why couldn't our loan officers function as quickly?

I began taking a stopwatch out to the villages, to time our loan officers in action. We looked at every possible place to shave even a couple of minutes off the meetings. . . . Today, if you were to sit in on an SKS borrowers' meeting, you'd see loan officers and borrowers moving smoothly and quickly through their scheduled tasks. We also make sure each loan officer's daily meetings are scheduled in villages that lie along a single road, so the employee can travel quickly between them.[49]

48. Akula (2010), 49.
49. Akula (2010), 100–03.

SKS was early among MFIs to computerize. Loan officers enter meetings with pre-printed, computer-generated lists of expected transactions. Transactions are quickly logged into a database. The uniformity in process makes it easier for managers to monitor the data so they can detect irregularities and send in "SWAT teams" to handle them. Irregularities can signify trouble or innovation on the ground that should be learned from.[50] SKS holds no monopoly on these practices; the efficiency of Bangladesh's ASA is what won it the top spot on the *Forbes* 50 list of MFIs in 2007.[51]

Branch staffing at efficient MFIs tends to be tight and uniform, with an organizational structure tailored to context and services delivered. The typical branch at Bank Rakyat Indonesia has four to ten workers: a unit manager, credit officers (responsible for loans), tellers (occupied primarily with taking deposits), bookkeepers (likewise), and sometimes a guard. These simple, standardized units facilitate growth. Typically, MFIs grow fastest through horizontal rather than vertical expansion, opening branches in new territory rather than increasing penetration in current territory. Standardizing roles and limiting overall functions allows branches to reproduce like cells, growing for a while by expanding local coverage, then splitting in two after territory and clientele reach a certain size. Each new unit can be staffed with a combination of veterans taking up their accustomed roles and new hires to whom they pass on their experience. The decision to split requires relatively little involvement from those further up the organizational hierarchy.[52]

The drive to streamline limits the non-financial services that can be bundled with microfinance. Anything more than a modest dose of teaching in basic subjects, such as birth spacing or accounting, will double the personnel cost—a new trainer to accompany each credit officer—or at least force the solo officer to spend more time with each group and visit fewer each day. As a result, most MFIs that bundle health and education with finance tightly delimit the topics their officers teach. Even within such limits, dedicated funding is often required for the add-ons.

Going to the Customer

Most people in rich countries relate to their banks impersonally. They pull cash out of ATMs, apply for credit cards online, mail checks to their power companies. Though mobile phones have begun to bring automated financial

50. Vikram Akula, chief executive officer, SKS Microfinance, Hyderabad, India, interview with author and Uzma Qureshi, April 16, 2006.

51. Matthew Swibel, "The 50 Top Microfinance Institutions," *Forbes,* December 20, 2007.

52. Rhyne and Rotblatt (1994), 31–35, 111–12.

convenience to the poor, so far microfinance has happened mostly face to face. The reasons will not be easily overcome, at least for credit. In poor countries, workers are cheap compared to computers. Also, the primacy of public peer pressure in group lending and the need for onsite inspection of businesses in individual lending—in other words, the very informality that characterizes microfinance—have made direct human interaction the substrate for microcredit.

From the lender's perspective, going to the customer helps build relationships, acquire information, and enforce compliance with loan terms. Given the general lack of credit histories and public documentation of assets and income, officers of individual lenders especially have to assess repayment capacity through indirect means: they can observe the lifestyles of clients, talk to neighbors about character and integrity, and visit business premises to ascertain repayment capacity. Even information regarding the drinking and gambling habits of clients can help the lenders judge default risk. Individual-loan officers of the now-defunct BANEX in Nicaragua would drop by borrowing businesses unexpectedly at the end of the day to check if the cash in the register was consistent with the business revenue claimed in the credit application. Because the financial statements in loan applications do not include the salary of the owner, they would estimate the "shadow salary" by looking for evidence of the borrowers' household spending, be it the presence of a new motorcycle or the size of a home.[53] MFIs also enforce repayment in person. A loan officer publicly collecting items pledged as collateral or demanding action on a late repayment in front of family, neighbors, or business associates is bound to exert pressure on borrowers even in urban neighborhoods, where social bonds are weaker than in tight village communities.

A major business challenge in doing microfinance, then, is bringing the banker and the banked together efficiently. Poor people cannot afford to travel long distances to meet their bankers. Public transportation can be expensive, as can missing a day of work. And poor people's lack of knowledge of the formal financial system can deter them from starting with microfinance in the first place. A loan officer who comes to the village or neighborhood and transacts in public reduces the transaction costs for the borrower even as he demonstrates to neighbors that financial services are within their reach.

Meeting the customer is cheap in cities and dense rural areas but a serious challenge in sparse regions. This partly explains why microfinance has succeeded more in populous Asian countries and the *favelas* of Latin America

---

53. Gabriel Solórzano, president, FINDESA (later BANEX), Nicaragua, interview with author and Uzma Qureshi, April 27, 2006.

Table 5-3. *Prevalence of Microcredit, All Developing Regions and Selected Countries, End-2009*

Region	Accounts/100 working-age adults	Population density (per km²)	Urban % of population
Sub-Saharan Africa	1.79	32	35
Ethiopia	5.24	75	16
Kenya	6.72	63	21
Middle East/North Africa	1.90	36	57
Morocco	4.34	68	55
Eastern Europe/Central Asia	0.80	18	64
Bosnia and Herzegovina	14.07	74	46
South Asia	5.06	310	29
Bangladesh	19.61	1,176	26
India	3.61	368	29
East Asia/Pacific	0.65	119	42
Cambodia	11.86	79	20
China	0.01	140	40
Indonesia	2.47	121	48
Mongolia	20.56	2	57
Latin America/Caribbean	3.66	27	78
Bolivia	14.99	8	64
Mexico	6.44	53	76
Nicaragua	11.29	45	56
Peru	16.59	22	71
Average over all	2.40	56	43

Sources: MIX (2010); World Bank (2011). See also www.themix.org/publications/mix-microfinance-world/2010/10/2009-mfi-benchmarks.

Note: Excludes some large institutions that are heavily subsidized or up-market on the credit side: Banco Caja Social Colombia, Banco Popular do Brasil, Kenya Post Office Savings Bank, Khushhali Bank of Pakistan, Postal Savings Bank of China, and Vietnam Bank for Social Policies. Data for Bank Rakyat Indonesia are for 2007.

than in less-urban Africa. It is another reason that microfinance does not often reach farmers. Table 5-3 shows that most countries where microfinance is popular are dense or urbanized relative to their region and all developing countries as a group.

Competition and Organizational Learning

This chapter has hammered home the point that microfinance has been designed to protect the provider's bottom line, even when that sacrifices convenience and choice for clients. But microfinance managers, who are generally committed to serving the poor, are not perfect judges of how many constraints they need to impose on customers for survival. The winners in the process of natural selection were the ones who erred on the side of caution, imposing more than necessary. Happily, over time, practitioners have found that they can loosen some strictures, such as forced savings. And they have found ways to cut costs, passing the savings on to clients. Pressure from clients, mainly through competition, has pushed MFIs along. Though finance certainly can be too competitive and free, the verity that competition empowers the consumer does apply to microfinance.

One apparent benefit to consumers is the tendency of interest rates to fall in competitive microcredit markets. Since most MFIs' profits are small or non-existent, the interest they charge cannot fall for long without steady gains in efficiency. A study of three countries with mature microcredit markets found that in two, rates had fallen and were likely to continue dropping.[54] Arguably the best measurement of pricing in the study is the excess of the average MFI rate over standard commercial bank rates, which removes fluctuations in the national interest rate environment. This difference fell ten percentage points in Uganda between 1999 and 2004, and 29 points in Bolivia between 1992 and 2003 (see figure 5-1). The margin also appears to have fallen slightly in Bangladesh in 1999–2004—but perhaps not enough to emerge clearly from noise in the data. Already low in 1999, it had less room to fall.

A less statistical examination of events confirms that MFIs in Bangladesh have been adapting to business pressures in ways that benefit customers. So much has microfinance evolved under competition there that the Grameen Bank no longer practices the system of credit it made famous. One instigator of change was ASA, the least-known of the Bangladeshi big three. ASA achieved its position because of its ability to learn. After its original strategy of social revolution failed, it switched to copying the Grameen Bank. "Being able to change course quickly was always our secret weapon," ASA founder Shafiqual Choudhury once said. "ASA has always shown an ability to adapt. But this has not always been appreciated as a virtue: I have often been accused of being an opportunist."[55] By the mid-1990s ASA had mastered microcredit, grown large and, in the confidence of its mastery, begun to tinker with the model. It formally dropped joint liability, though it generally stuck with group meetings to marshal peer pressure. And after Grameen borrowers in the Tangail district staged protests about their inability to access

54. Porteous (2006).
55. Rutherford (2009b), 97–98.

Figure 5-1. *Difference between Microcredit and Commercial Bank Interest Rates in Three Countries with Competitive Microcredit Markets*

Difference (percentage points)

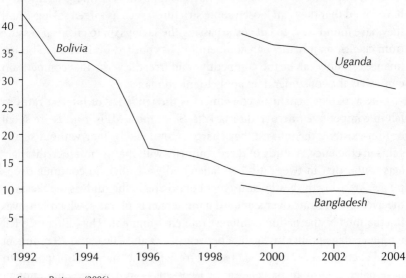

Source: Porteous (2006).

years of savings, ASA in 1997 freed up its forced savings accounts. Customers could now withdraw all savings in excess of 10 percent of their outstanding loans. ASA naturally feared an exodus of deposits; instead, as Thomas Malthus had predicted in 1807, the relaxation of rules attracted more savings.[56]

ASA's reforms having succeeded, they spread to other MFIs. At Grameen Bank, the adoption was ushered in by a crisis in the late 1990s. Attendance at meetings had been declining, and defaults were rising. Many Grameen villages, it seems, had fallen into what Rutherford calls the "unzipped state": default spread contagiously as women asked, "Why should I repay if she did not?"[57] But a liberal definition of "overdue" muffled the loan losses in Grameen's public statistics.[58] Terrible floods in 1998 dealt a further financial blow to clients and thus to Grameen while providing a face-saving way to write off the bad loans. In November 2001, weeks before being abducted by terrorists in Karachi, reporter Daniel Pearl joined his colleague Michael

56. Rutherford (2009b), 97–98, 134–44; Malthus (1809 [1807]), 475.
57. Rutherford (2009b), 132–34; Matin (1997a).
58. Rutherford (2006), 4, 9.

Phillips in exposing the troubles in the *Wall Street Journal,* tarnishing Grameen's international reputation.[59]

In fact, Grameen was by then well on its way to implementing the suite of reforms eventually dubbed "Grameen II," which clearly responded to the dissatisfaction of its members and would soon resuscitate the organization in extraordinary fashion.[60] The reforms removed some of the characteristic rigidity of microfinance and gave clients more financial options. In a letter to an unnamed American friend I infer to be Sam Daley-Harris, founder of the Microcredit Summit Campaign, Yunus reflected that the difficulties were a blessing in disguise: "Our repayment problem was temporary but has been very educational. In a way I am happy that it hit us. That gave us the opportunity to build it in a way which makes it stronger than ever."[61]

Like ASA, Grameen dropped joint liability—actually, it went so far as to assert that it had never used it.[62] Members were also no longer required to borrow. Those who borrowed still had to save, but the savings would go not into a group account but two personal accounts, one of which could be withdrawn from immediately. A particularly innovative change allowed for loans to be "topped up" anytime after the halfway point. A woman who had repaid $57 of a $100 loan, for instance, could borrow back that $57 instead of waiting until she had fully repaid before getting capital back out of the bank.[63] A wider variety of savings products was offered, including a commitment-savings "pension scheme," copied from upscale Bangladeshi banks, that paid 10 percent a year on savings accounts kept active for five years and 12 percent for ten years.[64] The Grameen Bank boomed. Having taken twenty-six years to reach 2.5 million members, it added as many again in thirty-one months.[65]

Similar changes occurred in Latin America in the mid-1990s as many MFIs dropped forced savings from their credit projects and converted to proper banks that could take voluntary savings.[66] Such evolutions, like falling interest rates in Bolivia and Uganda, offer hope that as the microfinance

---

59. Daniel Pearl and Michael M. Phillips, "Grameen Bank, Which Pioneered Loans for the Poor, Has Hit a Repayment Snag," *Wall Street Journal,* November 27 2001.

60. Dowla and Barua (2006), 71–104.

61. Muhammad Yunus, letter to "Friend," August 21, 2001 (j.mp/hJBy1G).

62. Rutherford (2008), 21

63. Rutherford (2006), 16.

64. Rutherford (2009b), 148.

65. Grameen Bank, monthly reports for January 2003 and August 2005 (j.mp/edr8rV and j.mp/eNpENh).

66. Elisabeth Rhyne, managing director, Center for Financial Inclusion, Washington, D.C., communication with author, February 4, 2011.

industry matures in more countries, more MFIs will relax the rigid terms of their financial products. Of course many of the adaptations described in this chapter still are essential to survival and will remain. Financial services for the poor will never be as flexible and individual as those for the rich. But the history of steady improvement in mature markets is a hopeful reminder that microfinance always has the capacity to improve. The search for ways to push back the frontier of the economically practical should never be abandoned.

Conclusion

The Darwinian perspective explains a remarkable amount about how microfinance is done: the focus on credit over savings and insurance; the tendency to work with women; the tendency to work in dense regions; the exclusion of the poorest; the small, regular payments mismatched to agriculture; the public nature of meetings in group lending; and more. Thus, a grand question about microfinance arises: to what extent are its business imperatives and social mission consonant, and to what extent are they in tension? On the one hand, charging enough to cover costs may price out the poorest, foiling the charitable mission. And accentuating credit may deprive people of services that would better address their needs to save and mitigate risks. On the other hand, the market test may be a sign of positive impact. For example, if women are more reliable when it comes to repayment, they may also be more reliable when it comes to putting the credit to good use. And meeting the market test lets an MFI grow and serve more people.

In the last four chapters, I have looked at the business of banking the poor from both sides of the teller window and watched it change over time. A symmetry emerges. The clients in front of the window and the workers behind it are all trying to solve workaday problems, like raising capital and balancing the books. By trial and error, they find their way to workable solutions. But each day brings changes and challenges, so their search continues. MFIs look for better ways to operate. Customers look for MFIs with the best services for the price. As has been the case for more than two centuries, market competition and philanthropic efforts drive the industry toward greater efficiency and quality.

The inherent tendency of microfinance, then, is to provide increasingly useful financial services to poor people on a large scale and in a business-like way. Like the drive of a species to survive, this nature can run amok but is fundamentally creative and constructive. That observation, I believe, must figure in any comprehensive assessment of microfinance—but it is not the end of the story. A constructive nature does not ensure constructive outcomes. It is time now to confront the question of impact. Does microfinance live up to the hype about lifting people from poverty? Can it live down the charge that it is merely a micro version of the subprime mortgage industry? In brief, how does the microfinance industry contribute to or detract from development? It turns out that the answer depends partly on what you mean by "development." The next three chapters seek answers to that question in light of three different conceptions of that word, which correspond to three live conceptions of success in microfinance.

six

Development as Escape from Poverty

What vast amount of misery, ruin, loss, privations [people's banks] have either averted or removed, penetrating, wherever they have once gained a footing, into the smallest hovel, and bringing to its beggared occupant employment and the weapons wherewith to start afresh in the battle of life, it would tax the powers of even experienced economists to tell.

—HENRY WOLFF, 1896[1]

Control groups in theory correct for the attribution problem by comparing people exposed to the same set of conditions and possible choices. However, control-group design is tricky, and skeptics hover like vultures to pounce on any weakness.

—ELISABETH RHYNE, 2001[2]

In January 2008 I visited Cairo, Egypt, for a few days. My official purpose was to speak at a United Nations conference whose premise I did not understand and did not try very hard to understand. It took place just off Tahrir Square, in a high-rise hotel with burly security guards and a clientele of Saudis who came to pursue pastimes more effectively proscribed in their own capital.

Outside the conference hall, I devoted most of my waking hours to two contradictory activities. On a laptop computer in the hotel room, I worked to reconstruct and scrutinize what was then the most rigorous and influential study of the impacts of microcredit on borrowers, one that Grameen Bank founder Muhammad Yunus often cited as showing that 5 percent of his

---

1. Wolff (1896), 4.
2. Rhyne (2001), 188.

borrowers climb out of poverty each year.[3] I found that as I progressed on the reconstruction, my doubts about the study intensified: it is one thing to show a correlation, another to prove causation. By extension, I increasingly doubted most other studies of the impact of microcredit, which were less rigorous. I began to see that after thirty years, there was little solid evidence that the microfinance movement lived up to its claims of reducing poverty.

But I also took time to visit a fast-growing microlender called the Lead Foundation. Happily, it was disbursement day at a branch office of the foundation in the poor district of Shoubra. Hundreds of women, clad modestly in hijabs, many towing their children, thronged the office lobby. The crowd overflowed into the hallways, down the stairwell, and onto the street. The women were waiting hours to get new loans. Some were there for the first time. The rest had just repaid smaller loans and were stepping up to the next. My Lead Foundation guide, who told me to call him George, ushered two groups of five women each into the branch director's office to talk with me. Through George's translation, I learned that every woman would use the credit to finance informal retail. In one group, Rasha and her sister Hala sold clothes and makeup, respectively; their cousin Doaa traded in women's accessories and scarves, while their aunt Samoh peddled clothing, too; and their neighbor in the same building, Anayat, sold bed sheets. Since the women spoke in the presence of bank employees, I only half-believed their stories. Possibly they were required to assert business activities in applying for the loans. But whatever they did with the credit, they sure seemed to want it.

I reflected on the absurdity of my situation. Should I tell these women, who seemed to be seizing loans to thread the gauntlets of their lives, that on a computer back in my hotel room, I had performed conditional recursive, mixed-process, maximum-likelihood regressions on a cross-section of household data from Bangladesh in the early 1990s, and *I wasn't so sure this microlending was a good idea?* Of course not. Unless I had compelling evidence that microcredit harms, which I did not, who was I to tell them how to live their lives?

At the same time, I believed that aid-funded projects should be rigorously evaluated. Billions of dollars are given away every year to fight poverty—including from the U.S. Agency for International Development to the Lead

3. For example, see Muhammad Yunus, "The Grameen Bank," *Scientific American*, November 1999, 118. The figure comes from Khandker (1998), 56, which extrapolates from Pitt and Khandker (1998).

Foundation—yet so little of this giving is guided by rigorous analysis of what works. Surely that is a recipe for massive waste.

So, in that branch director's office in the Shoubra district of Cairo, I hit a paradox. How could I square my concern about the lack of scientific evidence with the evidence before my eyes that something good was happening, something hard to gainsay?

My resolution of that paradox is the basis for the next three chapters, which confront head-on the question of whether microfinance "works." I realized that in the global conversation about microfinance are embedded three distinct notions of success in microlending. Each revolves around a different concept of development: as escape from poverty, as freedom, or as industry building. Each leads to different questions that tend to be tested with different kinds of data. If microfinance's success at eliminating poverty had been incontrovertibly proven, perhaps it would trump consideration of the other two concepts. But as this chapter explains, I believe the proof is lacking.

That makes the other two concepts essential to a full assessment of microfinance. One of these—development as freedom—focuses on the extent to which microfinance gives people more or less control over their circumstances: Does it empower women? Does it entrap some in debt? Development as freedom resonates with the client perspectives in chapter 2. The other conception—development as industry building—focuses on when microfinance institutions enrich the economic fabric of nations. It resonates with the business perspective of chapter 5.

About a year after returning from Cairo, I toured the websites of American microfinance groups, all of which evinced confidence that microfinance helps people out of poverty. Kiva invited me to "lend to a specific entrepreneur in the developing world—empowering them to lift themselves out of poverty." FINCA had launched a "historic campaign to create 100,000 Village Banks and lift millions out of poverty by 2010." The Microcredit Summit Campaign had set a goal to "help 100 million families rise above the . . . $1 per day threshold by 2015." Opportunity International stated simply, "Microfinance: A Solution to Global Poverty." Not to be outdone, Acción International invited me to visit lendtoendpoverty.org and "Ask the World's Economic Leaders to Make Microfinance a Focus."[4]

What to make of such claims? Common sense says that the effects of microcredit vary. If you lend three friends $1,000 each, they will do different

---

4. See Kiva (j.mp/kVVJ0L); FINCA (j.mp/kwd44i); Microcredit Summit Campaign (j.mp/iJShlg); Opportunity International (j.mp/ipbaCp); Acción (j.mp/kZv9ob).

things with the money and achieve different outcomes by luck or skill. One might pay heating bills. The other two might start catering businesses, one to succeed, one to fail. Credit is leverage. Just as bank loans let hedge funds bet bigger than they could with their capital alone, microcredit lets borrowers gain more and lose more than they could alone. Among the millions of borrowers, microcredit no doubt lifts some out of poverty even as it leaves others worse off. Less obvious are the *average* effects on such as things as household income and enrollment of children in school.

Academics respond to such claims and complexities by calling for studies. Their impulse, a good one, is to go beyond a few haphazardly collected stories of microfinance users. They go to "the field," gather data from a larger, more representative set of "subjects," and analyze it systematically from thousands of miles away. Some practitioners who work daily with appreciative customers roll their eyes at the researchers who seek enlightenment in such a stilted mode. But pursuit of empirical truth is what researchers are trained for, and just as they should hesitate to tell practitioners how to do their jobs, practitioners should acknowledge researchers' competence in measuring microfinance's social return.

Dozens of studies have attempted to measure average effects of microfinance.[5] Yet in the face of all that data collection, number crunching, and reporting, a recent World Bank review concluded that "the evidence . . . of favorable impacts from direct access of the poor to credit is not especially strong."[6] To help others understand that conclusion, in this chapter I introduce some statistical concepts that equip non-statisticians to view statistical studies in a properly critical light, and I then review the best studies.

Statisticians sometimes speak of research producing a "negative result." By that, they do not mean that they have found a clear negative impact, such as of smoking on health, but that they have failed to find evidence of impact positive or negative. In that sense, the conclusion of this chapter is doubly negative: most studies of the effects of microcredit on poverty are not capable of producing credible evidence one way or the other; and the few that are capable do not. On the limited high-quality evidence so far available, the average impact of microcredit on poverty is about zero. In contrast, the one high-quality study of microsavings does find economic gains. Overall, the verdict on microfinance from research that directly assesses the impact on poverty is muted.

5. Morduch and Haley (2002).
6. Demirgüç-Kunt, Beck, and Honohan (2008), 99.

The Challenges of Studying Impacts

The year 2009 was a milestone in the study of whether microcredit reduces poverty—and it was a tough year for those who said it did. In the summer of 2009, results from the first randomized studies of the subject reached the public. (At the same time, economist Jonathan Morduch and I released a paper questioning the leading non-randomized study, using the analysis on which I had labored in Cairo.) The new randomized studies, more rigorous than older ones, threw microfinance promoters back on their heels: at least over the first fifteen to eighteen months of availability, microcredit appeared to make no dent in poverty rates. Predictably, newspapers accentuated the negative. "Perhaps Microfinance Isn't Such a Big Deal After All," ran a headline in the *Financial Times*.[7] Said the *Boston Globe:* "Billions of dollars and a Nobel Prize later, it looks like 'microlending' doesn't actually do much to fight poverty."[8]

The next spring, recognizing an existential threat, six American microfinance groups banded together to release a joint statement on the power of microfinance. Going by word count, their largest countervolley was a sequence of vignettes of successful clients, one from each of the six signatories.[9] In Peru, Delia Fontela used loans to build a rental house and educate her daughters. In Afghanistan, Roqia started a tailoring business. To me, the document betrayed a misunderstanding of the purpose of research, which is the pursuit of responsible generalizations. I blogged:

> The question stands: what is the overall pattern of impacts?
>
> Think about how you might answer that question with stories. How would you go about collecting the stories by which to judge? Probably you'd start to think about how to build a representative sample; how big you could practically make the sample; and how to distill the core elements of each story into a few common terms in order to allow summary statements, such as the percentage that are success stories. This kind of thinking—not fancy statistical arguments—is what these new microfinance impact studies are really about. It's hard to see how to avoid it if you want to understand the impacts of microfinance.[10]

7. Tim Harford, "Perhaps Microfinance Isn't Such a Big Deal After All," *Financial Times*, December 5, 2009.

8. Drake Bennett, "Small Change," *Boston Globe*, September 20, 2009.

9. Acción International and others, "Measuring the Impact of Microfinance: Our Perspective," joint statement, April 8, 2010 (j.mp/lZ1n83).

10. David Roodman, "Microfinance Groups, Feeling Misunderstood, Misunderstand Research," *Microfinance Open Book Blog*, April 9, 2010 (j.mp/9TKsqH).

There is little reason to doubt the six stories in that statement. But there must be many other kinds of microfinance stories, which is what makes finding the right generalizations so hard. Take the case of a loan to a woman. She might invest in a calf, and the calf might die. Or she might invest in vegetable trading, depressing market prices for vegetables and reducing other women's earnings. She might substitute the loan for credit from a moneylender, cutting her interest payments, but not immediately augmenting her capital. She might not invest, as we saw in chapter 2, but instead buy rice to feed her family. She might be empowered by the loan, gaining a measure of freedom from oppressive, gender-based obligations within her extended family or patron–client relationships outside the family. On the other hand, the woman might "pipeline" the loan, handing the cash to her husband and gaining little new power for herself. The mutual dependence of joint liability might unify her and her neighbors into a local political force or oppress them with peer pressure. Some of these outcomes would be unfortunate; others would be fortunate but would not fit the archetypal story. Among fifty borrowers within a single slum or village, *all* these things could happen.

A researcher wanting to make sense of this complexity by measuring *average* effects of microfinance must take three difficult analytical steps. First, the details of people's lives must be observed. That is not as easy as it might seem. One can live in a village for a year or dispatch surveyors door to door, but the information gleaned will never be complete nor completely accurate. Second, researchers must estimate the counterfactual, what the lives of microfinance users would have been like without the microfinance. Measuring the world as it isn't is even harder than measuring it as it is. Third, since the complexity of the effects—different for each person—would exceed the grasp of the human mind, they must be distilled to a more manageable, yet ideally representative, set of stories and statistics.

Methods for Studying Impacts

In practice, then, social science research makes simplistic generalizations about variegated experiences using incomplete data about the world as it is and untestable assumptions about the world as it would have been. That does not make social science hopeless, but it does force choices in performing it. As in social science generally, researchers have studied the impacts of microfinance using several methods, which address the various impediments with varying degrees of success.

Researchers use two main methods to understand the impacts of microfinance. *Qualitative* research involves observing, speaking with, even living with, a few dozen or hundred people to grasp the complexities of a phenomenon of interest. Usually the core of qualitative research is a sequence of in-depth interviews with a defined set of subjects, such as women in a particular slum in Buenos Aires or vendors in a Ugandan market. The interviews can range from rigidly planned sequences of queries to natural conversations motivated by broad questions. Regardless, because of the intense exposure to one milieu, the researcher inevitably picks up extra information in unplanned ways.

All people do qualitative research to understand and navigate the world around them. Qualitative research exploits this innate human capacity to build up a rich picture of a particular setting. Done well, it penetrates the sheen of half-truths interviewees may serve up to transient surveyors. Its weaknesses are narrowness and subjectivity. "As the inclusion of the observer within the observed scene becomes more intense," anthropologist Margaret Mead wrote, "the observations become unique."[11] Two researchers living in two different villages—or even the same village—might perceive different realities; how then to generalize from one or two specks on the globe?

The other major approach to research is *quantitative*. Numerical data are collected on a set of "observational units" (people, families, villages, countries), and then avowedly dispassionate, mathematical methods are used to extract signals from the noise of local happenstance. Because the question that drives this chapter is about the measured, average impact of microfinance, I focus on quantitative research. The next chapter, on development as freedom, draws more on qualitative work.

Researchers collecting quantitative data (and this includes qualitative data) face a trade-off between depth and breadth. Expanding data sets to cover more people reduces vulnerability to distortion by a few quirky instances. That is why pollsters interview thousands rather than dozens. By using larger, more representative samples, large-scale quantitative studies can do better at the third research step, generalizing across instances. The cost usually is a shallower understanding of individuals studied. In contrast, more qualitative researchers can collect quantitative data on small sets of subjects, and because these quantitative data can be carefully observed, they can be of high quality. In exchange for depth (precision), they sacrifice breadth (representativeness).

Most heavily quantitative impact analysis is done on data from surveys of households or tiny businesses, collected through relatively superficial contacts between researcher and subject. At each doorstep, a surveyor pulls out

11. Quoted in Rahman (1999b), 28.

a sheaf of blank questionnaires and begins to rattle off questions. The surveys that generated the data I studied in my Cairo hotel room asked some 400 questions, many of them detailed and intrusive. Are you married? How much do you earn? Which of your relatives own at least half an acre of land? Are you in debt to moneylenders?[12] In asking many questions of many people, the surveyor might seem to dodge the trade-off I just asserted, between depth and breadth. But I can only guess how a poor Bangladeshi woman, perhaps illiterate, perhaps interrupted in her long gauntlet of daily chores, would greet such a peculiar visitor. Out of pride or fear, she might hide embarrassments or say what she thinks the surveyor wants to hear.

Debt in particular carries shame. Economists Dean Karlan and Jonathan Zinman wrote a paper called "Lying about Borrowing," in which they reported that half of South Africans who had recently taken a high-interest, short-term loan kept this information from surveyors when asked about it.[13] Such distortions, often hidden from the econometricians who analyze the data, make data collection an underappreciated art. A researcher for BRAC, a major microcreditor in Bangladesh, learned a surveying technique from her colleagues for determining whether a respondent borrows from more than one microcredit group. Since many adults answer "no" regardless of the truth—sensing that belonging to more than one group is frowned upon—a surveyor should ask the children: "Does your mommy go to Grameen meetings, too?" The little ones give extra meaning to the technical term for a survey respondent: "informant."[14]

But not all survey data are so artfully gathered. Journalist Helen Todd and her husband David Gibbons provide an interesting example by collecting the answers to the same question in two ways. Recall from chapter 2 that they followed the lives of sixty-two women in Bangladesh in 1992, forty of whom were Grameen Bank members. At the end of the year, they used their detailed knowledge to classify the women according to how much clout they wielded over their husbands in matters of money. "Managing directors" dominated financial decisionmaking. "Bankers" and "partners" made decisions jointly with their husbands; bankers had a slight upper hand, and partners had a more equal relationship. "Cashbox" women were responsible for holding money in the home but handed it to their husbands or other relatives on request. "Cashbox plus" women had some small say in domestic spending

12. Shahidur R. Khandker, "Household Survey to Conduct Micro-Credit Impact Studies: Bangladesh, Variables List," September 13, 2007 (j.mp/gPV2Kd).

13. Karlan and Zinman (2008a).

14. Mehnaz Rabbani, researcher, BRAC, Dhaka, interview with author, March 4, 2008.

Table 6-1. *Influence of Sixty-Two Bangladeshi Women in Household Financial Decisions, 1992*

Type	Grameen members	Non-Grameen members
No say	2	4
Cashbox	4	8
Cashbox plus	7	5
Partner	11	2
Banker	8	2
Managing director	8	1
Total	40	22

Source: Todd (1996), 86–89.

decisions. According to their study, twenty-seven of the forty Grameen Bank members were at least partners, while only five of the twenty-two non-members had achieved this status (see table 6-1).[15]

Back at the start of the year, Todd, Gibbons, and the rest of the research team had surveyed the same sample in a more conventional fashion. They asked each woman such questions as whether she had an equal say in decisions about purchase of land and schooling of children, then recorded the answers on a form with tick marks. "Looking back at them a year later, the ticks bore only limited relation to the reality we had come to know. If they had any usefulness it was to demonstrate a cultural idea—the way our respondent felt families *ought* to behave, rather than the way they actually did.[16]

Correlation versus Causation

Whatever balance researchers strike between breadth and depth of data collection, the second obstacle in analyzing impact remains: establishing the counterfactual. Indeed, this is probably the largest challenge to social science because it is at the heart of any attempt to understand causation. Somehow, the research must divine what a client's life would be like without microfinance.

Suppose a researcher finds, as Todd did, that borrowers earn more than non-borrowers. Absent certainty about how the borrowers would have fared without credit, many stories can explain this correspondence. Perhaps when women form their microcredit groups, they exclude the poorest as

15. Todd (1996), 86–89.
16. Todd (1996), 87. Emphasis in the original.

too risky—or the poorest exclude themselves—making borrowers richer on average to begin with. In fact, Todd saw this happen.[17] From the perspective of impact measurement, the influence of affluence on borrowing constitutes "reverse causality." Then there is the risk of "selection bias": people who succeed financially are more likely to make scheduled repayments and continue borrowing, while those who struggle and drop out may fall off the researcher's radar. Then, too, microfinance organizations may operate only in places of relative affluence. This "endogenous program placement" could create a misleadingly positive correlation between poverty and microfinance. More generally, there is the problem of "omitted variables," factors left out of an analysis that are simultaneously influencing both borrowing and income. For example, suppose that a woman's hidden entrepreneurial talent simultaneously makes her more apt to borrow and more likely to climb out of poverty, yet the borrowing has no effect on her welfare. It could appear that borrowing is helping her even though it is not—and even if she says it does. Unmeasured, her entrepreneurial talent would be omitted from the statistical analysis. As explanations for the correlation between borrowing and income, all these scenarios compete with the hypotheses that credit is making borrowers better off.

In sum, it is one thing to observe that borrowing and income go together but quite another to conclude that the first raises the second. Quantitative researchers have developed techniques to rule out such alternative causal chains, to attack what they call "endogeneity." Most of the techniques work worse in practice than in theory—and often worse than researchers seem to think, going by the write-ups in their papers.[18] In the late 1990s, for instance, the Assessing the Impact of Microfinance Services project of the U.S. Agency for International Development recommended comparing old borrowers (ones in a program for a few years) to new ones, on the idea that if the old borrowers had never borrowed, they would look the same as the new ones in such terms as income, spending, and family size. The new borrowers would stand in for the old borrowers' counterfactuals. Karlan pointed out several dangers in this approach. Old borrowers might differ systematically from new ones: perhaps they are the pioneering risk takers, while the new ones, being more cautious, held back from credit at first. And the passage of time may weed out the unsuccessful clients, as was the case in Todd's sample. This

17. Todd (1996), 171–74; see also Ito (1999), 138–64.
18. Roodman (2007a, 2009); Roodman and Morduch (2009).

makes it hard to attribute to microfinance any differences found between and non-borrowers and "surviving" borrowers, such as those in table 6-1.[19]

Fancy Math: Why to Doubt Most Microfinance Impact Studies

Quantitative microfinance impact research provokes two opposite reactions from those untrained in statistics: sweeping credulity and sweeping cynicism. Some confidently invoke the reports, intoning that standard phrase, "Studies show . . . " Others dismiss economists as divorced from reality. The problem with both views is that they are not properly discriminating. Indeed there are good reasons to be skeptical of statistical research. But some studies are better than others. And one needs to understand why in order to judge what the research so far tells about the effects of microfinance on poverty. Here, I will describe three foibles of econometrics: the black box problem, data mining, and the hidden assumptions needed to interpret statistical correlation as causation. The natural habitat for all these ideas is the world of numbers, but all can be explained with a minimum of technical jargon.

The Black Box Problem. In the 1980s and 1990s especially, the advent of powerful microcomputers and the fear of endogeneity led researchers to devise increasingly complicated mathematical techniques meant to purge endogeneity in its many forms. For example, in the study I scrutinized while in Cairo, Mark Pitt of Brown University and Shahidur Khandker of the World Bank deployed "Weighted Exogenous Sampling Maximum Likelihood–Limited Information Maximum Likelihood–Fixed Effects," which is as complicated and ingenious as it sounds.[20] Such analytical tools, typically packaged in bits of software, amplify some long-standing dangers in the application of statistics to the social sciences, known as econometrics.

Among the simplest statistical techniques is ordinary least squares, which can be visualized as finding the line that best fits a set of data points on a scatter plot of, for example, household income versus microcredit borrowing. The slope of this "regression" line—uphill, downhill, or flat—indicates whether the overall relationship between the two variables is positive, negative, or nonexistent. In fact, even this staple of undergraduate textbooks is complicated enough that it is hard to perform by hand. Computers make it easy, but in the process of hiding the complexity of the analysis, they also hide the complexity of that which is analyzed.

19. Karlan (2001). To be fair, the agency saw its approach as rough and ready—imperfect, but practical for microfinance groups to incorporate into their normal operations.
20. Pitt and Khandker (1998); Roodman (2011).

Figure 6-1. *Four Realities, One Best-Fit Line*

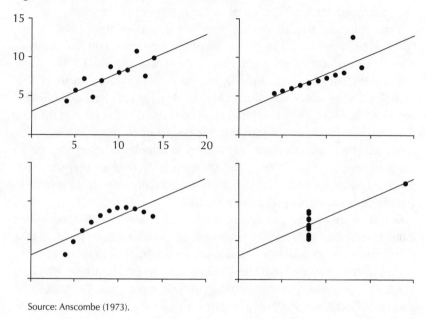

Source: Anscombe (1973).

Figure 6-1, based on a classic paper by Francis John Anscombe, illustrates.[21] Each of the four scatter plots shows a hypothetical set of eleven observations on two variables, one on the horizontal axis, one the vertical. Imagine them as total microcredit borrowing versus household income for eleven families. Each plot implies a different kind of relationship between the two variables. In the upper left, the data exhibit a linear relationship, if with some statistical noise. In the upper right, the linear relationship is perfect except for what looks like a data entry error. In the lower left, the relationship between the income and borrowing is also mechanical but curved rather than straight. In the bottom right, every household borrows the same amount except for one, whose income entirely controls the placement of the best-fit line. Here's the point of Anscombe's quartet: all four yield exactly the same numerical results if plugged into a computer program that does ordinary least squares line fitting. A researcher who merely looked at the numerical output could easily miss the real story. To look inside the black box, it's essential to make graphs like these. Unfortunately, more complicated

21. Anscombe (1973).

techniques are harder to check with graphs. As a result, they tend to obscure the underlying statistical challenges as much as they resolve them.

Data Mining. Another danger amplified by technical sophistication is "data mining," which is the process of sifting for certain conclusions, consciously or unconsciously. A statistical analysis can be run in a vast number of ways, varying the technique, the data points that are included, the variables that are controlled for, and so on. The laws of chance dictate that even if variables of interest are statistically unrelated, some ways of running the analysis will discover an improbable degree of correlation. Even a fair coin sometimes comes up heads five times in a row. And every step in the research process tends to favor the selection of regressions that show significant results, meaning those that are superficially difficult to ascribe to chance, even when they are random mutations.

A researcher who has just assembled a data set on microcredit use among 2,000 households in Mexico or a complicated mathematical model of how microcredit boosts profits will feel a strong temptation to zero in on the preliminary regressions that show microcredit to be important. Research assistants may mine data unbeknownst to their supervisors. Then, tight for time, a researcher may be more likely to write up the projects with apparently strong correlations, deferring others with the best of intentions. And if two researchers with the highest standards study the same topic in somewhat different ways, the one finding the more significant result is more likely to win publication in a prestigious journal.[22] Meanwhile, there is less career reward for spending time, as I have done, replicating and checking the work of others.[23] Economist Edward Leamer characterized the situation this way in his call to "take the con out of econometrics":

> The econometric art as it is practiced at the computer terminal involves fitting many, perhaps thousands, of statistical models. One or several that the researcher finds pleasing are selected for reporting purposes. This search for a model is often well intentioned, but there can be no doubt that such a specification search invalidates the traditional theories of inference. . . . [A]ll the concepts of traditional theory . . . utterly lose their meaning by the time an applied researcher pulls from the bramble of computer output the one thorn of a model he likes best, the one he chooses to portray as a rose. . . . This is a sad and decidedly unscientific state of affairs we find ourselves

22. Sterling (1959); Feige (1975); Denton (1985).
23. Tullock (1959); Hamermesh (2007).

in. Hardly anyone takes data analyses seriously. Or perhaps more accurately, hardly anyone takes anyone else's data analyses seriously. Like elaborately plumed birds who have long since lost the ability to procreate but not the desire, we preen and strut and display our *t*-values.[24]

Readers of research filter, too. Displaying a commitment to scientific evaluation unusual for a microfinance group, ten years ago Freedom from Hunger carefully studied its "credit with education" approach (see chapter 4) in Bolivia and Ghana. In Bolivia, the combination package apparently increased what the researchers termed intermediate indicators, such as breastfeeding. But with regard to the program's goals, "the evaluation research provide[d] little direct evidence of improved household food security and better nutritional status for children of mothers participating in the program." For example, young children of mothers who took microcredit did not appear to gain more weight than children of mothers who did not.[25] Yet a nine-page review of the literature on the impacts of microfinance published by CGAP cites only positive results from the Bolivia report, not mentioning the lack of evidence that Freedom from Hunger had reduced hunger.[26] "We do have some use for these studies," wrote Susy Cheston of Women's Opportunity Fund and Larry Reed of Opportunity International in a frank 1999 piece. "We quote liberally from them (as long as they are in our favor) when we apply for funding."[27]

Instruments and Assumptions. Alongside the black box problem and data mining stands one more side effect of technical sophistication: fancy math obscures crucial assumptions, giving econometric work a false appearance of objectivity.

One popular technique for assessing what is causing a correlation is "instrumental variables." For example, and simplifying, Pitt and Khandker's study that I pored over in Cairo posits the following causal chain in Bangladesh in the 1990s:

Owning less than half an acre → Microcredit borrowing → Household welfare

The left arrow says that owning less than half an acre of land makes a family poor enough to be eligible for microcredit, a criterion enshrined in the

---

24. Leamer (1983). *t*-values measure statistical significance.

25. MkNelly and Dunford (1999), 89.

26. Littlefield, Morduch, and Hashemi (2003).

27. Cheston and Reed (1999), 8.

law that created the Grameen Bank.[28] The right arrow says that how much a family borrows influences how well it does on such measures of poverty as total household spending per week. Roughly speaking, Pitt and Khandker's key assumption is that no causal arrow leapfrogs directly from landholdings on the left to welfare on the right: the characteristic of owning less than half an acre is related to welfare *only* through borrowing.[29] Thus if the two things on the ends of the diagram are statistically related, moving up and down in concert or counterpoint, both the intervening arrows must be at work—in particular, the right one: borrowing must be affecting welfare. Here, the characteristic of owning less than half an acre "instruments" borrowing; and having that arrow on the left lets us study the arrow of greatest interest, on the right.

Notice the reasoning. The authors assume that being below half an acre affects household well-being only through microcredit. That assumption plus data—an observed correlation between landholdings and welfare—leads to the conclusion that microcredit affects welfare. All reasoning proceeds this way: you have to assume something to conclude something. Euclid's classic tract on geometry begins with postulates, such as that any pair of points can be connected by a straight line. From that foundation, which is asserted, not proven, conclusions such as the Pythagorean theorem are deduced. Most social scientists, like Pitt and Khandker, make clear what they assume in order to reach their conclusions. Yet they often deemphasize the assumptions in abstracts and introductions, enough that the assumptions escape the notice of laypeople. This is unfortunate because some who lack the expertise to detect the assumptions are well qualified to check them.

There is an irony here. Implicitly or otherwise, social scientists evaluating microcredit chide the "believers"—those with fervent confidence that microcredit is a sure path to economic salvation. "You can't just make the leap of faith," the researchers say. "You have to look at the evidence." It turns out that social scientists take their own leaps of faith. And it is not always obvious that the assumptions they make are more credible than those of the "believers." A researcher assumes that landholdings affect welfare only through microcredit. A microfinance believer just holds faith that microcredit improves welfare. How different are social scientists from the practitioners, who also must forge ahead on assumptions and who also allow their own biases to creep into how they interpret the evidence they have? The

---

28. Grameen Bank Ordinance No. XLVI of 1983 (j.mp/nNoO2A).

29. More precisely, this is assumed to hold after linearly controlling for other variables, including log landholdings.

scientists do better only to the extent that their assumptions are more credible than the true believers'.

Randomization to the Rescue

So there are good reasons to distrust seemingly objective, quantitative studies of microfinance's effects. Is running the numbers therefore a hopeless
pursuit? No. In the last ten years, a new movement has swept into the evaluation of aid-funded social programs. The core idea is to not merely observe
reality but manipulate it—in a word, to experiment. Experiments can be
designed by the researcher, as when microfinance is randomly offered to
some people and not others, or they can arise "naturally," as when a charter
school admits students by lottery.[30] Either way, what differentiates these set-
ups is randomness in who gets access to the "treatment" (microfinance or
enrollment at a charter school). And that reduces or vitiates several econometric bugaboos.

Virtues of Randomization. In the physical sciences, one can perform
a controlled experiment with as few as two observational units if those
units can be made identical except in the characteristic of interest. One can
observe, for example, if black paper heats up faster in the sun than white. But
human beings are not so uniform and malleable, so experiments in the social
sciences, like tests of new drugs, work best with large samples and a dose of
randomness. Suppose an experimenter chooses 1,000 people in a slum, and
picks a random 500 for an offer of microcredit. No two individuals in this
"randomized controlled trial" (RCT) are identical when it begins, but those
offered credit would probably be *statistically* indistinguishable from those
not, having the same average income, number of kids, entrepreneurial talent,
and so on. Statistically, those not offered microcredit are the counterfactual for those offered. If systematic differences between the two groups then
emerge, the only credible explanation this side of the supernatural is that the
loans caused the difference.

Put another way, the computerized random number generator that
decides who gets the microcredit is an excellent instrument for credit:

Random number generator → Microcredit borrowing → Household welfare

Unlike with land ownership, one can safely assume that the random number generator on the left only affects household welfare through microcredit.
So if the two things on the ends prove statistically related, the experiment

---

30. Angrist and Pischke (2010). They also embrace high-quality non-randomized methods
such as regression discontinuity design.

makes a strong case that both causal arrows are at work. In particular, microcredit is changing welfare. Notice that the assumption here is much more obvious than the conclusion. In that difference lies the contribution to knowledge.

RCTs also have the virtue of mathematical simplicity, which shrinks the scope for black box confusion and data mining. Analysis can consist of little more than comparing average outcomes between the treatment and control groups, either across the whole sample or within subgroups, such as households headed by women. Elementary school children learn that kind of math. When a valid analysis can be done so simply, that reduces the impulse to explore baroque econometric variations, which can obscure the underlying reality and, through data mining, generate spuriously strong results.

For all these reasons, RCTs are the gold standard in medical research. A story shows why. By the late 1990s, half the postmenopausal women in America, on the advice of doctors, were taking artificial hormones to replace the natural ones dwindling in their bloodstreams.[31] Doctors drew confidence from non-experimental "cohort studies" that tracked thousands of women over time; the women in these studies who took artificial hormones had less heart disease. But beginning in 1991, the U.S. government funded a major RCT-based research program called the Women's Health Initiative (WHI), which studied, among other things, the estrogen–progestin combination pill in women who still had their uterus. So harmful did the hormones prove in that trial that the WHI halted it early. Women taking replacement hormones suffered *more* heart disease, as well as more strokes and invasive breast cancers. (Death rates within the study period, however, were not higher.)[32]

The contradiction with the older cohort study results mystified experts.[33] Perhaps women who responsibly reduced their risk of heart disease by eating well and not smoking were also more apt to follow the latest medical thinking by starting hormone replacement therapy, thus making it appear that the drugs reduced heart disease. After the RCT results were published, in 2002, drug companies slashed promotions of the drugs, and doctors slashed prescriptions.[34] Breast cancer incidence fell at unprecedented speed, from 376 new cases per 100,000 among women 50 or older to 342 a year later (see figure 6-2).[35]

31. Majumdar, Almasi, and Stafford (2004), 1987.

32. Writing Group for the Women's Health Initiative Investigators (2002).

33. Gina Kolata, "Hormone Studies: What Went Wrong?" *New York Times*, April 22, 2003.

34. Majumdar, Almasi, and Stafford (2004).

35. Altekruse and others (2010), Tables 4.7, 4.8.

Figure 6-2. *New Breast Cancer Cases per 100,000 among U.S. Women 50 and Older, 1975–2007*

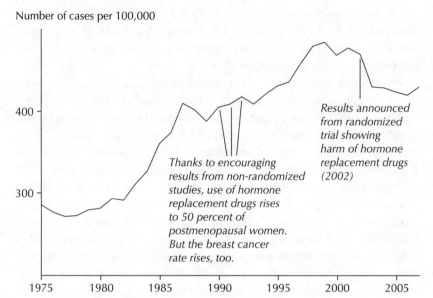

Number of cases per 100,000

Source: Altekruse and others (2010), Tables 4.7, 4.8.
Note: Includes invasive and in situ tumors. Excludes women who have had hysterectomies.

It is not certain that the release of the revolutionary findings caused the drop in cancer. However, a newer study tracked how fast heart disease, strokes, and cancer declined among WHI subjects who were taken off hormones after the original study was halted. Working backward, it estimated that hormone replacement therapy caused 200,000 extra breast cancer cases between 1992 and 2002 in the United States.[36] Non-randomized studies cause cancer.

Seemingly, RCTs also ought to be the gold standard when it comes to testing which social programs are safe to provide to poor people. In fact, over the last decade, RCTs became a hot trend in development economics, the ticket to tenure at elite universities for young stars studying everything from deworming of children to bed net distribution.[37] Given the weaknesses

36. Chlebowski and others (2009). Another theory attributes the rise to the declining rates of mammogram use, but the study finds that it cannot explain why the number of cancer cases fell so much once women were taken off the hormones.

37. Daniel Altman, "Small-Picture Approach to a Big Problem: Poverty," *New York Times,* August 20, 2002.

of non-experimental evaluations, the rapid rise of the "randomistas" seems fundamentally welcome. Today, hundreds of experiments are under way under the auspices of Innovations for Poverty Action in New Haven, the Abdul Latif Jameel Poverty Action Lab at Massachusetts Institute of Technology, and similar research centers. It was only a matter of time before they put microfinance to the randomized test.

Limits of Randomization. Yet the randomization movement also bears the marks of a fad and deserves a critical look. Indeed one mark is a brewing backlash. In the last few years, respected economists Angus Deaton, Martin Ravallion, James Heckman, and others have asked tough questions.[38] One challenge they pose is perhaps academic: are RCT researchers doing science if they do not model what makes people in their experiments respond in the ways the researchers observe them to do? Medical researchers confronted this question decades ago and reached a consensus that useful science runs along a spectrum. At one end are "pragmatic" studies that tell us the real-world harm and good done by a treatment. At the other are "explanatory" studies that help us understand the mechanisms that link cause and effect.[39] To apply that perspective to microfinance, it is worthwhile and practical to study the bottom-line question of whether financial services make people better off as well as intermediate questions, such as whether the cause is higher business profits or less-volatile spending.

A problem more inherent in experimentation is that randomized trials are by construction special cases. Running a microfinance experiment requires the cooperation of microfinance providers, many of which view manipulation of their offerings as administratively burdensome or immoral. Arbitrarily offering a service to some people goes against their professional grain. "A bank for the poor such as Grameen would find it hard to justify giving credit randomly to a group of poor people and declining credit to others for methodological convenience," explain Asif Dowla and Dipal Barua, two men associated with Grameen since its earliest days.[40] By contrast, the randomistas can argue that it is immoral *not* to rigorously test a potentially harmful social program on a small number of people before unleashing it on the general population, just as for drugs. But the randomistas cannot experiment without the practitioners, so they search for clever ways to randomize

---

38. Deaton (2009); Ravallion (2009); Heckman and Urzua (2009).

39. Schwartz and Lellouch (1967).

40. Dowla and Barua (2006), 34. Dowla studied under Yunus and served as the Grameen Project's accountant. Barua founded Grameen with Yunus and was its deputy managing director until 2010.

without withholding services. Karlan and Zinman, the ones who later wrote "Lying about Borrowing," persuaded lenders in South Africa and the Philippines to randomly "unreject" some people who had applied for loans.[41] No one was randomly *rejected*. Researchers at the Massachusetts Institute of Technology worked with the Indian microfinance group Spandana to randomize which neighborhoods got microcredit first as it expanded across the city of Hyderabad in Andhra Pradesh. (More follows on these studies.)

Such ingenious opportunism comes at some cost in representativeness. Since most microfinance groups do not allow researchers to interfere with their decisionmaking, those that do may be atypical. Then, too, any evaluation applies at once to an intervention and an intervener. Two microcreditors can implement the same program differently. Accepting that microcredit helps some more than others, the overall effect depends as much on the creditor's ability to select those it will help as it does on the potential effects on each borrower. Perhaps Spandana only got the kinks out of its Hyderabad operation after the researchers finished their eighteen-month data collection. Also, as described in chapter 5, microcredit tends to start out with small loans to test borrowers' reliability. The ramp-up may occur after researchers leave, so that microfinance is only evaluated at low doses. Finally, some contexts resist experimental evaluation altogether. In Bangladesh, most people already have access to microfinance, making it almost impossible to construct a control group. In the very Mecca of microcredit, the benefits cannot be rigorously demonstrated.

All these caveats show that even the gold standard has its blemishes. Every approach to knowledge in the social sciences—qualitative or quantitative, experimental or otherwise—is compromised. Each has particular strengths, so each generally deserves a place in the evaluator's portfolio. That said, my own examination of the research makes me distrustful of quantitative, nonexperimental studies that once garnered the most attention. I rank good qualitative research higher in credibility and randomized quantitative studies highest of all, and I look to both for insight.

Evaluating the Evaluations

With tongue in cheek, the late sociologist Peter Rossi once enunciated "The Iron Law of Evaluation and Other Metallic Rules." His Iron Law says that on average the measured impact of a large-scale social program is zero. (One reason: the most obviously successful programs don't need evaluation

41. Karlan and Zinman (2010, 2011).

studies.) His Stainless Steel Law warns that "the better designed the impact assessment of a social program, the more likely is the resulting estimate of net impact to be zero." Rossi conceded, "The 'iron' in the Iron Law has shown itself to be somewhat spongy" because some programs have been clearly shown to work, but:

> The Stainless Steel Law appears to be more likely to hold up. . . . This is because the fiercest competition as an explanation for the seeming success of any program—especially human services programs—ordinarily is either self or administrator-selection of clients. In other words, if one finds that a program appears to be effective, the most likely alternative explanation to judging the program as the cause of that success is that the persons attracted to that program were likely to get better on their own or that the administrators of that program chose those who were already on the road to recovery as clients. As the better research designs—particularly randomized experiments—eliminate that competition, the less likely is a program to show any positive net effect.[42]

Summarizing a career's worth of social program evaluation, Rossi's laws are food for thought as we turn to reviewing the available quantitative studies of the effects of microfinance. If the Stainless Steel Law holds up, the randomized studies will show smaller effects than the older non-randomized studies.

The Non-Randomized Studies: Less than Meets the Eye

Researchers and evaluators have performed dozens of microfinance impact studies over the last twenty-odd years.[43] There is no shortage of statistical "evidence." However, nearly all of it, in my view, is seriously flawed. I am indeed the sort of skeptic Elisabeth Rhyne wrote about, ready to pounce like a vulture on any weakness. But what can I say? I think the vultures are onto something. In my experience, the methodological weaknesses matter when it comes to deriving real-world meaning from statistics.[44] The problem is not simply that researchers are careless, though they may feel pressure to cut corners and publicize only favorable conclusions. The main problem is one already described, that it is hard to infer causation from correlation in social systems. In families, villages, and nations, everything, roughly speaking,

42. Rossi (1987).

43. Morduch and Haley (2002).

44. Easterly, Levine, and Roodman (2004); Roodman (2007a, 2007b, 2009); Roodman and Morduch (2009).

affects everything else. Causal arrows run every which way, competing to explain any superficial patterns discovered by number crunchers.

Here I review three non-randomized studies, the first by economist Brett Coleman, the second by Mark Pitt and Shahidur Khandker, the third solely by Khandker. One literature review published in 2007 speaks only of these three.[45] And the chapter on impacts in the authoritative academic text *Economics of Microfinance* casts the net only slightly wider, incorporating as well three studies from the Assessing the Impact of Microfinance Services project (the one that recommended comparing new and old borrowers)—but those mainly to illustrate the difficulties of measuring impact.[46] These precedents should head off the appearance that I am biasing my own account by dwelling on studies with problems.

Coleman's Studies of Village Banks in Northeast Thailand in 1995–96. Microfinance first caught the attention of Brett Coleman in the early 1990s while he worked in Burkina Faso for Catholic Relief Services (CRS). In 1992, he designed CRS's first microfinance project in the country. He then returned to academia for a Ph.D. in economics at Berkeley and decided to build his thesis around microfinance. He noticed that microcredit repayment rates are typically close to perfect but assumed that many members have trouble making every payment. As result, he wanted to study how villagers respond to borrowing peers in difficulty. Did borrowers informally insure each other, paying each other's loans from time to time? Did they lend each other money on the side? Or intensify the peer pressure? He also began to think about the question of impact on poverty.

While sitting in a Berkeley coffee shop, he hit upon a clever new way to attack the question. He then persuaded CRS to apply his method in a project run by two CRS-backed nongovernmental organizations (NGOs) doing village banking in Thailand. Normally, the NGOs visited villages slated for new banks to explain the program and help residents organize themselves into the groups. Then the NGOs would make the first loans. But in a handful of villages, at Coleman's request, the NGOs inserted a one-year delay: members were gathered into village banks in early 1995 but did not begin banking until 1996. That created the first *experimental* assessment of the impact of microfinance. During the one-year delay, Coleman could track the lives of the newly self-selected members, as well as their non-joining neighbors, both in villages with active banks and those with delayed banks. If members gained

45. Meyer (2007).
46. Armendáriz and Morduch (2010), 267–315.

more relative to non-members in villages where the credit was flowing than in villages where it wasn't, that would suggest that credit helps.

Matters worked out rather differently. Coleman found that CRS's village banking was not operating as intended.[47] Households in the villages with banks were richer than non-members even before receiving support from the village banks, with twice the average landholdings. "None of the villagers interviewed identified the village bank as a program that targeted the poor," Coleman explains. "Frequently, the village chief's wife was the village bank president or held another influential committee position, and other wealthy leading women in the village also usually became committee members."[48] These influential members took out the largest loans, often under several different names. Coleman could detect no impact of borrowing on the rank-and-file members, perhaps because their loans were so small. However, those with longer tenure on the governing committee, who apparently got the most credit, saved more, spent more on schooling for their boys, and bought non-land assets, such as cows. The women in these households spent more on and earned more from small business activities—and engaged more in moneylending.[49]

The good news in Coleman's study is that credit appears to have helped people. The bad news is that they were hardly the "poorest of the poor" CRS had targeted.

Pitt and Khandker's Studies of Solidarity Group Microcredit in Bangladesh in the 1990s. As I discussed earlier in the chapter, Pitt and Khandker ran what long stood as the most influential effort to measure the impacts of microcredit on borrowers. In 1991 and 1992, the World Bank funded the Bangladesh Institute for Development Studies to field a team of surveyors in eighty-seven villages and city neighborhoods in Bangladesh. The Grameen Bank operated in some of the villages, BRAC in others, and a government program, the Bangladesh Rural Development Board, in still others. Some of the villages studied had no microcredit program. Some of the solidarity groups were male and some were female. Some of the households that got knocks on the door from surveyors had participated in the microcredit programs; some could have, being considered poor enough, but did not; some formally could not, but did anyway; and some could not

47. Coleman (2006) refines the analysis in Coleman (1999).
48. Coleman (2006), 1619.
49. Coleman (2006), 1635–38.

and did not.[50] The surveyors visited these households after each of the three main rice seasons, asking up to 400 questions at each stop.

The first published study of the data was a *tour de force* of economic reasoning and econometric analysis, and it won publication in the prestigious *Journal of Political Economy*. Pitt and Khandker found that "annual household consumption expenditure increases 18 taka for every 100 additional taka borrowed by women . . . compared with 11 taka for men." This conclusion reinforced two beliefs about microfinance: it reliably reduced poverty and was especially effective when given to women.

Pitt and Khandker also found a complex and somewhat perplexing set of other effects. Lending to women made them less likely to use contraception and more likely to send their boys to school; and it reduced how much men in the household worked. Microcredit had no discernible effect on the work hours and non-land assets of women, or on the enrollment of girls in school.[51]

A pair of suppositions in the study set it apart from most that came before. These were the key assumptions that let the authors make the leap from correlation to causation. The first I already described: the rule barring those with more than half an acre of land created an artificial cut-off in the availability of microcredit. Intuitively speaking, households just under the line and households just over probably had similar economic prospects, yet officially one kind could get credit while the other could not. The comparison between them, as between Coleman's two groups, could reveal the effects of microcredit. Second, to differentiate the impacts of lending by gender, Pitt and Khandker used the fact that some villages had only male credit groups, some had only female, and some had both. They assumed that whatever determined the availability of credit to a particular gender also only affected welfare via microcredit borrowings.[52]

Not long after Pitt and Khandker circulated their findings, Jonathan Morduch obtained and reanalyzed their data. He had already published a detailed analysis of the costs of subsidies for the Grameen Bank from such donors as the Ford Foundation and the government of Norway.[53] Now he wanted to

50. In addition to the eligibility criterion that Pitt and Khandker focused on for purposes of statistical analysis—ownership of half an acre or less—the law creating the Grameen Bank also defined as eligible households with non-land assets worth less than an acre of land.

51. Pitt and Khandker (1998); Pitt and others (1999).

52. More accurately, the presence in a village of credit groups by gender, as well as the characteristic of being above the half-acre line, were assumed exogenous after controlling for various village, household, and individual characteristics.

53. Morduch (1999).

compare the costs to the benefits for poor people. In pursuit of a back-of-the-envelope grand total, he performed a variant of the Pitt and Khandker analysis that was much simpler and did not break out the impact by gender. To his surprise, the answer he obtained was, if anything, negative: credit seemed to do harm. Morduch investigated further and ended up questioning some of Pitt and Khandker's key assumptions. For example, 203 of the 905 households in the 1991–92 sample that owned more than half an acre used microcredit even though they were formally ineligible. They owned 1.5 acres on average.[54] Evidently, credit officers were pragmatically deviating from the claimed eligibility rule so they could lend to people who seemed reliable and were poor by global standards. The cut-off in credit availability at the half-acre mark was not obvious the way Pitt and Khandker had implied.

As is common in such debates, Morduch did not question the correlations that Pitt and Khandker had found as much as he did their interpretation as proof of microcredit's impacts. Morduch offered some findings of his own, though they were predicated on some assumptions he had just challenged. He found that microcredit was helping families smooth their spending from season to season, perhaps assuring that they had enough to eat more of the time.[55]

A year later, Pitt fired off a point-by-point retort. In general, he argued that the assumptions Morduch questioned did not need to hold as exactly as Morduch implied and that if the assumptions were relaxed, the original results held up.[56] This public debate became a sort of inconclusive trial: it lacked a judge and jury but had a big audience. The statistical arguments were beyond the ken of most people, like a duel between lawyers that degenerates into obscure points of procedure. And not even the litigants could fully explain what was going on because each used his own methods and did not, or could not, reconcile his results with the other's. Both their papers could be scrounged up on the Web, but neither was submitted to the verdict of a peer-reviewed journal.

As the American academics sparred to a murky draw in 1999, on the other side of the world the Bangladesh Institute for Development Studies fielded a new team to spread across the provinces and resurvey the 1,798 households last visited in 1992. For econometricians, tracking the same people over time creates tantalizing new analytical possibilities. In the case at hand, it allowed Khandker, writing on his own, to study how changes in microcredit use over the 1990s affected changes in household spending over the same years. To

---

54. Figures from Roodman and Morduch (2009).

55. Morduch (1998).

56. Pitt (1999).

appreciate the significance of this tack, remember the hypothetical woman who was my example for bias from omitted variables: her aptitude for entrepreneurship simultaneously increased her borrowing and her income, creating a false appearance that the borrowing increased income. Suppose that she was in Khandker's data and that her entrepreneurial talent affected her borrowing and income equally at both ends of the 1990s. To be specific, assume her entrepreneurial pluck raised her daily income by $1 at both ends of the decade, from the $2 of the average woman in the study to $3 in 1992 and from $3 to $4 in 1999; and that her pluck raised her borrowing by $100, from the $200 it would have been if she were average to $300 in 1992 and from $300 to $400 in 1999. Looking just at the 1992 data, as in the original Pitt and Khandker paper, she would manifest as someone with higher borrowing than average and higher income, potentially creating that false appearance of microcredit reducing poverty. But if we looked at changes over time, she would no longer stand out among her peers in that misleading way: Her income would increase $1 over time (from $3 in 1992 to $4 in 1999), while the average income also would increase by $1 (from $2 to $3). And her borrowing would increase by $100 over time (from $300 to $400), while the average borrowing also would increase by $100 (from $200 to $300). By looking at changes, Khandker eliminated bias from omitted factors whose effects on borrowing and welfare are constant.

Using the lengthened data set, Khandker's estimates of the impacts of lending to women roughly lined up with Pitt and Khandker's earlier ones. But in contrast to the earlier study, he found no clear impact of microlending to men.[57]

While Khandker's study was strong by the standards of the time, doubts could still be raised about it. Why would propensity for entrepreneurship have constant effects in a changing country? GrameenPhone, for example, arrived on the scene in the late 1990s, creating a radical new business opportunity: "phone ladies" could buy a mobile phone with Grameen Bank credit, then rent it out like a pay phone.[58] If our hypothetical woman's relative pluck had different impacts on her income or borrowing at different times, then the rationale for looking at changes over time broke down.

From my previous work on the effect of foreign aid on economic growth in receiving countries, I had learned not to trust a non-randomized econometric study until I had replicated and scrutinized it on my own computer. To make an informed judgment—to become an expert on the impacts of

57. Khandker (2005), 279.
58. Sullivan (2007).

microfinance so I could write this book—I felt compelled to approach the leading microfinance studies in the same way. I embarked on a project to pick up where Morduch left off—to obtain the raw data; rebuild the data matrix used in the famous analyses; program my computer to implement Pitt and Khandker's sophisticated methods; rerun the analyses of Pitt, Khandker, and Morduch; and check them all for problems. In particular, I aimed to resolve the confusing stalemate between Morduch and Pitt. For a while, I followed in Morduch's footsteps. But I trod fresher ground, too, writing a computer program that enabled other people to apply the techniques Pitt and Khandker had pioneered.[59] Eventually I joined with Morduch in improving the analysis, integrating it with his earlier work, and writing up the results.[60]

The tale from there took some unexpected twists. When, using my program, we ran the same methods on the same data, we got the opposite result from Pitt and Khandker. Taken at face value, our findings said that microcredit *hurt* Bangladeshi families when given to women. But we didn't believe that. Rather, additional statistical tests suggested that Pitt and Khandker's attack on reverse causation had not worked. The key pair of assumptions did not hold. That for us was the real bottom line, but it would have been stronger if we had closely matched the original results.

Then in the spring of 2011, Mark Pitt posted a reply, writing, "This response to Roodman and Morduch seeks to correct the substantial damage that their claims have caused to the reputation of microfinance as a means of alleviating poverty by providing a detailed explanation of why their replication of Pitt and Khandker (1998) is incorrect."[61] Pitt pointed out two key ways our "replication" departed from his original. Pitt and Khandker had documented the relevant technical details for one. Removing these discrepancies flipped our signs on credit back to positive, making it look once again as if credit helped. Probably if we had had access to Pitt's computer code the way he had access to ours, we would not have made these mistakes. For me, this vindicated the open approach to impacts research. By freely sharing our data and computer code online when we posted our working paper, we helped others find our mistakes and helped the research community reach more certain conclusions.[62]

---

59. Roodman (2011). The program is "cmp" and is freely available. It runs in Stata, a commercial statistical package.

60. Roodman and Morduch (2009).

61. Pitt (2011).

62. See David Roodman, "Response to Pitt's Response to Roodman and Morduch's Replication of. . . . etc.," *Microfinance Open Blog Book*, March 31, 2011 (j.mp/gwgo0g).

Pitt's helpful critique, however, did not confront our conclusion that the survey data collected in Bangladesh simply could not be used to determine the impacts of microcredit on poverty. In fact, by correcting our error, he helped us to at last put his regression under the microscope. We found that the stark contradiction on sign reflected a deeper problem: trying to estimate the impacts of female and male borrowing separately was pushing the data farther than they could go, making the complex statistical procedure in Pitt and Khandker unstable. It tends to produce strongly positive or strongly negative results, neither of which therefore deserves much credence. Small changes in the data can cause the results to completely reverse.[63]

In our 2009 working paper, we went on to replicate Morduch's 1999 analysis and Khandker's 2005 one. The story in each case is distinctive, but the bottom line is the same: these studies can show correlations but cannot credibly prove causation.

Randomized Studies

The growing recognition of such difficulties is what gave rise to the new movement built on the idea that randomization could slice the Gordian knot of causality. In 2009, the movement arrived at microfinance's doorstep.

Karlan and Zinman's Study of a "Cash Lender" in South Africa. If one defines "microfinance" broadly, the first randomized study of microfinance took place four years prior in South Africa. There, in 2005, Dean Karlan and Jonathan Zinman worked with a "cash lender," not unlike a payday lender in the United States. The lender made individual, four-month loans at an interest rate that worked out to 226 percent per year, or an astonishing 586 percent with compounding. To randomize offers of credit while avoiding the ethical pitfalls of arbitrarily depriving some poor people of services, Karlan and Zinman used a technique mentioned earlier. A computerized credit scoring system screened loan applications by taking into account such factors as the borrower's income and repayment history. (Branch employees, however, could override the computer's credit scoring.) The company agreed to tweak the computer program to randomly unreject some applicants whose credit scores fell just below the approval threshold. The unrejected turned out to have incomes of about $6.50 per day per household member.[64] That Karlan and Zinman studied people far

---

63. Roodman and Morduch (2009).

64. Karlan and Zinman (2010). Interest rates are author's calculations, based on a flat rate of 11.75 percent per month.

above the benchmark of $1–2 per day we usually imagine as the target for microcredit is not a flaw but is worth keeping in mind in generalizing from the study. And it reflects a limitation of randomized credit scoring: scoring entails too much time-consuming data collection to be economical when the smallest loans are made to the poorest people. This randomization technique does not get at the impacts of microcredit on the poorest clients, most of whom borrow through groups.

After setting their RCT top to spinning, Karlan and Zinman dispatched surveyors to the homes of accepted and rejected applicants alike. Neither the loan applications nor the surveyor visits took place all at once, so for given applicants, the space between the two events ranged between six and twelve months. To prevent borrowers from tilting their answers, the surveyors did not reveal their connection to the lender—indeed could not, for they were unaware of it themselves.[65]

The data revealed that applicants unrejected by the computers were no more likely to be self-employed than rejected ones with similar credit score. But they were 11 percentage points more likely to have a job. Apparently as a result, they were also 7 points more likely to be above the poverty line and 6 points less likely to report that someone in the household had gone to bed hungry in the last month.[66] These gains are all the more astonishing in light of the interest rate near 600 percent per year. Although the exact mechanisms by which credit improved well-being are unclear, the data, backed by stories from borrowers, suggest that the key lay in helping a subset of clients get or hold jobs. They might have used the loans to buy required uniforms, or sample kits for sales work, or fix or buy a vehicle to get to the job.[67]

In a separate study, Karlan and Zinman joined University of California, Berkeley, researchers Lia Fernald, Rita Hamad, and Emily Ozer to probe the psychological effects of borrowing using a battery of mental health assessment survey questions. Borrowers, especially men, appeared more stressed and depressed than non-borrowers.[68] Perhaps holding down a job and paying off a loan impose a psychological burden even as they boost economic

65. Karlan and Zinman (2010), Web appendix table 2. The $6.50 value is based on monthly household income of 4,389 rand for applicants with a 50 percent chance of being unrejected, an average 5.6 people per household, and a purchasing power parity conversion factor of 3.87 rand per dollar for 2005 from World Bank (2011).

66. Karlan and Zinman (2010), Web appendix table 2.

67. Dean Karlan, professor, Department of Economics, Yale University, e-mail to author, July 23, 2009.

68. Fernald and others (2008).

well-being. Or perhaps the stress effect came among people whom credit did not help to gain or retain a job.

In showing economic benefits, have Karlan and Zinman defied Rossi's Stainless Steel Law that the better the study, the less the impact found? Technically, no. Rossi wrote about social programs, interventions funded by governments or charities for the public good. But the South African company lent for profit. Still, the study does defy Rossi in spirit by showing how small loans can help some poor people, even at high interest rates. For understanding microfinance, the more important caveats are that the study subjects lived well above standard poverty lines of $1 and $2 per day, and their successes revolved around employment, not entrepreneurship, contradicting the popular image of microfinance. As we saw in chapter 2, a job is a distant dream for most of the world's poor. Overall, it is a striking finding: maybe small loans "work" best when they help moderately poor people get jobs rather than when they help the very poorest people start businesses.

Karlan and Zinman's Study of an Individual Lender in the Philippines. As this book was being written, more than thirty years after the birth of modern microcredit, the first results began emerging from randomized tests of what is more usually thought of as microfinance. In 2009 two studies of microcredit and one of microsavings appeared. So far the conclusions about microcredit *do* conform to Rossi's Laws.

Karlan and Zinman reprised their South Africa study in the Philippine capital of Manila with First Macro Bank, which makes individual microloans. Here, the typical borrower was a family with a *sari-sari* store—a corner store that sells cigarettes, basic foodstuffs, and other items. To merit consideration for a loan, thus inclusion in the study, applicants had to be "18–60 years old; in business for at least one year; in residence for at least one year if owner or at least three years if renter; and [have a] daily income of at least 750 pesos [$34]." Since the subjects were already in business, the study checked whether credit helps people who are already entrepreneurs, not whether it helps people become entrepreneurs. Also, the income floor put the study population well above the Philippine average, as in South Africa. Per household member, the average income in the study worked out to $8 per day.[69]

After follow-up waits ranging from eleven to twenty-two months, the survey teams succeeded in tracking down about 70 percent of applicants. The

---

69. Karlan and Zinman (2011). Figures of $34 and $8 use a 2006 purchasing power parity conversion factor of 22.18 pesos per dollar, the latter also using a mean monthly per capita household income of 5,301 pesos.

surveyors asked questions, observed the quality of borrowers' houses, and administered psychological tests. Karlan and Zinman checked some fifty-five outcomes for impact, ranging from whether someone in the household was working overseas to self-reported trust in acquaintances. Unlike in South Africa, almost none of the outcomes were perturbed by access to the credit. There was no apparent effect on household income, whether a household was above the poverty line, household food quality, whether the household included any students, and whether family members were prevented by lack of funds from visiting a doctor.

A few outcomes did appear to change. But most of these may be statistical mirages. For each variable, Karlan and Zinman checked whether the averages were different for accepted and rejected applicants. And they did so within five groups of people: all applicants, women only, men only, those above the median (50th-percentile) income, and those below. It emerged, for example, that computer-accepted male applicants were 18.5 percentage points less likely to have health insurance than computer-rejected men. In total, Karlan and Zinman performed 275 comparisons (fifty-five outcome indicators for each of the five groups).[70] For each, they used standard methods to estimate the probability that they could get a difference as big as they actually got—if in fact the real effect was nil. When that probability was low, say under 5 percent, they marked the difference "significant at the 5 percent level." But sometimes the improbable happens. If in fact First Macro's loans had no effect on anything, we would expect just by chance that among the 275 treatment-control comparisons, 10 percent (27.5) would be significant at 10 percent, of which 5 percent of the 275 (13.75) would be significant at 5 percent, of which 1 percent of the 275 (2.75) would be significant at 1 percent. Against these totals of 27.5, 13.75, and 2.75 are my tallies for the actual Karlan and Zinman significance results: 37, 17, and 5.[71]

Thus, most of the "significant" results in Manila are probably flukes and should not be taken literally. Instead, one must look for consistent and plausible patterns in the results. Overall, I am persuaded that access to the credit led entrepreneurs to borrow more from formal institutions, such as First Macro Bank (unsurprisingly); cut back on employees, house renovation, and perhaps health insurance (perhaps a sign of belt-tightening at the

70. I exclude total formal borrowing as an outcome because it is more directly affected by getting a loan.

71. Tallies are based on the initial working paper (Karlan and Zinman 2009), which included a large set of results that was distilled for final publication in Karlan and Zinman (2011).

time of a big investment partly financed by a new loan); express more trust in their neighbors (after experiencing that the bank is there to help); and borrow more easily from family and friends (having won the bank's seal of approval).

Banerjee, Duflo, Glennerster, and Kinnan's Study of Group Micro-credit in India. The other randomized study of microcredit that appeared in 2009 reached people usually thought of as targets for microfinance. Economists Abhijit Banerjee, Esther Duflo, Rachel Glennerster, and Cynthia Kinnan of the Poverty Action Lab worked with the India-based Centre for Micro Finance and the microfinance group Spandana to randomize the rollout of Spandana's lending in Hyderabad. Hyderabad is the capital of Andhra Pradesh, putting it at the center of what was then India's microcredit boom. Spandana chose 104 areas of the city to expand into and then, in 2006 and 2007, started lending in a randomly chosen 52. A year later, surveyors visited more than 6,000 households in all 104 districts, restricting their visits to families that seemed more likely to borrow: ones who had lived in the area at least three years and had at least one working-age woman. The time between the arrival of Spandana in a district and the arrival of surveyors averaged about eighteen months. Respondents reported living on $3 a day on average.[72] Twenty-seven percent of households in Spandana-served areas said they took microcredit, two-thirds of them from Spandana. In control areas, 18.7 percent took microcredit. The difference between these two rates of microcredit use, 8.3 percentage points, was the basis for assessing impacts.[73]

The impulse of microcredit did propagate through the lives of Hyderabad residents in ways picked up in the data, but not all the way to the indicators used to measure poverty. Households in Spandana-served areas were 1.7 percent more likely to have opened a business in the last year than in areas Spandana didn't serve. As a fraction of those who actually borrowed, the number opening businesses is closer to 5 percent. And households with more propensity to open their first business—as indicated by having more land, more working-age or literate women, and of course no business—were indeed more likely to do so if they were in an area Spandana served. Such households also spent more on "durables," such as sewing machines, and cut back on "temptation goods," such as snacks and cigarettes. Meanwhile,

---

72. Based on a control group mean of 1,419 rupees per month at a 2006 purchasing power parity conversion factor of 15.06 rupees per dollar.

73. Banerjee and others (2009).

existing business owners increased profits. But the study found no certain effects on measures of poverty: total household spending per person, women's say in household spending decisions, health spending per person, children having major illnesses, school enrollment, and school spending.

Of course, absence of proof is not proof of absence. Perhaps the team failed to find impacts on poverty because the treatment group had almost as much access to microcredit as the control group. One way to investigate this issue is to look at the confidence intervals around the estimated effects. For example, Spandana's measured impact on household spending (which, recall, averaged $3 a day overall) was not exactly zero. Rather, with 95 percent confidence, it was somewhere between –12¢ and +28¢ per household member per day, with the best estimate being at the center of that range, +8¢.[74] Thus even though the relatively modest difference in credit availability between the treatment and control groups reduces the power to detect impacts, the results were sharp enough to tell us that there is only a 2.5 percent chance that the true average effect is above +28¢ (and ditto for being below –12¢). Because zero is well within the 95 percent interval, standard practice in statistics is to conclude that convincing evidence of impact has not been found.

If microcredit clearly led to more businesses and more profits, why didn't household incomes rise with the same statistical obviousness? The survey data do not allow a definitive answer. One possible reason is that people who invested more money and time in their own businesses earned less outside the home. Another is that only about a third owned a business, so their gains waned once averaged over the whole sample. Perhaps a year was too short to wait to witness the full effects of credit. Or perhaps the welfare of those without enterprises went down as they borrowed to pay for televisions and makeup. Indeed, the microcredit market in Hyderabad blew apart in 2010 after the state government cracked down on the industry amid reports of overborrowing and suicide (more on that in chapter 8).

A Randomized Test of Microsavings. The brightest spot in the randomized impact research on microfinance also has been the least heralded—a trial of *savings* undertaken by two economists just finishing their dissertations. In the rural market town of Bumala, Kenya, on the road between the Kenyan capital of Nairobi and the Ugandan capital of Kampala, Pascaline

---

74. Technically, this statement is not quite correct because confidence intervals have a probabilistic interpretation relative only to the null hypothesis of no effect. Confidence intervals are ±1.96 standard errors, where a standard error is 46.221 rupees per month.

Dupas and Jonathan Robinson worked with a local village bank to offer free savings accounts to randomly selected "market vendors, bicycle taxi drivers, hawkers, barbers, carpenters, and other artisans"—in other words, existing microentrepreneurs. The accounts paid no interest and in fact charged for withdrawals, a feature that helped people who were looking for the discipline to save.[75] Uniquely, the research team followed up with the subjects not once, through the usual door-to-door survey, but daily over several months, through logbooks not unlike the financial diaries at the heart of the landmark 2009 book *Portfolios of the Poor,* introduced in chapter 2.[76]

Of the 122 people offered an account, about 67 opened one and actually used it, of which only 54 made more than one deposit in six months. A relatively small group, mainly female, made most of the deposits and withdrawals. That's a small cohort with which to study impacts, yet the authors find significant differences. Within six months, women had invested more in their businesses, increased personal spending from 68¢ per day to 96¢, and increased food spending from $2.80 to $3.40 (with a typical family having two parents and three children).[77] The savings accounts appeared to help women accumulate money for major purchases for their businesses, such as stock for their stores, which in turn may have increased profits. The pattern did not hold for men. The accounts may have helped primarily by giving women more control over their own impulses to spend in the moment or by giving them a way to deflect family requests for money. Especially if the latter, the women's gains may have come partly at the expense of relatives outside the study group.

Conclusion

The new generation of randomized studies marks a break with the past and holds real promise for revealing the impacts of microfinance. Yet each RCT makes only an incremental contribution to knowledge. It tells us a bit about what happened to particular groups of people at particular places and times. A good way to put such a study in perspective is to state its findings tightly.

---

75. The village bank here is a financial services association, a type of institution in Kenya that resembles the nineteenth-century village banks more than the ones devised by John Hatch, in that members buy shares. See chapters 3 and 4.

76. Dupas and Robinson (2009); Collins and others (2009).

77. Using a 2006 purchasing power parity conversion factor of 30.8216 shillings per dollar.

Take the Hyderabad study as example: In 2007–08, about eighteen months after Spandana began operating in some areas of Hyderabad, among households that had lived in their area for at least three years and had at least one working-age woman, those in Spandana areas saw no changes in empowerment, health, education, and total spending, on average, that were so large as to defy attribution to pure chance, compared to those in areas Spandana would soon expand into. That conclusion is a far cry from its interpretation in many newspapers that microfinance doesn't work. But more microfinance RCTs are under way, and as their results come in and patterns emerge, they will give us a richer sense of the impacts of microfinance on its clients, their families, and their communities.

I draw two main lessons from this tour of the evidence. First, poor people are diverse, and so are the impacts of microcredit upon them. Thus, microcredit undoubtedly helps many people. A distinction that appears particularly important in the latest results is between entrepreneurs, who are a minority, and everyone else. Microcredit in Hyderabad and commitment microsavings in Bumala helped active entrepreneurs.

And I conclude that there is no convincing evidence that microcredit raises incomes on average. While many have sought that Holy Grail and many have thought it found, it still eludes us. It is entirely possible that a majority of microfinance users do not invest in microenterprises but instead use the loans to smooth spending on necessities, as we saw in chapter 2. That could show up as *lower* spending (net of interest payments)—and getting to eat every day.

The ambiguity about average impact arises in part from an opaque mixture of four factors:

—Different people use microfinance different ways.

—Even people who use it in the same way can experience different outcomes.

—Families, villages, and neighborhoods are complex webs of causal relationships, which are hard to disentangle.

—Average effects depend as much on the ability of microfinance institutions to *select* those most likely to use finance well as it does on the potential effects on each user.

These complexities no doubt obscure the real impact of microfinance; yet their significance should not be exaggerated. That cash lending in South Africa at 586 percent helped people get or keep jobs shines through in Karlan and Zinman's data. If the average benefits of microcredit for poorer people without much access to steady employment are as clear-cut, they, too, should shine through in RCTs. Until that happens, prudence calls for skepticism of any claims about the systematic transformative power of microfinance. So does common sense: industrialization rather than financial services for poor people has historically reduced poverty. And until researchers understand better how many are made worse off by microcredit in particular, we cannot be sanguine about the ethics of the intervention. Suppose microcredit lifts 90 percent of borrowers just above the poverty line and consigns the rest to a spiral of indebtedness and destitution. Is that a reasonable trade-off, or a bargain with the devil?

This question brings me back to my encounter with the women in Cairo. Should I have told them they were making a mistake, risking their families' finances on an unproven intervention? Can 150 million microcredit borrowers around the world all be wrong? I think not. Absent strong evidence of harm, it would be the height of arrogance to dispute their judgment. On the other hand, absent strong evidence of *benefit,* it is reasonable to ask whether the intervention deserves my tax dollars.

Think of the paradox this way. In the last decade, the mobile phone has spread like wildfire in poor nations—for example, in the Democratic Republic of Congo, a vast and war-torn nation with shards of government. Few doubt that this is a fundamentally good thing. Scarce are the skeptics who demand RCTs to prove that mobile telephony helps the poor. While it must be the case that some Congolese are wasting money chatting on the phone, interconnection adds radical new possibilities to life. Iqbal Quadir, the original visionary of mobile phones for poor people and the driving force behind the founding of GrameenPhone, says that "connectivity is productivity."[78] One new possibility, in fact, is a way to do financial business, represented by the wildly popular M-PESA money transfer system in Kenya. Moreover, the triumphs of M-PESA in Kenya, of the telecommunications company Celtel in the heart of Africa, and of GrameenPhone in Bangladesh are sources of indigenous pride. Most of the countries that are today rich got that way thanks to just such business successes, repeated in a thousand industries.

But along with mobile phones, another Western export has also overspread the developing world: cigarettes. Few doubt that this is a fundamentally bad thing. The scientific evidence on the dangers of smoking should trump any attempt to cast tobacco addiction as a victory for consumer autonomy and entrepreneurship.

78. Sullivan (2007), 10.

So is microfinance more like cell phones or cigarettes? Unless or until randomized microfinance trials show strong average benefits or harm, the best answer to this question will come from evidence and analysis that is less compelling—but perhaps also more honest and insightful. The next two chapters explore two major themes in this vein, both hinted at in the mobile phone metaphor: the extent to which financial services give poor people more agency in their lives and the extent to which microfinance has enriched the economic fabric of nations.

seven

Development as Freedom

The availability and access to finance can be a crucial influence on the economic entitlements that economic agents are practically able to secure. This applies all the way from large enterprises . . . to tiny establishments that are run on micro credit.

—AMARTYA SEN, 1999[1]

BRAC, ASA, Grameen—they're all the same. You just have to pay. They *make* you pay. Sometimes they keep us sitting there all day. It makes my husband furious. That's why he's told me to leave. Everybody knows. Even if you have a dead body in the house that week you still have to pay.

—SAKHINA, NORTHERN BANGLADESH, 2004[2]

The microfinance movement cuts against old ideas about credit. In ancient texts on religion and philosophy, most references to lending are stern, especially when it comes to charging interest.[3] In the Koran it is written: "O believers, fear God, and give up the interest that remains outstanding if you are believers. If you do not do so, then be sure of being at war with God and His messenger. But, if you repent, you can have your principal."[4] In Leviticus, God spoke through Moses with lawyerly thoroughness, instructing, "When your brother-Israelite is reduced to poverty and cannot support himself in the community, you shall not charge him interest on a loan, either by deducting it in advance from the capital sum, or by adding it on repayment."[5] Such ancient proscriptions imply that lending money at interest to the poor

---

1. Sen (1999), 39.

2. As quoted by Rutherford (2006), 17.

3. Visser and McIntosh (1998).

4. Koran 2:275–80, as quoted in "Riba," Wikipedia.org (en.wikipedia.org/wiki/Riba [June 23, 2009]).

5. Leviticus 25:35–36 (New English Bible).

is the opposite of charity. It exploits their poverty to drive them further into it. Debts are *bonds*. Yet today lending to the poor is suffused with hope for the possibilities of capital. It is not micro*debt* but micro*credit*.[6]

The economic transformations of the last centuries have disposed us more than the ancients to perceive the possibilities in loans. In Biblical times, the sum of the economic game was zero: one family gained land if another lost it. Yet now even the poorest people have benefited from radical innovation within their lifetimes. Bicycles, mobile phones, and high-yield rice are all far more commonplace than they once were.[7] Half the world's people live in cities, whose air, goes the medieval saying, makes men free. Rich and poor alike can imagine the transformative possibilities in a loan more than they once could.

The absence of a clear statistical link between microfinance and poverty alleviation forces us to think more systematically about how delivering financial services to the poor can contribute to development. Indeed, it forces us to think more about what development is. This chapter turns to a theory associated with the Nobel-winning economist and philosopher Amartya Sen, who asserted that the essence of both the process and the outcome of development is increasing freedom. For him, "freedom" is not merely the libertarian concept of freedom from interference in one's affairs. Nor is it confined to the economic conception of freedom as greater consumer choice. It is about agency in one's life. Thus democracy, human rights, education, health, and income are all freedoms. Crucially, because freedoms can reinforce each other, any given kind of freedom is at once an end and a means to other freedoms.[8] The free press in India, Sen argues, prevented famines by making them impossible for leaders to ignore, while China lost 30 million souls in the disastrous Great Leap Forward of the early 1960s. Freedoms reinforce each other at microscale, too: a family earning more can invest more in education, and vice versa. In this way, Sen's conception is a broad theory about how development happens.

Applying Sen's theory to microfinance, if microfinance conclusively expands financial freedom, it is both an instance and a cause of development. The woman who gains more say in financial decisions, for instance, may use that power to put her daughter in school. A generation later, the daughter may earn more, defer marriage some years, and choose to have fewer children.

6. "Credit" descends from the Indo-European root for "heart," connoting trust and faith. Watkins (2000), 41.

7. Kenny (2011).

8. Sen (1999).

I believe this perspective helps resolve the paradox I hit in Cairo. Even though I had reason to doubt that tiny loans would lift the women I met out of poverty, I could see that they were reaching for an increment of control over their lives. Sen's philosophy makes sense of their striving, labeling it a kind of development.

In this chapter, I use the "development as freedom" frame to generate questions about the achievements of microfinance and critique its shortcomings. When does microfinance give people more control over their lives, and how much? What evidence do we have that lending to a woman gives her more say in family financial decisions, or helps her pay doctor's bills so her husband can return to work? Contrarily, how often does microfinance—microcredit in particular—*reduce* freedom by binding poor borrowers in the ways the ancients abhorred? Should we worry that microcredit interest rates sometimes exceed 40 percent per year? Are borrowing groups ever fonts of coercion rather than empowerment? Virtuous cycles, after all, can be reversed. The woman who pays a debt by selling the servitude of her son may slip into a downward spiral.

At one level, the outcome of the inquiry is not in doubt. As I wrote in chapter 2, it is in the nature of financial services to give people more control over their financial circumstances. And because being poor in a poor country means a life that is not only pinched but unpredictable, poor people need financial services more than rich people. Poor people weave together imperfect portfolios out of the low-quality options available to them as they strive to keep food on the table and kids in school. As Daryl Collins and colleagues write in *Portfolios of the Poor*, "Money management is, for the poor, a fundamental and well-understood part of everyday life. It is a key factor in determining the level of success that poor households enjoy in improving their own lives. Managing money well is not necessarily more important than being healthy or well educated or wealthy, but it is often fundamental to achieving those broader aims."[9]

What complicates the impacts of microfinance on agency is its dual aspect. Credit especially is both a source of possibilities and a bond. Even more confusingly, sometimes people turn to financial services precisely to bind themselves to certain commitments, such as paying down a mortgage. They exercise their freedom in order to reduce it. Accepting that the freedom-encroaching aspect of credit can be useful, in this chapter I first review factors that make a financial service more or less empowering for the client. I begin with the issue of price—that is, "usury." A rough estimate is that 83

9. Collins and others (2009), 3.

percent of microloans cost 35 percent a year or less. Is there a level at which high rates become unjust? Rather than trying to resolve this impossible question, I settle for noting that rates charged by financially self-sufficient lenders have generally fallen over time, indicating that a sense of mission on the part of lenders, as well as competition, are limiting exploitation. I then point to aspects of financial services other than price, including transparency, reliability, and flexibility, which also shape how microfinance enhances or restricts freedom. Microfinance has excelled on reliability, less so on the other two.

Next I review the research on how microcredit enhances or impinges on freedom. Though difficult to summarize, these in-depth, qualitative studies of families and villages suggest that individual microcredit is best at empowering borrowers. The images of group credit that emerge are more negative: women humiliated by loan officers, forced to sell off pots and pans to repay loans, or beaten by husbands in arguments over money.

Overall, the agency-enhancing potential of microfinance is inherent but not automatic; thus a top priority for the movement should be to evolve in directions that maximize that potential. Tactics include making the full cost of credit easier to understand, increasing the flexibility of credit products, deemphasizing credit in favor of savings and insurance, and using technology to deliver individualized services in new ways.

On Usury

Moral pronouncements against charging interest are a constant of history. Hindu and Buddhist traditions contain condemnations of lending at interest, while the New Testament joins the Old Testament and the Koran in prohibiting it. In the 1200s, the Scholastic theologian Thomas Aquinas argued that charging interest is unjust because it constitutes a charge for time, which no person can rightly own or sell.[10]

Another constant of history is the evasion of such pronouncements. Lending has met needs so great and opportunities so profitable that doing it for a fee has never been stamped out. The *Oxford Classical Dictionary* records that the formal repayment amounts on Athenian *eranos* loans sometimes exceeded the principal and were "used by Hellenistic Jews to evade the biblical prohibition of interest."[11] Centuries later, European Jews lent with interest to Christians, whom they conveniently viewed as other than "brother-

10. Visser and McIntosh (1998).
11. Cary and others (1950), 336. *Eranos* loans are described in chapter 3.

Israelites," thus exempt from God's prohibition on interest.[12] Muslims have developed banking methods that charge interest in effect if not in name. "When the law prohibits interest altogether," Adam Smith observed, "it does not prevent it."[13]

To Fee or Not to Fee

Lending money is like any other business in involving costs and risks. Unless those are covered in the price of credit, lenders will not lend much. And for the lenders most excoriated for high prices—the ones lending to the poor— the costs can be surprisingly high. Consider the moneylenders of Chambar, a market town in Pakistan on the Indus River, whom World Bank economist Ifran Aleem studied in the 1980s. Before extending credit to a new client, a moneylender would typically check the person's business references in the market, visit his village to check more references, and stop by the farm to see whether claimed herds and crops existed. The moneylender would then typically reject half the applicants, doubling screening costs per accepted client. And costs continued after the loan was extended. A small percentage of loans, typically less than 5 percent, were never paid back in full. Of those that were, a typical 10–20 percent were repaid half a year late—often with no extra interest and only after the lender spent several days searching for the debtor. After putting a reasonable value on the lenders' time and money, Aleem calculated that their costs averaged 79 percent of the capital lent, per year. That was exactly the average interest rate charged. High as their rates were, the lenders thus did not appear to be profiteering.[14] These numbers lend credibility to the words of a woman who quit moneylending, whom Sanae Ito met as a graduate student in the mid-1990s in Bangladesh:

> When I discussed moneylending with her, she grumbled about the difficulty of turning down persistent requests for loans because everyone in the village knew she was earning cash income every month: "You wouldn't know how difficult it is to ask these people to pay back loans. Oh, it's such a trouble. You have to go to them over and over again. Sometimes you almost have to beg. Even then, it's not always possible to get them to repay. I've finally decided never to lend to these people, no matter how hard they might try."[15]

12. Steinwand (2001), 48.

13. Smith (1812), 130.

14. Aleem (1990), 334–37, 345. Total cost figure is average cost for lenders when viewed as pursuing lending as their primary activity.

15. Ito (1999), 123.

In weighing the case against the moneylender, it is also worth recognizing how tempting they are to scapegoat. If a woman in a rich country loses her job, her family may hit the financial breaking point when the mortgage comes due. That makes even a low-cost lender an easy target for anger. And divisions along lines of class, caste, or religion can turn anger into hatred. Henry Wolff's 1890s description of how moneylenders were viewed in Germany reads chillingly in post-Holocaust retrospect:

> In [the United Kingdom] we have no idea of the pest of remorseless usury which has fastened like a vampire upon the rural population of those parts. . . . The poor peasantry have long lain helpless in their grasp, suffering in mute despair the process of gradual exinanition. My inquiries into the system of small holdings in those regions have brought me into personal contact with many of the most representative inhabitants . . . and from one and all—here, there, and everywhere— have I heard the self-same, ever-repeated bitter complaint, that the villages are being sucked dry by the "Jews." Usury laws, police regulations, warnings, and monitions have all been tried as remedies, and tried in vain. There are not a few Christians, by the way, among those "Jews," though originally the evil was no doubt specifically Hebraic— not altogether owing to a predilection of those who made a practice of it. They were practically driven into it. Germans do pretty well even now in the way of anti-Semitism. But that is nothing to the outlawry everywhere practised against the obnoxious race before 1848, when in scarcely any town were they allowed even to trade, except by sheltering themselves behind some friendly Christian, who could be brought to lend them the use of his name.[16]

Discarding the simplistic idea that credit should be free and scraping away the racism that has sometimes encrusted thinking about usury, what is the legitimate core of the antipathy, if any? It appears to be about the way that credit can make the rich richer and poor poorer. People with nothing to eat until the harvest may be willing to pay a lot for a loan: yes, the interest will cost them tomorrow, but if they do not eat, there will be no tomorrow. In economic parlance, the poor discount the future more than the rich, so credit tends to concentrate wealth. In ancient societies, most wealth was in livestock and land. People who defaulted on their loans lost their stock and became alienated from their land, having to rent it back from their former creditors. Sometimes, they had no choice but to sell their labor to repay their

16. Wolff (1896), 116–17.

debts, becoming slaves. Truly, moneylending was the first step in a descent from freedom. It was to reverse such inevitable, creeping inequality that the God of the Jews decreed periodic years of jubilee, in which all land titles were to be restored to their original holders, and all slaves freed.[17]

In Medieval Europe, the collision between the Christian ban on interest and the utility of credit must have intensified as city-states on the Italian peninsula became hubs of trade and banking. That seems to have led to a search for compromise. Within Christianity, "usury" shifted from referring to all interest to only that above some just price. In 1515, a papal council illustrated the newer conception in adjudicating the controversy that had erupted over whether the *monti di pietà*—the Italian charitable pawn shops of chapter 3—were usurious: "We declare and define . . . that the above-mentioned credit organizations . . . do not introduce any kind of evil or provide any incentive to sin if they receive, in addition to the capital, a moderate sum for their expenses and by way of compensation, provided it is intended exclusively to defray the expenses."[18]

The papal judgment has a remarkably modern resonance: most observers today acknowledge the legitimacy of cost-covering interest even as they feel twinges at the idea of charging poor people rates much higher than necessary to cover costs. Muhammad Yunus bristled when I once suggested that Grameen Bank's finances contain an element of subsidy.[19] To him, the bank's financial independence is paramount and requires passing all costs to the customers. The sordid history of heavily subsidized credit—in which the rich and connected capture cheap loans meant for the poor (see chapter 4)—also backs him up.

But is the search for the Golden Mean between zero interest and extreme interest more practical than interest bans? How do you determine when a rate is just? Almost uniquely within the movement, Yunus has been brave enough to offer a rule: no more than 15 percent plus the interest rate that the microcreditor pays on *its* loans from investors and big banks.[20] But the main thing Yunus seems to have proved with this proposal is how hard it is to come up with a rule that makes sense. Partly because microcredit is more expensive to deliver in Africa and Latin America than in South Asia, three

17. Leviticus 25:8–10 (New English Bible).

18. Translation appears in Tanner (1990).

19. Private discussion event, National Association of Home Builders, Washington, D.C., February 4, 2009. On historical subsidies to Grameen, see Morduch (1999).

20. Muhammad Yunus, "Sacrificing Microcredit for Megaprofits," *New York Times,* January 14, 2011.

quarters of today's microcreditors fall in the red zone of "moneylenders and loan sharks" according to Yunus's rule.[21] Even extremely high interest rates can be difficult to challenge. For example, Yunus attacked the Mexican microfinance bank Compartamos in 2007 after its founders issued stock in an initial public offering (IPO) and made millions, cashing in on profit flows from an interest rate of 85 percent a year (plus a 15 percent value added tax).[22] "Microcredit was created to fight the money lender," Yunus told *BusinessWeek*, "not to become the money lender."[23] But recall from chapter 6 that borrowers in the Karlan and Zinman experiment in South Africa gained income and employment while paying annual rates of more than 200 percent, or closer to 600 percent with compounding.[24] And informal savings and credit groups (ASCAs, in the terminology of chapter 3) often charge 10 percent a month for loans. Are these people, truly at the bottom of the financial services totem pole, also usurers?[25]

Another enticing and pitfall-ridden strategy for defining fair lending is to focus on profits rather than interest. Where delivering microcredit is expensive, high interest rates may be forgivable as long as there is no "profiteering." In India, the founder of the microlender Equitas has pledged to keep his company's profits below 5 percent of assets. Since the assets of Equitas are mainly loans, this is roughly equivalent to capping profits at 5 percentage points of interest.[26] Actually, even that is high by the standards of commercial banking, where a 3 percent return on assets is considered munificent. Perhaps a start-up like Equitas in an immature and controversial industry in a developing country looks risky to most investors, and therefore needs higher profits than established mainline banks to attract capital.

Carlos Danel, one of the Compartamos founders whom Yunus likened to a moneylender, builds on this idea. He told me that Compartamos, which was born out of a nonprofit group with a social mission, sought abnormally high earnings—currently at an astounding 17 percent on assets—to prove that microcredit is a legitimate business and draw in competition from

21. Gonzalez (2010a).

22. Rosenberg (2007).

23. Quote from Keith Epstein and Geri Smith, "Compartamos: From Nonprofit to Profit," *BusinessWeek*, December 13, 2007.

24. Karlan and Zinman (2010).

25. Wilson, Harper, and Griffith (2010), 5.

26. P.N. Vasudevan, managing director, Equitas, Chennai, India, conversation with author, November 16, 2010.

mainstream banks, among others.[27] Though self-serving, the argument was serious; it takes its cue from patents, which grant monopoly profits to innovators precisely to midwife new industries. Apple's pathbreaking iPhone raked in billions—and stirred competition that gave consumers new choices.

At any rate, because microcredit is labor intensive, even small layers of administrative fat can eclipse profits as drivers of interest rates. Among financially self-sufficient microfinance institutions (MFIs) in 2006, eliminating all profits and passing the savings on to customers would have cut interest charges by just a sixth.[28] Many MFIs are small and inefficient, some because they receive grants and feel minimal pressure to operate in a businesslike way. How sharp is the moral line between an efficient MFI that earns high profits and an inefficient one that charges the same rate and breaks even after covering a bloated payroll? In one case, affluent investors skim the cream. In the other, salaried and relatively educated MFI employees do, however unwittingly.

But Danel's defense of high profits does point a way out of the muddle by introducing the element of *time*. If increasing competition in Mexico drives rates down—as it seems to have done in Bolivia and Uganda (see chapter 5)—that will partly vindicate Danel. Indeed, Mexican microcredit competition does appear to have intensified since Compartamos went public, though whether that has reduced rates is less clear.[29] More generally, one of the best practical ways to judge whether the microcredit industry is serving the customer is to look at trends. Falling rates, especially relative to such benchmarks as government bond interest rates, are an encouraging sign that MFIs are becoming more efficient and passing savings on to borrowers in order to compete or serve their social mission.

Turning to the Data

So far in pondering what constitutes usury, we have collected half-answers: the impracticality of zero interest, the potential focus on profits instead of

27. Interview with author, June 24, 2008; MIX Market, "CompartamosBanco: Data" (j.mp/oRdUKj [September 3, 2011]).

28. Rosenberg, Gonzalez, and Narain (2009). Their sample consists of 175 MFIs that were self-sufficient in 2003 and 2006.

29. Kneiding and Rosenberg (2008), 3. Gross portfolio yields fell at all major Mexican microcreditors in 2009, the last year with good data at this writing; it is too soon to call this a trend. MIX Market, "Gross Portfolio Yield, Inflation Adjusted, Large Mexican MFIs, 2008–09," custom report (j.mp/oS4FlF [September 3, 2011]).

interest, and the importance of trends. What happens when these ideas are brought to the available data on microcredit?

The best analysis to date comes from Richard Rosenberg, Adrian Gonzalez, and Sushma Narain at CGAP, the autonomous microfinance research unit of the World Bank.[30] Their conclusions are reassuring. Figure 7-1 is inspired by one piece of their analysis. For each region of the developing world, it shows the "gross portfolio yields" of MFIs reporting to the MIX Market data warehouse. The portfolio yield is a rough measure of interest rates, the ratio of interest received during a year to the average amount of outstanding loans. I have adjusted the numbers upward for delinquent loans, which are carried on the books but earn less or no interest.[31] On the other hand, I have adjusted downward by netting out inflation. (A 20 percent loan is a bargain where inflation is 30 percent, since the currency borrowed is worth more than the currency paid back.)[32] While Latin America stands out for having more high-cost MFIs, only in the Middle East and North Africa, with the fewest MFIs, does the median (50th percentile) exceed 30 percent. Worldwide, 63 percent of MFIs, accounting for 83 percent of the loans, charge less than 30 percent over inflation.[33]

The CGAP researchers made other encouraging observations. Among financially self-sufficient MFIs, rates fell an average of 2.3 percentage points per year between 2003 and 2006. Profits and operating expenses fell. "Mission drift"—shifting to larger, more economical loans for richer people—could not explain the efficiency gains because costs fell per loan, not just per dollar lent.[34] The drop is good news in itself. It also indicates that some combination of competition and commitment to mission is driving the evolution of the microcredit market. This hardly looks like rampant exploitation.

That said, analyses based on portfolio yield probably understate interest rates somewhat because they do not capture the full cost of credit. As mentioned in chapter 5, many MFIs require clients to save even as they borrow, which reduces their net credit balance but not the interest charge and thus raises the effective rate. Many also overcharge for mandatory credit life insurance. (See the example in the discussion of credit life in chapter 5 and the next section's discussion of transparency.) In some countries, notably

---

30. Rosenberg, Gonzalez, and Narain (2009).

31. Following Gaul (2011), the formula is interest rate = gross portfolio yield / (100% − (write-off ratio + portfolio at risk, 30 days) / 2).

32. The formula is (100% + interest rate) / (100% + inflation rate) − 100%.

33. Author's calculations, based on sources for figure 7-1.

34. Rosenberg, Gonzalez, and Narain (2009); rates unadjusted for inflation.

Figure 7-1. *Microfinance Institutions (MFIs), by Region and Interest Rate, 2009*

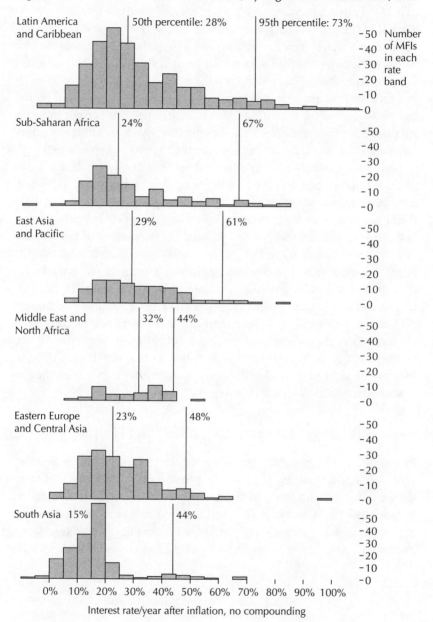

Source: Author's calculations, based on data from Microfinance Information eXchange (March 26, 2011) and World Bank (2011).

Note: Rates are gross portfolio yields, adjusted for loan losses and consumer price inflation. They do not factor in the hidden costs of compulsory savings and overpriced credit-life insurance.

Mexico, the government adds a value-added tax. An American nonprofit called MFTransparency, provoked into existence by the Compartamos lucrative sale of stock in 2007, began measuring interest rates more sharply, taking into account such complexities. According to my tabulation, in countries for which the group published data at this writing, the full, inflation-adjusted price averages about 5.6 percentage points higher than the portfolio yields in figure 7-1.[35] Mentally shifting figure 7-1 to the right suggests that typical inflation-adjusted microcredit interest rates are about 20 percent in South Asia and 30–35 percent elsewhere, after inflation. And, adjusting the earlier estimate, about 80 percent of microloans cost 35 percent a year or less.

Since usury will always defy precise definition, the best judgments one can make about the fairness of credit are relative and contextual. Overall, although microcredit interest rates are high by rich-world standards, once the higher cost of lending to poor people, the value of covering those costs in order to grow, the downward trend, and the immaturity of the industry in most countries are taken into account, most rates do not seem exploitative. The exceptions are a concern. Rosenberg, Gonzalez, and Narain conclude that "a few MFIs have charged their borrowers interest rates that may be considerably higher than what would make sense from a development perspective. Indeed, it would be astonishing if this were not the case, given the diversity of the industry and the scarcity of competitive markets."[36] The authors cite Compartamos as one of these institutions. But it is one thing to indict some players for crossing the line. It would be another—unjustified by the data—to indict the entire industry.

Beyond Pricing: Transparency, Reliability, Flexibility

In addition to that generally reassuring conclusion, the enquiry into usury points to a better way to judge whether lending is fair and freeing: focus less on a number and more on the relative power of borrower and lender. A monopolist MFI charging 40 percent should arouse more concern, for potentially abusing its market power at the expense of poor people, than a competing one charging the same rate. Taking that lesson to heart, we look

35. The countries are Azerbaijan, Bolivia, Bosnia and Herzegovina, Ecuador, India, Malawi, and Peru. Author's calculations, based on data from Microfinance Information eXchange and MFTransparency. For each MFI, MFTransparency computes interest rates for various loan products at various loan sizes. To aggregate, I took the median sample loan size tested for each loan product; then I averaged across loan products weighting by the number of clients for each.

36. Rosenberg, Gonzalez, and Narain (2009), 21.

next at aspects of lender behavior other than pricing that matter for whether credit bestows agency: transparency, reliability, and flexibility.

Transparency

Transparency in pricing is the motherhood and apple pie of microfinance, and rightly so. Microfinance institutions have a responsibility to assure that clients understand the costs and terms of their services, all the more so when the clients are illiterate or easily tempted into borrowing and buying things they cannot afford.

But many MFIs violate this ideal. And a client whose judgment is befogged by misleading information loses an increment of control over her financial circumstances. She loses freedom. One way MFIs violate the ideal is by imposing fees or other requirements that effectively raise interest rates without seeming to. Some charge one-time loan origination fees. Some require borrowers to deposit a percentage of each loan amount with the MFI in a savings account that pays interest (if any) at a rate lower than that on the loan. Some overcharge for life insurance bundled with the loan.

A rampant problem is that microcreditors often explain their contracts in ways that are incomplete, confusing, even misleading. In Bangladesh, for example, loan rules are often complex and not written down for clients. This gives the mostly male loan officers discretion to "interpret" the rules and gain power over their mostly female clients. The loan officers can be expected to use this power in response to the incentives they face for keeping repayment rates high. Formally, a lender's rules might say that forced savings are available for withdrawal at any time. Informally, a loan officer might resist releasing the savings to increase his leverage in cajoling repayment and buffer against late payments when his leverage fails.

In Dhaka in 2008, Stuart Rutherford introduced me to a client of his *Safe*-Save microfinance project who lived in the slum around the corner from a branch office. He took pride in showing me the rules for the woman's loan and savings accounts: in plain Bengali, on a single sheet of paper folded into her passbook. She could not read it but she and Rutherford took further pride in showing me that her school-age son could. Through its transparency, *Safe*Save implicitly criticized business-as-usual microfinance in Bangladesh.

Another oft-criticized practice (now more common outside Bangladesh than in) is to charge interest on the full loan amount even as the outstanding balance declines over the repayment cycle. Such "flat-rate" interest effectively doubles the interest rate: on a $100 loan steadily repaid over a year, $20 of interest may look like 20 percent but is in fact 40 percent of the average balance of $50.

MFIs can make pricing less opaque via simplification or distillation. Simplification is straightforward: it entails getting rid of such things as origination fees and tacked-on credit-life insurance premiums. Distillation is a more complicated business: how does one express the economic burden of a loan repayment schedule in a single number? It turns out there is no one right way, but a few in combination can work well.

Among those steeped in finance, the reflexive response to fine—or invisible—print is to demand to know the annual percentage rate (APR), the number that sums all costs and expresses them as an interest rate over a standard time frame, such as a year. In the first half of the twentieth century, for example, the Russell Sage Foundation became convinced that much of the harm of informal "loan-sharking" lay in its lack of transparency. The foundation eventually persuaded two-thirds of U.S. states to pass versions of a Universal Small Loan Law, which offered loan sharks a deal perhaps worth imitating today: the laws exempted them from interest rate caps provided they disclosed their charges simply and transparently.[37] In our era, MFTransparency carries the torch for the APR as a tool for understanding the true cost of microcredit.[38]

While any move to make fees transparent is laudable, APR disclosure on its own is probably not ideal for borrowers. Consider the 1931 defense of the Morris Plan's pricing scheme (see chapter 3) by a top Morris Plan executive named Ralph Pitman. Pitman responded to a critique of the plan by Clyde Olin Fisher, an economist of the day. Fisher had studied the practice of the Morris Plan of deducting a flat 8 percent interest charge up front and calculated that it yielded a 17.3 percent APR, mainly because of the doubling phenomenon just explained. "No useful purpose," he wrote, "is served by confusing the nominal and the real rate of interest paid by the borrower."[39] Pitman retorted:

> If he had stated that our advertising was to the effect that a Morris Plan loan costs 8 per cent interest per annum, then his point would be well taken. If he will inspect the bulk of Morris Plan advertising, however, he will find that this statement is never made and the only reason that we tell the public that a $100 loan costs $8.00 is that this statement is

37. Carruthers, Guinnane, and Yoonseok (2007), 3.

38. MFTransparency, "Why We Need Transparent Pricing in Microfinance" (j.mp/oaQ9Bi [August 31, 2011]).

39. Fisher (1929), 500. The balance on a loan with a face value of $100 would descend from $92 to $0 over a year, for an average balance of $46. Of that balance, $8 of interest is about 17.3 percent. An internal-rate-of-return calculation yields slightly more than 18 percent with compounding.

plainer to the average borrower than would the statement be that our charge mathematically figures 17.3 per cent. . . . He will also find that frequently Morris Plan banks publish charts showing the face amount of the loan, the amount deducted, the amount to the borrower and the weekly, semi-monthly or monthly payments. We believe we are safe in asserting in this connection that our advertising does not intend to deceive and that it does not deceive.[40]

In other words, Pitman claimed that regular Americans don't understand APRs. Instead, the Morris Plan told clients, "if you borrow $100 from us, we keep $8 but you pay back $100 in small, even installments over a year," Even if borrowers did not think in APRs, Pitman argued, they understood the deal, and the cause of transparency was served. In fact, even an economist like Fisher needed to pull out a slide rule to compute an APR, which said something about how natural they were to the human mind.

Recent research has vindicated Pitman. University of Chicago economists Marianne Bertrand and Adair Morse arranged for an American payday lender with operations in many states to experimentally place three separate educational graphics on cash envelopes that clerks pass to patrons. One graphic compared the APR of different types of loans, showing that the charges on the two-week loans—$15–17 per $100—worked out to more than 400 percent per year with compounding. Another compared how the interest or fees on a $300 payday and credit card loan add up over a three-month period. And one showed how often people slip into serial borrowing (see figure 7-2).

Bertrand and Morse checked whether exposure to the images changed how often and how much people borrowed in the following months. The APR message had little or no effect on rates of borrowing in subsequent pay periods. The third graphic also had minimal impact. But the second, adding up the interest charges in a simple way, cut the frequency of reborrowing in future pay cycles by roughly one-tenth. How lower debt played out in the lives of the subjects is unknown. The presumption should be that translating fees into terms that people could easily understand—highlighting that borrowing $300 for three months cost $270—helped them make better decisions.[41] And if they saw the message every time they took a two-week loan instead of just once, as during the experiment, it might help them even more.

Transparency is in the eye of the beholder. Disclosure only succeeds if people understand the message. To work, disclosure must be designed to

---

40. Quoted in Persons and others (1931), 16.
41. Bertrand and Morse (2009).

Figure 7-2. *Three Experimental Messages on Cash Envelopes for Clients of Payday Lenders*

Annual interest rates on different types of loans

	Median Annual Interest % (from government surveys)
Payday Loan	443%
Installment Car Loans	18%
Credit Card	16%
Subprime Mortgages	10%

How much it will cost in fees or interest if you borrow $300

PAYDAY LENDER (assuming fee is $15 per $100 loan)		CREDIT CARD (assuming a 20% APR)	
If you repay in:		If you repay in:	
2 weeks	$45	2 weeks	$2.50
1 month	$90	1 month	$5
2 months	$180	2 months	$10
3 months	$270	3 months	$15

Out of 10 typical people taking out a new payday loan...

| 2 1/2 people will pay it back without renewing | 2 people will renew 1 or 2 times | 1 1/2 people will renew 3 or 4 times | 4 people will renew 5 or more times |

Source: Bertrand and Morse (2009).

overcome the foibles of human cognition, which the ascendant subfield of behavioral economics is helping us understand. Most people overestimate their own luck and skill. Optimistic, we yield to temptation and sometimes take on debts we cannot handle.[42] APRs may play into that bias by obscuring concrete future costs of today's choices. Needless to say, our brains did not evolve intuition about APRs. "For the past few million years it has been much more important to think fast than it has been to think accurately," writes Mike Dixon of the Institute for Public Policy Research in London. But "the short cut can sometimes lead to the wrong place."[43]

Still, APRs can be useful, too, which is why the United States and other countries require them to be disclosed as part of loan offers. They are a helpful metric for comparing credit offers with different terms. If two loans have the same total cost but one requires more payment toward the beginning, its average balance will be lower over the term, and the ratio of interest paid to average balance will be higher. APRs capture that, assigning a higher rate to the latter.

A three-step plan for making microcredit pricing transparent would simplify fee structures; disclose cost in two or three intuitive ways, such as payment per week and total payments; and state APRs to allow comparisons. The microcredit industry does best on the second of these by quoting "flat" rates, which let people calculate installment payments as fixed percentages of the opening loan amount. But complex fee structures still hide the full cost, and APRs are not typically quoted. Surely this is low-hanging fruit if a goal of microcredit is empowerment.

Reliability

Akin to the notion of transparency is that of reliability: commitments should be not only clear but honored. Here, microfinance generally excels. MFIs operate at the boundary between the formal economy, where institutions conduct business through legal documents, and the informal one, where businesses are hardly distinct from families and transactions are recorded in people's heads. When formal MFIs sell services to people who work primarily in the informal economy, they bring a more contractual style of business than their clients usually experience. In the ideal, participants in these financial relationships are legal persons, parties to a contract that precisely stipulates obligations.

42. Slovic (1987).
43. Dixon (2006), 49–50.

Thus MFIs are more dependable financial partners than friends, family, moneylenders, and moneyguards (who hold savings for a fee). If the Grameen Bank says a client will be eligible for a new loan if she maintains her payment record for seventeen weeks, she can bank on it. The authors of *Portfolios of the Poor* extol microfinance for its rule-bound reliability:

> It represents a huge step in the process of bringing reliability to the financial lives of poor households. For many poor people, having to deal with unreliable financial partners is just part of a general environment of unreliability that they must live with every day. Institutions that they interact with in other aspects of their lives are unreliable as well: the police and the courts, for example, or the health and education services. . . .
>
> [The Bangladeshi microfinance] loan officers came to the weekly meetings on time, in all kinds of weather; they disbursed loans in the amount they promised at the time they promised and at the price they promised; they didn't demand bribes; they tried hard to keep passbooks accurate and up-to-date; and they showed their clients that they took their transactions seriously.[44]

In the spirit of diversification, argue the authors, poor people welcome this distinctive style of finance into their portfolios, along with informal services.

Informal financial relationships, by contrast, are more embedded in social relationships, which is both a curse and a blessing. The curse is the precariousness this brings to economic life. Will your brother pay back? Will the "merry-go-round" Rotating Savings and Credit Association (see chapter 3) keep spinning until your turn? Will the moneyguard abscond? The blessing is flexibility. When your brother lends *you* money, you have some control over when you repay.

Flexibility

Thus, to an extent, flexibility is the flipside of unreliability. The social context that lubricates informal dealings at once complicates them and softens their rough edges. Contrarily, microfinance offers more reliability to clients and usually demands more of it from them. By nature, it is reliable and inflexible.

Classic microcredit disburses once every six or twelve months and demands regular repayment, but calamities don't befall people on such a neat schedule. So even those who can get microfinance also borrow and save elsewhere, mainly from less formal sources. Moneylenders, it turns out, may

---

44. Collins and others (2009), 26–27.

be more expensive, but they are there when you need them, and they are surprisingly flexible about repayment. Recall that in Pakistan, World Bank researcher Ifran Aleem discovered that 10–20 percent of clients of money-lenders repaid late, generally without incurring extra interest.[45] The authors of *Portfolios of the Poor* discovered the same leniency in the financial diaries they helped poor people maintain for a year in Bangladesh, India, and South Africa. Late payments and wangled interest forgiveness often dramatically reduced the effective rates paid to moneylenders. In this way, the flexibility of informal finance begat freedom. And in this light, favorably comparing microcredit interest rates to the higher ones of moneylenders is misleading. The two credit relationships differ fundamentally.

Microcredit is famous for high repayment rates. Until a government smackdown in 2010, India's high-flying SKS Microfinance in India boasted a repayment rate of more than 99 percent.[46] If the Compartamos IPO in Mexico was the touchstone controversy for the debate over whether micro-credit interest rates are too high, then the SKS IPO in India's Andhra Pradesh state and the imbroglio that followed have been the rough counterpart for repayment rates. In both countries, the most thoughtful observers have been unable to dismiss the charge that rates—interest rates in Mexico, repayment rates in India—were too high.

In fact, the controversy in India began years before the SKS IPO. A major theme has been whether microcreditors were too inflexible in their pres-sure for repayment. In 2006, authorities in the Krishna District of Andhra Pradesh padlocked the local offices of Spandana and SHARE Microfin (then India's largest MFIs), jailed loan officers, and announced that clients need not repay their loans. In 2010, just months after the IPO, the state government ambushed the industry with a law that effectively shut it down. It threatened to arrest MFI managers and board members, and again put out word not to repay, this time statewide. Alongside headlines about the tens of millions of dollars SKS founder Vikram Akula and his investors had made in the IPO, newspapers and television stations carried sensational stories of debtors committing suicide. Undoubtedly bureaucratic interests were at work, too, given the rivalry between the fast-growing MFIs and an equally ambitious self-help group program backed by the government and the World Bank.[47]

45. Aleem (1990), 337.

46. SKS Microfinance, "FAQs" (sksindia.com/faq.php [May 21, 2011]), answer to "Is over-indebtedness a problem among microfinance borrowers?"

47. Ghate (2007).

While the interest rates of SKS, Spandana, SHARE, and other big players were regularly attacked, by global standards, they were low at 25–35 percent (15–25 percent above inflation).[48] The real problem seemed to be a combination of eagerness to lend and aggressiveness in collecting. Before the 2010 crisis, the three S's all reported "portfolio at risk"—amounts owed by people behind on their loans—of 0.2 percent or less, which is extremely low even by microfinance standards. Well before the crisis, a leading authority on Indian microfinance, Prabhu Ghate, worried aloud about the repayment pressures bearing on India's poor:

> The point at which peer group pressure becomes coercive is an extremely difficult one. However one clear lesson . . . is that the policy of 100 percent repayment and "zero tolerance" for default carried a very high cost in terms of client dissatisfaction, and provided ample material to be exploited by interested parties. Clearly there is a need for flexibility to accommodate cases of extreme distress in which a borrower is unable to pay because of critical illness, hospitalization, and so on. A second lesson is that there is a great need for action research to provide answers to the question of how flexible MFIs can afford to be, even in cases of lesser distress (such as failure of a business) in rescheduling loans, without affecting repayment discipline generally, and how much operational costs would go up to introduce such flexibility.[49]

His successor as author of the annual *Microfinance India: State of the Sector Report,* N. Srinivasan, concurred: "It's possible through coercive action to get the borrowers (or their group guarantors) to repay the instalments, regardless of their income flows. But this causes acute stress on the poor households, especially when the weekly payments have to be continued at a time when personal misfortunes befall the poor families. Under such conditions, one wonders whether microfinance has a soul and whether such credit mechanisms really serve the vulnerable."[50]

The Andhra Pradesh crises raise an important question: must microfinance demand the same mechanical reliability that it supplies? Or can it be both reliable and flexible? Prabu Ghate voiced hope, and the trade-off is theoretically avoidable. The "cash credit" that originated in Scotland in the 1700s was at once flexible and reliable (see chapter 3). So are lines of credit today. True, the business imperatives of mass-producing small-scale services

48. MFTransparency, "India" (j.mp/jjtrMs [May 21, 2011]).

49. Ghate (2007), 169–70.

50. Srinivasan (2010b), 11.

for the poor do crank up the tension. Dealing with late payers can cost more than the loans themselves are worth, so delinquency must be avoided. But there is scope for improvement.

The best proof of the potential is the package of innovations the Grameen Bank adopted in 2001, "Grameen II" (see chapter 5). At the time, Yunus characterized classic Grameen microfinance, the kind imitated in India and dozens of other countries, with remarkable frankness:

> The system consisted of a set of well-defined standardised rules. No departure from these rules was allowed. Once a borrower fell off the track, she found it very difficult to move back on, since the rules which allowed her to return were not easy for her to fulfill. More and more borrowers fell off the track. Then there was the multiplier effect. If one borrower stopped payments, it encouraged others to follow.[51]

Grameen II aimed almost entirely at making the bank more flexible, by tweaking existing services and adding new ones. It let clients open flexible individual savings accounts. They could "top-up" loans that were at least half paid off—that is, they could borrow back the amounts just paid in, making Grameen loans more like lines of credit. In work behind *Portfolios of the Poor*, Rutherford tracked the finances of some households in Bangladesh under Grameen II. Ramna's story exemplifies how the reforms freed clients from the traditional one-year loan cycle:

> Ramna . . . and her husband were completely landless, sheltering on her brother's land and trying to bring up two school-age sons. The husband had few skills and was in poor health, and though he tried day laboring, working in a tea stall, and fishing for crabs, he was never able to maintain steady income during the three years we knew them.
>
> Ramna had . . . taken a loan of $83 used to buy food stocks in a lean period. She was repaying weekly from a variety of sources including her husband's income, interest-free loans from family and neighbors, and her own Grameen II personal savings. In April 2003 she "topped up" her Grameen loan and used it to buy grain to keep in reserve for the coming monsoon period. . . . Then in October her father-in-law died and they financed the funeral with another top-up, worth $67. They managed to make repayments during the winter dry season, so that in May 2004, when she was eligible for another top-up, she took it and stored it with a moneyguard, from whom it was later recovered

and used to pay down a private loan that had been hanging over them for some time. She topped up with another $75 once more in December, the month of the main rice harvest, and it was spent on stocks of grain and on medical treatment for her husband, with a portion held back to make weekly repayments. They struggled to repay in early 2005 because her own father was ill and they had to find money to pay for his treatment, but in early July she was able to top up again ($65), this time paying school fees as well as restocking with food.[52]

Ramna and her husband fought to keep up with their debts. Indeed one wonders whether the bottom half of her repeatedly topped-up Grameen loan will ever be paid off. Yet it would have been even harder for them to mesh their sporadic income with volatile spending needs without the ability to borrow and save flexibly. If the Grameen Bank had insisted on a strict annual schedule, that would have pushed Ramna further toward more flexible but expensive informal services. Grameen II may well have given Ramna a precious increment of freedom.

The credit relationship has price and non-price aspects. Price gets the press when microcreditors are accused of usury. But if the goal is to maximize the agency of borrowers, most microcreditors appear to have more room for improvement in the non-price aspects of transparency and flexibility.

Group Dynamics

Yet another aspect of the microcredit experience for most users is the dynamic of the group. It is often said that the microcredit groups empower their members. When a woman brings home a loan, yet remains accountable to other women for the management of that money, she may gain leverage with her husband. When she does business in public, in going to these meetings, she may defy cultural restrictions on her sex. If she and her peers meet regularly, they may come to support each other in times of need. They may collectively agitate for their rights within the community. Solidarity groups carry the hope of empowerment in their name. Self-help groups (SHGs) do, too, once "self-help" is understood to tap into Gandhi's philosophy of collective grassroots action.

It is not hard to see how groups could empower women in these ways. Most poor societies restrict women's roles outside the home, perhaps the more so the poorer the society. Bangladesh again provides the classic

52. Collins and others (2009), 163.

example; there, the custom of *purdah* prohibits women from seeing or talking to men outside their extended family.[53] Even when not obeyed literally, *purdah* inhibits women from acting in public fora and engaging in commerce. Amid such paternalism, a space for women to convene in public, to pass money from hand to hand and discuss business affairs, is inherently radical. And one can imagine how these tight-knit groups, meeting weekly over the years, could become platforms for mutual aid and subversion in the best sense. A story from an authoritative 2006 report on SHGs by Frances Sinha conveys the idea:

> Traditionally, married women were never allowed to stay away from home for an entire night and if they even tried doing it they knew they could be beaten up or even thrown out by their husband. . . . [T]raining programmes for SHG members sometimes involve their stay[ing] overnight at another village.
>
> When this happened in Manikhera village (Orissa), soon after the SHGs were formed 6 years ago, one of the SHG members was locked out [of] the house by her husband when she returned from two nights out at a training programme. But, when the other SHG members rallied round, and said they would report the matter to the police, the man gave in and accepted her back. This early success was a source of strength to the group, building their confidence that they could support each other and act together to deal with issues within the family.[54]

On the other hand, as asserted in chapter 5, the *raisons d'être* for groups has less to do with empowerment than with discipline and efficiency. Joint liability substitutes for collateral as a way to persuade borrowers to repay. Group meetings save microfinance officers time compared to going door to door—but by the same token impose on borrowers' time. The peer pressure of joint liability is inherently coercive. Thus, when group microfinance expands people's freedom and when it contracts it are unclear, making it one of the most difficult issues to generalize about in this book. Compelling stories are told on both sides—some of which you will read in a few pages.

Multiple Borrowing: A Paradox of Plenty

In November 2010, five weeks after the government of Andhra Pradesh issued a surprise death sentence to private microcredit within its borders, I

53. Rahman (1999a), 80.
54. Sinha (2006), 79.

visited the village of Yarvaguda 20 miles west of the state capital, Hyderabad. In a functional one-room concrete building that is used for SHG meetings, I met seven women, all SHG members. My guide and I sat cross-legged on a woven mat, the only furnishing, with our backs against a wall. The women formed an arc around us. We spoke for about an hour. I would ask a question, my guide would translate, much discussion would ensue, and he would occasionally toss an answer my way. Obviously, I missed the richness of the conversation.

I was interested in the extent of multiple borrowing—borrowing from several MFIs at once—as a marker for potential overlending and overborrowing. It emerged that before the previous year, BASIX had been the only MFI lending in the village. BASIX is at once the forebearer of the other, pure-credit MFIs and, as described in chapter 4, an exemplar of providing additional, bundled services. The newer MFIs were, by all accounts, a different breed. They did just credit, had been growing blisteringly fast, and stood widely accused of many crimes, including misleading disclosure of interest rates, loan pushing, and aggressive loan collection. Three came to Yarvaguda: SKS and Spandana (among the biggest), and one called L&T.

Among the seven women, two were too old for microcredit as a matter of policy or practice. The rest had two to four MFI loans in addition to their SHG ones. I focused on inventorying these formal loans, asking for names of lenders and initial and current amounts outstanding (shown as vertical pairs of numbers in table 7-1).

Average formal debt for these five women was 51,000 rupees, or $1,130. In comparison, the Andhra Pradesh poverty line was placed at 433 rupees ($9.60) per capita per month for rural areas and 563 ($12.50) for urban.[55] Using the higher figure because proximity to Hyderabad may lift prices and wages in Yarvaguda, multiplying by a typical four members per household, and doubling again since the women, as SHG members, were probably not the poorest gives a monthly household income of $100. So on average they had formal debts worth perhaps a year's income.

My guide said that most of the loans were intended for investing in crops. Ellamma, though, used hers to pay off a moneylender loan that financed her daughter's wedding. This probably helped her in lowering the interest rate. Overall, the women said, about half the borrowings went to consumption needs—school and clinic fees, food. They also explained that unusual rains had ruined their cotton crops (in the same year as the Pakistan floods). Apparently it normally stops raining in early October, but I witnessed a few

55. Government of India (2009), 17.

Table 7-1. *Formal Loans, by Borrower and Lender, for Five Women in Yarvaguda, Andhra Pradesh, November 2010*

Thousands of rupees (1,000 = $22)

Name	Self-help group (SHG)	BASIX	New microfinance institutions (MFIs) SKS	Span-dana	L&T	Total current debt	Notes
Rukkama (Original loan value ↓ Current balance)	15 ↓ 5		12 ↓ 4	20 ↓ 20	12 ↓ 12	41	Had trouble sleeping before weekly MFI payments due; defaulted on SHG one to two months ago but paid a fine and now servicing
Santosha	? ↓ ?					?	SHG loan only; forgot to ask how big; too old for MFIs as a matter of policy or practice
Ellamma	20 ↓ 15		22 ↓ 14	15 ↓ 15		44	Refinanced moneylender loan for daughter's wedding; maybe not so poor
Vijaya	30 ↓ 28	20 ↓ 12	20 ↓ 14	15 ↓ 15	15 ↓ 15	84	President of village SHG organization; maybe not so poor; defaulted on SHG one to two months ago but paid a fine and now servicing
Lakshmi	20 ↓ 15	15 ↓ 15	12 ↓ 4	15 ↓ 15	12 ↓ 12	61	
Khajabhi	? ↓ ?					?	SHG loan only; forgot to ask how big; too old for MFIs as a matter of policy or practice
Bhavani	12 ↓ 4		12 ↓ 4	12 ↓ 4	12 ↓ 12	24	SKS agent and center leader, organizing five-member borrowing groups

Source: Author's calculations.

Note: In number pairs for each name, upper numbers are original loan amounts and lower ones are current amounts.

squalls even in mid-November. The flooded crops fell prey to a fungus that turned the maturing cotton black and robbed it of commercial value. The crops they had counted on to pay their loans were lost.

I heard no suicide stories. So I asked the women how they felt about their debt burdens and the payment holiday the government had effectively declared. Lakshmi said the stress of repayment gave her a fever. More credibly, Rukkama said she had trouble sleeping on nights before weekly meetings of the new MFIs. They were relieved about the holiday. These women may not have been representative—indeed, I think they were asked to speak to me precisely because of their multiple loans—and it was impossible to know whether credit added to or merely deferred their distresses. But they put a human face on reports I heard while in Andhra Pradesh. MFIs were said to be so numerous in many villages and slums that women referred to them by the day of the week on which they met. Some places ran out of days of the week. It was easy to see how a fraction of women would have been enticed into borrowing more than they could easily repay and how, given the pressure in microcredit for on-time repayment, that would generate stress.

For me, the encounter in Yarvaguda exemplified an obvious contradiction in the nature of credit: on the one hand, offering a loan gives people a new option, an increment of freedom; on the other hand, easy credit can be a debt trap. That contradiction will always be with us, and so it is perhaps not worth too much philosophizing in itself, except to note that other financial services, done properly, do not contain the same lurking threat of diminished freedom. More concretely, the encounter revealed that microlending goes overboard when many lenders expand rapidly in the same areas without knowing clients' total borrowings.

The history of microfinance is dotted with such outbreaks, but the industry has usually learned and recovered. In the 1990s, Bolivia became an early exemplar of microcredit—and of the pitfalls of multiple lending. Years of rapid growth in microfinance attracted a new breed of creditor, the consumer lender, which extended credit primarily to help people buy expensive goods, such as televisions and refrigerators. The consumer lenders sprang onto the scene in the late 1990s and then collapsed almost as quickly—but not before strewing overindebtedness in Bolivian cities and infecting MFIs with repayment problems. Multiple borrowing also has been common in Bangladesh since the late 1990s and may have contributed to the payment troubles Yunus acknowledged at the Grameen Bank.[56] And in the lead-up to microcredit crises in Bosnia and Herzegovina, Morocco, Nicaragua, and

---

56. Prevalence in late 1990s from Chaudhury and Matin (2002).

Pakistan, 30–40 percent of borrowers had more than one loan, meaning that the majority of loans went to multiple borrowers (see chapter 8).[57]

Multiple borrowing is a particular challenge just where failure to manage it can harm the most: among the poorer clients, who take group microcredit. Group methods are designed to offload the job of monitoring borrowers onto the borrowers themselves. But it also amounts to a constitutional ignorance about how much customers do and should borrow. As a result, in group credit it has traditionally been up to borrowers to keep tabs on how many loans their peers have, how much they owe, and whether they can keep up with the payments. The solvency of major group microcreditors and their clients thus depends on the good judgment of those clients. Unclear is how reliable that judgment remains as multiple borrowing becomes the norm, especially if quickly. Human beings are eminently capable of collective delusion about the realism of whole classes of financial claims. The worry is that where borrowing becomes common, an upward bias will creep into people's intuitions about how much debt their peers can handle. "Everyone is borrowing from multiple MFIs," they may think, "and nothing bad has happened to them, so it must be OK."

On the other hand, Bangladesh's example seems reassuring: more than a decade of multiple borrowing—overlapping, as they call it there—has not led to a meltdown. Exactly how well people are managing their multiple loans, though, is unclear. In 2002, BRAC's Imran Matin and fellow researcher Iftekhar Chaudhury found that in a handful of villages in Tangail district, 90 percent of BRAC-only borrowers were regular loan repayers, compared to just 50 percent of those who borrowed from BRAC and at least two other MFIs. As usual with such figures, causality is hard to pin down. Borrowing from several MFIs may have gotten people into debt trouble, or trouble may have led them to borrow from several MFIs, like people juggling credit card balances. The seeming good news was that most people did eventually pay off their loans. But here, too, the interpretation is uncertain. Behind statistics showing full repayment may lie a haphazard pattern of paying off old loans near the end of each one-year cycle, possibly via bridge loans from moneylenders, in order to quickly obtain new ones.[58]

The best way for lenders to monitor and manage multiple borrowing is to share information about borrowers among themselves. Normally this is done through a credit bureau. Microcreditors are increasingly computerized, so they should be able to share information cheaply. Perhaps a high-tech

57. Chen, Rasmussen, and Reille (2010), 7.

58. Chaudhury and Matin (2002).

makeover is possible to allow even group creditors to economically track their borrowers. One key would be a reliable way to establish people's identities and prevent them from borrowing from different MFIs under different names. India, for one, has no national identification system, but it has launched an ambitious project to build one. The system will reportedly use biometric technology, such as digital fingerprinting. If such a system indeed can identify a billion Indians, perhaps it can work anywhere.

The Evidence on Microcredit and Freedom

So far in our inquiry into whether microcredit empowers, we have focused on what creditors do: what interest rates they charge, how they disclose costs, how reliably and flexibly they serve customers, and where their client rolls overlap. This exploration has led to some rough conclusions: Interest rates *can* be harmfully high, but given the general downward trend and the high cost of lending to low-income people, abuse appears exceptional. Transparency, reliability, and flexibility may be at least as important. And the greatest threat to the freedom of clients may lie in a combination of easy credit, multiple lending, and strong repayment pressure.

These are useful guides from broad, conceptual reasoning. But how microcredit intersects with the freedom of human beings is ultimately an empirical question that requires a focus on the borrowers. Researchers have studied them and reported back a diversity of experience. We turn to their data now. The ambiguous results show that microcredit does not automatically enhance development as freedom. Its contribution to freedom must be striven for rather than assumed.

Quantifying Empowerment

Chapter 6 explained the relative strengths of quantitative and qualitative research. Researchers have applied both brands to the microcredit-empowerment link. Quantification is perhaps less suited to the complex and diffuse issue of empowerment but does force one to think concretely about this nebulous concept.

One influential quantitative article, "Who Takes the Credit?" by Anne Marie Goetz and Rina Sen Gupta, focused on whether female borrowers decided how their loans were used, or whether their husbands or brothers took control once the women returned home with the cash. Goetz and Sen Gupta judged that in their early-1990s Bangladesh sample, 63 percent of women exercised partial, very limited, or no control over the use of loan funds.[59] The finding suggests that to a large extent credit flows along existing power channels within the family rather than cutting new paths. On the other hand, that 37 percent of women in a sexist society *did* retain full or significant control may have been a victory for empowerment. It is particularly hard to interpret this study without the counterfactual, what life would have been like for the women studied in the absence of microcredit. Logically, Goetz and Sen Gupta could not compare borrowers and non-borrowers on their power over loan use.

Syed Hashemi, Sidney Schuler, and Ann Riley improved on Goetz and Sen Gupta by devising a much broader metric of empowerment and applying more sophisticated statistical methods. In the early 1990s, the trio developed an index of individual empowerment that includes eight headings, each elaborated with fine rules giving a woman points for ability to "purchas[e] pots and pans," "knowing the name of a local government official," and so on. To apply the metric, the research team interviewed 120 households in villages served by BRAC or the Grameen Bank. Some households had microcredit borrowers and some did not, allowing comparisons between the two kinds. Hashemi, Schuler, and Riley concluded that BRAC lending did empower women and Grameen lending even more so. They supplemented such findings with quotes from in-depth interviews. This is an example:

> Several of the women . . . told the field investigators that through Grameen Bank they had "learned to talk," and now they were not afraid to talk to outsiders. In both programs some members have the opportunity to play leadership roles. One woman told the researchers, "I have been made the [borrowing group] Chief. Now all of the other women listen to me and give me their attention. Grameen Bank has made me important."[60]

Still, the skepticism I voiced in chapter 6 about the capacity of non-experimental quantitative analysis to determine cause and effect applies full force here. The three authors do take steps to rule out reverse- and omitted-variable causation (concepts explained in chapter 6) but express appropriate humility about their limitations. Perhaps women who were more empowered to begin with were readier to borrow, thanks to their relative wealth and voice. And weekly messages from loan officers may have indirectly coached borrowers to give the "right" answers to the researchers' questions.

---

59. Goetz and Sen Gupta (1996), 49. Rahman (1999a, b) has similar findings.
60. Hashemi, Schuler, and Riley (1996), 648.

Because empowerment is among the hardest to quantify of the potential impacts of microfinance, it is particularly suited to qualitative research by those who spend months getting to know a small group of people. Remember from chapter 6 that when Helen Todd and her husband surveyed women about their influence in domestic decisionmaking, their answers seemed to say less about how the women lived than what they thought researchers wanted to hear. A year of watching and talking to people led Todd to much richer insight—and different answers to the survey questions.[61] So I devote the rest of this chapter to qualitative studies that are deeply observed and intelligently written. To reduce the dangers of selective storytelling, I cull findings from all the studies that I judge relevant and credible. Unfortunately, almost all the research comes from South Asia, which makes it hard to generalize to the rest of the world.

Debt Traps

From the point of view of development as freedom, the biggest worry about credit is that it becomes a trap, a repayment difficulty so great that it sends the borrower spiraling downward. This occurs when a debt burden pushes a borrower to liquidate a source of livelihood, such as land or a cow, mortgaging her future. How often does this happen? Among more than 150 million borrowers, the answer is not "never." Bad luck throws even the most far-sighted borrowers off track sometimes. But in reading through the academic studies, I found it hard to go beyond this elementary certitude. There appear to be no convincing studies of how frequently borrowers are left substantially worse off.

That leaves us with little more than stories. One can find stories of all varieties. Helen Todd provides a good one about a woman called Begum and her husband Shakeeb, who climbed out of financial trouble thanks to microcredit:

From the very beginning—when Shakeeb was still working out his labor contract—this couple has systematically used the GB [Grameen Bank] loans to acquire land. The first two years they leased in 10 decimals [10 hundredths of an acre] and then 15 decimals—which they sharecropped out because Shakeeb could not work it while he was contracted to his landlord. Meanwhile, with the balance of the loan amount they bought paddy, which Begum boiled, husked and resold, using the profit to make her repayments. After Begum took her third loan, she bought a cow and Shakeeb left the labor contract and came

61. Todd (1996), 87.

home. Now he worked the leasehold land himself, using the cow for ploughing (borrowing another cow to make a pair from another GB family) and doing daily labor to meet their cash needs.

Begum worried at first about the leasehold land and kept very quiet about it, because it was against the GB rules. But they both wanted to salt this unaccustomed capital away into investment—into the "pure value" of land. Shakeeb says:

> If we had put all the loans into paddy, that would make us lazy, it would take away our impulse to work. We agreed to put as much as possible into land. Of course, it was hard to get through the months until the harvest. Often we didn't have enough to eat because we used our cash to make the repayment. It was very difficult in those early years but we had that land and added to it.

For the past four years, Begum has done less paddy husking and invested in cows. She sold a cow to buy a plough and used her group loans to buy fertilizer. In the process she has helped turn Shakeeb into a leaseholder and a sharecropper, since both the cows and capital for inputs make him an attractive prospect for landlords wishing to share-crop their land.

Their joint ambition is to release Shakeeb from daily labor altogether and to turn him into a full-time farmer. During the year of data collection he was half way there. He farmed 59 decimals of sharecrop and 45 decimals of leasehold, which took almost half his time. There was always ample paddy in stock for the family's food needs, as well as surplus for Begum to husk and sell. It is hard to overestimate the satisfaction and security that a full store of paddy gives to someone like Begum, who remembers the hunger of herself and her children.[62]

There are sad stories, too. University of Manchester's David Hulme, the inventor of the financial diary, points researchers to microfinance dropouts to learn more about the harmful side of microcredit:

> Because of circumstances beyond their control (sickness, flood, drought, theft and so on), lack of skills and knowledge or taking bad decisions, a proportion of poor borrowers encounter great difficulties in repaying loans. While MFIs suggest that such problems are overcome through "social support" in some painless way this is often not the case—talk to the dropouts of MFIs! Many (though presently we

62. Todd (1996), 42–43.

have little understanding of exactly what proportion) report being threatened by group members and MFI staff or having their possessions (pots and pans, roofing iron) seized. In Bangladesh, MFI debtors have been arrested by the police (this came to light in 1997 when a police vehicle carrying such debtors crashed and the individuals concerned were killed) [and] are threatened with physical violence.[63]

Lamia Karim, an anthropologist at the University of Oregon, spent a year in Bangladesh and in 2008 published disturbing accounts:

I saw that credit-related strife amongst members and their families were routine occurrences. Women would march off together to scold the defaulting woman, shame her or her husband in a public place, and when she could not pay the full amount of the installment, go through her possessions and take away whatever they could sell off to recover the defaulted sum. In circumstances when the woman failed to pay the sum, which happened several times a month in the NGOs [nongovernmental organizations] I studied, the group members would repossess the capital that the woman had built with her loans. This ranged from taking away her gold nose-ring (a symbol of marital status for rural women, and removing it symbolically marks the "divorcing/widowing" of a woman) to cows and chicks to trees that had been planted to be sold as timber to collecting rice and grains that the family had accumulated as food, very often leaving the family with no food whatsoever. The women who committed these acts did so at the exhortations of NGO officers, but they also considered these acts to be "protecting their investments," and the defaulting woman as someone who had "broken faith with the community." These acts were committed with the full knowledge of NGO officers, but the officers did not participate in these collective acts of aggression. Instead, they threatened to withhold future loans unless the defaulted money was recovered.

In instances where everything had been repossessed because of a large default, members would sell off the defaulting member's house. This is known as house-breaking (*ghar bhanga*) and has a long history in rural society.[64]

Karim also related a conversation with a prosperous moneylender and microcredit client:

63. Hulme (2007), 19–20.
64. Karim (2008), 18–19.

Jahanara proudly told us that she had broken many houses when members could not pay. "We know when they cannot pay, so we take a carpenter with us to break the house." When I asked Jahanara, "Why do you break the houses of kin?" Jahanara became indignant at first. Her initial comment was "Why shouldn't we? They have breached their trust with us. If they cannot pay, then we will have to pay. Why should I pay for them?" Then she became quiet and said after a while, "It is not good to break someone's house, but we are forced to do it. This is how we get loans from Grameen Bank and other NGOs. They put pressure on us to recover the money, then we all get together and force the defaulting member to give us the money. We don't care how we do it."[65]

It is exceedingly hard to determine from the evidence at hand—most of which comes from one country—the extent of debt trouble among microcredit clients generally.[66] Most likely the reality is what common sense would suggest: just as in rich countries, most of the time borrowers in poor countries manage their debt loads without capsizing. Through storytelling, microfinance promoters disarmed this common sense, persuading the public that, as in the title of one book, "the poor always pay back."[67] The reality is more complex.

Individual Microcredit

Individual microcredit is a particularly intriguing object of study for us because it helps us isolate the effects of finance from the effects of groups. Like Helen Todd, Naila Kabeer of the Institute of Development Studies brilliantly details the effects of microcredit on women in a few Bangladeshi villages in her writings. But unlike Todd, Kabeer studied a government-supported program called the Small Enterprise Development Project (SEDP) that made subsidized individual loans to women with at least half an acre of land. In contrast, classic solidarity group credit in Bangladesh aims to minimize subsidy while serving those with less than half an acre.

Overall, Kabeer's assessment of the project is the scholarly equivalent of upbeat. Despite the landownership minimum, many of her subjects were poor by any reasonable standard, and for them access to credit could still mean a great deal. Said one:

65. Karim (2008), 23. On housebreaking, see also Ito (1999), 159.
66. On the fragmentary but worrying data on dropouts, see also Montgomery (1996).
67. Dowla and Barua (2006).

If I had not gone to that SEDP meeting, had not taken a loan, had not learnt the work, I would not get the value I have, I would have to continue to ask my husband for every taka I needed. Once I had a headache, I wanted one taka for a bandage to tie around my head, I wept for eight days, he still would not give me the money. Just one taka.[68]

Kabeer saw little sign that borrowers became more active politically as a result of microcredit, but many reported more power and respect in the home. The few who were married to particularly abusive husbands either gained more independence from them or established a less violent power balance with them. While Kabeer's work is not exempt from the potential for statistical (and human) biases, several subtle and contrarian observations give her work credibility. Kabeer questions authors who equate empowering women with challenging cultural and legal norms. Some women (though not all) told her that they used loans to comply with *purdah*. They stopped working in the fields for day wages and instead bought and raised cows near home, elevating themselves in the eyes of their neighbors by hewing closer to cultural norms.[69] Kabeer also delineates how women's experiences with individual and group credit differed:

There was general agreement among SEDP loanees, including those who had previously borrowed from BRAC and Grameen, that there were greater stresses and strains associated with repayment of loans from poverty-oriented programs. These often spilt over into conflict, sometimes between husband and wife . . . sometimes between "irresponsible" loanees and other group members worried about their future creditworthiness . . . but most often between loanees' families and program officers seeking to recover repayments. . . .

The discipline built into poverty-related lending, which gave rise to the stresses remarked on by the loanees, reflected a concern with loan recovery and with long-term sustainability on the part of these programs. SEDP could afford to run a more relaxed lending regime because a concern with sustainability had not been built into program design while its loan recovery efforts were backed up by the perceived authority of a government bank. It was one of the constant ironies thrown up by the fieldwork that relatively well-off households could access loans at subsidized interest rates with greater flexibility built into

68. Kabeer (2001), 71.
69. Kabeer (2001), 69, 74.

their repayment schedules while all around us, poverty-focused credit organizations were lending far smaller sums of money to much poorer sections of the population at much higher interest rates with far more inflexible weekly repayment schedules. Indeed, the pressure of meeting weekly repayments was mentioned as the single most important source of the tensions generated by poverty-oriented lending.[70]

It would be easier to apply Kabeer's conclusions to commercial microcredit if the SEDP were not significantly subsidized; perhaps that is the main reason the freeing side of credit came to the fore. But another interpretation is that individual credit is more apt to enhance agency than group credit. If correct, this may be because the individual credit is free from peer pressure or because those taking it are better positioned to leverage the credit into yet more control over their lives.

Solidarity Groups in Bangladesh

Group microcredit was peripheral to Kabeer's study. Others, like Karim (above), have focused on it directly. What have they seen?

A remarkable World Bank study offers a rare international comparative perspective on our subject. In this effort, researchers collected life histories from thousands of people in fifteen nations in Asia, Africa, and Latin America, aiming to understand what causes people to rise out of, fall into, or stay in poverty. In addition to collecting stories, the researchers performed structured interviews about whether people felt control over their lives. Here is what they observed in Bangladesh:

> Unlike many women in the other study regions, who said that they felt powerless, inferior, or trapped, women in the Bangladesh study villages often appeared confident and assured. They dressed well, spoke up, participated in household decisions, and stepped out of the house to markets. Some felt confident enough to enter the public sphere, marching to local politicians to speak out against injustice. These changes in women also forced the men in their communities to change. Some applauded women's empowerment, but others appeared anxious and resentful. They longed for bygone times when the rules were simple and women did what they were told.[71]

70. Kabeer (2001), 78–79.
71. Narayan, Pritchett, and Kapoor (2009), 134.

Being so prevalent, group microcredit may deserve credit for bolstering the stature of women. On the other hand, the authors do not directly analyze this link, so it is hard to know quite what to conclude about it.

Other researchers have focused more directly on the link. Helen Todd was one of the first to do so with in-depth qualitative research. Sure enough, she found stories of women clawing their way up economically and gaining stature within their families like that of Begum and Shakeeb. The storyline was not universal, but it was common enough to tilt Todd's assessment toward the positive. As noted in chapter 6, one caveat for generalizing is that Todd chose not to study dropouts. The borrowers she followed had all been with Grameen at least ten years, and may have been a somewhat rarified cohort.

Yet even with her optimistic assessment, Todd tagged as myth the idea that solidarity groups foster solidarity. They did not cause women to look after each other in times of need and fight patriarchy with joined fists. Empowerment came through economic success, not alongside it:

> The fundamental meaning of these two centers is not a collective one for their members. They go to the meetings and keep the discipline in order to keep open a regular line of reasonably priced credit. For the same reason, to keep their eligibility for loans, members would help others with repayment, so long as they did not ask too often, and pressure each other to follow the rules and keep the good name of the center. Their purpose is not a group purpose but an individual one, firmly rooted in self-interest and based squarely on their primary loyalty to their immediate family.[72]

Another qualitative researcher, Sanae Ito, arrived at a bleaker view of the microcredit-empowerment link. The traditional microcredit group emerges from Ito's writing, as from Karim's, as an assemblage in which women placed strong pressure on one another when necessary while Grameen employers presided like more or less benevolent dictators. In running the mandatory weekly meetings, the branch managers exercised discretion created by the opacity of the loan approval rules. Ito describes:

> Two recent cases in which several centre members raided the houses of the members in arrears, under pressure from the branch manager. One of them was Kateja. She went into arrears when her son, who drove an auto-rickshaw in Dhaka, fell ill and could not send her remittances.

72. Todd (1996), 175–76.

Several members went to her house, took away her cow and yoked it at the front yard of the branch office as a punishment. Kateja could not stand the embarrassment for too long. She borrowed money from her brother, repaid her loan, got her cow back, and sold it immediately to pay her brother back. In Rehena's case, her husband spent her general loan on purchasing a motor to start a rice husking business. When the motor failed to work, Rehena immediately got into repayment difficulties. The branch manager at first threatened to ask the union chairman to intervene if she did not bring her repayments up to date, a standard tactic used by the branch manager in such situations. When it did not work, he went to the centre meeting and suggested that the members should go to Rehena's house to persuade her to repay. When members showed reluctance to do so, he reportedly declared: "All right then. All of you will pay back her loan together." Upon hearing this, several . . . went to her house, and verbally threatened to take away her assets. One of the members managed to steal a torch light [flashlight] from Rehena's house . . . though it was later returned through the mediation of the branch manager.[73]

A pair of studies commissioned by the international charity CARE used quantitative and qualitative methods to study how families in Bangladesh manage credit—one study in the southeastern part of the country, the other in the northwest.[74] The most powerful pieces of the reports are the short anecdotes drawn from qualitative interviews. (The writers use initials to protect confidentiality.) Some of the stories are happy:

One woman, LB (husband GU) improved her economic condition by taking an NGO loan as well as a *mohazan* [moneylender] loan. She and her husband now own a cow, fishing net, and a boat. GU can fish in his own boat and does not need to share his fish with the boat owner. . . .

Wife of AH reported that in the beginning they had no assets, but in seven years time they accumulated seven cows and two betel leaf gardens. She also mentioned that after receiving the loan, she wanted to buy a nose pin for herself but her husband said that "we cannot consume this money, we will buy a nose pin from the profit."[75]

73. Ito (1999), 159.

74. Gillingham and Islam (2005a, 2005b).

75. Gillingham and Islam (2005a), 19.

But most of the stories are not happy. Here is one:

> If the wives of the . . . poor households fail to pay the NGO weekly installment, they are humiliated. NGO staffs and group members scold them, and the group members come to their houses to seize their assets. One woman of an always poor household related: "After being insulted by group members, I made a promise, in the name of Allah, that I would never take another loan. After a few years, my husband is again asking me to take a loan. He says that he will bear the sin of breaking my promise."[76]

Another passage relates:

> Most households take two meals a day instead of three for 9–12 months. For the two days prior to loan installment, they starve themselves or just take rice mixed with water. For paying off the *mohazans,* some households minimize their meals 7–10 days ahead of time. . . .
>
> The participants informed that they do not mortgage or sell their land at first; they try many different options and use their land as a last strategy. They referred to one M.U., who first borrowed from a *mohazan* for his medical care and household food during his sick days. He failed to pay back the *mohazan* from his income and he borrowed from an NGO to clear the *mohazan* debt. Then he could not pay the NGO installments regularly, and his debt burden increased to the point that he sold three decimals of land and mortgaged out 10 decimals to repay NGO loan. Now he hardly can manage three meals a day.[77]

The most negative assessment I have seen of traditional Grameen group credit comes from Aminur Rahman, introduced in chapter 5, who spent a year in a Bangladeshi village in the mid-1990s focusing on the connection between microcredit and violence against women in the home. Rahman's native fluency in Bengali language and culture brought him closer to his subjects, but he was distanced from them by his gender. In an effort to draw out women as interviewees, he hired a full-time female assistant. Like Todd, Rahman found that certain members exercised more power within the credit groups—for better and worse. Sometimes they arranged for one group member to lend money to another to cover a weekly payment; other times, they exacted retribution in a personal dispute by blocking a loan

76. Gillingham and Islam (2005a), 21.
77. Gillingham and Islam (2005b), 26–27.

request. Rahman's verdict is harsh: "In the study community, many borrowers maintain their regular repayment schedules through a process of
loan recycling that considerably increases the debt-liability on the individual households, increases tension and frustration among household members, produces new forms of dominance over women and increases violence
in society."[78]

On the subject of bank worker–orchestrated peer pressure, Rahman
reported:

> Often there are one or two members in every loan center who, because
> they were unable to arrange their instalments, did not come to center
> meetings. . . . Other regular members in the center are forced to sit on
> their bare feet on a mud floor for several hours until all instalments
> are collected. If the absent member is available in the village, her peers
> persuade her to come to the center. The appearance of the absentee . . .
> usually releases an outburst of anger toward her by fellow members
> and the bank worker.

One woman, Ramena, sat through those extra hours only to return home to
a beating from a husband furious at having to wait so long for his breakfast.
The husband had invested her loan in a brown sugar business that was not
earning enough to cover the interest, which no doubt added to his stress. In
another case, a woman named Yuri had her husband get a two-week moneylender loan to bridge her from one Grameen loan to the next. But the center
chief, a fellow borrower, blocked her request for the new Grameen loan. The
reason? Yuri refused to pass part of her new loan to the chief's mother. Again
the result was a beating for the cornered wife. Toward the end of his time,
Rahman surveyed 120 women in the village. All said that they experienced
some violence in the home. Eight-four said they had suffered more since
joining Grameen Bank while eighteen reported less. Of course, some caveats
apply: they may have tilted their answers according to what they thought
Rahman and his assistant wanted to hear, and the pair may have phrased
their questions in a leading way.[79]

Regardless of their generalizability, Rahman's conclusions about how
some women experience microcredit seem fundamentally plausible. As
noted, Sen's argument that freedom begets freedom also works in reverse:
loss of freedom in one domain causes loss in another. In a society where

78. Rahman (1999a), 67.
79. Rahman (1999a), 72–74.

domestic violence is endemic, when a woman loses financial freedom because of failure to stay on top of a loan, she can also lose the freedom of personal security. By the same token, though Rahman does not say this, when women gain financially through loans, they probably also find home life safer.

In sum, a fairly consistent picture of the empowerment effects of classic solidarity group microcredit emerges from the most credible studies, the qualitative ones. Among women who succeed economically through borrowing, greater freedom from want probably spills over into other freedoms—greater health, better education for the children, less abuse from the husband. For those who fall into debt trouble, the opposite is true. These effects occur through the use of the loan rather than the group-based process of obtaining it. The peer pressure implicit in group credit appears more oppressive than liberating. Arguably this is to be expected of a lending system that intertwines people's burdens and was honed less to empower women than to efficiently mass-produce credit for the poor.

Self-Help Groups in India

In contrast, the distinctive Indian variety of collective finance, the self-help group, appears to have been designed and implemented much more deliberately to help women perceive and attack the injustices done to them. As described in chapter 4, Indian nonprofit organizations organize groups of ten to twenty women at a time into SHGs. They help the members save into a shared bank account and then obtain a loan from the same bank. Using government or charitable funds, many of these nonprofit "promoters" also invest considerable energy in teaching members to see themselves as victims of pervasive sexism who can find power in collective action. Here's an account from one middle-aged SHG member, related via sociologist Paromita Sanyal:

> [The program director] asked us, "Say for instance, the husband earns Rs [rupees] 50 and he thinks that his wife doesn't even earn Rs5. But that is not the case. Women too earn Rs50! But, from where? Let me see if any of you can tell me, from where?" Some of the women tried, some were incorrect, some couldn't even think of anything. Then he explained, "Consider this, women tend to their cows, goats and hens throughout the day. How much do they earn daily doing that? Or, consider how much you'd have to pay someone if you employed the person to do all the household chores? But husbands never have to pay their wives anything! That money is extra, so that is what women

earn!" But we'd never thought in that manner before, we'd never perceived it in that way. Then he said, "OK let's take independence, men
have all the freedoms. Why don't women have any freedom? Because
they can't protest!"[80]

In time for the United Nations–declared International Year of Microcredit, 2005, the United Nations Development Program and a major banker
to SHGs, ICICI, commissioned an edited book of qualitative studies of the
groups.[81] Most of the chapters are studded with anodyne generalizations with
little systematic documentation of the underlying evidence, but an exception
is the chapter by Shashi Rajagopalan, a pillar of the cooperative movement in
India, on an SHG promoter called Lokadrusti. It operates in one of the poorest parts of India, the state of Orissa. Within 20 of the 146 villages in which
Lokadrusti worked, Rajagopalan commendably chose fifty-five women at
random to interview. She also held meetings in each of the twenty villages
with representatives from all local SHGs, including some that had defaulted
on their collective bank loans. Her report mixes good and bad news in a way
that suggests critical thinking and representativeness of real-world complexity. She concluded that "the women appeared to have gained very significantly in terms of mobility, self-confidence, widening of interests, access to
financial services, building of own savings, competence in public affairs, and
status at home and in the community."[82] On women's mobility, she writes:

> Almost all women spoke of the widening of their world because of
> the SHG. They said that it was not as if they had not been out of their
> villages earlier. More than the geography, it was the agenda for which
> they now travelled [to visit a bank], and the fact that they travelled, not
> with family members, but with friends from other castes, that made
> them feel that their world had become larger.[83]

She also describes their collective power when supported by the SHG promoter Lokadrusti:

> In one village, the local priest had felt threatened by the SHG and
> warned the women of tragedy befalling their children if they contin-
> ued to work as an SHG, or used the community-cum-storage centre

80. Sanyal (2007), 13.
81. Burra, Deshmukh-Ranadive, and Murthy (2005).
82. Rajagopalan (2005), 281–82.
83. Rajagopalan (2005), 262.

built for them by Lokadrusti. The women, despite their collective strength, felt overwhelmed, and were unwilling to challenge him. They did, however, work on him with Lokadrusti's help, did overcome their fears, and finally began to conduct meetings inside the new centre.[84]

But Rajagopalan's critical eye also picked up the SHGs' loose financial culture, which they acquired along with the loans from the government bank. One SHG member explained:

> The government has taught us to ask for [30–40,000 rupees] under various schemes. When it says that such money is available and that we should try and access it, it is too much to resist, even though we are all conscious that we will not be able to absorb such a large loan. Also, the government has given indications that it does not expect its loans back; so those of us who know the art of accessing such "loans" do get such loans, and do not think of them as repayable.[85]

Not surprisingly, "default was not frowned upon by Lokadrusti, even though it was worried about it, as was true of many voluntary development organizations and government agencies. . . . Most . . . do not have a system where a defaulter pays a price for default. Default is explained away: drought, illness, and so on."[86] It is easy to see how a tacit license to default would be empowering even if it sets a costly example of bringing financial services to the poor. This suggests a trade-off between financial and empowerment goals in group microfinance.

An excellent and more comprehensive work whose conclusions resonate with this portrait is *Self Help Groups in India: A Study of the Lights and Shades* by Frances Sinha. Sinha and her research team drew on the experiences of 214 SHGs in four states. The report sets a worthy example by devoting a whole section to dropouts, counting them and their reasons for leaving, and telling their stories. Some of those stories signal troubles with SHGs (a woman loses her savings because of fraud), some do not (through no fault of her SHG, a woman falls ill and leaves the group, taking her savings).[87]

The report strikes a more positive note on the empowerment training that SHG promoters provide. The studied SHG promoter in Andhra

84. Rajagopalan (2005), 270.
85. Rajagopalan (2005), 273.
86. Rajagopalan (2005), 273.
87. Sinha (2006), 51–52.

Pradesh, for example, "appears to have been very successful in educating women about their rights, and raised their consciousness on dowry, desertion, domestic violence, property and other issues affecting women to their disadvantage."[88] The women sometimes turned those ideas into community action, if "not as frequent[ly] as might be hoped for."[89] The report tabulates instances in which members collectively intervened in domestic disputes, such as by confronting a wife-beating husband, or in community issues, such as by pressuring local leaders to shut down alcohol shops. An example from Andhra Pradesh:

> Kamala ... was married to Narayana of Pantulapally village three years ago. Kamala brought with her a sum of [50,000 rupees] as dowry. Narayana, dissatisfied with the dowry, mistreated her and asked her to return to her parental home.
>
> His parents found him another match—with a dowry deal of [200,000 rupees] cash, a vehicle and 120 [grams] of gold. The arrangements for the wedding commenced. On the advice of the NGO ... Kamala told Narayana that unless he divorced her he could not remarry and warned him that if he went ahead with his second marriage, she would lodge a police complaint. Narayana ignored her and his family continued with his wedding arrangements. On hearing this, and irked by the greed for dowry, all the SHGs of Pantulapally went on a rally to the [local government] office in Nallabelly. They staged a *dharna* [protest], expressed solidarity with Kamala and demanded that justice be done to her. They submitted a memorandum saying that the matter was grave and action must be taken immediately against Narayana. ... Narayana was arrested and imprisoned for three months. After his release, he and Kamala resumed their married life, and they now have a child.[90]

As with Lokadrusti, the NGOs that formed the SHGs were central to organizing such actions: generally, they did not arise spontaneously. Meanwhile, financial management seemed lax: "In relation to financial transactions,

88. Sinha (2006), 79.

89. Sinha (2006), 77. SHGs had agitated on community issues in 40 of the 108 villages studied. Since the SHGs were at least five years old on average, that works out to roughly eight events per year in the 108 villages—and must be deflated further since Sinha's team deliberately sought socially active SHGs for the sample.

90. Sinha (2006), 79.

books and records need to be well maintained with systems in place to verify the records and as a basis for transparency with group members. This is largely not happening."[91]

These studies of SHGs suggest that the training component of the SHG package is working to the extent that SHG members are standing up for themselves somewhat more, corroborating the thesis of Linda Mayoux, a longtime writer on the subject. She argues that microfinance does not automatically empower, but it can if designed to do so.[92] Ironically, though, laxity within SHGs facilitates default, which is certainly liberating but undercuts financial viability.

Conclusion

A simple question—does microfinance expand or contract freedom?—leads to complex answers rooted in debt's double aspect as a source of possibility and obligation. The theory and evidence generate several conclusions, some more certain than others.

By decoupling when something is bought from when it is paid for, financial services inherently give people more control over their financial lives—more "freedom" in Amartya Sen's terms. Savings and insurance services grant such freedom without imposing future obligations the way credit does, so they seem more benign if they are provided free of fraud, price-gouging, and recalcitrant disbursement. But this chapter looked almost exclusively at credit because the movement has emphasized it and its impacts on freedom are more ambiguous.

Evidence on how microcredit affects people's freedom is fragmentary and comes mostly from South Asia. It supports a few generalizations. First, doing financial business with poor women empowers them mainly through any economic success they achieve rather than in parallel to it. Women gain more autonomy from successful investment or spending management than they do from entering into solidarity with jointly liable borrowers. Yet Indian self-help groups go well beyond pure financing to run activities organizing women to fight oppression and can leave a stronger imprint. The same may hold for the "credit plus" programs of BRAC and Freedom from Hunger, which train and teach as they lend (see chapter 4).

91. Sinha (2006), 107–08.
92. Mayoux (2006).

Second, the more a microcreditor pursues financial self-sufficiency, the more it imposes on the freedom of its clients in the short term. The financially loose SHGs and the subsidized SEDP program that Kabeer studied seem to score best on empowerment.

Finally, collateralizing one's reputation through group credit may be more oppressive than a more conventionally collateralized individual loan—for those who have a choice.

Viewing development as freedom validates the provision of financial services to the poor in general as a contribution to development. The contribution looks modest next to the goal of eliminating poverty, but if it is commensurate with the costs, if any, to donors and social investors, then it is worthwhile. Just as everyone deserves clean water, sanitation, and electricity, everyone deserves access to financial infrastructure.

However on any given day, in any given place, the immediate business interests of the lender conflict with the agency of the borrower. As laid out in chapter 5, business imperatives have driven the microfinance industry toward inflexible services that put the banker's responsibilities on clients. The poorer the clients, the greater the pressure on costs and the greater this need to impose. To a substantial extent, this trade-off is unavoidable and worth making. Being poor means having access only to lower-quality services, which are often better than nothing. And if by doing business in ways that reduce clients' autonomy at the margin, MFIs grow to make loans available to more people when they need them, the net benefit for freedom may well be positive.

Fortunately, the short-term trade-off between the lender's bottom line and the client's freedom is not an iron law. In fact, MFIs have found many ways to dodge the trade-off—for example, by making loan repayment terms more flexible and taking savings. Mobile phones, smart cards, and other technologies are opening up radical new possibilities in this regard by cutting the cost of individualized service and giving financial institutions better data about clients. In Kenya for example, the phone company behind the M-PESA money transfer service has teamed up with the country's leading MFI, Equity Bank, to provide savings accounts and loans. For loans, computers score applicants based on their cash flow history. That judgment obviates the need for traditional group arrangements and peer pressure.[93]

93. David Roodman, "Glimpsing the Future in Kenya," *Microfinance Open Book Blog*, May 21, 2010 (j.mp/9Qm8Bm).

The practical message of this chapter's analysis is to embrace microfinance as fundamentally freedom enhancing while recognizing its potential to restrict freedom and working to maximize its positive potential. Ironically, that means deemphasizing to the extent practical the very model that made the movement so successful. The stripped-down South Asian solidarity group loan appears least intrinsically empowering. Social entrepreneurs and investors should thank the microcredit pioneers for building a global movement to bring financial services to the poor—and live up to the spirit of that movement by experimenting with and scaling up alternatives.

eight

Development as Industry Building

Are not all these distinctly useful services? Is not the country the richer, the happier, the better endowed with producing power for them? Unquestionably banks of this class, which will neither give nor take anything for nothing, which scrutinise their member-customers with a keen, selfish, discerning eye, which think nothing of educating, of elevating the poor, which apply only the hard, cold principle of purely economic co-operation, have rendered perfectly inestimable services to the small trading classes, the agriculturists, the working population of their countries, and have strengthened the social fabric of their nations just where strength was most needed and tells to best effect.

—HENRY WOLFF, 1896[1]

It is impossible for the large capitalist to come into direct contact with the small cultivator. The capitalist has no local knowledge of the individual, he has no agency for collecting small loans, and he could not keep millions of small accounts. There must be some intermediate organisations.

—WILLIAM GOURLAY, 1906[2]

It is far better to build the capacity of the financial system than to provide a substitute for its inadequacies.

—ELISABETH RHYNE, 1994[3]

When I think of vaccination in developing countries, I see a baby getting a shot. I hardly see the nurse who gives the shot, much less the health ministry she works for. When I think of the provision of clean water, I see a mother working a hand pump to fill a bucket. I do not see the nonprofit that drilled the well.

1. Wolff (1896), 44–45.
2. Gourlay (1906), 217.
3. Rhyne (1994), 106.

When I think of the delivery of financial services to poor people, I see a cluster of women in colorful saris seated on the ground, gathered to do their weekly financial business. But I also see a young man, the loan officer in Western clothes who is the nucleus of the gathering. And I wonder whom he works for: perhaps the Grameen Bank in Bangladesh? CASHPOR in India? The institution enters the image.

There is no Grameen Bank of vaccination. One does not hear of organizations sprouting like sunflowers in the world of clean water supply, hiring thousands and serving millions, turning a profit and wooing investors. Yet one does in microfinance. Stuart Rutherford observed that "most poor Bangladeshis now have routine access to a basic banking service that is often more reliable than the educational and health services that they commonly encounter. Nowhere else in the world has this yet happened."[4]

More than any other domain of support for the global poor, microfinance comprises spectacular indigenous institutions. At the end of 2009, thirteen microfinance institutions (MFIs) belonged to the million-borrower club and eight had a million or more voluntary savings accounts. And though self-sufficient today, many once relied on outside support. Money now flows into MFIs through a variety of channels: dedicated investment funds, commercial bank loans, issuances of bonds and securitized microcredit loans, and initial public offerings (IPOs) of stock. The majority of the flows are public money, but the private share has risen steadily.

So distinctive is microfinance's transition from charity to industry that some observers have argued that success in microfinance should be defined as success in building organizations and industries.[5] They are not purists: they do not argue that this is all that matters. The perspectives in the previous two chapters, which center on reducing poverty and expanding freedom, matter too. But as we have seen, those measuring sticks are deceptively hard to apply to microfinance and so far have produced fragmentary, ambiguous, and muted results. Meanwhile, it seems inherently good to cultivate self-sufficient, customer-oriented, domestically owned organizations serving poor people. So often foreign aid fails precisely because local people do not take ownership of whatever intervention is tried. Absent decisive evidence that microfinance is harming its clients on average, microfinance supporters should aim for and judge themselves against the goal of birthing MFIs that thrive independent of aid.

---

4. Rutherford (2009b), 191.

5. For example, Rhyne (1994).

This point of view can be rooted in ideas as established as Amartya Sen's definition of development as freedom. Joseph Schumpeter was an Austrian-born economist who moved to the United States in 1932 to escape Nazism, then taught at Harvard for his last 18 years. In 1911, in his late twenties, Schumpeter published his *Theorie der wirtschaftlichen Entwicklung*. When translated into English in 1934, it gained the title *The Theory of Economic Development*.[6] *Entwicklung* might better have been translated as "evolution" instead of "development" to convey the original German sense of continual, internally driven change.[7] For Schumpeter, who lived in a time of accelerating industrialization, the interesting question in economics was not why prices settle at levels that balance supply and demand, but why the economic balance was constantly disrupted by new technologies, firms, and trade patterns. The ambient metaphor for the paradigm of equilibration, the farmers' market, was a terrible model for the economic churning he witnessed. Schumpeter concluded that the heroes of economic evolution and the objects of greatest scientific interest were entrepreneurs. They were agents of creative destruction, finding new ways to make valuable things: people like Henry Ford—and Muhammad Yunus.

In fact, for Schumpeter, entrepreneurs did not need to be individuals. Organizations, too, were entrepreneurial if they developed and spread "new combinations of the means of production."[8] In the Schumpeterian view, then, the arrival of self-sufficient MFIs, such as BancoSol in Bolivia, Equity Bank in Kenya, and Bank Rakyat Indonesia (BRI), *is* economic development, full stop.

The success of the microfinance movement in building dynamic institutions and industries is the brightest spot in this book's assessment. Accepting this success, the practical question, just as with conventional finance, is how to limit the damaging side of microfinance and help it realize its potential to deliver freedom-enhancing services to billions of people. Like most financial industries, microfinance is prone to mania. But just as it would be a step backward to ban the mortgage industry on account of its faults, so would it be to shut down microfinance. How can we assure that creative destruction is more creative than destructive? Metaphors from ecology inspire some broad answers. A species enriches its ecosystem when its natural growth is roughly checked by constraints and its linkages to other species are multiple: predation, competition for food, symbiosis, and so on. Likewise, MFIs enrich the

6. Schumpeter (1934).
7. "Evolutionary Economics" (wikipedia.org/wiki/evolutionary_economics [January 8, 2010]).
8. Schumpeter (1934), 74–75.

economic fabric most when their growth is checked within certain rough limits and they provide multiple services, for example taking savings as well as making loans. But pouring millions into microfinance can cause microcredit disbursements to grow dangerously fast and discourage lenders from taking savings. Mythologizing microfinance, by attracting large investment flows, has sometimes undermined true success.

Learning from Professor Schumpeter

"Development" in English signifies both outcome and process. Outcome has been drilled into many minds by the Amartya Sen–inspired Human Development Index, which scores each country on the income, health, and education of its populace. But process is truer to the word, which, like "evolve," comes from the Latin *volvere*, "to roll." Chapter 6, with its focus on measurable impacts, worked under the outcome definition. Chapter 7 blended the two conceptions, taking freedom as both end and means. This chapter hews to the process sense of the word, and more concretely than in Sen's broad reasoning. My starting point is recognizing that through the process of industrialization, certain societies have become rich over the last few centuries, not merely by enhancing various mutually reinforcing freedoms, but by enduring long processes of economic churning in which new ways of making things continually displace old.

One practical question that drives this book is how much good can be done by investing in microfinance, whether with $25 or $25 million. Judging success relative to the Schumpeterian reference point is fairly easy: investors and advisers have made microfinance what it is today. But whether such success improves the lives of poor people is less certain. Making that link as best we can requires a broad understanding of the process of national economic development and the role of finance within it.

In the history of economics, Schumpeter is the leading proponent of the view that development is an evolutionary process fueled by finance. Now, his theory is incomplete: even today, why certain countries begin industrializing at certain times is not fully understood.[9] But he did observe correctly that when economic evolution is under way, the rise of new technologies is often associated with the rise of new corporations—makers of steel, software, and so on. "It is not the owner of stage-coaches who builds railways."[10]

---

9. Commission on Growth and Development (2008), 33.

10. Schumpeter (1934), 66.

To use yet another word from that Latin root, development is a series of revolutions, brought about by the continual birthing of new institutions. In fact, these new institutions need not be corporations. Nonprofits, such as the Red Cross, and institutions of governance, such as the British Parliament, also arise to put their stamp on society. They produce new things that people value or old things in new ways. A society that ceases to nurture such institutional revolutions ceases to develop. To describe the process of renewal in his 1942 book, *Capitalism, Socialism and Democracy*, Schumpeter popularized the term "creative destruction":

> The history of the productive apparatus of a typical farm, from the beginnings of the rationalization of crop rotation, plowing and fattening to the mechanized thing of today—linking up with elevators and railroads—is a history of revolutions. So is the history of the productive apparatus of the iron and steel industry from the charcoal furnace to our own type of furnace, or the history of the apparatus of power production from the overshot water wheel to the modern power plant, or the history of transportation from the mailcoach to the airplane. The opening up of new markets, foreign or domestic, and the organizational development from the craft shop and factory to such concerns as U.S. Steel illustrate the same process of industrial mutation—if I may use that biological term—that incessantly revolutionizes the economic structure from within, incessantly destroying the old one, incessantly creating a new one. This process of Creative Destruction is the essential fact about capitalism.[11]

In the earlier *Theorie der wirtschaftlichen Entwicklung*, Schumpeter laid the groundwork for the idea of creative destruction by describing an imaginary economy called the "circular flow." I imagine it as a seaside town in medieval Italy, with winding, stone-paved streets. In the circular flow, little changes. The farmer sells to the butcher, who sells to the baker, who sells to the candlestick maker, who sells to the farmer. Income and expenditure course in predictable ways, day to day, year to year. Methods of production remain static. Credit is useful but inessential. Schumpeter knew that no economy is completely static, but he used the circular flow as an artifice. It lined up with a paradigm he wanted to revolt against: the iconic graphs of supply and demand that Alfred Marshall, the nineteenth-century dean of economics, had popularized.

11. Schumpeter (1976 [1942]), 83.

The important question, Schumpeter wrote, is not what makes this equilibrium, but what breaks it: "Carrying out a new plan and acting according to a customary one are things as different as making a road and walking along it."[12] How do economies change? Where do Model Ts and microcredit come from? His answer: the essential agent is not the scientist nor the inventor but the entrepreneur, the one who strikes out to combine labor and materials in novel ways and so reroute the circular flow. "Development in our sense is then defined as the carrying out of new combinations," he wrote.[13] Profits exist only to reward such entrepreneurship.

The people and organizations whose stories were told in chapter 4 are Schumpeterian heroes—the Okas in Indonesia, Yunus in Bangladesh, the creators of BancoSol in Bolivia. They did not invent joint liability and mass production of financial services for the poor any more than Henry Ford invented the automobile. But through luck, vision, persistence, ingenuity, and trial and error, they made small economic revolutions. They brought new possibilities to poor customers. They created jobs. They were copied. In response to competition, they innovated again. They enriched the institutional fabric of their nations, creating new possibilities for thousands of people as employees and millions as customers. In this sense, their contribution to development is incontrovertible. This praise may seem hollow because it does not assert that microfinance is reducing poverty or even expanding clients' freedom. But consider that replicating the success of microfinance institutions in a thousand other lines of business, creating dynamic industries in everything from soap to software, would make a country rich. Except for oil fields, nothing else ever has.

Interestingly from the point of view of a book about microfinance, Schumpeter saw a special role for finance. Development could take place within the business of financial services, but far more importantly, economic development occurred because of financial services. Credit is not merely a useful thing to sell to people, like food and shirts. It is the lifeblood of *entwicklung*: to fashion economic novelties, entrepreneurs need purchasing power with which to hire workers and obtain materials. One of the more mind-boggling everyday facts in economics is that banks create money (but not wealth) out of thin air. You put your money in a savings account and it is still yours. The bank hands most of it to a borrower, who can spend it: one dollar becomes two. If the borrower invests the money in successful economic activities,

12. Schumpeter (1934), 85.
13. Schumpeter (1934), 66.

then the growth in money is matched by growth in wealth produced. (Otherwise, inflation may result, as an expanded money supply chases the same amount of goods and services.) Without the money created through credit, Schumpeter submits, the entrepreneur could not obtain purchasing power to outbid the traditional employers of capital and labor and disrupt economic patterns. Under socialism, government planners could substitute for this mechanism through command and control, and perhaps guide development more effectively. But in the capitalist system, the hero behind the hero is the banker:

> The banker . . . is not so much primarily a middleman in the commodity "purchasing power" as a producer of this commodity. . . . He has himself become the capitalist par excellence. He stands between those who wish to form new combinations and the possessors of productive means. He is essentially a phenomenon of development, though only when no central authority directs the social process. He makes possible the carrying out of new combinations, authorises people, in the name of society as it were, to form them. He is the ephor of the exchange economy.[14]

Schumpeter overreached somewhat. Sometimes innovative companies are launched with savings rather than credit. And while economic development may be impossible without finance, it would be equally impossible without many other things, such as scientific advance, rule of law, and a healthy environment. A play with the banker in the leading role is a pallid allegory for the extraordinary processes of technological change of the last few centuries. Perhaps this is why Nobel-winning economist Robert Solow once remarked, "Schumpeter is a sort of patron saint in this field. I may be alone in thinking that he should be treated like a patron saint: paraded around one day each year and more or less ignored the rest of the time."[15] But the core idea seems right: significant innovation requires people to invest effort before reaping returns, and that takes finance. The financial industry is both a locus and a source of economic development.

Is microfinance worthy of the exalted status of hero behind the hero of capitalism? Probably not. If you leaf again through chapter 2, I think you'll see that financial services for the poor do not disrupt the circular flow of a national economy as much as smooth it. Perhaps when reading Schumpeter's

---

14. Schumpeter (1934), 74. The ephors of ancient Sparta were elected magistrates of the king.
15. Solow (1994), 52.

depiction of the circular flow, I should have imagined a slum in Peru instead of a town in medieval Italy. To the extent that takers of tiny loans invest in businesses, they largely do so in low-tech subsistence activities, such as retail. They rarely hire or innovate. Yunus may be a Schumpeterian hero, but he is wrong as a practical matter to see himself in his clients.[16] Microfinance flows only in the capillaries of the body economic.

A Burgeoning Industry

If the real Schumpeterian success story is about the financial institutions rather than the clients, then finance *for* microfinance *is* an example of the transformative power of credit. Those who invest in microfinance are central to its successes and failures, in enriching and disrupting the institutional fabric of nations. As a result, in the by-the-numbers review of the microfinance industry that follows, MFIs and investors are both prominent.

Microfinance Institutions

No doubt about it: the microfinance movement has built some big institutions. The twenty largest microcreditors with data on the Microfinance Information eXchange are shown in table 8-1, going by number of loans. They break roughly into three groups. Clustered at the top are large, established MFIs in Bangladesh and Indonesia whose days of fast expansion are over. (Indeed, ASA and BRAC pulled back in 2009.) Next down are the recent hyper-growers of India, led by SKS. Filling out the list are big MFIs in Africa and Latin America.

The top twenty exhibit a variety of institutional forms. The Grameen Bank and Caja Popular Mexicana, a credit union, are owned primarily or solely by their members. BRI was government owned when it entered microfinance and has since sold a minority of its shares to investors. ASA and BRAC are nonprofits. Notably, fifteen are owned by non-member investors, suggesting that outside finance is the surest way to scale.

Table 8-2 shows the top twenty on voluntary microsavings accounts. BRI looms over all, with more than 21 million accounts. The Bangladeshi big three again join BRI near the top. Below them appear microfinance institutions from many countries and of many legal structures. Notably absent are

---

16. Yunus (2004), 207: "I believe that all human beings are potential entrepreneurs. Some of us get the opportunity to express this talent, but many of us never get the chance because we were made to imagine that an entrepreneur is someone enormously gifted and different from ourselves."

Table 8-1. *Number of Borrowers and Growth Rates, Twenty Largest Lenders of 2009*

Name	Country	Ownership	Borrowers (thousand)	Average growth/ year (%)
Grameen Bank	Bangladesh	Members, government	6,430	12
BRAC	Bangladesh	Nonprofit	6,241	9
SKS	India	Investors	5,795	139
Bank Rakyat Indonesia	Indonesia	Investors, government	4,461	9
ASA	Bangladesh	Nonprofit	4,000	8
Spandana	India	Investors	3,663	57
SHARE Microfin	India	Investors	2,357	45
Bandhan	India	Investors	2,301	125
Compartamos	Mexico	Investors	1,503	37
AML	India	Investors	1,340	60
Financiera Independencia	Mexico	Investors	1,236	35
SKDRDP	India	Investors	1,226	60
BASIX	India	Investors	1,114	65
BCSC	Colombia	Investors	976	19
Equitas	India	Investors	889	438
Capitec Bank	South Africa	Investors	802	26
Caja Popular Mexicana	Mexico	Members	786	7
Grama Vidiyal	India	Investors	772	69
Equity Bank	Kenya	Investors	716	65
ACSI	Ethiopia	Investors	680	14

Source: Author's calculations, based on MIX Market, "Trends for Microfinance Institutions" (j.mp/6bjcLM [March 15, 2011]).

Note: Excludes Postal Savings Bank of China and Vietnam Bank for Social Policies because they do not emphasize financial self-sufficiency. Growth rates taken over up to five years, subject to data availability. Bank Rakyat Indonesia figure is for 2008.

the big Indian MFIs, which are barred from taking savings.[17] Most savings-taking MFIs are regulated to assure that savers' money is handled with care. The exceptions are in Bangladesh and Sri Lanka—though with recent government moves to take control of Grameen, *laissez-faire* may be coming to an end in Bangladesh.

Arguably a truer sign of Schumpeterian transformation than the growth of institutions is the arrival of industries populated in each country by competing players. We saw instances near the end of chapter 5 where competition

17. MIX Market, "Trends for Microfinance Institutions" (j.mp/4RMKJj [January 15, 2010]).

Table 8-2. *Number of Voluntary Savings Accounts, Twenty Largest Account Providers, 2009*

Name	Country	Ownership	Regulated?	Accounts (thousands)
Bank Rakyat Indonesia	Indonesia	Investors, government	Yes	21,229
Grameen Bank	Bangladesh	Members	No	7,970[a]
ASA	Bangladesh	Nonprofit	No	6,613[a]
BRAC	Bangladesh	Nonprofit	No	5,447
Equity Bank	Kenya	Investors	Yes	4,038
Caja Popular Mexicana	Mexico	Members	Yes	3,514
Khan Bank	Mongolia	Investors	Yes	2,500
Capitec Bank	South Africa	Investors	Yes	1,297[b]
UNACOOPEC	Côte d'Ivoire	Members	Yes	925
Crediscotia	Peru	Investors	Yes	808[a]
BURO	Bangladesh	Nonprofit	No	747
FECECAM	Benin	Members	Yes	708
RCPB	Burkina Faso	Members	Yes	673
ACSI	Ethiopia	Investors	Yes	612
CMS	Senegal	Members	Yes	607
ACLEDA	Cambodia	Investors	Yes	586
PRODEM	Bolivia	Investors	Yes	568
WDB	Sri Lanka	Investors	Yes	555
BancoEstado	Chile	Government	Yes	504
Sabaragamuwa	Sri Lanka	Investors	No	448

Source: Author's calculations, based on MIX Market, "Trends for Microfinance Institutions" (j.mp/6bjcLM [March 15, 2011]).

Notes: Excludes the Banco Caja Social Colombia and the Kenya Post Office Savings Bank as institutions that do not emphasize financial self-sufficiency.

a. Includes an unknown number of involuntary accounts, required as part of borrowing. Number of depositors rather than accounts.

b. Number of depositors rather than accounts.

has pressed MFIs to cut costs, improve and expand services, and even lower interest rates. One study found that heightened competition from conventional banks moving downmarket into microfinance led to dedicated MFIs pushing farther downward, too.[18] Within the microfinance industry, competition does appear to be increasing in most countries. One standard measure of industry concentration, often used in anti-trust enforcement, is the Herfindahl-Hirschman index. As in the statistics I presented at the beginning

18. Cull, Demirgüç-Kunt, and Morduch (2009).

Figure 8-1. *Concentration of Microcredit Market Based on Numbers of Borrowers, Selected Countries with Substantial Industries and Necessary Data Available*

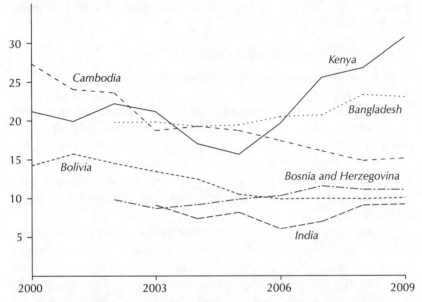

Average market share of a client's lender (%)

Source: Calculations by author and Scott Gaul of the Microfinance Information eXchange using underlying data from MIX Market, "Trends for Microfinance Institutions" (j.mp/6bjcLM [January 15, 2010]).

of chapter 5, it is the average market share of a borrower's lender. So if 100 people borrow from Lender A, 100 from B, and 200 from C, then half the loans come from lenders with a 25 percent market share (A and B) and half from one with 50 percent share (Lender C), for an overall average of 37.5 percent. The index reaches 100 percent under monopoly and approaches 0 with a swarm of tiny firms. In most countries with substantial microfinance industries and the necessary data available, the index is below 25 percent, which is equivalent to having at least four big institutions of equal size (see figure 8-1).[19] The major exception in the figure is Kenya, where Equity Bank has grown explosively and without serious rival.

Microfinance being a business, its measure also ought to be taken in financial terms—amounts of money lent as distinct from number of loans

19. For more details and caveats, see David Roodman, "Should Industry Concentration Cause Consternation?" *Microfinance Open Book Blog*, January 15, 2010 (j.mp/5GuheZ).

made. Here, too, the historical trend is upward. A Geneva-based company called Symbiotics publishes the most detailed data on investible MFIs. Total microloans outstanding of the "SYM 50" group of MFIs climbed steadily from about $1.5 billion at the end of 2005, paused around $4.5 billion after global credit markets froze in late 2008, and then climbed to $5.4 billion by the end of 2010.[20]

Linking Microfinance to Capital Markets

Modern microfinance began in the nonprofit world, seemingly the antithesis of capitalism. But after Muhammad Yunus and the Grameen Project proved in the early 1980s that microcredit could reach thousands in short order, the movement felt its way toward sustained, commercial-style expansion. The journey to commercial maturity involved three major steps: turning nonprofit institutions into for-profits, building an ecosystem of financial intermediaries to channel capital to them through tailored deals, and issuing standardized securities such as bonds and shares of stock for trading in public markets.

Transforming Institutions from Nonprofit to For-Profit. To open branches, hire staff, and expand client rolls at a steady pace, most MFIs need money up front. They can borrow it, but if they remain nonprofit, they tend to run into two limits. The first has to do with leverage. If a nonprofit with $1 million in cash reserves borrows another million from an aid agency and lends it to poor families, a 10 percent loss on those loans will cost $100,000, a manageable 10 percent of the $1 million reserve. If it borrows and on-lends $10 million, a 10 percent loss will spell bankruptcy. That precious $1 million reserve is the nonprofit's equity, and a ten-to-one debt-equity ratio is dangerously high.

The other limit nonprofits may hit is the willingness of outside investors to lend to institutions subject to little government supervision. Government oversight of banks is meant to prevent overextended credit operations, protect depositors' savings, and guarantee timely and accurate disclosure of the bank's financial situation. When the rules are rickety, as they often are for nonprofit financial institutions, investors may stay away.

Both limits have compelled some nonprofit MFIs to transform into regulated, for-profit financial institutions. For-profits can add to their equity by selling shares to outside investors. These shares entitle investors to a say in management and a fraction of earnings. For MFIs, equity off-loads risk onto investors who are better able to absorb it.

---

20. For the latest figures, see www.syminvest.com.

The first transformation of a nonprofit MFI into a for-profit took place in Bolivia in 1992. Five years before, the U.S. Agency for International Development (USAID) and Acción International had helped Bolivian business leaders and philanthropists found Prodem, a nonprofit solidarity group lender. Elisabeth Rhyne of Acción described what throttled Prodem's growth:

> Prodem had some access to commercial loans from banks, but these were too limited to maintain its desired rate of expansion. In 1991 . . . it had a total of $710,000 in commercial loans [, which] covered less than one-third of Prodem's total funding requirement. That year Prodem issued about $2 million in loans each month, expanding its portfolio from $2.4 million to $4.6 million. . . . Acción International's Bridge Fund, a guarantee mechanism set up with funding from USAID, Ford Foundation, and others, guaranteed repayment of [Prodem's loans from banks]. Without guarantees, Prodem's "collateral" for a loan from a bank was its own loan portfolio, which consisted of unsecured loans that bankers and banking authorities considered too risky to use as security. Moreover, no bank wanted to face the unpleasant possibility of chasing down an NGO whose aim was to lend to the poor and whose owners were not liable for the organization's assets. Unless Prodem were to enter the financial markets as a full-fledged member, it could not hope to gain access to the amounts of finance it would need.[21]

The idea for transforming Prodem into a commercial bank for the poor was a businessman's. Canadian Martin Connell came into his fortune as a third-generation chief executive of his family's mining company and had engaged with friends in venture capitalism. He empathized with microentrepreneurs he met on travels in poor countries. In 1983 he created the Calmeadow Foundation, and, after an encounter with Acción's Jeffrey Ashe, who pioneered solidarity-group lending in Latin America, Connell found a mission in a commercial vision of microfinance.[22] He became involved with Prodem and helped persuade its board members and other backers to take the leap to for-profit status.

After several years of planning and studying Bolivian law, Prodem transformed into BancoSol, a for-profit bank. Formally, Prodem gave its loan portfolio to the new legal entity BancoSol. In return, Prodem got a large ownership stake in the for-profit microbank.[23]

21. Rhyne (2001), 107.

22. Calmeadow Foundation (2005), 17–18.

23. Prodem lived on as a nonprofit lender specializing in rural areas and then transformed a second time, into the for-profit Prodem FFP.

Initially, BancoSol raised equity capital from mission-driven institutions, including Calmeadow, Acción, and the Inter-American Investment Corporation, an arm of the Washington, D.C.–based Inter-American Development Bank. In their willingness to take risks that profit-oriented investors still shunned, these institutions provided a stepping-stone to commercialization. Since then, other MFIs have grown and transformed in the same way, including Compartamos and some Indian microlenders in table 8-1.

The transformation of nonprofits may have been necessary historically as the pioneers felt their way to capitalism, but perhaps today's MFI founders need not repeat history. If the destination is profit-making, why not just go there directly? That is the philosophy of the German ProCredit Group. Today ProCredit owns banks in twenty-one countries. One of the first began in Bolivia under the name ProCrédito, as recounted in chapter 4, just when Prodem was transforming into BancoSol. ProCrédito, too, began as a nonprofit but transformed in just three years. Most newer ProCredit banks, from Armenia to the Democratic Republic of Congo, have simply started as for-profit financial institutions.[24]

The Microfinance Investment Bankers. True to Schumpeter's thinking, another sign of the commercialization of microfinance is the increasingly diverse financial ecosystem supplying it with finance. Here, too, the history begins in Bolivia—and yet traces its inspiration back much farther. Connell recounts:

> The board meeting of BancoSol in early 1993 . . . was a positive one. The bank was showing healthy growth in assets and profits, and the feeling coming out of the meeting was energizing and optimistic. Considering that BancoSol had only been open for a little over a year, the small group of board members at the courtyard bar outside the meeting room had reason for a moment of self-congratulation. . . . What next, we mused?
>
> It was Ernst Brugger who then tossed in his vision of an investment fund that would help create more BancoSols. . . . Our response was electric and instantaneous—we must do it![25]

Brugger was a Swiss who ran FUNDES, a foundation focused on Latin America created by the early visionary of environmentally sustainable business, Stephan Schmidheiny. Today Brugger chairs BlueOrchard, the leading specialist microfinance investment company. Looking back on those early

24. ProCredit Holding (2011).
25. Calmeadow Foundation (2006), 1.

days, Brugger described his inspiration: "It seemed like a good time for that, like Europe in the 19th century, when the *sparkassen* were first established. I could see that these microfinance institutions were well planned, but they needed strong partners to grow."[26] As a partner, however, a microfinance investor would play a role quite different from that of the municipal governments that backed those old savings banks. Instead of guaranteeing the safety of savings, they would finance loans.

With Connell's support, the world's first microfinance investment vehicle (MIV), ProFund, opened its doors in 1995. The purpose was to demonstrate that microfinance investors could earn respectable returns and eventually get their capital back, or "exit," by receiving full repayment on loans made or selling outstanding claims to other investors. The plan was to raise funds from noncommercial institutions like those that had invested in BancoSol, purchase equity in Latin MFIs, continue for ten years, then sell all its holdings and shut down. No one knew if it would work. Each investment in an MFI was a novel and complex legal deal. ProFund's director, Alex Silva, had to pound the pavement in search of investors, rather opposite the situation today. ProFund eventually placed $23 million in fourteen MFIs. Some did lose money, especially in dollar terms. Investors in Latin America in 1995–2005 faced fierce headwinds: financial crises in Paraguay and Ecuador; political chaos in Haiti and Venezuela and Bolivia; and depreciating currencies all around that eroded returns in dollars. But enough MFIs did well to earn the fund an average 7 percent a year over the decade. The big gainers were BancoSol, Mibanco in Peru, and Compartamos.[27] The return was low for the risk, considering that a super-safe U.S. money market fund earned 4.3 percent annualized over the same time.[28] Yet it proved microfinance a serious enough play to attract investors whose risk-return calculus included a "social" bottom line.

As intended, ProFund spawned an industry. At the end of 2009, more than 100 MIVs operated, along with a handful of other funding intermediaries, including ProCredit Holding. The five biggest fund managers together had $3.7 billion in assets and the entire class held $8 billion, nearly 350 times ProFund's capital (see table 8-3). Some MIVs, such as ProFund's younger sister AfriCap, specialize in one region, while others are global. Some stick to debt, many favor equity, and some do both. Most chase the top-tier MFIs

---

26. Calmeadow Foundation (2006), 7.

27. Calmeadow Foundation (2006); Silva (2005).

28. Based on 1995–2004 returns from the Vanguard Group; see Vanguard, "Vanguard Prime Money Market Fund Institutional Shares" (j.mp/9ltfO6 [February 15, 2010]).

Table 8-3. *Top Microfinance Asset Managers, End-2009*

Asset manager	Assets (million $)
Oppenheim Asset Management (for European Fund for Southeast Europe)	907
BlueOrchard	866
Credit Suisse	801
Oikocredit	770
SNS Asset Management	375
Total, top five	3,719
Industry total (approximate)	8,000

Source: Reille and others (2011).

that can absorb capital most readily. Others invest in less-established, dicier MFIs, typically sharing ProFund's desire to help young ones mature.

As a group, MIVs appear to be doing roughly as well as ProFund did. The Symbiotics "SMX" index, which tracks the performance of a group of MIVs mostly investing in debt, returned 34.1 percent over 2004–10, equivalent to 4.3 percent a year with compounding. That is 2.4 percentage points above the U.S. dollar money market return during the period, a bit less than ProFund's margin of 3.7 points. Earnings in terms of the euro were lower because it climbed against the dollar (see figure 8-2). Performance was poor in 2009–10; it remains to be seen whether this was a transient consequence of the global financial crisis or the arrival of a new era in which a capital glut depresses earnings.[29]

Issuing Securities. The final step to the capital markets has been for MFIs to issue securities, transferable promises to pay out money to the holder under specified conditions. These have been of two main kinds. One is modern and complex, yet familiar for its role in creating housing bubbles: the securitized loan. In their details, loan securitizations are 100 times more intricate than I could convey in a paragraph. At base, MFIs sell microloans on their books—IOUs of poor people—to investors. The MFIs get cash now and the investors get future cash flow. The MFIs continue to collect debt service on those bundled loans, keep much of it to cover costs, and pass the remainder to investors. Meanwhile, having increased their reserves, MFIs are free to make more loans—and sell those, too, in a continuing cycle. In the hands of financial engineers, loan-backed securities can take many forms.

29. For the latest figures, see www.syminvest.com.

Figure 8-2. *Performance of Symbiotics Microfinance Index in Dollar Terms, 2004–10*

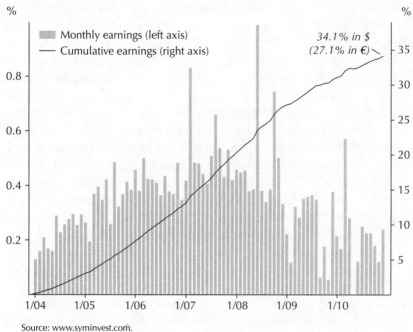

Source: www.syminvest.com.

Repayment flows can be split into principle and interest or junior and senior tranches, the junior ones taking the hit first from partial defaults. Another wrinkle: donor agencies have often guaranteed some or all of the promised payments in order to nurture such innovation and support microfinance.

The first microfinance securitizations took place in 2006. In May of that year, ProCredit Bank Bulgaria sold €48 million of its loans to institutional investors. A few months later BRAC created a structure through which it is selling $180 million in loans over six years. They are denominated in Bangladesh's currency, the taka, so foreign investors rather than BRAC bear the risk that the MFI's home currency will lose value.[30] Securitizations have become most popular in India.

The guarantors and investors in microcredit securitizations are taking on more risk than it would seem at first. Daniel Rozas, a microfinance industry analyst, has shown that when an MFI goes bankrupt, its loan portfolio tends to disintegrate. People stop repaying current loans if they think it won't help

30. Swanson (2008).

them get access to future ones, as it wouldn't if the MFI goes defunct.[31] Contrast that with mainstream finance, where a bank can collapse yet sell off its loans at 100 cents on the dollar. That happened to me once, in a way: in the bubbly days of the U.S. mortgage market, a hot Internet-based lender called DeepGreen gave me a home equity line of credit with a great interest rate—maybe too great because not long after the company went under. It sold my loan, at a price that I assume reflected my good credit history and adequate collateral, to PNC Bank. I had never met PNC before but kept paying the interest so as to keep my home. But imagine how quizzically a Peruvian slum dweller would gaze upon a loan officer from Microcreditor B who showed up at the door asking for the payments on her loan from Microcreditor A. Microcredit's "collateral" cannot be repossessed. It is embedded in relationships built over time among borrowers and loan officers. Thus microcredit portfolios are like sand castles: they can be large and elaborate, but without constant maintenance, they can quickly fall apart. And they are very hard to transport from lender to lender. In the language of finance, securitized microcredit loans contain equity risk because their value remains tied to that of the issuer.

The class of microfinance security is traditional: bonds and stocks. One important, early issuance in this category came in 2004 when Compartamos borrowed 500 million Mexican pesos by selling bonds. Because of doubts about whether investors would risk lending to a young business in a commercially unproven industry, the World Bank's International Finance Corporation (IFC) partially guaranteed Compartamos's payments to bondholders.[32] Five years later, the Mexican MFI had earned enough investor confidence to issue 1.5 billion pesos in bonds without an IFC assist.[33]

Stock issuances have occurred less often, served different ends, and generated more controversy. To date, flotations have mostly not raised capital for MFIs.[34] Rather, they have allowed existing owners to exit, selling what was once their private equity to the public, often at great profit. In 2003, the century-old, government-owned BRI became the first publicly traded MFI after the government sold 30 percent of its stake on the national stock

31. Rozas (2009). See also Christen, Lyman, and Rosenberg (2003), 27.

32. Citigroup, "Citigroup/Banamex Leads Financiera Compartamos Bond Issue in Mexico with a Partial IFC Credit Guarantee; Standard & Poor's, Fitch Assign Investment-Grade Country Rating," press release, August 2, 2004 (j.mp/oxJ5gz).

33. CGAP, "Deal of the Month: Compartamos Diversifies Its Funding (August 2009)," November 16, 2009 (j.mp/qA60a0).

34. CGAP (2009a), 10.

exchange.[35] The IPO of Kenya's Equity Bank in 2006 arguably matters more historically because it was the first debut of a young modern-wave MFI on a public stock market. For AfriCap, the African ProFund equivalent, the IPO and subsequent run-up turned $1.6 million into $32 million.[36]

Two other IPOs have strained the microfinance movement like nothing else in its history. The first came in 2007: Compartamos went public. Acción, the IFC, and other early investors sold 30 percent of the company, together earning $450 million for stakes that had cost $6 million.[37] The founding co-CEOs of Compartamos became the "first microfinance millionaires," in the words of Morgan Stanley's Ian Callaghan.[38] The fortunes made by charging the poor 100 percent interest reignited ancient debates over usury, as noted in chapter 7. Compartamos defended the sale as helping the microfinance industry mature and grow: its profits would attract competition in Mexico.[39] Acción said that it wanted to exit the bank in order to invest its gains ($135 million) in younger institutions in poorer places.[40]

Although the event was explosive within the international movement, it was never that controversial within Mexico, and the country's microcredit industry continues to grow apace. In contrast, the 2010 IPO of SKS in India, also introduced in chapter 7, triggered a domestic backlash that has brought the industry to its knees there. That flotation earned founder Vikram Akula and famed venture capitalist Vinod Khosla more than $80 million each, at least at peak stock prices.[41] No one had ever made anything close to such sums by banking the world's poor. Investors paid so dearly for the shares because of SKS's track record of rapid growth, its streamlined operating methods, and the vast Indian market still untapped. But on October 14, 2010, amid a media drumbeat about microcredit-induced suicides, the government of Andhra Pradesh ambushed the industry with a law that essentially shut it down in the state. Andhra Pradesh was India's microcredit hotbed, with 6.2 million of the country's 29 million microloans and $1.2 billion of $3.9 billion in outstanding amounts.[42] The MFIs, their creditors, and their investors will

35. BRI, "History," February 2, 2010 (j.mp/c1BkOg).

36. Diouf (2010), 1; "Investor Reaps Sh2.5b from Sale of Equity Bank Shares," *70.71 Group Blog,* January 11, 2009 (j.mp/d9JW2s), using exchange rate of 77.47 Ksh/$ from XE, "KES Rate Table," January 8, 2009 (j.mp/cS2ytf).

37. Rosenberg (2007).

38. Ian Callaghan, "Let Me In!" *Forbes,* December 20, 2007 (j.mp/qQIsLj).

39. Danel and Labarthe (2008).

40. Rhyne (2010), 4.

41. Chen and others (2010), 8, 15.

42. Srinivasan (2010a), 49.

Table 8-4. *Cross-Border Financing for Microfinance, by Destination, 2009*

Region	Cumulative total, end-2009		Net new commitments, 2009	
	(million $)	*(% of total)*	*(million $)*	*(% of total)*
East Asia & Pacific	1,546	7	230	8
Eastern Europe & Central Asia	6,188	29	1,099	37
Latin America & Caribbean	4,724	22	743	25
Middle East & North Africa	787	4	29	1
South Asia	4,064	19	33	1
Sub-Saharan Africa	2,544	12	441	15
Multiregion	1,461	7	381	13
Total	21,313	100	2,956	100

Source: CGAP (2010b).
Notes: "Net new commitments" include exchange rate effects. For donors, "commitments" are funds committed to active microfinance projects, whether or not disbursed, whenever disbursed. Outstanding funds to projects now considered inactive are not counted. For investors, "commitments" include all funds placed. Loans are counted in full until repaid in full.

probably have to write off most of that $1.2 billion. We'll come back to that story later in this chapter.

Investment Flows

As financial channels proliferated—MIVs, private equity, loan securitizations, bonds, IPOs—the funds flowing through them swelled. CGAP calculates that at the end of 2009, donors and international investors had poured at least $21.3 billion cumulatively into microfinance institutions, an increase of $3.0 billion from twelve months earlier. In dollar terms, most of the new investment went into Eastern Europe, Central Asia, and Latin America (see table 8-4).[43]

Historically, nearly all this foreign investment has come from institutions and individuals with social missions (see table 8-5). Traditional donor agencies, including USAID and Germany's Gesellschaft für Technische Zusammenarbeit, accounted for 7 percent of the cumulative end-2009 total. International agencies, including the parts of the World Bank that lend to governments, held 20 percent. Foundations and other private donors had 5 percent. "Development finance institutions," which are agencies that invest

43. CGAP (2010b).

Table 8-5. *Cross-Border Financing for Microfinance, by Source Type, 2009*

Entity	Cumulative total, end-2009 (million $)	(% of total)	Net new commitments, 2009 (million $)	(% of total)
Public entities	**14,603**	**69**	**1,443**	**49**
National aid agencies	1,585	7	–138	–5
International aid agencies lending to governments	4,166	20	–312	–11
National and international agencies investing in private sector	8,852	42	1,893	64
Private entities	**6,710**	**31**	**1,514**	**51**
Foundations and nonprofits	1,116	5	229	8
Individual and institutional investors	5,594	26	1,285	43
Total	21,313	100	2,957	100

Source: CGAP (2010b).
Notes: "Net new commitments" include exchange rate effects. For donors, "commitments" are funds committed to active microfinance projects, whether or not disbursed, whenever disbursed. Outstanding funds to projects now considered inactive are not counted. For investors, "commitments" include all funds placed. Loans are counted in full until repaid in full.

public money in the private sector, made up the largest category, at 42 percent of outstanding funds. That left just 26 percent in the hands of private investors, probably most of whom invest in pursuit of the "double bottom line" of modest profit and social betterment. They include Khosla, New Zealand billionaire Christopher Chandler, who bought a controlling stake in India's SHARE Microfin for $25 million in 2007, and Kiva, the website that lets users lend as little as $25.[44]

The numbers in table 8-5 suggest that the hand-off from public to private investors long envisioned by the proponents of commercialization is occurring. In 2009, probably for the first time, net flows from private investors exceeded those from public, in a 51–49 ratio. In fact, aid agencies, as distinct from official agencies that invest in the private sector, divested on net in

44. Legatum Ventures, "Legatum Invests over 100 Crore (Us$25 Million) for Majority Interest in Share Microfin Ltd., India's Leading Microfinance Institution," press release, May 15, 2007 (j.mp/q0NFSo); "SKS Microfinance Raises $75 Mn," *Financial Express* (India), November 10, 2008.

2009. Meanwhile, of the 51 percent private share, 43 percent came from individual and institutional investors, as distinct from charitable donors.

MFIs also raise capital from investors at home, though little is known about how much. Good numbers are available for India and deserve mention because they are large enough to be globally significant. A long-standing Indian policy of "priority-sector" lending requires domestic banks to devote 40 percent of their credit (and foreign banks 32 percent) to certain groups, such as self-employed people; certain activities, such as agriculture; or certain financial channels, including MFIs and self-help groups (SHGs).[45] The lending to microfinance has been small within the priority-sector lending landscape but large from the point of view of the microfinance industry, in which it fueled fast growth. As of March 31, 2010, loans to MFIs totaled at least 138 billion rupees ($3.1 billion). Those to SHGs were 272.66 billion rupees ($6.1 billion).[46] It is this easy access to credit that so tantalized venture capitalists. Every rupee they put into an MFI could easily leverage 5–8 rupees in bank loans.[47] All the profit from those loans went to the equity investors.

When Is Creative Destruction More Creative than Destructive?

Besides the commercialization of microfinance, I can think of only two comparable instances where philanthropy and foreign aid have helped develop a global industry and a supporting financial ecosystem in order to serve poor people: the savings bank and credit cooperative movements of the nineteenth century (see chapter 3). It seems a constant of history that the poor need financial services, are willing to pay for them, and yet are underserved by reliable institutions. Foreign aid and philanthropy have catalyzed industrial flowerings that respond to the need.

Still, especially in the wake of the debacle in Andhra Pradesh, it is impossible not to question the hot trend of microfinance. Is the commercialization of microfinance, with its promise to bring reliable services to billions, a dangerous capitalist fantasy? Is it—to use an epithet popular among British intellectuals—destructively neoliberal?[48] As with so much in microfinance, the truth is ambiguous.

45. Reserve Bank of India, "FAQs" (j.mp/iMMR05 [February 19, 2010]).

46. Srinivasan (2010a), 131, 133.

47. MIX Market, "Indicators for Microfinance Institutions," data on debt-equity ratios for Indian MFIs, 2009 (j.mp/hqzNfe [April 18, 2011]).

48. Bateman (2010).

To organize our thinking about this question, this section offers two framing ideas. Both are inspired by ecology. The first is the distinction between growth and development. The second is about the value of linking microfinance institutions to their environment in multiple ways.

Herd Mentality

Jutting out of the Bering Sea halfway between mainland Alaska and Siberia is St. Matthew Island, a 30-mile-long landscape of rolling hills, subarctic tundra, freshwater lakes, and dizzying cliffs where seabirds nest.[49] The island's isolation and harsh winters have prevented Westerners from permanently settling it. In 1944, the U.S. Coast Guard installed a radio beacon on the island as part of an advanced navigation system for pilots at air and sea called LORAN. It was the GPS of its day. Along with the equipment, nineteen cooks, medics, engineers, and other personnel were stationed on the island. For an emergency back-up food source, the Coast Guard also shipped in twenty-nine reindeer and loosed them to browse on the isle's thick mats of lichen. But World War II soon ended and the men left. The reindeer stayed behind, on what science writer Ned Rozell described as an "ungulate paradise." Over the next twenty years, the animals fattened off the land and, free of predators, multiplied into the thousands. In a famous research paper, U.S. government biologist David Klein captioned a 1957 photograph of four bulls with a comment on their health: "Note the rounded body contours and enlarged antler size."[50] Recalling an expedition to study the herd in 1963, Klein said, "We counted 6,000 of them. They were really hammering the lichens."[51]

But then the paradise became a purgatory. In Rozell's words:

[Klein] heard a startling report from men on a Coast Guard cutter who had gone ashore to hunt reindeer in August 1965—the men had seen dozens of bleached reindeer skeletons scattered over the tundra. When Klein returned in the summer of 1966, he, another biologist and a botanist found the island covered with skeletons; they counted only 42 live reindeer, no fawns, 41 females and one male with abnormal antlers that probably wasn't able to reproduce. During a few months, the reindeer population of St. Matthew had dropped by 99 percent.[52]

49. Winker and others (2002), 493.
50. Klein (1968), 356.
51. Rozell (2003).
52. Rozell (2003).

In his research paper, Klein concluded that dwindling food supply, with an assist from an extreme winter in 1963–64, doomed the herd.[53] Storms in February brought wind gusts as high as 63 miles per hour (101 kilometers per hour) and sustained wind chills below –40°F (–40°C) for days on end. The state of development of fetal skeletons, found nestled within the skeletons of their mothers, dated the die-off to that same month.[54]

Although the severe weather magnified the effect, the rise and fall of the reindeer of St. Matthew Island is a classic illustration of the idea of overshoot. In the beginning, a positive feedback loop generated fast growth: the more reindeer there were, the more fawns were born each year. Then a negative feedback loop kicked in: the more animals, the less food per animal, and the less ability to survive and reproduce. If the population somehow could have gauged and adjusted to its distance from the maximum sustainable population level—as pregnant rabbits can by reabsorbing embryos—then the herd might have coasted smoothly to that limit. The upper left of figure 8-3 shows a simulation of this ideal, marking the sustainable level as 100. The rate of increase at any point along the curve relates to two factors: current population and distance from the sustainable level of 100 ("headroom").[55] Increasing the number of fawns per litter in the simulation causes faster growth (upper right of the figure), and the population slams into, but still remains within, the ecological limit.

But on St. Matthew Island, feedback about limits arrived late. This is simulated in the diagrams by making growth at any given time depend on headroom in the past rather than the present. It turns out that when litters are small—when the growth drive is low—the feedback lag does no harm, because headroom in the recent past nearly matches headroom now. Information is accurate, and the herd still coasts to equilibrium (lower left). But if the drive for growth is high *and* information about limits is delayed, the population repeatedly overshoots and collapses (lower right). In the abstract example in the figure, even without savage blizzards, the population plunges 79 percent, from 188 to 39.

This is why ecological economists have long distinguished between growth and development. Herman Daly, eminent in the field, explains, "To *develop* means 'to expand or realize the potentialities of; to bring gradually to a fuller, greater, or better state.' When something grows it gets bigger. When something develops it gets different. The earth ecosystem develops (evolves),

53. Klein (1968).
54. Klein, Walsh, and Shulski (2009), 36–37.
55. Mathematically, absolute increase is proportional to the product of these two distances.

Figure 8-3. *How Fast Growth and Delayed Feedback about Limits Cause Overshoot*

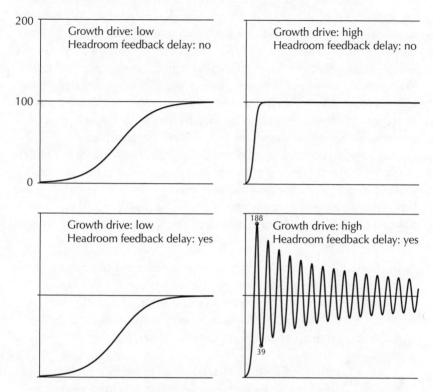

Source: All panes plot $\Delta x_t = g \frac{x_{t-1}}{100} \left(1 - \frac{x_{t-1-L}}{100}\right)$ with $x_t = 1$ for $t \le 0$, $g = 1$ for slow growth and 10 for high growth, $L = 0$ for no delay and 15 for delay.

but does not grow. Its subsystem, the economy, must eventually stop growing, but can continue to develop."[56]

Growth *can* constitute development, making it worthy of the label "healthy growth." Children should grow as they develop; those who do not have developmental problems. The growth of the mobile phone industry in poor countries also seems developmental. In that case, development first occurred within the industry as entrepreneurs solved technological and business problems, thus becoming more sophisticated about how to do their jobs. Then, by scaling up and creating new possibilities for connection, the industry brought development to society as a whole.

56. Daly (1993 [1990]), 268.

But growth can be unhealthy beyond certain bounds: think of those reindeer, the childhood obesity epidemic in the United States, and the expanding appetite for coal and oil that is causing climate change. Daly calls this uneconomic growth. "Growth for the sake of growth," declared eco-radical Edward Abbey, "is the ideology of the cancer cell."[57] In fact, what we usually refer to as economic development consists of both development and growth as Daly means the words. It involves both increasing complexity and expanding economic activity. The expansion has occurred above all in the amount of energy consumed, and while it has literally fueled much development, it is overrunning ecological bounds, making it partly uneconomic.

Daly's homily on growth and development puts microfinance in an interesting light. Microfinance certainly has grown. To what extent is it leading to development, in the sense of complexification, within the industry and beyond? After all, it is always dangerous to *push* loans. Think of microcredit as you read this quote from economist John Kenneth Galbraith on herd mentality in finance:

> In all speculative episodes there is always an element of pride in discovering what is seemingly new and greatly rewarding in the way of financial instrument or investment opportunity. The individual or institution that does so is thought to be wonderfully ahead of the mob. This insight is then confirmed as others rush to exploit their own, only slightly later vision. . . .
>
> As to new financial instruments, however, experience establishes a firm rule . . . that financial operations do not lend themselves to innovation. What is recurrently so described and celebrated is, without exception, a small variation on an established design, one that owes its distinctive character to the . . . brevity of the financial memory. . . . All financial innovation involves, in one form or another, the creation of debt secured in great or less adequacy by real assets. . . . All crises have involved debt that, in one fashion or another, has become dangerously out of scale in relation to the underlying means of payment.[58]

To connect this with the lessons of figure 8-3, a financial market overshoots when information about its "scale in relation to the underlying means of payment" is unavailable or unheeded and when its drive for growth is aggressive. Neither ingredient alone is necessarily destructive.

57. Abbey (1977), 183.
58. Galbraith (1993), 18–19.

But both have been abundant in microcredit. As for the first, the ample investment flowing into the industry has fueled fast growth. The social motivation behind this capital adds to the danger by dulling business sensibilities. And once aggressive lending starts at one MFI, it is contagious within a country. Initially conservative managers abandon caution in order to keep up with their peers. And they find that the easiest way to recruit new customers is to offer microloans to people who already have them. Such people understand how microcredit works—and might want a new loan to pay off an old one. Yet sustainable lending calls for a delicate balance of risk taking and conservatism. To maintain that balance, MFI managers need training programs for new workers, pay formulas that do not overly reward disbursement, and internal data systems for tracking portfolio health. All take time to build and refine.[59] Growth that outpaces this internal development is the growth of a weed tree. As one MFI manager in Bosnia rued, "We were focused on competing instead of building our capacity."[60]

The other crisis-inducing ingredient is a lack of robust ways to judge whether clients can handle the debts they have contracted. Multiple microcredit borrowing is fine within bounds. Out of conservatism, each microlender may impose a rigid repayment schedule and give less credit than people need and can handle. By overlapping loans from several sources, borrowers can blend the individually rigid loan schedules to meet their needs.[61] But especially when lending is growing fast, it is hard for clients to judge when credit has become too much of a good thing. The classic solution is for microlenders to share information, such as through a credit bureau. But many poor countries lack effective credit bureaus that cover poor people.

This problem is especially rampant when MFIs lend through groups. When Yunus and his students devised their form of solidarity lending, when Ashe and his staff did the same in the Dominican Republic, and when John Hatch and his associates devised village banking, their clients had no comparable alternatives. Recall from chapter 5 that group microcredit cuts costs by offloading onto clients the tasks of selecting and monitoring each other. Thus the financial health of group microcreditors depends on the judgment of their borrowers. It is unclear whether that judgment remains reliable as multiple borrowing becomes the norm. One can imagine that much as mortgages with teaser rates became common in some American

59. Roodman and Qureshi (2006).

60. Chen, Rasmussen, and Reille (2010), 10.

61. Krishnaswamy (2007), 5; Jonathan Morduch, "Debunking the Microfinance Bubble," *Financial Access Initiative* blog, August 28, 2009 (j.mp/DiplS).

communities, multiple borrowing becomes dangerously normal in a micro-credit-saturated milieu. Everyone accepts multiple borrowing for no better reason than that everyone does it.

As with banking generally, the history of microcredit is sprinkled with implosions. And as with banking generally, while all have been regrettable, none has been fatal. Bolivian microcredit experienced an early instance in 1999. As mentioned in chapter 7, years of rapid microcredit expansion had attracted an aggressive new breed of consumer lender that helped people with salaries buy goods such as televisions. Elisabeth Rhyne described the dynamic:

> Poaching clients from other institutions through the offer of larger loans has proven to be an extremely successful marketing technique in Bolivia, as elsewhere. And it has been shown repeatedly that clients are not good judges of their own debt capacity. Apparently credit is like good food: when seated at the table in front of a feast, many people eat too much and regret it later. . . . The truly unfortunate dynamic is that if over-lenders are successful at luring clients away from more responsible lenders, the responsible lenders are virtually forced to follow suit. The pressure to lend more to keep good clients is nearly as irresistible as the client's desire to borrow more. Worse, if clients begin using one loan to pay off another, the game becomes . . . "Who collects first?" In short, the sector as a whole starts to become one big Ponzi scheme.[62]

The good news is that the Bolivian microcredit industry survived the crisis, the wiser and stronger for it. One key improvement was a credit bureau. Lenders who had resisted sharing information about their clients agreed to do so in order to get a fuller picture of each borrower's debts.[63] Daly has written about the need to move from an "empty world" mentality that treats natural resources as inexhaustible to a "full world" one that accepts limits.[64] In effect, the creditors in Bolivia recognized that their ways of doing business, which were developed in an empty world, had to be adapted to the full world of a mature microcredit market. They needed better feedback about how close they were to their clients' borrowing limits. So do microcreditors in other countries.

62. Rhyne (2001), 155.

63. Campion (2001).

64. Herman E. Daly, "Economics in a Full World," *Scientific American*, September 2005, 100–07.

Connections

When does microfinance enrich the economy? When we think of an economy as an island ecosystem and microfinance as a species within it, the growth–development distinction provides a partial answer. But the focus on scale is rather one-dimensional. The ecological metaphor can be plumbed for a richer understanding of the potential constructive role of microfinance. We can say more generally that a species enriches its ecosystem when it links to other species in diverse ways, such as through competition, predation, and symbiosis. By the same token, a financial institution contributes the most to its host economy when it links to other economic actors in diverse ways. Notice that the Bolivian microcreditors survived the crisis by linking more strongly to each other, in sharing information. Multiple ties add resilience and stability to the financial industry and to the economy as a whole.

This might seem like fuzzy analogizing. But it is precisely the propensity to connect that puts financial services at the heart of economic development. Each loan, savings account, and insurance policy is a link between two or more parties. The more such threads an MFI spins, the greater its contribution to the economic fabric. With some services, such as money transfers and checking accounts, the connective nature is explicit. With others, interconnection seems to arise as a side effect, as when banks use the funds of savers to finance borrowers. Historically, just as the invention of movable-type printing accelerated the flow of information and ideas, the rising sophistication of financial institutions accelerated the circulation of two other intangibles—purchasing power and risk—opening the way for industrialization and affluence. Today, an industrial country's financial system includes banks, brokers, insurers, regulators, credit bureaus, bond raters, mutual fund companies, stock and bond exchanges, and a bevy of other institutions. After the international financial crisis, you might smirk at such enthusiasm for the wonders of the financial system. But the credit market freeze-up was aptly compared to a heart attack. After wars, natural disasters, and epidemics, nothing does more economic damage than a financial crisis.[65] In the long run, a healthy financial system helps keep the rest of the body economic healthy.

Ross Levine, an economist at Brown University, counts five ways that a financial system connects to and supports economic development.[66] First, it mobilizes savings. Every economy has people who have saved more than they

---

65. I credit this observation to my colleague Liliana Rojas-Suarez.
66. Levine (1997), 691.

want to invest in their own businesses and people who have good ways to invest more than they have saved. Often, the investors need large sums over the long term, while savers individually offer small amounts and want the option to withdraw on short notice. Banks, stock and bond markets, investment funds, and brokers bring savers and investors together to mutual advantage, providing companies with patient capital while promising savers liquidity to the degree they need. Walter Bagehot, who edited *The Economist* early in its history, wrote about this process. He observed the fluidity with which London bankers and brokers issued and bought bonds to finance seafaring traders and American steel plants. He asserted that Lombard Street, the locus of these dealings, was a key to British economic dominance: "A million in the hands of a single banker is a great power; he can at once lend it where he will, and borrowers can come to him, because they know or believe that he has it. But the same sum scattered in tens and fifties through a whole nation is no power at all: no one knows where to find it or whom to ask for it."[67]

Levine enumerates two other functions closely related to savings mobilization: allocating capital and holding the users of capital accountable. Bankers do not mechanically disburse the savings they mobilize; rather they check credit histories, scrutinize investment proposals, analyze market risks. They serve the economy by channeling capital to where it ideally will produce more value. Meanwhile, the arm's-length split between the providers and users of capital increases accountability. Investors' demands for upright accounting and proactive management prod companies toward efficiency and innovation.

Fourth, just as the financial system pools savings, it pools risk, in part for the same reason: to move that which is pooled to those who can manage it better. A deep-pocketed insurance company, for example, can absorb the $100,000 shock of a cancer diagnosis more easily than a middle-class family, so it makes sense for the family to pay the company to take the risk. Even better, pooled risks sometimes cancel out. To an actuary, an insurance company's commitment to cover cancer risks for a million people might be costly but is not risky: the number of claims submitted each year is predictable. By the same token, mutual funds allow even small investors to reduce risk through diversification, letting them buy fractions of a thousand companies with a thousand dollars. Diversification hardly eliminates the risk of investing in the market, but it reduces it and thereby makes it easier for *all* companies to attract capital.

67. Bagehot (1897), 5–6.

Finally, through electronic transfers, paper checks, trade credit, and currency and commodity exchanges, a financial system lubricates commerce. The easier it is for companies to buy in the market what they do not make themselves, the more they can specialize. And division of labor, as Adam Smith famously observed of a pin factory, raises productivity.

Financial systems often perform these five functions poorly. They are unruly, bedeviled by the unpredictable interplay of greed and fear, faith and doubt, fads and contrarianism. Complete government control of banks and elimination of financial markets might squelch these worst tendencies—but at the cost of market discipline over who gets finance. So in most countries, the financial system is an awkward and flawed mix of public and private players.

The microfinance industry will probably never play a central role in the transformative economic processes that increase productivity, create jobs, and lift people from poverty. But the example set by the mainstream financial system is, broadly, the one to follow: microfinance institutions will contribute most to economic development when they become full intermediaries, taking funds from some locals and placing them with others. The more diversely they connect to their context, the more they will help the economy move "gradually to a fuller, greater, or better state." And the more the potential extremes of their behavior will be checked. This means taking capital from investors at home as well as abroad. It means taking savings. It can even mean channeling microsavings into loans for entrepreneurs a step or so up the economic ladder—who might hire the savers.[68] "Long evidence (even back to 16th century Europe)," observes microfinance expert Marguerite Robinson, "indicates that financial intermediaries are more stable, profitable, and sustainable than credit-focused organizations."[69] The historical pattern seems to hold for microfinance. Not least because of regulatory oversight, companies are more cautious when they on-lend the savings of the poor than when they on-lend funds from rich social investors from the other side of the world.

Emulating mainstream finance in its propensity to connect also means moving into the money transfer business. For example, in the market of Kisumu, Kenya, on Lake Victoria, I saw stall owners using the mobile money system M-PESA to pay for long-distance shipments of goods. By providing a safer way to make cross-country payments, it was reducing the frictions of domestic trade. More precisely, by democratizing access to a service formerly available only to the elite, it was allowing poorer people to engage in trade.

---

68. See Patten, Rosengard, and Johnston (2001), 1057, on BRI.
69. Robinson (2002), 137.

Given the role that trade has played in economic history, this unexpected effect of mobile money seems profound.[70]

Recent Travails of Microcredit

After years of steady expansion and good press, microcredit ran into serious trouble in a handful of countries in 2009 and 2010. The exact circumstances differ by country, but a common and most likely essential thread can be discerned: fast, credit-dominated growth. In general, the growth was driven by a mix of motives. The pursuit of profit was one, especially in India, where MFIs brought in private-equity investors looking for high returns. But as we have already seen, most of the investment in microcredit has been socially motivated. Profit has not been the main lure. Thus these bursting bubbles may be the first in history filled more by generosity than greed.

This section reviews a sampling of these events in order to illustrate the difference between growth and development and the value of multiplying connections.

Before the debacle in India, in 2008–09, the microcredit industries in Bosnia, Morocco, Nicaragua, and Pakistan all crashed.[71] According to a CGAP review, typically 30–40 percent of active microcredit borrowers had more than one loan in these nations (or in Pakistan, in certain districts), which meant that multiple borrowers accounted for the majority of loans. Yet until early 2008, all seemed well, going by the numbers. One standard measure of loan portfolio health is the portfolio at risk over 30 days (PAR 30)—the share of outstanding loan amounts owed by people at least 30 days delinquent. PAR 30 stood at a tranquil 3 percent in Nicaragua and 2 percent in the rest. Yet eighteen months later PAR 30 had shot up. Most of the increases took place in the first half of 2009 (see table 8-6).[72] As figure 8-4 shows, by the end of 2009, microcredit portfolios had shrunk in Bosnia, Nicaragua, and Morocco, somewhat reminiscent of the overshoot and crash in the herd simulations in figure 8-3. Comparable data were not available for Pakistan.

The CGAP report cited three common causes, all symptoms of fast growth combined with an inability to detect and respond to information

---

70. See David Roodman, "Connectivity Is Productivity," *Microfinance Open Book Blog*, May 29, 2010 (j.mp/9kBv9K), included in appendix.

71. In Nicaragua and India, politicians accused the industry of usury and took destructive government action. The attacks in turn made it harder to tell whether the industry had damaged itself or merely had been damaged by its critics.

72. Chen, Rasmussen, and Reille (2010).

Table 8-6. *Anatomy of Four Microcredit Crises*

Country	Annual growth rate of loan stock, 2004–08 (%)	Share of borrowers with loans from multiple lenders, 2009 (%)	Share of portfolio at risk over 30 days (%)		
			12/07	12/08	6/09
Bosnia	43	40	2	3	7
Morocco	59	29	2	5	10
Nicaragua	33	40	3	5	12
Pakistan	67	30[a]	2	2	13

Source: Chen, Rasmussen, and Reille (2010).
a. Crisis districts.

about how much more credit borrowers could safely handle: "concentrated market competition and multiple borrowing," "overstretched MFI [management] systems and controls," and "erosion of MFI lending discipline."[73] The clients' ability to handle debt is an external limit MFIs must stay within, but they also face an internal one: the ability to blend incentives and oversight to keep lending on an even keel. Since quality of management matters, there is no universal speed limit for MFI expansion.

Bosnia and Herzegovina

After peace was achieved in Bosnia and Herzegovina in 1995, western agencies funded the creation of several MFIs that emphasized individual loans for small businesses. Loans at ProCredit's bank, the first to enter, quintupled in total value between 2001 and 2007. EKI, an affiliate of the American NGO World Vision, grew by a factor of eighteen in the same years, and Mercy Corps's bank, called Partner, expanded twenty-fold.[74] Then the bubble burst. Al Jazeera reported:

> In pursuit of commercial scale and personal gain, microfinance lenders issued more loans than ever, expanding their loan book and earning the loan officer involved a personal commission.
>
> These loans were increasingly spent by borrowers on consumer goods rather than the modest business assets for which they were intended. Rather than equip a hairdresser, buy a van or a cow, they now more often than not went on weddings, cars or TVs.

73. Chen, Rasmussen, and Reille (2010), 2.
74. MIX Market, "Trends for Microfinance Institutions" (j.mp/4RMKJj [March 15, 2011]).

Figure 8-4. *Total Value of Outstanding Microloans in Bosnia, Morocco, and Nicaragua*

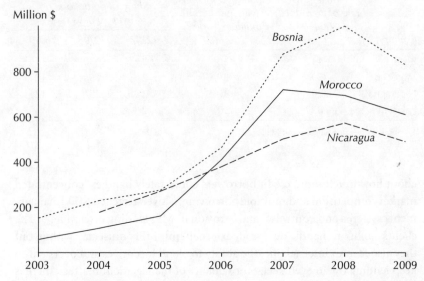

Source: Author's estimates, based on MIX Market, "Trends for Microfinance Institutions" (j.mp/4RMKJj [March 15, 2011]).

"The clients were aware that there are many microfinance lenders offering loans and wherever they could go they could get it. They were attracted by the possibilities and rushed into it without thinking," says [Selma Cizmic of the nonprofit MFI LIDER].[75]

Recently, the European Union and the World Bank's IFC injected new funds to prop up some of the struggling MFIs.[76]

India

In the first draft of this book, I described India as being on everyone's watch list. In late 2010, it came off the list. The drama in Andhra Pradesh state has been an ambiguous interplay of growth, competition, ideology, and politics. Thanks to ample finance from investors of various stripes—public and private, profit and nonprofit, domestic and foreign—the state's MFIs and SHG programs posted nearly unprecedented growth numbers in recent years (table 8-1). In Andhra Pradesh, multiple borrowing became common

75. Phil Cain, "Microfinance Meltdown in Bosnia," Al Jazeera, January 4, 2010 (j.mp/9BOHhZ).
76. Microfinance Enhancement Facility (2011).

because MFIs found it easier to shadow their peers, starting groups where people were already familiar with microcredit, than to strike into virgin territory.[77] In fact, MFIs reportedly piggybacked on each other's organizing efforts, making loans to groups formed by their competitors or, in the case of SHGs, doing the same after breaking the SHGs into smaller groups.

Yet if MFIs were eager to hand out money, they remained true to their organizational character when it came to getting it back. Smooth, quick weekly meetings remained essential to efficiency. Delinquency was dealt with swiftly lest it spread. This appears to have had two fateful consequences. First, stories began to emerge in the local papers and television channels of people hounded by loan officers to the point of suicide. The truth seemed murky. Some media outlets had ties to politicians who spied an opportunity for electoral gain by pinning responsibility on their opponents. Farmer suicides are nothing new in India, sadly. And people so desperately in debt as to end their lives typically owe to many kinds of creditors, including friends, family, and moneylenders. Yet after visiting the state in November 2010, a month after the government all but shut down microcredit there, I became convinced of the broad plausibility of a microcredit–suicide link. As noted in chapter 7's section on multiple borrowing, microcredit is distinguished among sources of finance available to the poor in its rigidity—its persistent demand for on-time payment; this insistence can lead to a triggering event for suicide, such as a humiliating public hectoring by a loan officer.

The second fateful consequence of aggressive collection on the part of private MFIs was the unraveling of government-backed self-help groups. As also noted in chapter 7, SHGs are culturally more elastic and less aggressive about loan collection. Thus when cornered by loan officers from both directions, women would default on SHGs first. The managers of the SHG program watched as their funds leaked into the coffers of for-profit MFIs. Combined with the record windfall from the IPO of SKS Microfinance and the suicide stories, the unraveling of SHGs became intolerable. These same managers wrote the law enacted in the fall of 2010 to rein in MFIs.[78] The explicit purpose of the law was to protect SHGs, which were "being exploited by private [MFIs] through usurious interest rates and coercive means of recovery resulting in their impoverishment & in some cases leading to suicides."[79] As the

---

77. On multiple borrowing, see Johnson and Meka (2010), 27.

78. B. Rajsekhar, CEO, Society for the Elimination of Rural Poverty, Hyderabad, India, interview with author, November 20, 2010. See David Roodman, "When Indian Elephants Fight," *Microfinance Open Book Blog*, November 24, 2010 (j.mp/gL4lDe), included in the appendix.

79. Andhra Pradesh Micro Finance Institutions Ordinance, approved December 2010 (j.mp/q2Em3n).

leader of commercial microfinance in India and the chairman of BASIX, Vijay Mahajan, put it to me, the government became both a player and a referee.[80]

But while assailing the crackdown as a biased overreaction, Mahajan was quick to say that it overreacted to a real problem. In chapter 7, I told of meeting with women in a village west of Hyderabad, the capital of Andhra Pradesh, where the number of MFIs had jumped from two to five. I also told of hearing about villages where MFIs became so numerous that they ran out of days of the week on which to hold meetings. It was not hard to see how the sudden influx of credit would get some people in trouble. Such destructive and self-destructive growth was the opposite of development as industry building. As Graham Wright, India office head for the research firm Micro-Save, had warned a year before:

> The poor have moved from having no access to credit (except from extortionate moneylenders) to being able to access loans from 3–4 MFIs at the same time. This change has occurred in the space of 2–3 years. It might be that the poor took loans from as many MFIs as were offering them, *because* they were available, without really understanding the implications of having to repay all these loans and the stress that this would incur in the lean season. In their pursuit of growth, MFIs' staff do little or no due diligence and simply leave this to the groups. They should have found out about the existing debt burden of the borrowers.[81]

At an industry conference weeks after the Andhra Pradesh law was enacted, there was an eerie sense of the walking dead. Almost no one had anything good to say about India's commercial microfinance industry. Most quietly wondered whether some of India's biggest MFIs, with high exposure in Andhra Pradesh and small equity cushions to absorb losses, would go under. A couple of weeks later, Vineet Rai, a prominent social investor in microfinance, declared, "No logical person would invest in microfinance right now, because there is no microfinance right now."[82]

Although the Andhra Pradesh microcredit industry did not simply pop under its own weight like a classic bubble would, the overshoot-and-collapse paradigm captures aspects of what happened. Much less obvious is that the

80. Vijay Mahajan, chairman, BASIX, interview with author, Hyderabad, India, November 18, 2010.

81. Transcript of roundtable discussion, Hyderabad, India, August 10, 2009, in Srinivasan (2009), 17.

82. Ruth David, "Temasek Snared in India as Crackdown Slows Microfinance IPOs," Bloomberg, December 2, 2010 (j.mp/fbyJ8D).

other ecological pattern I offered earlier—enrichment through connection—does, too. In an insightful analysis, Elisabeth Rhyne explains:

> Although large MFIs were allowed to convert from non-profits to commercial institutions, they were not licensed to take deposits, in part because they would have become competitors to the public sector banks. Deposit-taking, properly supervised, would have allowed the MFIs to raise funds locally, both from clients and others in their neighborhoods. It would have created a balanced portfolio of products and revenue sources, rather than exclusive reliance on the micro-loan mono-product. Instead of unbalanced mono-product giants, MFIs like SKS might have grown up to look more like Mibanco in Peru, Equity Bank in Kenya or BRI in Indonesia, all with solid loan and deposit bases. When clients have a place to save (and banks have an interest in promoting savings) they may be less likely to fall into debt traps.[83]

In addition, Rhyne points out that unlike in Bolivia, where the nonprofit Prodem became a major shareholder of its for-profit offshoot BancoSol, Indian law barred nonprofits from holding stakes in for-profits. The original nonprofit SKS, for example, got no shares or board seats on the for-profit SKS. If that connection had not been severed, it might have tempered the pressure from venture capitalists on the board to hit short-term growth targets so they could sell their shares at a high price through an IPO.[84]

Nicaragua

Industry consultant Barbara Magnoni gives a glimpse of the story in Nicaragua:

> At [a conference] in El Salvador in 2007, I knew there was a bubble as I watched investment funds competing to get face time with a number of Nicaraguan MFIs. Already, the market had grown substantially since 2004; Findesa (now Banex) had a loan portfolio of US$125 million, up from US$33 million at the end of 2004. I wondered why it made sense to lend to so many small MFIs in one country with 5 million people, 600,000 informal sector workers and 300,000 credit clients. . . .
>
> I visited Findesa later that year in Managua and asked the CFO what the institutions' main competitive advantage was. His answer reinforced my fears. He said, "We are very good at raising money from

83. Elisabeth Rhyne, "On Microfinance: Who's to Blame for the Crisis in Andhra Pradesh?" *Huffington Post*, November 2, 2010.

84. On board seats, see Chen and others (2010), 8.

foreign investors." Debt financing was clearly flowing to Nicaragua, with high profile, fast growing institutions like Findesa bringing in the bulk of the money; yet how would these MFIs' loan portfolios grow? Mostly, by trying to compete for each other's clients, ultimately adding to the clients' debt burdens. Implicit in this strategy is a loosening of credit methodology.[85]

A borrower's revolt soon gelled in Nicaragua, the *Movimiento de No Pago* ("No-Pay Movement"). President Daniel Ortega backed it. BANEX eventually succumbed, declaring bankruptcy in 2010. ProCredit's bank survived, if wounded, perhaps thanks to the financial reserves of its parent company. So did MFIs that had expanded more conservatively.[86]

Pakistan

As late as June 17, 2008, prospects looked sunny for the Kashf Foundation, a major microlender in Pakistan. On that day, the Japan Credit Rating Agency issued an upbeat analysis: "While maintaining controls and asset quality against the backdrop of rapid growth is critical, KF is considered to be well poised to take on this challenge in view of its tested lending methodology and tailor-made software which ensures effective monitoring."[87]

The number of outstanding loans had increased tenfold during 2003–07, from 29,655 to 295,396. But by the end of 2008, Kashf recognized a shocking 22 percent of its loan portfolio as at risk. It set aside $15 million, more than a third of the start-of-year portfolio, for write-offs. But it was not forthcoming about its financial fiasco.[88] Its 2008 annual report admitted the truth only where it could not be avoided, in a few key lines of the income statement. An independent report from the Pakistan Microfinance Network revealed more but shied away from mentioning Kashf or other MFIs by name: "[MFIs'] internal controls lagged expansion: Because of pressure on staff for quick outreach, coupled with multiple responsibilities of loan officers, inadequate staff incentive systems, and weak internal monitoring and control systems, some microfinance loan officers across various key [MFIs] appeared to be

85. Barbara Magnoni, "Bubble Bubble Banex Trouble," Financial Access Initiative blog, August 25, 2010 (j.mp/ pnncm4).

86. Magnoni (2011).

87. Japan Credit Rating-Vital Information Services, "Kashf Foundation," rating report, June 17, 2008 (j.mp/eX2dwk).

88. Kashf Foundation (2009), 32.

short-circuiting operational procedures and risk control systems."[89] Laxity opened the way for blatant abuses:

> Group leaders and activists get an opportunity to turn into commission agents primarily because the [MFI] staff, lending through solidarity groups, tend to delegate [a] significant portion of their client selection responsibility to group leaders or activists. Having a de facto power to accept or reject a potential borrower in a group, the group leader has the power to provide or refuse access to financial services to potential clients. This power allows group leaders to charge [a] commission from borrowers for access into a group. . . .
>
> Often, the group leader had accessed more loans from an [MFI] than the [MFI] had record of by borrowing through a "dummy" or "ghost" borrower. In some cases the group leader and the "ghost" borrower had subdivided the loan amount and thus the repayment responsibility as well.[90]

This kind of out-of-control, free-wheeling lending is just what you might expect when the profit motive takes over microcredit. But the Kashf Foundation is a nonprofit, and most of its money came from three institutions not known for profiteering: a New York–based social investment fund called Acumen Fund, the Grameen Foundation, and the World Bank.[91] Because motives other than profit can drive unsafe microlending, it is more useful to focus on the pace and quality of growth than its drivers.

In Search of Developmental Growth

The recent difficulties in microcredit industries across four continents—especially those in India—have pushed the pendulum of public opinion against microfinance. Many now ask, does microfinance actually work? Or is it on to the next hot thing in philanthropy? In the context of this careful investigation, the question is whether microfinance can be more creative than destructive. The answer depends in part on how much hope there is for structural changes to steady the industry. This section looks at two changes that already put microfinance on a more even keel in some countries: credit bureaus and deposit taking.

89. Burki (2009), 4.
90. Burki (2009), 6.
91. Kashf Foundation (2008), note 14.

Credit Bureaus

Business people generally resist sharing information about clients with competitors, so credit bureaus arose in rich countries only after bitter lessons about their necessity. Just so, information-sharing systems are being established or strengthened in Bosnia, India, Morocco, and Pakistan.[92] As in Bolivia before, such new institutions enrich the economic fabric in the Schumpeterian spirit of development. They make new information-sharing connections between lenders, with consequences for their relationships with borrowers.

An effective credit bureau provides better information, and in so doing, better incentives. It gives lenders a fuller picture of current debts, thus about clients' "headroom" for additional borrowing. Although it is impossible to know exactly whether a person has too much debt, because capacity to repay depends on the uncertain future, with better data a lender can exercise better judgment. It can combine information about a client's outstanding debts and credit history with conservative rules of thumb—for instance, that mortgage payments should not exceed a third of income. A credit bureau also allows lenders to infer reliability from credit histories, which in turn encourages clients to borrow conservatively and repay diligently for fear of compromising their access to finance.[93]

A major prerequisite to building a credit bureau is a way to reliably identify people, in order to match up records from various lenders and prevent fraudulent use of multiple names. Everyone must have a number. The poorer the country and the poorer the people within it, the less likely they are to have been incorporated into such a unique identification system. Fortunately, breakthroughs may be imminent. As discussed in chapter 7, in 2009, the Indian government launched an ambitious project to create a national identification system and tapped famed Infosys cofounder Nandan Nilekani to run it.

Of course, America had three credit bureaus—and a mortgage meltdown. In Andhra Pradesh, MFIs already knew that multiple borrowing was ubiquitous. But just because credit bureaus are not sufficient, that does not make them unnecessary.

---

92. Chen, Rasmussen, and Reille (2010), 14; Vijay Mahajan and P.N. Vasudevan, "Microfinance in India: Twin Steps towards Self-Regulation," *Microfinance Focus*, January 10, 2010 (j.mp/afJCHX).

93. De Janvry, McIntosh, and Sadoulet (2010)

Taking Deposits

As we reach the end of my assessment of microfinance, a recurring theme becomes apparent: the value of microsavings. The first notion of success we examined is development as escape from poverty. In that context, a randomized study found that offering a commitment savings account to market vendors in Kenya raised spending among the female vendors.[94] No randomized studies have found such impacts from microcredit. As for development as freedom, it is hard to see how voluntarily saving too much would lessen a poor person's control over her life, as long as the savings are safe. Once again, the same is not true for credit. And regarding development as industry building, an MFI that complements credit with savings services becomes a financial intermediary, a new node in the economic web connecting those with money to set aside with those who have immediate uses for it.

Happily, many MFIs have become true microbanks, doing both credit and voluntary savings. Their savings accounts take various forms. Some are completely liquid, allowing deposits and withdrawals of any amount at any time, or nearly. Others are time deposits, like certificates of deposit, which are locked up for agreed periods and pay higher interest in return. In between are semi-liquid accounts, like the ones in the Kenya experiment, which limit the number, amount, or both of transactions per month through rules or penalties. The global goliath of microsavings, BRI, offers all three.[95] Partly inspired by BRI, the Bangladeshi groups ASA, BRAC, and Grameen got serious about voluntary savings in the late 1990s.[96] Grameen in particular accumulated large sums through commitment savings accounts. Some Pro-Credit banks are also seriously into savings, as are Equity Bank in Kenya, and BancoSol and other MFIs in Latin America.[97]

Yet in many countries, microcredit still overshadows microsavings. I can see good, tough reasons for the disparity. Letting people put in and take out money when they please cuts against the mass-production strategy of microcredit, as explained in chapter 5. It makes microsavings accounts more expensive to administer than microloans of the same size. In addition, in Latin America especially, many people shudder at memories of

94. Dupas and Robinson (2009).
95. Robinson (2002), 266.
96. Rutherford (2009b), 144; Wright, Hossain, and Rutherford (1997), 315–21.
97. On Latin America, see Westley and Palomas (2010).

hyperinflation, which destroyed monetary savings and taught people to save in gold and goats.

Finally, and perhaps most importantly, start-up nonprofits generally should not be entrusted with what is referred to in the trade as other people's money; yet the organizations can give out loans the day they open their doors. While there are some notably successful examples of unregulated deposit-takers (see table 8-2), the global consensus is for supervision because government banking experts are better positioned than ordinary savers to judge whether their money is being used prudently. The problem is that supervision is costly for all concerned. Small institutions may lack the administrative and financial capacity to comply with complex rules and liquidity requirements. And underfunded supervisors in poor countries may not have the staff to track more than a handful of large institutions.[98] So the general thrust in financial regulation is toward conservatism in granting permission to take savings. Most progress in microsavings has occurred in the countries where microfinance flourished earliest, such as Bolivia, Indonesia, and Peru. Perhaps credit is a pioneer species, the lichen that colonizes bare rock so that the successor, savings, can take root. Perhaps expecting MFIs to take savings in their earliest days would be like expecting oaks to root in bare rock.

Perhaps—but that is not the whole story. In general, MFIs can raise funds for lending from three sources: retained profits from lending; outside finance, including loans and equity capital; and customers' savings. Usually they will do whatever is easiest—and outside finance has been pretty easy since the mid-2000s. Why should a microfinance institution bother with the administrative and regulatory hassle in maintaining thousands or millions of small savings accounts when it can raise grants and low-interest loans from investors? This observation leads to what Dale Adams, emeritus economics professor at Ohio State and longtime savings advocate, calls Shaw's Law, after the American economist Edward Shaw: "Deposits will only be mobilized when there is little or no outside funding available to potential deposit takers."[99] Adams recounts:

In the early 1990s I saw a dramatic example . . . in Egypt where [US] AID spent a good deal of money trying to reform a traditional agricultural bank, including stimulating more deposit mobilization. These efforts were later undercut by a large World Bank loan that provided funds to the bank more cheaply than the bank could obtain them from

98. Adams (2009), 9–10.
99. Adams (2002), 5; Shaw (1973). See also Christen and Mas (2009), 282.

depositors. The agricultural bank quickly lost interest in the difficult task of mobilizing voluntary deposits.[100]

Around the same time, perhaps wanting to associate with success, the World Bank attempted to lend to BRI. Dennis Whittle, who later left the World Bank to co-found the online charity marketplace GlobalGiving, sketched the story in a comment on my blog: "I worked with the World Bank in Indonesia back in the late 1980s and early 1990s, when BRI's microcredit program was already booming. During that time, I tried repeatedly to lend BRI $100 million at subsidized rates to expand their microcredit program. BRI's answer: 'No thanks, that would screw up our discipline.'"[101]

A detailed study in Latin America confirmed that borrowed funds undercut deposit-taking on price, if less so among larger MFIs that can administer savings programs more cheaply per dollar held. Typically the loans MFIs take from domestic government agencies and foreign investors are at submarket rates, which is shifting the balance away from deposit taking (see table 8-7).[102]

As a rule, then, the more money investors pour into microcredit, the less microsavings is taken. Accepting that savings should be the province of institutions of a certain age and size, the practical thrust of Adams' complaint is that outside money is lulling big institutions into savings avoidance and little ones into merger avoidance. To be fair, easy finance is not the only inappropriate hindrance to microsavings. Regulations in many countries impede entry into savings through rules that are explicitly prohibitory, as in India, or impractically vague. Still, banking regulations are political outcomes. Larger institutions that are hungry for savings can lobby to accelerate the adoption of favorable rules.

The lack of microsavings in turn appears partly responsible for a lack of moderation in microlending. It seems unlikely, for example, that credit-dominated MFIs in India or Bosnia would have grown so recklessly if they had been on-lending the savings of the poor rather the investments of big banks, aid agencies, and millionaires. Some combination of regulation, conscience, and fear of angering customers and politicians would probably have installed caution. Thus easy money from investors simultaneously provides the fuel for fast credit growth and reduces the compunction about burning it. In fact, if one sorts a list of the major microfinance countries by the

100. Adams (2002), 5.

101. Dennis Whittle, February 4, 2010, comment on David Roodman, "Charting Growth," *Microfinance Open Book Blog*, February 3, 2010 (j.mp/cUAobc).

102. Maisch, Soria, and Westley (2006).

Table 8-7. *Costs of Various Funding Sources as Share of Amounts Saved or Lent, Selected MFIs in Latin America, Circa 2004*

MFI	Country	Size of MFI (deposits, million $)	Deposits			Bor- rowing	Stock issu- ance	Bond issu- ance
			Admin- istration	Interest paid	Total			
CMAC Pisco	Peru	3.0	11.6	7.9	19.5	13.0	4.1	
CMAC Chincha	Peru	3.9	14.7	7.6	22.3	12.1	31.5	
CRAC Señor de Luren	Peru	11.5	6.6	7.1	13.7	6.5	17.8	
Procredit	Nicaragua	12.5	6.9	1.5	8.4			
CRAC Nor Perú	Peru	14.4	4.8	5.0	9.7	5.7	21.1	
Finamérica	Colombia	15.5	12.5	1.8	14.3	5.7	4.6	
FPP FIE	Bolivia	22.2	5.2	5.0	10.2	5.1	23.6	
FFP Caja Los Andes	Bolivia	48.3	3.9	4.1	8.0	4.3	14.3	
CMAC Arequipa	Peru	91.7	7.7	4.4	12.1	13.0	29.1	
CMAC Piura	Peru	96.5[a]	8.1[a]	3.6	11.7	10.6	32.6	
Compartamos	Mexico							9.4
Mibanco	Peru							9.1
Average			8.2	4.8	13.0[b]	8.4[b]	19.8	9.2

Source: Maisch, Soria, and Westley (2006), 36, 51, 95.
a. Taking savings tends to get cheaper with scale.
b. Loans to MFIs are often subsidized, which undercuts savings.

fraction of microcredit financed with borrowings from investors, a remarkable pattern emerges. All the countries recently in credit crisis are near one end, taking little in microdeposits and much in loans from outside investors (see table 8-8).

In sum, easy outside money for microcredit aggravates two ills: overemphasis on credit (to the point of inflating bubbles) and underemphasis on savings. The consequences of the first have been graphically illustrated in news coverage of Andhra Pradesh. In contrast, the underemphasis on savings is a kind of silent tragedy. Perhaps the best indicator of the size of that tragedy is BRI's record, noted in chapter 4. At the end of 2007, the bank had six depositors for every borrower (21.2 million savers, about 15 percent of Indonesian adults, versus 3.5 million borrowers). And 21 percent of BRI's non-borrowing customers lived below the poverty line, compared to just 9 percent of its borrowers.[103] Doing the multiplication, we see that BRI had twelve times as many non-borrowers as borrowers living below the official

103. Johnston and Morduch (2007), 29.

Table 8-8. *Financing Structure of MFIs in Twenty-Five Countries with Most Loans, 2009*

Country	Number of loans	% of financing Borrowings from investors	% of financing Deposits	% of financing Equity	Graph
Morocco	919,025	81	0	19	
India	26,629,123	76	4	19	
Nepal	586,952	67	24	9	
Bosnia and Herzegovina	374,966	64	18	18	
Nicaragua	391,375	64	21	16	
Egypt	1,112,892	49	0	50	
Pakistan	1,111,720	49	26	25	
Brazil	820,728	45	25	30	
South Africa	805,449	37	42	21	
Mexico	4,508,747	29	47	24	
Philippines	2,680,065	28	53	19	
Peru	3,088,620	25	59	16	
Cambodia	1,110,687	24	60	16	
Nigeria	439,902	23	48	29	
Ecuador	667,696	22	61	17	
Ethiopia	2,312,408	21	39	40	
Bangladesh	20,571,831	20	55	25	
Mongolia	384,317	20	72	9	
Bolivia	872,655	17	70	13	
Colombia	2,227,876	16	65	18	
Uganda	431,439	15	65	21	
Kenya	1,458,809	13	65	22	
Sri Lanka	911,029	11	75	13	
Paraguay	404,874	9	78	12	
Indonesia	3,597,450	5	89	5	

Source: Author's estimates based on Mix Market, "MFI Indicators" (j.mp/aDBhal [June 4, 2010]).

Note: Countries recently in crisis are boldface. Equity is total assets, including outstanding loans, minus borrowings and deposits. Data for Indonesia are from 2006. Excludes four large state-run institutions for which financial viability is not a primary objective: Banco Popular do Brasil, Kenya Post Office Savings Bank, Khushhali Bank of Pakistan, Vietnam Bank for Social Policies.

poverty line.[104] Absent the deposit option, some BRI savers would switch to credit as an inferior, risky substitute while others would drop out altogether. Through deposit-taking, BRI is providing a higher quantity and quality of services to the poor. Replication of its model in more countries would improve the financial lives of hundreds of millions of people.

Conclusion

I began this chapter with the idea that there must be something right in a charitable project that repeatedly and uniquely produces such impressive organizations. Rather than trying to pin down the direct link from the development of such institutions to poverty reduction and empowerment, I have argued that sustainably extending the financial system to poor people *is* development, appropriately defined.[105] Poor people deserve access to financial infrastructure just as they deserve access to clean water, sanitation, and electricity. Throughout history, most extensions of the financial system to new customers have been led by private institutions, from merchant banks to industrial life insurers. Fundamentally, the microfinance movement is about carrying that tradition forward to the planet's majority through the construction of businesses and businesslike institutions. This is not to assert that success in extending financial access has always worked out well. Nor is it to say that growth of industries is all that matters—if it were, then the cigarette industry would be a boon to progress. The point is that microfinance must be appraised from this viewpoint as part of a rigorous overall assessment.

In light of this conception of success—and in light of the various crises of 2008–10—microfinance looks flawed. That is a problem, but it should be no more fatal in our judgment of microfinance than recent credit troubles in rich countries should be for mainstream finance. If the global rich still deserve access to mortgages, the global poor still deserve access to small loans.

In fact, the greatest strength of microfinance has been in building industries that enrich the fabric of nations. Chapter 6 concluded that evidence of the direct impact on poverty is spotty and muted. Chapter 7 discovered that the firsthand reports on when microcredit empowers and when it oppresses are also disturbingly mixed. But in chapter 8, there is no disputing some basic, impressive facts. Where there were no MFIs a few decades ago, now there are thousands, serving millions. The big ones are businesses or operate like them. The industry's history is one of constant innovation, from the

104. Twenty-one percent of (21.2–3.5) million versus 9 percent of 3.5 million.
105. Prahalad (2006).

basic credit delivery methods to various forms of savings, from pen-and-paper bookkeeping to Palm Pilots, from foundation grants to securitized loans and IPOs. This success does not appeal to the imagination as much as lifting a woman out of poverty would. But it is more certain and should be recognized as economic development.

Accepting that microfinance has "worked" overall in this way, the practical question is how to make it work better. In particular, what is the proper role for would-be supporters? Here, the conclusion is more cautionary. On the one hand, there might not be a microfinance movement were it not for outside donors and socially motivated investors. Yet precisely because the idea is introduced from the outside, like the reindeer on St. Matthew Island, microfinance can easily undermine itself and hurt those it is meant to serve. For growth in microfinance to be healthy, the growth impulse must be counterbalanced by restraints, such as credit bureaus, nonprofit ownership of for-profit institutions, and supervision of deposit-takers. And microfinance institutions must connect diversely to capital markets and clientele. In particular, *less* investment from investors, notably foreign ones, will in many contexts make microfinance *more* successful, by encouraging more responsible lending and the taking of savings.

A big lesson is that mythologizing microfinance has distorted funding for it, undermining the industry in precisely the aspect in which it has most inborn capacity to succeed. Foreign money came easily because of microfinance's exaggerated reputation for fighting poverty and empowering women, extending some MFIs beyond their capacity. Now the pendulum is swinging against microfinance. As long it does not swing too far, lower expectations may bring greater success.

nine
Billions Served

Neither a borrower nor a lender be;
For loan oft loses both itself and friend.
And borrowing dulls the edge of husbandry.
This above all: to thine own self be true,
And it must follow, as the night the day,
Thou canst not then be false to any man.

—*HAMLET* 1.3.75–80[1]

In the last eight chapters, I have examined microfinance from more angles than ever before in one place. I have placed modern microfinance in the flow of history. I have shared the viewpoints of the user at the metaphorical teller window and the manager behind it. I have surveyed the diversity of microfinance and investigated the strongest claims for its virtues: microfinance as abolisher of poverty, enhancer of freedom, and builder of industry. Now I sum up the lessons, ponder what lies ahead, and advise how to influence it.

You know the popular image of microfinance: it was invented by that guy in India who won the Nobel Prize; it gives loans so people can start businesses and lift themselves out of poverty. My job in the first part of this book was to peel back that image and discover a more credible, complex story. Modern microfinance is not merely another foreign-aid fad foisted upon the poor, as a cynic might have it, doomed by its naïveté to fail. If it is a fad, then it is the longest in the history of overseas charity. What explains its persistence is its remarkable success on the market test: poor people are willing to pay for reliable financial services. Microfinance is best seen as arising organically from several sources: the real needs of poor people for tools to manage tumultuous financial lives; a long historical process of experimentation with ways to deliver such tools; the creativity, vision, and commitment

---

1. G. Blakemore, ed. 1974. *The Riverside Shakespeare* (Boston: Houghton Mifflin). "Husbandry" might be "economy" in modern English.

of the pioneers, including Muhammad Yunus; and the business imperatives of mass producing small-scale financial services.

The scene having been set, I then delved into the evidence on microfinance's role in development, airing its most serious defenses. I tried, in the words of my colleague Ethan Kapstein, to be critical but not cynical. In tackling these chapters, I realized that I needed to look at the question of impact within several conceptions of "development," each leading to different questions and types of evidence. In particular, while randomized impact studies have recently and rightly received much attention, they do not tell the full story—no more than a randomized trial of mortgages in the mid-2000s would have told us everything we needed to know about the impact of the mortgage industry.

The lessons from chapters 6–8 distill to these:

—Credible evidence on microfinance's success in *development as escape from poverty* is scarce. At this writing, essentially two credible studies of microcredit and one of microsavings are in the public domain. The two of credit found no impact on indicators of household welfare, such as income, spending, and school attendance one to two years out. But the celebrated sequence from credit to enterprise is more than a myth. The study of group credit in Hyderabad, India, spotted an increase in profits among the 31 percent of households that already had a business, as well as more business starts among households of relative education and wealth.[2] Meanwhile the randomized study of a commitment savings account in Kenya found that this service, too, helped existing business owners invest in their enterprises. Unlike with microcredit, the boost to entrepreneurship showed up as improvements in household welfare.

—The evidence is mixed on whether microcredit in particular spurs *development as freedom,* strengthening poor people's tenuous control over their circumstances. Financial services inherently—but not automatically—enhance agency. Poor people whose incomes are volatile and who can't work when injured or sick need financial services more than the global rich so they can put aside money in good days and seasons and pull it out in bad. Loans, savings accounts, insurance, even money transfers can help. Researchers who have spent weeks or years with borrowers have collected a range of stories about microcredit's effects. Some women have found liberation by doing financial business in public spaces. Others have been made to sit in meetings until all dues are paid. And even more disturbingly, some have had their cows or chicks or trees taken by peers in order to pay off their debts.[3] These

2. Banerjee and others (2009), 17.

3. Rutherford (2004), 30; Karim (2008), 19.

contradictions are not hard to understand because credit is both a source of possibilities and a bond. Overall, it is hard to feel sanguine that stories of empowerment are the whole story.

—The success on which microfinance can stake its strongest claim is in *industry building*. With time, the microfinance industry has increased in size, efficiency, and diversity of offerings, partly because of competition. More institutions are becoming domestic intermediaries, taking deposits from and lending to locals. In few realms can foreign aid and philanthropy point to such success in fostering Schumpeterian development. But this success still leaves scope for critique. The enthusiastic supply of credit for microcredit has distorted the industry, undermining the drive to take savings and spurring unwise lending, even bubbles. Enthusiasm for credit appears inherently destabilizing in competitive markets where microfinance institutions (MFIs) can grow fastest by poaching each other's clients, leading people to take several loans at once, and where no credit bureau gives MFIs the full picture.

Overall the great strength and hope of microfinance lies in *building self-sufficient institutions that can give billions of poor people an increment of control over their lives,* control they will use to put food on the table more regularly, invest in education, and, yes, start tiny businesses. The least realistic expectation is that it will provide an escape hatch from poverty. We would not expect access to reliable electricity to lift people from poverty, and we should not expect access to reliable financial services to do so, either.

Because poor people are willing to pay for financial services, MFIs can serve many from a modest base of charitable funds. Thus while the benefits appear modest compared to traditionally high expectations, the costs can be modest, too. Rich Rosenberg once recalled his oversight while at the U.S. Agency for International Development of "a few million dollars of donor subsidies in the mid-1990s" for Bolivia's Prodem. Along with its offshoot BancoSol, Prodem held 234,000 credit accounts by the end of 2009 and a remarkable 893,000 savings accounts.[4] Rosenberg diagrammed the "value proposition" of microfinance this way:

Small one-time subsidies
    leverage large multiples of unsubsidized funds
        producing sustainable delivery year after year of highly valued services
            that help hundreds of millions of people
                keep their consumption stable, finance major expenses, and cope with shocks
                    despite incomes that are low, irregular, and unreliable.[5]

4. MIX Market, "Number of depositors and active borrowers, mature Bolivian MFIs, 2009," custom report (j.mp/qK7kFj [September 19, 2011]).

5. Rosenberg (2010), 5.

This chapter reflects briefly on why that realistic value proposition was shouldered aside in many minds by an unrealistic one about escape from poverty. Then it sketches ways for the microfinance movement to best realize its real potential to build dynamic industries that bring freedom-enhancing services to billions.

The Effects of Causes

A big idea in chapter 5 is that microfinance as we observe it is the outcome of an evolutionary process. "Natural" selection explains the emphases on credit, groups, and women. The evolutionary perspective also explains a trait little noted in chapter 5: the mythology that promoters have woven around the workaday business of disbursing and collecting loans. Pankaj Jain and Mick Moore called it the "orthodox fallacy"—the idea, for example, that the poor pay back reliably because they all succeed in business.[6] Almost no development project has held such strong and multidimensional appeal as microcredit. It appeals to the left with talk of empowering women and the right by insisting on individual responsibility. As the cliché goes, it offers a hand, not a handout. And because the currency of microcredit is currency itself, not textbooks or trainers, supporters feel that the money they contribute goes directly to the poor. To this extent, the intermediary disappears in the mind of the giver, creating a stronger sense of connection to the ultimate recipient. Peer-to-peer lending sites such as Kiva post borrowers' stories and pictures to strengthen this psychological bond.

Just as it hardly matters from the evolutionary point of view whether joint liability was invented or copied in the 1970s, it hardly matters whether microfinance promoters believed the mythology. What matters is that donors and investors who finance microfinance rewarded those who told certain stories, creating a selective environment that favored the promoters best at telling them. That microfinance leaders should accentuate the positive should not surprise. All of us who believe in our work tell the best stories we can to show how we believe we help. Jain and Moore put it well:

> We are not suggesting here that the leaders of the big [MFIs] perpetrated some kind of fraud. . . . The picture is far more complex than that and notions of blame or of individual responsibility are irrelevant to our objective of obtaining practical understanding of why and how [MFIs] have been so successful. Our limited evidence suggests that the

6. Jain and Moore (2003), 28.

orthodox fallacy blossomed and spread in large part because that is what people in aid agencies wanted to hear, thought they had heard, or asked [MFI] leaders to talk about and publicise. To the extent that [MFI] leaders did foster a particular image, this could be seen simply as targeted product promotion in a "market" of aid abundance. . . .

To justify the continuing flow of that money to their own particular organisations and to the microfinance sector as a whole, [MFI] leaders and spokespersons have gradually found themselves, through a combination of circumstances and pressures, purveying a misleading interpretation of the reasons for their success. They emphasise a few elements in a complex organisational system, and are silent on many key components.[7]

Perhaps the mythologizing of microfinance was historically necessary to build support for the good cause of delivering useful financial services to billions. But in addition to being largely wrong, the mythology has damaged the microfinance movement in several ways. First, it has amplified the emphasis in favor of one service, microcredit, delivered in ways conceived at one time, about three decades ago. Second, the mythology has spread the idea that investing in microcredit, putting poor people in debt on a large scale, is automatically good for them. In 2004, for example, the U.S. Congress acceded to a campaign run by the nonprofit group RESULTS to require that half of all U.S. microfinance aid go to "very poor" people, despite the lack of evidence that the poorest wanted and could safely handle such credit.[8] Third, the global acceleration of funding for microcredit since the mid-2000s, effectively predicated on the idea that more is always better, is also a cause of the debacles in India and elsewhere, which now haunt the movement. Last, now that high-quality studies have emerged that contradict the high-flying myth, the public standing of microfinance may dive, like Icarus after he flew too close to the sun. In short, the mythology has brought bubbles and backlash. The question now is whether microfinance will survive its own success.

This book is an attempt to develop a more honest story of microfinance, so that Icarus will neither fly too close to the sun nor brush the waves, and so that the movement will realize its fullest potential to serve poor people. How well it succeeds, along with other efforts to bring realism, depends on how

---

7. Jain and Moore (2003), 28–29.

8. The law defines "very poor" as living on less than $1,000 per annum in Europe and Eurasia in 1995 dollars, under $400 in Latin America, and under $300 elsewhere. Microenterprise Results and Accountability Act of 2004, Public Law No. 108–484, §252(c).

much the supporters of microfinance change their behavior. If people continue to channel billions to the best storytellers, they will continue to distort the very thing they mean to support. But if they recognize how their choices have been part of the problem, then they can become part of the solution.

You Can't Have It All

Economics is sometimes defined as the study of the optimal allocation of scarce resources. Really there is more to it than that—resources are rarely allocated optimally anyway—but the definition is apt in that dismal scientists often think in trade-offs. Rejiggering a factory produces more toasters but fewer microwaves. In chapters 6–8, I reviewed microfinance in light of each of the three notions of success. But that sequential analysis is only an input to a broader synthesis. Having built the evidence base by scoring microfinance against various standards, it is time to think across them. One useful way to do so is with the notion of trade-offs.

Microfinance versus Everything Else

Trade-offs await on two levels: in comparing microfinance to other charitable projects, and in comparing styles of microfinance. On that first, broad level stands the grand question of this book: Does microfinance deserve all that praise and funding? Or should supporters channel their charity and aid elsewhere?

Since there's not much evidence that microfinance lifts people from poverty or even reliably empowers them, it might seem sensible for funders and investors to dump it and move on. But the degree of our ignorance about its effects is not unusual. The impacts of building clinics or training judges or digging wells are also variegated, uncertain, and poorly studied. Thus, limited evidence is not a strong argument against microfinance and for other activities.

I think that financial services for poor people do deserve a place in the world's aid and social investment portfolios, for two reasons. First, microfinance has compiled impressive achievements in building institutions that enhance the freedom of millions and could do the same for billions. These achievements come with the caveats already noted, but because microcredit is generally safe in moderation and encompasses more than microcredit, the caveats are not fatal. Second, a principle of diversification applies: given the uncertainties about the impacts of microfinance or anything else, and given that poor people need many things, it is wise to invest in several strategies at once. That said, I will argue below that from the perspective of delivering appropriate financial services to poor people, microfinance's slice of public aid and private charity—about $3 billion in 2009, as noted in chapter 8—has grown too large. Microfinance would do better on its own terms if less money went into it. To this substantial extent, then, there is no trade-off between microfinance and other kinds of aid. Less money for microcredit and more for bed nets would be a double win.

Microfinance versus Microfinance

Within microfinance, trade-offs are harder to avoid. In the late 1990s, specialists hotly debated the trade-off between taking subsidies in order to serve the poorest and weaning MFIs off subsidies so that they could grow to serve more people, even if that meant bypassing the poorest. Economist Jonathan Morduch called the split between the "poverty" and "sustainability" advocates the "microfinance schism." Within this breach, however, a seedling of thought grew that questioned the inevitability of the trade-off: businesslike sustainability, the argument went, need not cost much in depth of outreach to the poorest. Bangladesh was Exhibit A. But, true to his training, Morduch doubted that the choices could be dodged so easily.[9] With coauthors, for example, he demonstrated that increasing a microcredit interest rate 1 percent (not 1 percentage point) in Dhaka, the capital of Bangladesh, reduced borrowing by slightly more than 1 percent on average. The implication is that even in Bangladesh, cutting subsidies to an MFI might make it more self-sufficient but would also put formal financial services beyond the reach of some poor people.[10]

The evidence gathered in this book also hints at trade-offs, especially in the short term between development as freedom and development as institution building. Recall the end of chapter 7: "On any given day, in any given place, the immediate business interests of the lender conflict with the agency of the borrower." MFIs can do credit more easily than savings or insurance, yet credit by nature curtails freedom more. Imposing constraints on borrowers, such as through group meetings and weekly payments, protects an MFI's bottom line. Higher interest rates may boost the profitability of MFIs and the dynamism of the industry—and flirt with "usury." Inversely, layering nonfinancial services on top of financial ones may enhance women's agency but also requires subsidies.

If it is easy to point out choices, it is harder to make them. The advantages and disadvantages of building subsidy into microfinance, such as through low-interest loans from social investors, vary over time and space according to formulas that can only be vaguely estimated. Even if we knew exact

9. Morduch (2000).

10. Dehejia, Montgomery, and Morduch (2009).

consequences, ethical imponderables would arise. How are we to weigh cheaper services for a smaller group against more expensive services to a larger group?

In the face of such unknowns and imponderables, I suggest two principles of judgment. First, a project is mostly likely to achieve its potential when it follows its natural constructive tendencies. If your daughter were a piano prodigy, you would get her piano lessons. But note the emphasis on "constructive": you would probably not nurture her tendency to sociopathy. By this principle, microfinance is likely to do the most good when it plays to its strength: turning modest amounts of aid into substantial industries that provide reliable services. Among charitable projects, microfinance is in this respect truly prodigious.

In contrast, aid for microfinance does not stand head and shoulders above the rest in reaching the poorest, let alone lifting them out of poverty. The (limited) evidence suggests the contrary, that microcredit is more likely to help those who already have businesses or who, because they are better off to start with, can start a business more easily. With respect to Morduch's "schism," I therefore favor those who seek to do microfinance in a self-financing, businesslike way in order to responsibly maximize reach. This may sometimes mean making choices that reduce the freedom of clients, such as lending to the poorest through groups rather than individually. However, the history of microfinance, short as it is, includes many examples of businesslike MFIs evolving their products to increase freedom, such as in moving to savings.

And that leads to the second principle of judgment: don't give up hope on dodging trade-offs. The dictatorship of hard choices is only absolute if MFIs are squeezing every possible ounce of productivity from the capital and labor they consume and technology is static. But perfectly efficient firms reside only in textbooks, and technology is always improving. Thus the choices in microfinance today are not entirely dismal. The chief opportunity spied by some of the sharpest observers today, including the Bill & Melinda Gates Foundation, is in taking savings, perhaps especially through high technology (see below).

Too Much Credit for Microcredit

The financial innovations channeling billions into microfinance are marvels. Yet because the ample and cheap finance feeds mostly into microcredit portfolios, it has at least two downsides. It dulls the initiative to take savings as an alternative source of funds. And it encourages microfinance organizations to grow faster than they can safely manage—indeed, drives them to do so, because of the way competition favors the most aggressive players in the short run. Fast microcredit growth is not always bad.[11] But if there is some maximum amount of microcredit that a populace can sustainably absorb, the faster that line is crossed, the worse. Recognizing these risks while accepting that credit for microcredit has its place forces hard practical questions. How should investors collectively define and enforce Aristotle's golden mean? If they can define it in some way, can they legislate it in practice, divvying up the limited investment pie among themselves? Or if moderation cannot be enforced, would the next-best option be to browbeat certain classes of investors into withdrawing altogether?

Drawing the line to minimize either side effect of excessive lending to MFIs is inherently arbitrary at the margin. As for the concern about undermining the incentive to take savings, most MFIs cannot and should not emulate the purity of Bank Rakyat Indonesia (BRI) circa 1990, which as a century-old government-owned bank was stout enough to resist the World Bank's offers of credit. Even mature MFIs should diversify across funding sources because each source has its costs and risks. Accepting that borrowing *by* MFIs is reasonable in principle, it is hard to pinpoint the right amount. Perhaps it should go more to young MFIs, then taper as they grow. But according to what formula?

As for the second concern about ample finance—that it will cause dangerous credit expansion, even bubbles—drawing lines is notoriously difficult here, too. Bubbles are certain only in retrospect. To ground my thinking about this challenge, my research assistant Paolo Abarcar and I set out to answer an impertinent question about the microcredit bubbles that popped in 2008–09 (see chapter 8): Who inflated them? We combed through the annual reports of the largest MFIs in four relevant countries.[12] In Bosnia, Nicaragua, and Pakistan, it turned out, foreigners supplied most of the $1.46 billion in credit for the bubbles. And most of that money seems to have come from loans that were made or guaranteed by public agencies. (In the latter case, private entities make the loans, but public ones assume some or all of the risk of default.) Number one in Bosnia was the European Fund for Southeast Europe, a conduit for European government donors. In Pakistan, the top lender was the Asian Development Bank, followed by the Pakistan

---

11. Gonzalez (2010b).

12. Where one institution had guaranteed another's loan—promising to pay it if the borrowing MFI did not—we attributed the amount to the guarantor. The U.S. government's Overseas Private Investment Corporation is an example of a guarantor.

Poverty Alleviation Fund, which passed through credit from the World Bank. Some big lenders were private companies that manage funds from both public and private investors. BlueOrchard, for example, was number one in Nicaragua and number two in Bosnia (see table 9-1).

One important message from these tallies has to do with their novelty. Laboring to answer the question of who inflated the bubbles, I realized: almost no one knew. The data summed here were incomplete, uncertain in some respects and, at one to two years of age when gathered, out of date next to the tempo of hypergrowth. But they were the best that were publicly available. In the years before the bubbles burst, hardly any investor saw the big picture because hardly any had tried. Perhaps key people at BlueOrchard and other intermediaries understood the situation. If so, they seem not to have advertised it heavily.

A Credit Bureau on Investment in MFIs

This story should sound familiar: A set of borrowers, microcreditors in this case, are taking loans from many sources. Total borrowing is expanding rapidly. No one is tracking all this activity, much less whether the borrowers can reasonably be expected to handle all the debts they have contracted. And the easy credit is hiding the very problems it creates, since unpayable loans are quickly refinanced with new ones. In other words, the cross-country microcredit financing scene resembles the within-country microcredit market in some places, with untracked multiple borrowing creating the risk of overborrowing. In the mid-1990s, Alex Silva struggled to raise a few million dollars for the first microfinance investment vehicle, ProFund (see chapter 8). Now microfinance investment managers are struggling to place the funds they have on hand.

One response within the microfinance world to the excesses of lending has been to attack the manifestations. The Smart Campaign, a joint project of CGAP and Acción International's Center for Financial Inclusion, has signed up more than 600 MFIs to endorse six principles of responsible lending: avoidance of overindebtedness; transparent and responsible pricing; non-coercive collection practices; proper staff behavior; mechanisms for redress of grievances; and privacy of client data.[13] The organizers well understand that fine words do little in themselves. But they can help change the culture, for example by giving social investors a benchmark against which they can hold MFIs accountable.

13. Smart Campaign, "Campaign Mission & Goals" (j.mp/oYQ0dY [September 2, 2011]).

Table 9-1. *Top Five Creditor/Guarantors to Top Five Microfinance Institutions with Data, Four Countries with Microcredit Crises*

Creditor/guarantor	Money source[a]	Outstanding loans and guarantees (million $)
Bosnia and Herzegovina, end-2008		
European Fund for Southeast Europe (EC, Austria, Denmark, Germany, Switzerland)	Public	86
BlueOrchard	Mixed	57
European Bank for Reconstruction and Development	Public	35
Instituto de Crédito Oficial, Spain	Public	34
responsAbility	Private	29
Total, all creditors and guarantors		532
Morocco, end-2008		
Instituto de Crédito Oficial, Spain	Public	143
Banque Populaire du Maroc	Private	104
Banque Marocaine du Commerce Extérieur	Private	48
Agence Française de Développement	Public	34
Société Générale Marocaine de Banques	Private	32
Total, all creditors and guarantors		468
Nicaragua, end-2008		
BlueOrchard	Mixed	46
Central American Bank for Economic Integration	Public	33
ProCredit Holding	Mixed	28
Financiera Nicaragüense de Inversiones (Germany/KfW)	Public	27
responsAbility	Private	19
Total, all creditors and guarantors		326
Pakistan, end-2007		
Asian Development Bank	Public	71
Pakistan Poverty Alleviation Fund (World Bank)	Public	32
Domestic money market	Private	8
Habib Bank, MCB Bank, ABN Amro	Private	7
U.S. Overseas Private Investment Corporation	Public	6
Total, all creditors and guarantors		131

Source: David Roodman, "Who Inflated the Microcredit Bubbles?" *Microfinance Open Book Blog,* March 27, 2010 (j.mp/9bRASO).

a. "Mixed" institutions are privately run conduits for mixes of public and private money.

Unfortunately, the history of financial manias teaches us that a heavy tide of capital will overtop or sweep away all but the sturdiest embankments. In the United States, the trillion-dollar buildup to the crisis of 2008 tossed aside ratings agencies and central bankers—supposed agents of restraint—like so much flotsam. Only jurisdictions with the firmest regulatory restraints on lending, such as North Dakota and Canada, held back the tide. The Smart Campaign and other such efforts, while constructive, are not powerful enough to stop the problem of overeager lending. Something else is needed to attack the problem closer to its source: a campaign aimed directly at credit for microcredit, with the goal of restraining it.

What should be the demands of such a campaign? How should moderation be defined and enforced? Within nations, one corrective for overeager lending is the credit bureau. By analogy, investors in microcredit at least need to establish ways to share information at high frequency, such as quarterly, on the financial obligations of MFIs in which they invest. This could happen informally. A credit bureau with information on microcreditors could publish high-frequency data on investment flows into MFIs and lending flows out of them, aggregated where necessary to protect the confidentiality of individual deals. The body could develop indicators of individual, regional, and national lending growth. Based on soft standards analogous to the rule of thumb that mortgage payments should not exceed a third of income, it could issue warnings of various severity levels. (Think of yellow and red traffic lights.) These external reference points would help microfinance investment managers resist higher-ups, politicians, customers, and citizens who are eager for them to pour more money into microcredit. The body also could gather data relevant to when credit for microcredit undermines the initiative to enter the savings business. It could analyze whether a given MFI realistically could obtain permission to take savings, study the cost of taking savings, and compare that cost to that of external capital in order to gauge the distortion from cheap credit.[14]

Like ordinary credit bureaus, such a centralized brain for the microcredit investment business would reduce but not eliminate problems. The toughest problem might be imposing the restraint implied by a serious commitment to savings: would microfinance investors support a body that advised them to slash their operations, to stop picking the plum MFIs? They might if they saw it as essential to the industry's survival.

14. Liliana Rojas-Suarez, senior fellow, Center for Global Development, Washington, D.C., conversation with author, April 30, 2010.

Public versus Private Investment

An alternative to regulating the sizes of the flows is to regulate who can emit them, favoring those more apt to act with care. In a 2007 report called *Role Reversal*, Damian von Stauffenberg, founder of the first microfinance ratings firm, MicroRate, and industry consultant Julie Abrams argued that public investors ought to exit MFIs when private ones enter. The job of public investors (which they call international financial institutions, or IFIs) is to "go where the private sector does not yet dare to tread; to assume risks that private capital would find unacceptable." Yet that's often not what has happened. Table 9-1 shows that substantial amounts of public *and* private money entered Bosnia and Herzegovina, Morocco, and Nicaragua. To explain why, von Stauffenberg and Abrams pointed to the incentives at work in public agencies that favor disbursement for its own sake:

> Whether top decision-makers are aware of it or not, there are powerful incentives for IFIs to maximize their microfinance exposure, and to do so by concentrating on the largest and safest borrowers. Microfinance has acquired such a positive image, that a sizeable exposure in this sector has become a sign of an IFI's commitment to development. This is reinforced by an IFI's need to disburse its microfinance budget each year. Since IFIs are not primarily profit-driven, their success is often defined by the amounts that have been lent. If a budget has been allocated to microfinance, that budget must be spent—and spending it on a few large loans to top MFIs is far quicker, cheaper, and less risky than lending to, and nurturing immature institutions.[15]

On its face, the rule that public investors should exit when private investors enter is blunt and has a fuzzy rationale. It is not obvious why private social investors pursuing that "positive image" should behave more constructively than public social investors doing so. Private investment funds also feel pressure to get money out the door and associate with success; many of them are not primarily profit-driven.

But conversations with industry insiders have persuaded me that the public–private distinction has teeth. The nub of the matter is that most private investors are small specialists. Bad calls can permanently damage their reputations. Such mortal risk focuses the corporate mind. As private companies with staffs numbering in the dozens rather than thousands, they are much less rule-bound, more agile. In contrast, major public investors such as the

15. Abrams and von Stauffenberg (2007), 1.

International Finance Corporation (IFC) are muscle-bound generalists. After the recent crises, the private investors seemed quicker to recognize and respond to troubles than the public investors; they even gently discouraged prospective investors in their funds. By contrast, in the last, dark days of 2008, when global financial Armageddon seemed nigh, the IFC and Germany's KfW joined forces to announce the Microfinance Liquidity Facility. It was meant to prevent a sudden scarcity of capital from choking sound microlenders. It would inject up to $500 million into MFIs via leading fund managers such as BlueOrchard and responsAbility. Although it was a smart, swift, and bold proposal, it took five months for the first of the money to trickle out and another four before operations were in full swing. By the time the money fully arrived, in September 2010, private microfinance fund managers were struggling with a surplus rather than a deficit. Despite the excess of liquidity, the facility created more of it, disbursing $76 million over the rest of 2010.[16]

Given the dangers of surfeit and the continuing dominance of public investors, curtailing the flow of public money into microcredit portfolios would probably make the world a better place. It is a practical proposal: a relatively small group of actors, including heads of development banks and parliamentarians holding the purse strings, could make it happen.

If the microcredit investment industry cannot be run in a way that minimizes harm to the goals of responsible lending, safe deposit-taking, and healthy institutional growth, it probably should be shut down altogether, save for a catalytic role in developing new MFIs through seed capital and training grants. Because of the dangers of aggressive lending, too little direct financing of microcredit portfolios is better than too much. A fundamental problem is that the evidence of microcredit's overall impact on poverty and freedom is ambiguous. If it is this hard to assure that such investment does more good than harm, the movement may be barking up the wrong tree. Helping microfinance play to its strength, building lasting institutions, calls for less investment, not more.

Deliberately Seeking Savings

The lives of the poor are full of risk. Their incomes fluctuate sporadically by day and season. They are more prone to injury and illness, yet more

16. Microfinance Enhancement Facility (2011); Martin Holtmann, head, Microfinance Group, Global Financial Markets Department, International Finance Corporation, Washington, D.C., interview with author, May 5, 2011. Interpretation of the facts is the author's.

dependent on physical health for their livelihoods than wealthy people. If poor people's chief financial problem is managing unpredictability, then seemingly insurance is the financial service they need most. Certainly, exploratory efforts to insure the poor should be supported, and successes should be applauded. Going by the history of today's rich countries, life insurance is the most promising avenue for takeoff. The prospects are perhaps best in South Asia where, just as with microcredit, skilled staff are cheapest relative to the incomes of those to be served. However, as we saw in chapters 4 and 5, insurance is inherently more complex than credit and savings, which cuts against the microfinance industry's imperative to streamline. On balance, microinsurance for the billions appears a less practical ideal than microsavings for the billions.

Savings is a conceptually simpler service, with much going for it. Shifting toward savings and away from credit should help microfinance perform better on all three of the senses of success considered in this book. Experience and common sense say that the poorest are more willing to save than to shoulder the risk of credit. Meanwhile, as we saw in chapter 2, savings can do almost anything credit can. People can save to start a business, pay tuition, finance a funeral. And like insurance, it can buffer families against financial shocks. It lacks the leverage of insurance—a dollar a year in premiums can instantly buy $100 in life insurance, but a dollar a year in savings only adds a dollar a year to shock absorption capacity. Yet savings has the advantage of accessibility in the case of any misfortune, not just certain insurable ones.

To achieve its full potential, savings needs to be offered in a variety of forms, perhaps including ones that haven't been invented yet. In principle, accounts can be completely liquid, for maximum flexibility, though in practice these are costly to administer. Commitment savings better approximate the discipline and rhythmic efficiency of loans. Exploration beyond those standard product types deserves the same energy historically poured into elaborating and refining microcredit. An interesting credit-savings hybrid is Stuart Rutherford's "P9," which he is piloting through *Safe*Save's rural sister in Bangladesh, Shohoz Shonchoy. It is designed to eliminate two barriers to saving: lack of discipline and lack of periodic lump sums of income, such as paychecks, from which to set aside money. At the same time, it strives for flexibility. A customer starts with a zero-interest loan of 2,000 taka ($28), of which the bank disburses just two-thirds, putting the rest in a zero-interest savings account; the loan becomes the lump sum from which to save. Despite having received less than 2,000 taka, the customer pays back that much so that she ends up with a net savings balance. She repays on a schedule of her choosing. She then repeats with optionally larger amounts, so that after a typical seven cycles, her savings exceed her loan balance. Once she reaches 20,000 taka in savings, she can withdraw it all, continue to "borrow to save," or just save conventionally, now with interest.[17]

One big responsibility is assuring the safety of deposits. Informal, small-group savings arrangements meet the responsibility through witness. In a Village Savings and Loan Association of thirty women, as described in chapter 4, every member can watch as the three key holders secure the group's lock box. But when clients are too numerous for direct witness, government supervisors are usually needed. It sounds like a simple step, but when an external body assumes responsibility for the safety of savings at an MFI, it causes a massive departure from credit-only microfinance. Regulators and supervisors take an interest not only in the savings side of the operation but the previously ignorable credit side, too, since the lending puts the deposits at risk. Overseers must devise and enforce formulas to govern MFI behavior. One such formula is the "capital adequacy ratio"—for example, a ratio of 10 percent means that for every $10 in outstanding microloans, the MFI must have at least $1 on hand in its own cash or some other ultra safe form ready to absorb losses on the loan portfolio and protect deposits. The government also may regulate the lending in order to assure that it is aboveboard and prudent, for example by requiring that the banks keep files with specified documentation on each borrower. They may impose constraints on the ownership and board composition of the MFI to prevent crony capitalism and assure that if the MFI needs to call in more capital, owners will have deep enough pockets to comply.[18]

This is the stuff of conventional banking regulation. Bringing it to microfinance requires surmounting several challenges. One is that enforcing and complying with all these rules costs the MFIs and the government money. As noted in chapter 8, for MFIs, collecting the required documentation and filing the required reports drives up the cost of taking savings. In an authoritative review of regulatory issues in microfinance, Rosenberg and colleagues write that it is not unusual for compliance to cost 5 percent of assets in the first year and 1 percent or more per year thereafter. Likewise, especially in poor countries where government agencies are chronically underfunded, supervisors may lack the staff to monitor all of a country's MFIs and other deposit-taking institutions. And because most MFIs are too small to undermine confidence in the banking system generally, MFIs are a low priority. Recognizing such limits, the authors point to a trade-off: only allow a few

17. Stuart Rutherford, "Product Rules" (j.mp/epwJlh [April 24, 2010]).
18. Christen, Lyman, and Rosenberg (2003).

MFIs to take savings, or allow more to do so, bringing financial services to more people, but with little or no supervision. However supervisors make this trade-off, they should take care not to overestimate their own capacity to effectively oversee the MFIs they license, and they should require any unsupervised MFIs to inform customers that no guardian angel is watching.[19]

Recent events in Nigeria show what can happen when supervisors overreach. In 2007–08, the central bank defined a new type of financial institution, the Microfinance Bank, and issued an absurd 800 licenses to start them. The banks could do both savings and loans. The unit assigned to supervise them was woefully understaffed. The result was unsurprising: 800 little institutions taking depositors' and investors' money; growing fast, making sloppy loans; paying rich salaries to top officials; and running up records of fraud, default, bank runs, and failure. At this writing, the central bank has revoked more than 100 licenses.[20]

The other challenge in keeping savings safe is adapting conventional regulation to microfinance. Although poor savers deserve the same protections as rich ones when it comes to capital adequacy, the job of setting guidelines is easily botched. Some traditional rules can undermine the microcredit approach, for example by requiring all loans to be backed by collateral or viewing a nonprofit MFI that would own the majority of its for-profit offspring as a crony capitalist.[21]

Chapter 8 laid out the argument for young MFIs to start with credit, then branch into savings. This path is not the only one available. Among the exemplars of microsavings, the largest and smallest, BRI's unit *desa* system in Indonesia and Rutherford's *Safe*Save in Bangladesh, took savings from the start and so far have rewarded their clients' trust. Many of ProCredit's banks took savings from birth or moved into it quickly, exploiting the financial muscle of their parent organization. But accepting the credit-then-savings path as reasonable, it follows that at any given time not every MFI should be expected to do microsavings.

And just as not all MFIs are suited for savings, not every organization that does microsavings needs to be an MFI. Institutions of different form, with a comparative advantage in reliability, can also do the job: Village Savings and Loan Associations; credit cooperatives and their more formal and regulated cousins, credit unions; and established savings banks, public and private. If

19. Christen, Lyman, and Rosenberg (2003), 19, 28.

20. Rozas (2011), 16–17; Central Bank of Nigeria, "CBN Grants Provisional Approval for New Licenses to 121 MFBs," press release, October 21, 2010 (j.mp/lMNDP7).

21. Christen, Lyman, and Rosenberg (2003).

the end is the expansion of microsavings, promoters and regulators should be ecumenical about the means.

Along with keeping savings safe, a primary task in making microsavings work is controlling cost. A study by the Inter-American Development Bank of MFIs in Latin America found that for microsavings accounts, defined as those under $100, holding $1 in deposits cost an astonishing $2 per year, mainly in bank tellers' time handling tiny deposits and withdrawals. Clearly the economics of banking impose limits on how small the accounts and how poor the people that can be offered savings accounts. Happily, the situation is not as bleak as this statistic suggests. Just as microcredit is expensive in Latin America (partly because of the high cost of employees relative to loan sizes), so should we expect microsavings to be. The economics are probably better elsewhere. Meanwhile, despite the high costs, the Latin MFIs maintained many of these costly, small accounts, and for reasons: a sense of mission to serve the poor; an expectation that many balances would rise over time; and the use of the savings relationship as a platform to sell insurance, money transfers, and credit.[22] Although the economics are probably better elsewhere, cost remains an impediment. The great hope for reducing it lies in modern technologies, such as mobile phones and smart cards.

The Technological Frontier

For economists, the flavors of microcredit that started the microfinance revolution—solidarity and village banking, individual microcredit—are technological advances. Although they were low-tech in the everyday sense of the word, in context, they were fresh ways to extract more value from a given amount of labor and capital, providing services at a lower price than previously possible. Since those days, circa 1980, microfinance has not changed so much as a retail product. SKS in India does group microcredit much as Muhammad Yunus and his students invented it, albeit with a computerized back office. Compartamos in Mexico does village banking more or less as John Hatch and FINCA refined it. But new, high-tech ways of connecting people and transmitting information may bring a second revolution to the movement.

People often use new technologies first as slot-in replacements for their predecessors. The desktop computer began in many offices as just a fancy typewriter, a new machine for preparing printed documents. It takes a while for societies to discover wholly new uses, such as e-mail, that make the initial uses seem quaint. In the microfinance world, an early response to advances in

22. Maisch, Soria, and Westley (2006).

communications and computing was to use them to make standard models more efficient, such as by keeping records at group meetings with Palm Pilots.

But the future of microfinance appears to differ radically from its past. In the mid-2000s, Brazil used satellite links and barcode readers to extend its banking system to all of the country's 5,561 municipalities, including 2,300 that had never been banked before. Post offices and corner stores now operate as "banking correspondents," agents who can handle transactions on behalf of regular banks far away. They handle the conversion between paper and electronic money, so that customers can, for instance, arrive with cash and make a water bill payment that is transmitted electronically to the utility. The system has handled trillions of dollars in payments.[23] In South Africa and Namibia, a company called Net1 delivers government welfare payments to nearly 4 million people by charging their smart cards. Cardholders can convert balances to cash at any store with the appropriate point-of-sale card reader. The cards look like ordinary credit cards, and the machines that read them look like ordinary card readers. But inside, the technology is more advanced: The cards and readers are designed to operate in decentralized fashion to accommodate unreliable power and communications infrastructure. They contain chips that store encrypted transaction histories of their owners and the owners of other cards or readers that they have recently touched, allowing them to pass around and back up securely encoded transaction histories like ants passing chemical signals. When the readers do connect by phone to central computers, they synchronize everything they have. And because the cards are computers, they can provide extra services when passed through readers, such as extending a loan on the fly, based on on-card data about the cardholder's history of welfare payments and servicing of past loans.[24]

The greatest potential for technological revolution in microfinance comes from one stupendous fact: some 5.3 billion people now tote mobile phones.[25] Access to connectivity is converging to universality. Put otherwise, there are now 5.3 billion people with globally networked computers in their pockets. What can they do with those besides talk and text? Access financial services, for one.

In fact, a phone company created one of the most successful financial services for poor people yet. Called M-PESA, the phone-based money transfer system was launched in 2007 by Kenya's Safaricom with the help of a

23. Gallagher (2006).
24. Schwarzbach (2006).
25. ITU (2011).

£1 million challenge grant from the U.K. Department for International Development. Although the service was born out of the microcredit movement, in pilot tests ordinary Kenyans began doing something other than credit transactions with it: sending money to each other. As Safaricom developed the system, it realized that the "killer app" for M-PESA was not patching a 1990s communications technology onto a 1970s financial technology, but *sending money home*. In Kenya, many rural families send a husband or son to Nairobi to work and support the family from afar. Before M-PESA, physical transport of cash was costly and dangerous. One could spend a day or so taking cash home oneself and get robbed on the way. One could pay informal money carriers, again risking theft as well as fraud.[26] M-PESA offered a radically safer, more reliable way to send money over long distances. In just three and a half years, M-PESA reached some 13 million, or 60 percent, of Kenyan adults.[27] It handles more transactions than Western Union.[28]

The first thing Kenyans usually want to do when they receive electronic money is cash it. This they do by visiting any of the 23,000 M-PESA shops scattered among the markets, slums, and villages, which like Western Union storefronts convert between the old and new forms of money for a fee.[29] The shops are franchise businesses, operated by entrepreneurs in agreement with Safaricom. Almost all the shops I visited during a trip in 2010 were run by women. For these business people, providing the on-demand conversion between paper and electronic money takes work and involves risk. They must staff their shops, project demand for cash, keep enough on hand, and transport it between the shops and the bank at the risk of robbery. In return, these entrepreneurs keep 70–80 percent of the commissions, the rest going to Safaricom.[30] As that split suggests, the M-PESA shopkeepers are the muscle and bones of M-PESA.

The phone-based electronic interface is the skin: it holds the system together. Understanding how gets to the core departure from traditional microcredit. For one, the phones allow the managers behind M-PESA to monitor transactions in real time and anticipate cash demand efficiently.[31] As well, the phones make M-PESA's e-money seem real and trustworthy. The

26. Hughes and Lonie (2007).

27. Jack and Suri (2011), 4.

28. Mas and Radcliffe (2010).

29. Jack and Suri (2011), 4.

30. Eijkman, Kendall, and Mas (2010), 3.

31. For more on the management structure behind M-PESA, see David Roodman, "Make New Media of Exchange, but Keep the Old," *Microfinance Open Book Blog*, May 26, 2010 (j.mp/c3tbXx).

instant a customer deposits cash into his phone account, Safaricom verifies his new balance with a text message, which stays in his phone's memory. More generally, the phones let customers hold Safaricom and its agents accountable for promises of service to a degree impossible in informal ways of sending money. When someone sends money home, both he and the recipient get text messages, which prove that Safaricom representatives are obliged to surrender the funds to the recipient upon request.

That accountability in turn allows the delegation and professionalization of cash transport. Before M-PESA, village women might have gone individually, by foot or by bus, to the nearest market town to pick up cash sent home by husbands. Now an M-PESA agent can do it for all of them, all at once, saving time.[32] When I visited Kenya, my fellow travelers and I were taken to the market at the crossroads in the town of Holo, not far from Lake Victoria. Before M-PESA, we were told, people trekked 25 miles by foot or bus to Kisumu, on the shores of the lake, to get their cash—and spent much of it in the market there. Now the cash comes to them through M-PESA, and they spend it locally. And so the Holo market is bustling.[33] Access to the new mobile money technology has increased access to the old mobile money technology, cash.

M-PESA shows how information technology can create new efficiencies and empower clients. It brings a more conventional banking experience to a poorer clientele, offering an alternative to the power relationships of traditional microcredit, in which bank employees lean on clients to lean on each other and the ultimate sanction is the loss of future access to loans. With mobile-phone based payments, the relationship is less credit centered, thus more freeing. In contrast with a microloan, which can be viewed as a locked-in sequence of transactions, each small mobile transaction stands on its own, with fees measured in pennies. Such tariffs give clients complete control over the flow of payments in and out while guaranteeing the provider a profit at each step. Ignacio Mas, who jumped from the world's largest mobile phone company, Vodafone, to the world's largest philanthropy, the Bill & Melinda Gates Foundation, explains that charging by the transaction "is analogous to prepaid airtime for mobile operators: a card bought is profit booked."[34]

I suspect that we are on the cusp of a technological revolution in microfinance. Mobile payments look to me like a kind of infrastructure, like electricity supply and the Internet. Technology connects people in a radically new way

32. Eijkman, Kendall, and Mas (2010).

33. Frederik Eijkman, cofounder, PEP Intermedius, Kisumu, Kenya, conversation with author, May 18, 2010.

34. Mas (2009), 57.

and creates possibilities that will take years for human ingenuity to discover. It will disrupt every field that it touches. The week I was in Kenya, Safaricom launched a partnership with Kenya's dominant MFI, Equity Bank. With a few key presses, M-PESA users can now move electronic money into an Equity savings account that pays interest. They can apply to get automatic loans too, just as with Net1's system. And they can buy personal accident insurance.[35]

Overall, as seen in Brazil and Kenya, technology is rearranging the economics of banking the poor, centralizing core banking functions while decentralizing the interface to the customer. The new approach splits retail from wholesale while linking via wires and radio signals. The retailers are local shopkeepers who provide the interface between paper and electronic money. They substitute for the loan officers of traditional MFIs, but they do not hold clients' money. That job is performed by regulated institutions behind the scenes. Recall how one major impediment to safe savings is the limited capacity of governments to supervise banks. Communications technology is accommodating this limitation in a new way, making it more economical to link the poor directly to traditional, supervised banks. The digital interface of a card or a phone doesn't make the human interface obsolete; rather, as with M-PESA, it provides a new way to delegate customer service to people who can do it more cheaply than brick-and-mortar banks can do.

Coming Full Circle

I began this book with two opposing stories. One was about Murshida, who climbed out of poverty on a ladder of microcredit. The other was about Razia, who slipped down a rung after taking loans. I did so to expose how storytelling forms the public image of microfinance and to make the case for serious research that tests such stories. Good research brings us as close as we can come to the truth about something as diverse as the microfinance experiences of 150 million people.

Though I have examined services other than credit and notions of success other than escape from poverty, there is no denying that the grain of sand that seeded the imperfect pearl of this book is the common belief that microcredit cuts poverty. As a child of bitterly divorced parents, it goes against my grain to choose sides. I see the world in grays. While I cannot dismiss traditional microcredit as pure hype, I also cannot defend direct investment in microlending as a great way for aid agencies, philanthropists, and social

---

35. Ignacio Mas, "M-KESHO in Kenya: A New Step for M-PESA and Mobile Banking," Financial Access Initiative blog, May 27, 2010 (j.mp/je9Pse).

investors to help poor people. Microcredit is one thing; outsiders financing microcredit portfolios in bulk is another. Consider:

—While microcredit gives people a new option to manage their complex and unpredictable financial lives and helps some build businesses, it also leaves some worse off and has a potentially addictive character. On the creditor side, it often pays to keep lending to clients in a continual cycle. On the borrower side, the need to pay off one loan often leads people to take out another. Overlending and overborrowing become more likely as creditors multiply and compete, often by lending to the same clients.

—Although good studies show microsavings and microcredit stimulating microenterprise, those on microcredit so far have found no impact on poverty.

—Qualitative studies by people who immersed themselves in a village for a month or year corroborate this ambivalence. Some women find liberation in doing financial business in public. Others find entrapment in the intertwining debt obligations and peer pressures.

—Enthusiastic flows of money into lending are inherently dangerous. They can reward overly rapid lending and, in competitive markets, nearly force it through a vicious cycle in which each lender strives to keep up with its peers. The microfinance movement has compiled a rather long list of disasters in recent years: Bosnia, India, Morocco, Nicaragua, Nigeria, Pakistan. Probably none will be fatal, but together they point to a deep problem of instability.

Credit is undoubtedly useful in moderation as a way for people to discipline themselves into setting aside money for big purchases. It becomes dangerous when it is pushed too hard. Thus, the mythology that has grown up around microfinance is not just deceptive but destructive.

How much support for microcredit is too much? Incomplete evidence cannot support a certain answer. But choices today must be made on the evidence available today. To the practical question of whether social investors ought to keep pouring billions of dollars per year into microcredit, I say no. Seed money for pilots and start-up MFIs is one thing; large-scale, submarket financing of microcredit portfolios is another.

The long-term goal should be to create balanced, self-sufficient institutions that offer credit in moderation, help people save and move money safely, and push the envelope of practicality on insurance. If these goals can also be achieved through institutional forms less associated with traditional microcredit, such as commercial banks and phone companies, that should be encouraged. While such paths may superficially contradict the credit-centered mythology advanced by some of the founders of modern microfinance, it is the truest realization of their vision: building businesses that serve the bottom of the pyramid, giving billions of people more leverage over their difficult financial circumstances.

Nimble social investors have helped build such institutions with money and advice, and they can do so again. Indeed, the history of microfinance reviewed in chapter 4 shows that small amounts of intelligently placed aid were invaluable to the microfinance movement. The Ford Foundation and the U.N. International Fund for Agricultural Development gave crucial early support to the Grameen Project. The U.S. Agency for International Development worked behind the scenes in Indonesia and Bolivia, as did Germany's Gesellschaft für Technische Zusammenarbeit in India, on the self-help group program. The United Kingdom's aid department made a tiny but timely challenge grant to launch the M-PESA pilot. The focus for outsiders should be making such critical, opportunistic investments, in the failure-accepting spirit of venture capital. It should not be building giant machines for indebting the poor.

At the end of day, I cannot dismiss Razia's story as immaterial to the morality of favoring credit. Nor can I dismiss the story of Eva Yanet Hernández Caballero, whom Compartamos featured on its website until her knitting business unraveled and she began missing payments on loans with triple-digit interest rates.[36] I cannot dismiss chapter 7's story of Jahanara, the microcredit borrower and moneylender who boasted "that she had broken many houses when members could not pay."[37] I cannot dismiss the story of families in Andhra Pradesh who lost wives or husbands, mothers or fathers, to suicide after they fell into debt—debt that included microcredit.[38]

But neither can I dismiss the manifest hunger of poor people for reliable tools to manage their money, nor the extraordinary success of some microfinance institutions in creating and serving this market. The best way forward is to celebrate what is good in this achievement and build on it.

Better banking will no more abolish poverty than better clinics or schools ever have. By and large, what ends poverty is not the direct delivery of services to poor people but industrialization, in all its disruptiveness. Over the

36. Keith Epstein and Geri Smith, "Compartamos: From Nonprofit to Profit," *BusinessWeek*, December 13, 2007.

37. Karim (2008), 23.

38. For example, see Soutik Biswas, "India's Micro-finance Suicide Epidemic," BBC News, December 16, 2010 (j.mp/hq6S8U); Yoolim Lee and Ruth David, "Suicides in India Revealing How Men Made a Mess of Microcredit," *Bloomberg Markets Magazine*, December 28, 2010.

last third of a century, judicious support from donors and social investors for microfinance has contributed to such economic transformation in a small but respectable way, catalyzing innovations, institutions, and industries, and reaching millions. Over the next third of a century, donors and investors can go much farther. They can help build a global industry to give billions of poor people the tools they need to manage their wealth.

appendix
A Sampling of Blog Posts

Here are a dozen of my favorite posts from my *Microfinance Open Book Blog* (blogs.cgdev.org/open_book). You can still post comments there.

Help Me Write This Book
February 16, 2009

I am using this blog to share the process of writing my book about microfinance (the mass production of small-scale financial services for the poor). The book asks and attempts to answer bottom-line questions about what we know about the impacts of microfinance and what that implies for how governments, foundations, and investors should support it.

For, oh, the last millennium, the standard way to write a book has been to hide the text from all but a few people until it is frozen, then unleash it and await a reaction. As I drafted chapter 5 last December, I realized that from the point of view of interacting with the audience, you can't get much more stilted than that. Why work that way in the Internet age? Why not share drafts online, and start conversations between writer and readers while the text is still in play? One of CGD's technology gurus, **Dave Witzel**, pointed me to the blog as a natural vehicle. (Down the road, CGD may use more Talmudic mechanisms that let you annotate paragraph-by-paragraph. See **twobits.net**.) Through this blog, I will share and seek feedback on chapters I have drafted, documents I have found, and burning questions on my mind.

This blog will not keep you up-to-the-minute on microfinance with a fire hose of news—see the blogroll down on the right side of the **blog home page** for channels more like that. But by the same token, it will give you an opportunity to talk back to the content and influence the final product: a book that should help us all see deeper. I hope you will take that opportunity. Some books are written by experts wanting to share their expertise. In contrast, I am writing this book in order to *become* an expert. Writing it is a voyage of discovery.

We at CGD are inventing our "open book" blog process as we go. I will upload chapter drafts in Microsoft Word (.doc) and Adobe Acrobat (.pdf) formats. I will create a main blog post for each chapter, with the idea that commenting on these posts will be the best way for you to comment on the drafts they announce. You can also send me marked up files by **e-mail**, which we might post publicly. (I don't want to commit since this is all so new.) The "Contents" list on the right margin of the **blog home page** will help you navigate the book's content.

This "open book" blog marries an old writing form with a new one. Although books predate the printing press, that technology of mass production endowed books with a new and transformative power. An author could ponder the world—filter information, weigh competing views, test ideas against data—then broadcast his or her conclusions more quickly, to more people, and across greater distances than ever before. Much the same can be said of the Internet and bloggers today, even if this time around the technology predated the medium. Blogs will never drive books into extinction, but the two might interbreed. I suspect this blog is part of that historical development, whose full consequences will take time to unfold.

The Anti-Bono: Microfinance Is Not Aid
February 22, 2009

Zambian-born economist Dambisa Moyo has a new book coming out called *Dead Aid*. In the lead-up to the launch, she is doing interviews with outlets such as the **New York Times** and **Financial Times**. She appears to make an old and serious argument, going back at least to **P.T. Bauer**'s 1971 *Dissent on Development*, that foreign aid does harm by reducing the accountability of government to the governed. The potential harm is especially great in Africa, where many states get large percentages of their budgets from aid. (For a couple of CGD works on this theme see Moss, Pettersson, and van de Walle's **Aid-Institutions Paradox** and Birdsall's **Do No Harm**.)

In case you hadn't noticed, one thing that distinguishes Moyo from Bono, Geldof, Sachs, and Easterly is that she is not a white guy. She is African. So she is powerfully positioned to shoulder her way into that constellation of figures, each of whom has to some extent gained fame by becoming a caricature of an extreme position in the grand debate over whether aid "works." (OK, some of those guys also wrote some good songs.)

Unclear to me is whether it is her goal to join them or forge a more nuanced image.

Her *NYT* interview did raise my eyebrows. I would hate to have my comments to reporters taken too literally, so I will try not to do that to her, and await the book before judging **statements like these**:

What do you think has held back Africans?
I believe it's largely aid. You get the corruption—historically, leaders have stolen the money without penalty—and you get the dependency, which kills entrepreneurship. You also disenfranchise African citizens, because the government is beholden to foreign donors and not accountable to its people.

If people want to help out, what do you think they should do with their money if not make donations?
Microfinance. Give people jobs.

But what if you just want to donate, say, $25?
Go to the Internet and type in **Kiva.org**, where you can make a loan to an African entrepreneur.

If you'll forgive a little math geekiness, this yields a system of two equations:
(1) Aid ≠ Microfinance
(2) Microfinance = Jobs
As for equation (1): In fact, a lot of foreign aid, as grants and loans, has supported microfinance in Africa and elsewhere. That includes (in my mind) **a lot of official-agency investment**, which occurs on below-commercial terms, accepting low returns for the perceived risk, and so contains a subsidy element. So is this good aid? If so, what distinguishes it from bad aid? Is aid for microfinance, just by virtue of being for microfinance, better than aid for education or health or roads? Or is the key that the microfinance support she likes goes around the government? Or that microfinance charges for what it provides? . . . in which case would education and health and road-building aid be equally meritorious if they did the same?

As for equation (2), I am aware of no credible evidence that microfinance creates jobs, on average. Of course it has in some cases, but we don't know how representative they are, nor how many jobs are destroyed at enterprises out-competed by micro-financed ones. To the extent that borrowers use microfinance for microenterprise, as opposed to, say, paying school fees, they tend to invest it in small, self-employing ventures—corner stores, vegetable trade—that do not hire. That's not to knock Kiva or suggest that financial services are useless to the poor.

I look forward to reading her book, where perhaps she recognizes these complexities.

Review of *Portfolios of the Poor: How the World's Poor Live on $2 a Day*
May 23, 2009

If you want to understand how poor people in poor countries manage money, invest in **Portfolios of the Poor**. The new book's four authors— Daryl Collins, Jonathan Morduch, Stuart Rutherford, and Orlanda Ruthven—took up an idea of **David Hulme**, to compile **financial diaries** of poor households. A researcher visits a poor household repeatedly, say, every fortnight for a year, and gathers detailed information on what its members earned, spent, borrowed, and saved since the last visit. Through the data collection and the associated conversations she pieces together an intimate portrait of the household's financial life. "[F]inance is the relationship between time and money . . . to understand it fully, time and money must be observed together." (Disclosure: I am coauthoring a **CGD paper** with Morduch.)

Much glory in the social sciences goes to those who study causality, who (seem to) show that A causes B. Yet the most enlightening work is often just plain *descriptive*, coming from a good, long stare at A or B. Of course, to do good descriptive science, you have to know what to ask and how to ask it:

> The intensity of getting to know the characters in the financial diaries informed our perspective on financial behavior as much as our scrutiny of the data we collected. We and our field team got to know not only which respondents were using what financial devices, but also gained a deeper and more personal understanding of who these people were: who was often confused about their finances, who had family disagreements that guided their decisions, who was not coping with the circumstances they found themselves in. Money is powerful, particularly when you don't have a lot of it, and it was only by going to the "coal face" of financial interactions between the people themselves that we felt we could understand how and why the poor managed money the way they did.

Rutherford and a small team he led compiled the first diaries, from 42 Bangladeshi households in 1999–2000. Ruthven did it in India in 2000, with 48 households. And in 2004, Collins collected diaries from some 94 families in South Africa.

Some themes of *Portfolios of the Poor* will be familiar to readers of Rutherford's *The Poor and Their Money* (**free early version**). Rutherford is not the sole author of the new volume of course, but might be said to be its soul author, his influence being clear. (For more on Rutherford and his earlier book, see the draft chapter 2 on my own **"open book" blog**, where I am writing a book about microfinance in public.) In the earlier book, Rutherford showed how poor people look to all financial services—savings, credit, insurance—to turn small, frequent pay-ins into occasional, large pay-outs. The pay-ins can be weekly savings deposits, loan payments, even insurance premia, while the pay-outs can be large withdrawals, loan disbursements, and insurance indemnities. People deploy lump sums so assembled for investing in enterprise, yes, but also for doctor's bills, school fees, funerals, weddings, even dowry. The poor's use of financial services involves much more than microcredit for microenterprise.

The new book builds on these ideas. It emphasizes that being poor in a poor country means having an income that is not just low but variable and unpredictable. At least as much as a family's average level of income (such as $2/person/day), the volatility around the average drives how the poor manage money. If you make $1 today, $4 tomorrow, and nothing the day after, but need to put food on the table every day, you will engage in complex patterns of borrowing and saving to smooth the mismatch between your income and outflows. Thus out of necessity poor people deploy *more* complex financial strategies than do the rich. The book tells stories of families who are constantly juggling small loans to and from friends and family; saving with local "moneyguards"; participating in savings and insurance clubs (such as burial clubs in South Africa); buying groceries from the local shopkeeper on credit; and otherwise patching together an extraordinary diversity of financial devices in order to get by.

Portfolios of the Poor also shows the embedding of these informal financial relationships in social relationships, which is both a blessing and a curse. The blessing is flexibility: an interesting discussion of moneylenders' interest rates, for example, shows how often late payments, defaults, and wrangled interest forgiveness effectively reduce rates that might otherwise seem usurious. When out of social obligation a lender forgives the debt of a woman who has just lost her husband, the lender absorbs some of the risk of the woman's life in a way that formal bankers are less wont to. The curse of socially embedded informal finance is the tincture of precariousness. Will your brother pay back? Will the **"merry-go-round"** savings club, in which one person takes the pot each week, keep rotating till your turn comes around? Will the moneyguard abscond?

In the view of the book's authors, "semiformal" microfinance—the kind you've heard of—stands out in the financial lives of the poor for its rule-bound reliability. If the Grameen Bank says you will be eligible for a new loan in 17 weeks if you maintain your payment record, you can bank on it. In the spirit of diversification, poor people welcome this distinctive style of finance into their portfolios, along with informal services. The book's emphasis on this point helped me appreciate that the essence of formality is abstraction from social context. In the ideal, participants in a formal financial arrangement are legal persons, parties to a contract that precisely stipulates obligations. Whether the persons are rich or poor, giant corporations or tiny families, should not matter.

That great strength is also, as so often, a great weakness: in this case, rigidity. Classic microcredit disburses once a year, but husbands do not fall sick on such a neat schedule, which is why other forms of finance must still fill in. Yet the authors are optimistic that microfinance can become more flexible, mainly because it already has at the Grameen Bank, whose "Grameen II" reforms in the early 2000's transformed it more than most realize. Savings can now be withdrawn at any time . . . except from a popular new "pension" savings plan through which clients bind themselves to contributing a sum such as $1/month for 5 or 10 years in return for 12%/annum interest at maturity. Loans can now be "topped up": halfway into a one-year loan repayment, you can borrow back to the full amount. The book closes by calling for more such reforms in Bangladesh and beyond, so that reliable microfinance can cater to the true financial needs of the poor. Even as they laud the changes at Grameen, they ask for more:

> The interface with the microfinance institutions remains the weekly village meeting, a breakthrough of the 1970s that is now looking somewhat stale: meetings consume too much precious time, there is no privacy, individual needs go unrecognized, the male workers tend to patronize the women members, and more and more members skip the meeting if they can, preferring just to show up and pay their dues as quickly as possible. Working almost exclusively with women may well have started as a commendable attempt to right a gender imbalance, but . . . more and more critics point to the failure to find ways to serve men. Many microfinance institutions say that they have abandoned joint liability, but field staff, fearful of loan arrears, continue to impose some forms of it. Similarly, despite attempts to make repayment terms and schedules more flexible, most loans are still for one year with equal invariable weekly payments that cannot be prepaid. . . . Most clients are still routinely pressured into taking out a fresh loan as soon they have repaid an earlier one.

For me, this quote highlights two major lacunae in the book. The first is a full-bore discussion of gender. The authors make explicit that their unit of analysis is the household not the individual. Yet surely they gained insight into how men and women within a household cooperate and vie in managing money. Microfinance's long-time focus on women is predicated on the belief that women are more likely to invest extra resources in the health and education of the family, and repay loans more reliably. Did Collins *et al.* see that in their microscope? Or have men gotten a bad rap?

The second gap, more understandable since it lies farther from the core contribution of the book, concerns the business imperatives of microfinance. These I came to appreciate in writing **Microfinance as Business**. If microfinance officers still pressure people to borrow, they probably do so out of an institutional need to maintain the flow of business. Historically, the focus on women arose in part because they proved more pliable to the peer pressure of credit groups, which made them cheaper to lend to. The need to keep costs in line with the small transactions of the poor limits how far microfinance groups can go in providing quality service. Grameen II pushed the frontier in Asia beyond where most might have guessed it could go, and new technologies may push it farther, but the principle seems essential for understanding how much microfinance can help the poor manage their money. The gulf between what the poor need and what they get will always be with us.

Read this book somewhat backwards. The authors make great use of other people's stories, but hide their own story till Appendix 1. That plus the conceit, which seems quaint in the blog age, that four authorial voices are one gives the main text a slightly ethereal quality. Read the story of the financial diaries themselves and peruse diarists' stories in Appendix 2, in order to appreciate the lessons in the main text.

I close with my favorite display in the book. It shows the average recorded discrepancy between total inflows and total outflows for each household in South Africa on each biweekly visit. It typically took 6 visits—three months—to get the discrepancy close to zero and convince researchers they were seeing the whole picture. Lots got left out early on. That is a cautionary tale for those who study data from one-shot surveys of households. The truth is an elusive thing. *Portfolios of the Poor* shows the power of financial diaries to pursue it.

Debt = Rope
May 26, 2009

Strong stuff from anthropologist **Parker Shipton**:

> Juloo, "rope" to a Mandinko, means several things at once. It can refer to a small-scale trader, or to credit or debt. Every Mandinko knows the meanings are related. Traders are also lenders, and their loans, while

sometimes useful like a rope ladder, also tie down a farmer like a rope around the neck. When rural people in The Gambia speak of juloo, in any of these uses, they consciously or unconsciously connote slavery. The Mandinko and other peoples of this small and impoverished West African river nation, an ancient trade route winding thinly through southern Senegal, have had occasion in history to learn quite a bit about ropes and involuntary servitude, and about debt. The linked images and overtones are not empty of emotion.

The source is a 1990 World Bank working paper, **How Gambians Save**, which commenter **Kim Wilson** pointed me to. For the book **What's Wrong with Microfinance**, Kim contributed a provocative piece called "The moneylender's dilemma" about rise and fall of Catholic Relief Services' involvement in microcredit.

Shipton's point is not that all debt is bad, but that poor people are often wisely wary of it and like to save too. I'm confronting the dual nature of credit/debt now as I think about usury and the ethics of lending.

The rope metaphor is linked to the Jubilee 2000 movement's call to "break the chains" of third world debt.

Hammer Blows or Pinpricks? Stories vs. Statistics in Microfinance
July 22, 2009

It's been a tough season for the **proposition** that "microfinance is a proven and cost-effective tool to help the very poor lift themselves out of poverty and improve the lives of their families." In May came a **randomized trial of microcredit in Hyderabad** finding no impacts on poverty 15–18 months out. In June came a **paper** challenging the leading older-generation studies that seemed to show that microcredit had cut poverty in Bangladesh in the 1990s. Now in July we have **another randomized trial**, of microcredit in Manila, also finding no impact on bottom-line measures of household welfare.

A couple of people, including **Tim Ogden**, have raised a good question with me in the last few days: What does this mean for microfinance? Has a myth been debunked? Is the whole movement about to implode in a ball of fire? More precisely, will this research perturb the dominant narrative about microfinance in the public mind, about microenterprise as a reliable ladder out of poverty?

I'm reminded of two Mark Twain saws—the one about lies, damned lies, and statistics; and the one about the reports of his death being greatly exaggerated.

Reasons this isn't quite a David (ahem) and Goliath story:

- The new and randomized trials of credit, though credible, have produced only fragmentary knowledge. On the one hand, that does undercut the assertion that microcredit is a proven anti-poverty tool. On the other, it doesn't prove that microcredit rarely helps. The Karlan and Zinman Manila sample is predominantly middle class—people who were already out of poverty. Their earlier South Africa study looked at four-month loans to people who (I think) could show pay stubs, and who worked in a system that implicitly expected them to borrow in order to pay for on-the-job training. (See **previous post**.) The one full-bore study of microcredit for poor people without jobs, in Hyderabad, does not look at outcomes beyond the first 15–18 months.
- The **Dupas and Robinson randomized study** found benefits from *savings*—again out of sync with myth, but good news for microfinance more broadly.
- Also appearing in the last few months is the great book, **Portfolios of the Poor**. It makes no claim that microfinance raises income on average. But it does argue that microfinance is valuable in helping people *smooth* that income (for a price). To put this more personally, I mentally file all those statistical studies in one chapter of my book, "development as measured impact." But since our knowledge of the actual impacts in millions of lives is doomed to be limited, I also devote chapters to other notions of success. The ideas in *Portfolios of the Poor* fit into my "development as freedom" chapter. And into my "development as institution-building" chapter fits the thesis that a chief contribution of microfinance is its enrichment of the institutional fabric of nations.

In other words, the challenge to microfinance per se is far from mortal. But I do think the new studies pose a test for the *story* that microfinance promoters have so effectively constructed. Are we approaching a tipping point, the precipice of a sort of **Kuhnian** revolution in public perception? Will the new research combine with the recent and dramatic demonstrations of the dangers of debt to depose one image of microfinance and seat another in its place? I of course don't know. But I am launched in this book project in the belief that such change is possible and healthy.

Kiva Is Not Quite What It Seems
October 2, 2009

This post is so long it needs an:

Executive summary/long story short

Kiva is the path-breaking, fast-growing person-to-person microlending site. It works this way: Kiva posts pictures and stories of people needing loans. You give your money to Kiva. Kiva sends it to a microlender. The lender makes the loan to a person you choose. He or she ordinarily repays. You get your money back with no interest. It's like eBay for microcredit.

You knew that, right? Well guess what: you're wrong, and so is **Kiva's diagram**. Less that 5% of Kiva loans are disbursed *after* they are listed and funded on Kiva's site. Just today, for example, Kiva listed a loan for **Phong Mut in Cambodia** and at this writing only $25 of the needed $800 has been raised. But you needn't worry about whether Phong Mut will get the loan because it was disbursed last month. And if she defaults, you might not hear about it: the intermediating microlender **MAXIMA** might cover for her in order to keep its Kiva-listed repayment rate high.

In short, the person-to-person donor-to-borrower connections created by Kiva are partly fictional. I suspect that most Kiva users do not realize this. Yet Kiva prides itself on transparency.

I hasten to temper this criticism. What Kiva does behind the scenes is what it *should* do. Imagine if Kiva actually worked the way people think it does. Phong Mut approaches a MAXIMA loan officer and clears all the approval hurdles, making the case that she has a good plan for the loan, has good references, etc. The MAXIMA officer says, "I think you deserve a loan, and MAXIMA has the capital to make it. But instead of giving you one, I'm going to take your picture, write down your story, get it translated and posted on an American web site, and then we'll see over the next month whether the Americans think you should get a loan. Check back with me from time to time." That would be inefficient, which is to say, immorally wasteful of charitable dollars. And it would be demeaning for Phong Mut. So instead MAXIMA took her picture and story, gave her the loan, and then uploaded the information to Kiva. MAXIMA will lend the money it gets from Kiva to someone else, who may never appear on kiva.org.

Moreover, the way Kiva actually works is hidden in plain sight. On the right of **Phong Mut's page**, you can see that MAXIMA lent her the money on September 8 and listed her on Kiva on September 21. So while Kiva is feeding a misunderstanding, it isn't technically hiding anything.

And finally in Kiva's defense, its behavior is emblematic of fund-raising in microfinance and charity generally, and is ultimately traceable to human foibles. People donate in part because it makes them feel good. Giving the beneficiary a face and constructing a story for her in which the donor helps write the next chapter opens purses.

Our sensitivity to stories and faces distorts how we give, thus what charities do and how they sell themselves. What if the best way to help in some places is to support communities rather than individuals? To make roads rather than make loans? To contribute to a disaster preparedness fund rather than just respond to the latest earthquake? And how far should nonprofits go in misrepresenting what they do in order to fund it? It is not an easy question: what if honesty reduces funding?

The big lesson is that the charities we observe, the ones whose pitches reach our retinas, are survivors of a Darwinian selection process driven by our own minds. An actual eBay venture called MicroPlace competes with Kiva; but MicroPlace is more up-front about the real deal. Its page for sample borrower **Filadelfo Sotelo** invites you to "invest in the organization that helped Filadelfo Sotelo: Fondo de Desarrollo Local" (FDL). This honesty is probably one reason MicroPlace has badly lagged Kiva. Who wants to click on the FDL icon when you can click on a human face?

Nicholas Kristof once **tweeted** that he "Just made a new microloan on www.kiva.org to a Nicaraguan woman. Great therapy: always makes me feel good." We should not feel guilty about the pleasure of giving. It should not just be eating your brussels sprouts. Indeed, Kristof might argue that Kiva.org's ability to make the user feel good is its greatest strength, for it draws people into an experience that stretches their horizons, educates them about global poverty, and entices them to contribute money they might otherwise spend on potato chips.

Still, we should take responsibility for how our pursuit of that pleasure plays out. Surely it is better to invest in an institution such as FDL without requiring it to incur the expense of posting pictures and stories of every borrower. Historically microcreditors have scaled to reach millions of people by cutting costs to the bone. Surely it would be better for us to give in a way that allows the microfinance institutions to put more of their limited energies into helping poor people manage their difficult lot and less into making us feel good.

I do not know the full answer to this conundrum, this tension between the need to draw donors and operate efficiently. Still, subtle dissembling makes me uneasy, perhaps because good intentions so often go awry. If a charity obscures how it operates, should we trust its claims about its impacts?

Long version

My wife Mai heard someone say that the world needs both playwrights and critics—if more playwrights. I treasure this observation because, as this blog must make obvious, I'm a critic. I can testify that being a critic can be bruising, especially when the playwrights you critique are alive. It's solace to think that the world needs me.

But the observation also helps me appreciate playwrights. They are the people who create things that weren't there, the people who are a tad insane in the sense that they confuse fantasy and reality. They see something in their mind's eye and believe they can make it real. Precisely because I am not like them, I hold playwrights—visionaries—in some awe. The most skillful, passionate, and lucky of them "put a dent in the universe" as Steve Jobs **said**. (An early employee described Jobs's uncanny ability to create a **reality distortion field** that altered bystanders' perceptions of the technologically possible.) Without playwrights, we might be still living in caves. At least, we wouldn't have iPhones.

We also probably wouldn't have the Grameen Bank, BRAC, and dozens of other successful microfinance institutions (MFIs) made by driven visionaries. And we wouldn't have **Kiva**, the person-to-person microcredit web site founded by Matt Flannery and Jessica Jackley.

On the other hand, without critics—analysts driven to understand the world rather than change it—we might not have mastered electricity. So we needed them too to get to iPhones. Critics and playwrights are yin and yang. Of course the two essences exist within all of us.

Critics seem to parse matters into quantities and concepts while playwrights seem to speak, and perhaps think, more in pictures and stories. (Or am I over-reaching here?)

The Kiva story

Like most innovations, Kiva is not entirely new. Rather, it is an ingenious fusion of older ideas. One is **child sponsorship**, which Save the Children **pioneered in 1940**. A family in a rich country sends $10 or $20 each month to a designated child in a poor country via a charity. In return, the family receives a photo and an update at least once a year. When I was perhaps eight, my family sponsored Constance, a Greek girl about my age, through Save the Children. I remember looking at her solemn face in two successive black and white portraits, trying to judge how much she had grown in a year.

Child sponsorship grew explosively in the United States in the 1990s, thanks mainly to groups with names like the Christian Children's Fund, Children International, and Childreach (now Plan International). Then an exposé in the *Chicago Tribune* in March 1998 brought it crashing down (hat tip to **Tim Ogden**). Starting in 1995, editors and reporters at the paper sponsored a dozen children in such countries as Guatemala and Mali. Then the reporters tracked down the children:

> The Tribune's yearlong examination of four leading sponsorship organizations . . . found that several children sponsored...received few or no promised benefits. A few others received a hodgepodge of occasional handouts, such as toothpaste, soap and cooking pots. Some got clothing and shoes that frequently did not fit.
> Sick children were sometimes given checkups and medicine, but not always.
> One child, a 12-year-old Malian girl sponsored through Save the Children, died soon after being sponsored, although the charity continued to accept money on her behalf for nearly two years after her death. A subsequent investigation by Save the Children found that at least two dozen other sponsors had sent the charity money on behalf of dead children in Mali for varying periods of time, in two cases as long as five years.

There was more to the story. Clover and John Dixon of Bellingham, Washington, **received faked New Year's letters** from a West African child who had died in a donkey cart accident. Sponsorship peddlers sent heart-string-tugging appeals for extra $25 contributions on birthdays, Christmas, Easter, and the **purpose-built** International Hug Day. Childreach ran a **disastrous experiment** in Ecuador with a novel intervention called "micro-credit." Local workers embezzled funds; in protest, borrowers burned loan documents.

Undoubtedly some hard-sell charlatanry was at work. But the problem was deeper than that: a tension between creating the psychological experience of connection that raised money and the realities of fighting poverty. Often the fairest and most effective way to help poor children is by building assets for the whole community such as schools, clinics, and wells. Often charities contract with locals to build these things. Often things go wrong because of corruption, bad luck, or arrogance among outsiders thinking they know what will work. In the best cases, charities learn from failure. All these factors break the connection between giving and benefit, sponsor and child. But admitting that would have **threatened the funding base**:

> "For a segment of the public, there will be nothing else that will reach those people the way that child sponsorship does," says Charles

MacCormack, the president of Westport, Conn.-based Save the Children, the nation's oldest and best-known sponsorship agency.

. . .

As MacCormack puts it, "An awful lot of people who sign on to a personal human being will not sign on to a well."

. . .

"[The charities] are addicted to it, because if they stop, they lose their identity as Save the Children," says Michael Maren, a veteran aid-agency worker in Africa and author of "The Road to Hell," a book critical of private foreign assistance organizations including Save the Children.

"That's their thing," Maren says. "They invented it. That's their problem. The Catch-22 is that the only way to raise money is sponsorship, but that is not the way to development. The show is the biggest part of what they do. So, they say, let's keep the show going, but try to find ways to make it better."

Within a year of the Tribune series, the Missouri attorney general had **slapped restrictions on Children International** while the nonprofit umbrella group **InterAction committed to developing a set of voluntary industry standards**. Many of the rule changes related to how clearly the charities disclosed how they operated.

Matt Flannery penned a **history** of Kiva's first two years for MIT's *innovations* journal in 2007. Two years later, he wrote a **second installment** in the same periodical. Flannery's authentic, conversational voice makes both articles readable and engaging. As he tells his own story, he comes across as an approachable man of vision, passion, and action.

Flannery tells how another Kiva ingredient, microcredit, first mixed in his mind with child sponsorship. Fittingly, it happened through hearing a story:

One night, [Jessica] invited me to come hear a guest speaker on the topic of microfinance, Dr. Mohammed [*sic*] Yunus. Dr. Yunus spoke to a classroom of thirty people and shared his story of starting the Grameen Bank. It was my first exposure to the topic and I thought it was a great story from an inspiring person. For Jessica, it was more of a call to action that focused her life goals.

Some months later, Jessica went off to East Africa to perform "impact evaluations" for the **Village Enterprise Fund**, which works intensively with poor farmers, providing grants (not loans) and training to help them start business activities. Jessica's work gathered data on indicators of poverty among participants, asking "questions like 'Do you take sugar with your tea?' and 'Do you sleep on a mattress?'" The couple kept in touch by phone. Then came the epiphany:

> When the words "Sponsor a Business" entered our phone conversation, it set off a chain of ideas. We had both grown up sponsoring children in Africa through our church and families. Why not extend the core of that idea to business? However, instead of donations, we could focus on loans. This seemed like a dignified, intellectual, and equitable extension that appealed to us at this point in our lives. Instead of benefactor relationships, we could explore partnership relationships. Instead of poverty, we could focus on progress.

Soon after, Matt joined Jessica in Africa. He brought his video camera, which embodied the third key ingredient in Kiva, information technology. "I planned to spend most of my time making a short documentary of small business stories. I was also intent on investigating the viability of our new idea."

Back in the United States Matt and Jessica began their impressive passage across the desert in pursuit of their vision. She networked for advice and support. He built the website after-hours, and eventually quit his job. Together they wrote the business plan.

> Once the site was ready, we needed loan applications in Africa to post on the site. That's where our friend Moses came in. Moses Onyango is a pastor in Tororo, Uganda, whom Jessica had stayed with after I left. Moses is a community leader in Tororo and is highly connected to the Internet. We had been in close contact over the past year and Moses was ready to post and administer the loans of seven entrepreneurs in his community. . . .
>
> Once Moses had posted the seven businesses, the site was ready to go. We sent out an email to our wedding invite list and waited to see what would happen. We emailed about 300 people, and all seven businesses were funded in a weekend. That was April 2005, and we raised $3,500 in a few days. We were blown away; everything worked.

Right there, Kiva hit the tension in the sponsorship—more currently, "person-to-person" (P2P)—model: the need to find and post enough stories to keep up with demand. It led instantly to fraud, though Matt Flannery didn't know it when he wrote the two-year history. As he recounts in the four-year history, a Kiva Fellow (volunteer) sent to Uganda discovered that Moses was producing many stories about individual borrowers the easy way, from whole cloth. Flannery flew to Uganda:

> I spent two weeks organizing a clean-up operation. We hired accountants and lawyers. I spent hours with Moses, trying to figure out exactly what happened. He was very apologetic, but our conversations didn't go anywhere. The money had vanished into a series of bad investments and a new house. Moses had a growing family. His new son was named for me: Matthew Flannery Onyango.

Admirably, Kiva went public with the information:

> . . . we alerted our users that not all of their funds made it to the intended recipients. . . . The reaction from our user base was telling. Overwhelmingly, they thanked us for our honesty and poured their refunds back into loans to other MFIs on the site. They reinforced an important lesson: whenever possible, be completely transparent. Transparency pays huge long-term dividends.
> . . .
> If you are running an organization and are considering withholding valuable information from your customers, just don't. There are a million reasons to withhold information. Lawyers will warn you about liabilities. Marketing people will preach about tarnishing the brand. Investors will encourage you to look bigger and better than you are. Most of this is just tired and outdated thinking.
> Operating transparently is a great way to keep an organization accountable for its actions. Before you act, ask yourself: would you be OK doing this if you had to tell your entire user base about it? Would you be proud if your actions were described on the front page of the New York Times? These are great tests that I often use to vet a decision.

Flannery describes the "story factory." Running one—collecting and posting stories—imposes a significant expense on MFIs but is evidently offset by the ~~low 2%~~ 0% (hat tip Ben Elberger) interest rate that Kiva charges on capital:

> Out in Cambodia, I got to watch firsthand how a sophisticated MFI gets content on the site. It is quite an operation. . . .
> In the field, loan officers carry Kiva questionnaires along with a host of other loan documents. When they visit a village, they gather

women and tell them about the opportunity to apply for a loan. If a woman decides to apply, the loan officer takes down information on paper—some for the Kiva site and some for other business purposes. The Kiva questionnaire asks for information that interests lenders. For instance, how many children do you have? And how will the loan make an impact on your family? This is all done in the local language—Khmer. They also take photos of the applicants.

Returning to the branch, the loan officer enters the data into a computer and sends the information—via Yahoo! Messenger—to the Kiva coordinators at the headquarters in a major city. Kiva coordinators are typically young, Internet-savvy males who get paid a few thousand dollars a year. It is a desirable job and about ten of them are now working in Phnom Penh. We train them in the art of synthesizing the Kiva questionnaire into a readable narrative; then they spend their days writing stories and uploading pictures.

. . .

As a kid, I would write letters to [sponsored] children a few years younger than me in Africa and South America. I imagined my letters being delivered to a thatched-roof hut halfway around the planet. It sparked my imagination and gave me a sense of connectedness. Through Kiva, we can provide some of that to a new generation of kids.

Looking back now, I imagine that the transaction wasn't as simple as I had thought. A lot of intermediaries were involved, lending a certain production quality to the experience. Plus, it was expensive. Delivering the child sponsorship experience was often as expensive as the child sponsorship itself. At Kiva, it's not as simple as it seems, either. . .

The back-story
Innovations invited Sam Daley-Harris, who was central to teaching Americans about microfinance and serves on Kiva's advisory board, to **comment** on Flannery's four-year retrospective. While praising Kiva's "profound contribution to the field of microfinance and international development," he worried about the transaction costs, and noted one other concern:

> . . . there is still a bit of deception in the notion that the moment that a loan is funded, the client in Kenya or Cambodia receives his or her microloan with those particular dollars. Indeed, there are real people receiving real loans to start or grow real enterprises, but if a client in

a remote village qualifies for a loan, the MFI will not likely make that client wait for the Kiva lenders to put up that last $25. Said another way, loan funds are fungible, and a larger MFI on Kiva's website will use Kiva's loans as one important source of their lending pool, but it's not actually those precise dollars going to that precise client.

As I noted at the top, Sam is right. In fact, I wrote a little program in Excel to extract data from kiva.org. It **shows** that for September 2009, only 4.3% of loans were disbursed after Kiva users had fully funded them through the site. And probably some of those the local lender had already *committed* to make before Kiva users had funded them. And in a **new report** on what happens to investors when microfinance institutions collapse, Daniel Rozas computed from **data on kiva.org** that the failure of just three lending institutions caused 93% of all Kiva defaults to date. No doubt many of those institutions' *borrowers* were faithfully repaying at the time of collapse. Conversely, if a borrower defaults, the lender will often cover for him in order to maintain a good reputation on Kiva. So whether you get your money back as a Kiva user depends overwhelmingly on the solvency of the lenders, not the borrowers.

Kiva deserves kudos for being transparent enough for Rozas and myself to extract such data. But I wondered whether Kiva might become the Save the Children of P2P microcredit, the reasonably responsible pioneer who is imitated and overtaken by less scrupulous actors who pull the whole industry down a muddy slope into hucksterism. So I checked out **MYC4**, **Wokai**, and **Babyloan** (motto: "micro credits, great stories"; and no, it doesn't make loans to babies: it's French). To my surprise they were **more honest** about the P2P relationships they (seem to) forge. Here's Babyloan in enjoyably imperfect English:

> Note: Babyloan works as a REfinancing platform and not as a direct financing system. It can happen that the MFI already "advanced" the microcredit to the entrepreneur when you make the online social micro loan. Indeed, as we are still in a launching phase and particularly for seasonal projects , we did not want to make the realisation of the project "dependant" on the Internet users' good will and click. Babyloan is no microfinance reality show of ! However, we limit the funding time of the project not to create too much time discrepancy between the project and your micro loan, so your money is really used to finance the project. After the delay of 3 months maximum , we send all the money even if the funding has not been completed by the Internet users. The MFI will complete the funding.

So these sites are refinancing mechanisms. Kiva-linked microlenders make loans, then "sell" them to Kiva and its users. Might we rescue the P2P conception by observing that the lenders make their loans *anticipating* refinancing on Kiva? Yes, but only partly. Kiva limits itself to providing at most 30% of any lender's capital. So a lender will make at least three loans for every one it chooses to post on Kiva (hat tip to **Molly's dad**).

The end
Kiva brings microcredit and microchips to child sponsorship. Like sponsorship charities, it is all about stories: it was inspired by them and it succeeds by telling them. As a result, it operates in a pincers between the giver's desire for personal connection and the costs and constraints that imposes on business of serving poor people. In fact Kiva can be seen as an ingenious finessing of this old tension. Technology has brought down the cost of transmitting stories and images.

Indeed, Kiva's P2P connections are more solid than those of child sponsorship 15 years ago. The people in the pictures, we can assume, really do get microcredit. Following in the *Tribune*'s footsteps, Nicholas Kristof tracked down one of his borrowers, a **Kabul baker, with little difficulty**.

On the other hand, the P2P connection comes at a cost, is one-way, and is partly synthetic. The baker was surprised by the encounter because he had never heard of Kristof. For his part, Kristof might be surprised to learn that most of the Kiva **loans he helped fund** were disbursed before he saw them on Kiva. And the cost of collecting the baker's story, translating it into English, taking his picture,and uploading it over a balky Internet connection may still be significant relative to the small loans and the great needs in Afghanistan.

Is it so terrible that Kiva modestly misleads in order to raise money for a cause about which it is passionate? No. But as a critic I offer these points:

- As I have **discussed** in connection with the interest rates on loans, the test of disclosure is whether people get the message. Technically, you see on Kiva's site that most loans are disbursed before they are funded. But the **How Kiva Works page** creates the opposite impression, and my casual survey of Kiva users reveals widespread misunderstanding. In the wake of the *Tribune* scandal, sponsorship organizations adopted **standards** on disclosure, among other things, in order to "preserve and protect the trust of sponsors and other donors by ensuring the accuracy and transparency of each [child sponsorhip organization]'s approach to child sponsorship and the manner in which its sponsorship funds are used." In this respect, Kiva is violating its stated ideal of transparency and ignoring a lesson from its family history.

- Kiva may fear that complete honesty would undermine growth. If so, they might be right. But I am optimistic that Kiva will make and survive the leap of faith in its users. So take this interesting, small hypocrisy as the camel's nose under the tent, a way into the larger theme of how our behavior as donors rewards charities for distorting and contorting themselves. Why has Kiva succeeded by doing microfinance as opposed to community-level projects such as well and school construction? Such construction would stray from the P2P construct. Why has it succeeded by doing just credit despite the longstanding idea that services such as savings are at least as valuable and less dangerous? Because only well-regulated institutions should hold other people's money; building them is hard and is neither photogenic nor atomizable into P2P.

- And why has Kiva, like most other microcredit fundraisers, succeeded while **mythologizing the power of microcredit**? You already know: storytelling works. Indeed, the most misleading thing about kiva.org is not obfuscation about sequencing that this post has dwelled upon but the smooth telling of the simplistic story about microcredit. In this Kiva is not unusual. The borrowers are all "entrepreneurs" even though we know the poor often use loans to pay for food or school. Meanwhile, as I have discovered over the last year, the evidence on the effects of microcredit on **poverty** and **empowerment** is rather ambiguous. "Kiva lets you lend to a specific entrepreneur, empowering them to lift themselves out of poverty." What part of that home page slogan is grounded in reality?

- Carol Adelman, among others, has **argued** that private philanthropy is superior to government aid in many respects because it is more flexible and subject to a market test. But we see here that we all, as private philanthropists, have our irrationalities too. Private aid therefore cannot perfectly substitute for public aid. No doubt it is best to do some of each, while striving to improve both.

Is Microfinance a Schumpeterian Dead End?
May 15, 2010

Last month, Lant Pritchett, the invariably instructive scholar of development, had to sit twice through my spiel about the different notions of "development" I employ in my book to evaluate microfinance and my **curiosity**

about extending this analytical thread beyond microfinance. Lant serves on both our **Advisory Group**, a group of leading academics, and our **Board of Directors** (ex officio).

The thing bothered him. If you've ever seen him in action, you know what I mean, and I mean that in the best way. I had a good but truncated conversation with him during a break in the Board meeting. I'll represent his skepticism, or what I gleaned from it, as well as I can.

First, the whole **development as freedom** riff rubbed him wrong. I think he sees the emphasis on outcomes such as health and education as ends of development as having led to muddy thinking: the Millennium Development Goals, the idea that development can be bought with more aid ($50 for each child in school, say), and the obscuring of the importance of industrialization in reducing poverty. I reply (or replied) by arguing with none of that, but saying that an intervention that is giving millions of people an increment of control over their financial lives is doing something right, not bad by the standards of foreign aid. Perhaps he would say that he holds aid to a higher standard: it is wasting its potential if it does not contribute to economic transformation—industrialization—which promises to not merely ameliorate poverty but reduce it. Of course, accelerating transformation with aid is easier said than done.

Lant also disputed my characterization of microfinance as a **Schumpeterian success**, an example of aid building a thriving, disruptive industry that enriches the institutional fabric of nations. Rather, I think he argued, microfinance should be seen as an unfortunate work-around for the failure of mainstream financial systems to serve the poor. It's like the private water industry in New Delhi that sells water to slumdwellers at far higher prices than the rich pay for piped supply. I said, "So it's a Schumpeterian dead end?" He said, "Yes!" He told a story of visiting a self-help group (an example of a distinctively Indian microfinance) while working for the World Bank. After he and other visitors had finished asking questions of the members, all women, someone asked them if they had questions too. One member asked, "So how do self-help groups work where you come from?" The answer: we don't have them.

It's an interesting idea, microfinance as a Schumpeterian dead end. It strikes me that the claim imposes a pretty high burden of evidence though. Economic developments often takes circuitous routes. I recall Jane Jacobs's thumbnail history of Detroit, I think in *The Economy of Cities* (I can't check my bookshelf because I am travelling). It began as a tiny copper mining town; then moved into flour milling; then, using its accumulated expertise in machinery, boat repair (it being on the shore, connected to America's internal maritime transport network); then boat manufacturer; then, in time, almost inevitably, the hub of the American auto industry. Only when it became a single-industry town, seemingly extraordinarily successful, did it economically stagnate. So the question is, how can you tell with reasonable confidence whether a new industry represents a dead end? Several big financial institutions today—Bank of America, Metropolitan Life, the Prudential (in the U.K. and its namesake in the U.S.)—started by serving the poor, arguably the microfinance institutions of their day. It's not clear to me that work-around-for-deviation-from-the-ideal is a useful criterion for Schumpeterian dead end. Maybe Lant or others can chime in to continue the debate.

Update May 21: I just returned from Kenya, where I saw M-PESA, the mobile phone–based money transfer system with 9 million customers. It began as an idea: to use phones as an add-on to microcredit. Thus did a great new business start with a spark from an old one. More to come.

Akula v. Yunus: Commercial Microcredit = Just Profit or Unjust Profiteering?
September 28, 2010

Did you catch the microcredit debate at the Clinton Global Initiative conference last Tuesday? OK, I wasn't invited to the ex-president's annual gathering either. But, rather amazingly, I watched the debate live on my Droid while being a soccer dad. You can watch the whole thing at the bottom of this post. It was a good show. It put on one stage the two leading (disagreeing) voices in the hottest controversy in microfinance. And it helped me think through some of the ideas in my **Development as Industry Building** chapter . . . but that chapter's still in draft, so I'd be interested in your thoughts.

Vikram Akula reignited the debate over commercialization and profit in microfinance when he took **SKS Microfinance** public this summer. SKS is on track to surpass Bangladesh's **Grameen Bank** as the world's largest microcreditor, measured in number of loans outstanding—if it hasn't already. SKS got big fast by **going for-profit in 2005**. It raised several rounds of investment from venture capitalists, which allowed it to quickly open thousands of branches implementing its streamlined version of the Grameen's traditional microcredit system. The SKS initial public offering (IPO) this July allowed those early investors to sell their shares at high multiples of original cost. In fact, even before the IPO, Akula sold enough shares to other investors to become a microcredit millionaire and **India's 9th-largest taxpayer**.

As I **blogged, Muhammad Yunus**, famed founder of the Grameen Bank, has criticized the SKS IPO as he did the Compartamos IPO in 2007. "This is pushing microfinance in the loansharking direction. It's not mission drift. It's endangering the whole mission."

Last Tuesday in New York, NPR's Adam Davidson moderated a panel that included Akula and Yunus, as well as Mary Ellen Iskendarian, head of **Women's World Banking**. I was at once delighted by the subtleties that emerged in the debate, especially in Yunus's position, and disappointed about an issue left unmentioned. Here, I offer you two quotes (more or less), a pointer on how bank finances work, then three thoughts.

(Some of the transactions affecting ownership of SKS even before the IPO have been controversial too, not to mention complicated—I don't understand them and don't approach them here. CGAP has just begun **a new stream of work** that I suspect will become the definitive analysis of SKS's journey to the capital market.)

At 14:32 in the video, Akula tells a story about how he concluded that microcredit needed to bring in big investors:

Before starting SKS Microfinance I actually worked for one of these small NGO microfinance institutions, basically as a loan officer. I would give out these small loans and see this tremendous impact that Professor Yunus has written about and shown the world. And what would happen is, women from more remote villages would come to us and say, "Can you start in our village?" And we'd always have to say no, it's grant-run, so we don't have funds, and we'd have to turn them away, and they'd walk away disappointed. Now, on one particular day, a very poor woman—emaciated, torn sari, no chappals—she had clearly walked quite a distance to ask me the same question. And again I said, "We don't have funds. We can't come into your village." But unlike the other women who simply walked away disappointed, she looked me in the eye and said something that I'll never forget. She said, "Am I not poor too? Do I not deserve a chance to get my family out of poverty?" Now, for me this was a jarring question because here I was thinking I'm doing something to help eradicate poverty. But this woman's question basically put me in my place, basically said: Look, what are you doing if you're only doing this in a handful of villages and not doing it in the next set of villages? It's as if you're sending one child to school and holding one back. . . . How do you design microfinance in a way so that you never have to turn away a poor person who's simply asking for an opportunity?

Akula's answer: Go to the capital markets. Bring in big money in exchange for a share of the profits. Grow fast.

At 18:28, Yunus replies with an interesting distinction:

> You imply that I am somehow opposed to profit. I am not. Grameen Bank is a for-profit organization. We want to make profit. So we are not [an] NGO. We are a bank. But: ownership is the question. The Grameen Bank is owned by the borrowers. So we make profit. Profit goes back to them. So we protect that part. So what we are opposed to when you say "profit" or "commercialization" is the money of the poor going out to somebody else. And you may say, "Well what's wrong with taking a small amount of profit?" Then I'll say, "Is it small? Who defines what is 'small'? Do you have any rule that will keep it restricted to this percentage? You do not." It's an open thing. So anybody who makes profit can do that. So today you may say well we are only making small profit, but tomorrow because of the system you have, you like to maximize your profit. It's the wrong direction . . . .The moment you say "profit" the sky's the limit. You saw what happened [in] this financial crisis.

Yunus goes on to emphasize that the Grameen Bank is owned by its clients. And it gets funding not from outside investors, but from the villages it serves, mainly by offering savings accounts:

> Grameen Bank is created by the local money. Each branch is created by the local deposits . . . We live in an ocean of money . . . We have so much money we don't know what to do with the money.

To which Akula basically answers: that's great, but the Indian government won't let us take savings.

So if I understand right, Yunus is *not* criticizing commercialized microfinance merely because it makes some people rich. He does not seem to directly begrudge Akula his wealth even though almost every rupee of it came out of the hands of poor Indian women. Rather, Yunus says that outside ownership drives a microcreditor to hurt the customers for the sake of the owners by, say, raising interest rates on loans. I think this is how Yunus links outside ownership to moneylending. A traditional for-profit corporation can be expected to commit usury. Ergo, the customers should be the owners: ownership should be *cooperative*.

This argument has to be taken seriously: I don't know anything about Indian corporate law, but I'm guessing that SKS now has a legal duty to maximize shareholder returns. There are thus margins at which client and shareholder interests conflict. And in making this argument, Yunus is harking back to the origins of microcredit perhaps more than he realizes. As I've documented in the draft **chapter 3**, Bangladeshi microcredit traces to German credit cooperatives that began in the 1850s. They were partly inspired by the **"first apostle of cooperation in borrowing and finance,"** Victor Aimé Huber, who in turn drew inspiration from Robert Owen in England, **an originator** of the idea that corporations will serve society better when owned by their clients.

So a cooperative *bank* like Grameen takes two kinds of money from its customers: savings and equity. As for the first, Grameen members **have to save some of their borrowings**, and many members and non-members voluntarily deposit additional sums with Grameen. (At SKS, loans from big banks take the place of savings, encouraged by a law that requires those banks to lend to **"priority sectors."**) Like any bank, Grameen pays interest on these savings according to set formulas and needs to protect the savings at all costs.

As for "equity": new Grameen members have to buy a 100 taka ($1.44) share in the Bank. And like ordinary shares of stock, the returns to owning these shares are unpredictable. Grameen began paying dividends in 2006 and has paid 30 taka/share the last two years—a good return. On the other hand, if a lot of Grameen loans went bad, the shares could lose all their value. The shares have to take the hit in order to protect the savings. This would be sad, but not catastrophic: that's what's great about equity. But—to illustrate the difference between savings and equity—if even more loans went bad, Grameen might become *insolvent*, unable to return all its savers' money. That could be catastrophic. That's what **happened to Adam (Davidson)'s Bank** when NPR producer Caitlin Kenney defaulted on her dollhouse mortgage. The job of equity is to cushion savings against loan losses.

Understanding that, I'd make three points:

1. The distinction between these two kinds of money is hidden in the way Yunus talks about things. You can't just finance a bank with savings. The "ocean of money" has been almost all savings: **83.3 billion taka in deposits** against just 0.5 billion taka from sales of those 100 taka shares. In fact, Grameen's total equity cushion, which includes accumulated profits, has not been growing as fast as its loan portfolio, so that the cushion now **verges on illegal thinness**. It seems that Grameen now needs to sell many more shares to its members. Will they buy? Maybe if purchase is required

for new loans or deposits. Grameen and its members have succeeded unconventionally many times before. Otherwise, Grameen
will have to scale back its lending . . . or go to outside investors
like SKS.

2. I think it's easy to overestimate the power of Grameen's shareholders over Grameen's management, and to underestimate another
check on management: competition. Putting it another way, Grameen's members may exercise more power when they vote with
their patronage (of competing microcreditors) than when they vote
their shares to elect board members. Grameen has a strong, autonomous leader, to say the least. I'm not suggesting that Yunus wants
to profiteer off the poor, just that Grameen is hardly a persuasive
model of how a cooperative structure with millions of members—
rather than dozens, as in the original cooperatives—bends management to the will of clients. **My reading of Stuart Rutherford's
history** is that competition is mainly what has led Grameen and
other big Bangladeshi microcreditors to serve clients better, such as
by improving savings options.

3. So it seems to me that Grameen and SKS resemble one another
more than last week's debate suggests. Both swim in oceans of
money: with its high growth, SKS can easily raise more loans and
equity; with its attractive interest rates, Grameen can easily pull in
more savings deposits. Both Grameen and SKS face serious competition. Both are growing. Neither is really governed by the poor.
. . . which leads me to that "issue left unmentioned." Here we have
two lending operations, growing steadily, egged on by competition, fed by easy money. Have you heard that story before? If I
had been in the audience, I would have asked Akula and Yunus:
How do you know when *growth* is *development*? (Vikram, if you
are reading, I think you know **this distinction from Herman Daly**.)
When does multiplication of microcredit constitute a fine contribution to the economic fabric of nations, and when is it a prelude to
bubbles? When should we become concerned that microcredit is
doing harm by luring many poor into borrowing more than is good
for them? I know this question has no easy answer. But it has to be
confronted **in India** and in Bangladesh.

My prior is to favor commercialization and competition in microcredit
as maturation of an industry, **as true economic development**. Most poverty reduction has been caused by similar processes of economic change
repeated a thousand times over in various nations and industries, what we

call industrialization. But lending is a special business. Here, without proper restraints, commercialization and competition can do a lot of harm. I wish both sides were more persuasive in their implications that their way will work just fine. I'm not predicting doom, just saying that the debate on ownership structure is distracting from something that matters more, and that at least conceptually puts the two sides in the same boat.

What do you think of this? And what do you think about the question *I* ducked: when is it just to get rich off the poor?

When Indian Elephants Fight
November 25, 2010

I've been pretty oblique in recent posts about my evolving opinions of the Andhra Pradesh (AP) crisis. I've been trying to share my thought process with you. But that seems to have left me open to **misinterpretation** and **criticism for poor construction**. Perhaps I have taxed your patience. So let me be clear: in a week of talking to people in India about microfinance, I heard almost no one defend the behavior of the microfinance institutions (MFIs) in the villages and slums. Those actions appear indefensible. Loans were made too easily; interest rates were opaque, as they are in most of the world (though according to **Chuck Waterfield**, they are among the *lowest* in the world); collection practices were often aggressive; profits were disturbingly high. And that, I am now confident, is the core story. Whether the government response is ideal (when is it ever?), whether MFI leaders were cartoon tycoons acting on pure greed, the extent of the suicide link, the role of politics and the vested interested of the government-led self-help group (SHG) program—all those are more complex issues on which I think I am increasingly getting a grip.

The story behind the ordinance

On Saturday, my last day there, I had an enlightening interview with B. Rajsekhar, the CEO of the **Society for the Elimination of Rural Poverty**. SERP, it turns out, was at the center of the Andhra Pradesh government's smackdown of the microcredit juggernaut in the form of that October 14 **Ordinance**. SERP was created a decade ago to implement the World Bank–financed *Velugu* program that provides finance and many other services to self-help groups in Andhra Pradesh. Through a hierarchy that mirrors the geographic divisions of the state (district, mandal, village) it bridges between the government and about 1 million SHGs with 10–15 members each.

Formally it is non-governmental. But the state government funds it and the Chief Minister **chairs its governing board**.

Rajsekhar began with a soliloquy on *intent*. He pointed out that five years ago, before the MFIs had grown large, AP was already home to a huge number of self-help groups that help the poor save and borrow. If MFIs were truly committed to bringing financial services to those who lack, why didn't they go to states with fewer SHGs? Clearly, the MFIs are driven by greed. "Intent is not poverty alleviation. The intent is profit maximization on the MFI side." It was cheaper for MFIs to piggyback on SERP's years of hard labor organizing a million SHGs: the MFIs could just poach the SHG members, who were already screened for creditworthiness, organized into groups, and accustomed to credit. "It's like SERP have cooked the food; it's ready; MFIs can just come serve themselves and start eating."

He then told me the story of the Ordinance from his point of view. As early as the spring of 2010, local TV channels were broadcasting reports of microcredit-linked suicides. The coverage was sensational (whether sensationalized, I don't know): women spoke on camera of being pushed into prostitution. In response—and illustrating the key role of the media—SERP constituted task forces in each of AP's 23 districts to investigate such stories and file criminal charges where appropriate. The big MFIs resisted however, arguing that they were regulated under national, not state, law.

The media drumbeat intensified in July and August, focusing the minds of politicians and policymakers. One apparent reason was an unusually strong monsoon (think of the **floods in Pakistan** and, again, of global weirding). Under the impressive **National Rural Employment Guarantee Act** of 2005, the national government promises 100 days of paid work to every rural adult in the country. Most of the labor is unskilled and relates to public works, but it appears to have become a valued source of security for the poor. It pays weekly, which is convenient for people with loans requiring weekly payments. Sowmya Kidambi, a former activist now working for the program in AP, praised NREGA for getting cash into the countryside and preventing hunger this year despite higher global food prices. But it's hard to build earth works in a heavy monsoon. So some expected wages did not come. Another factor, which Rajsekhar did not mention but Sowmya did, is political unrest. A flyer into Hyderabad arrives at a huge and beautiful new airport, then rides into town on a divided highway through fallow pastures. On my way back to the airport, I traveled on the still-under-construction ring road. The flip side of all this investment catering to foreigners and the well-to-do, I was told, is the complete starvation of investment for the rest of the state, and that has stirred separatism. Activists want to split the state. Storefronts have been looted and buses set on fire. And political groups have called for *bandh*'s—general strikes that shut down the region. Once more the poor get stomped on: wage laborers lose days of work. (See M. Rajshekhar's **Economic Times article** on both factors.)

Since intolerance for late payment is in the DNA of MFIs, pressure began to build on borrowers. Probably, in fact, the pressure had been building on many people for months and been held at bay with new borrowings. But that of course had to end.

Also in July, SKS went public. What was once cloaked was now spelled out with numerical precision in the papers: the investors and managers of SKS were making millions off the poor.

In August, the AP government formed the committee that would ultimately draft the Ordinance. It was led by Reddy Subramanyam, principal secretary of the state's rural development ministry, but staff at this nongovernmental entity, SERP, did the bulk of the work. Rajsekhar described the committee as "racing against time." Despite the rush, they managed to study existing laws, consult their own legal department, and get input from legal luminaries.

Did they consult MFIs? "We didn't feel that we needed to discuss with them." When I asked why, he first cited lack of time. When I pointed out the inconsistency in this rationale, he referred to some bitter history. In fact, tensions have simmered between SERP and the MFIs for more than five years. In early 2006, they boiled over in the coastal Krishna district. An official seized the records and closed 57 offices of Share and Spandana, then the country's two largest MFIs. In a response to the attacks, and an apparent attempt to fend off regulation, the microcredit industry group Sa-Dhan announced a voluntary code of conduct for its members. Prabu Ghate **recounts**:

> The RBI [Reserve Bank of India, the central bank] expressed its concern to the state government that the action it had taken could have wider repercussions by vitiating the MFI repayment culture in other parts of the state, . . . It set up a Co-ordination Forum to discuss issues of concern to stakeholders and resolve them as soon as possible. At a meeting of the forum held on April 20 [2006] it was claimed that the MFI movement was "eating into the SHG movement", MFI practices were "barbaric" and posed a serious law and order problem, and that even the lower interest rates suggested in the March 20 code of conduct of 21–24 per cent were usurious and illegal. Spandana and SHARE announced a reduction in their interest rates, including those on current loans outstanding, to 15 per cent on a declining balance basis. It was left to a respected MFI leader [must be Vijay Mahajan]

to state that this rate was unacceptable to other Sa-Dhan members because it was not sustainable, and pointed out that the state government had no business to stipulate rates for [Non-Banking Financial Companies] regulated by RBI.

Having bared their fangs, the state government officials mostly retreated, effectively accepting the MFIs' promises to behave better and lower interest rates. (And, I am told, taking pay-offs from the MFIs.) So in Rajsekhar's view, the MFIs were given ample chance, five years, to behave themselves. And they blew it. Worse, some of them promised interest rates they could not deliver, making themselves liars. Meanwhile, the MFIs presumably resented the impossible demands for low interest rates and the state's fundamental misunderstanding of the cost-covering, commercial approach to microcredit. Thus by 2010, it seems that neither side respected the other. That's being polite: I suppose they held each other in contempt.

So in 2010 the government chose to ambush the MFIs with the Ordinance. The minister for rural development, of whom many spoke highly, briefed the Congress party's high command in Delhi, as well as the leadership in Hyderabad. A special state cabinet meeting was called on October 14, the first in history, Rajsekhar said, with one agenda item. The proposed Ordinance was approved in an hour. Since the legislature was not in session, the bill went next to the state's Governor (a sort of head of state, as it were) for interim approval on October 15, pending a vote in the legislature. The torpedo was launched.

I don't know that this little story has been aired before.

Critique of the Ordinance

The Ordinance required MFIs to immediately halt operations, to register, and to await processing of their registrations by an obviously hostile government before resuming. A court quickly **granted** MFIs the right to continue operating. However, through channels I do not understand, word went out to local officials to block all MFI employees from entering villages. The women I **met in Yarvaguda**, for example, were told two weeks ago to stop paying. This sub-legal directive is perhaps more important than the Ordinance, for it has frozen the MFIs in Andhra Pradesh and could bankrupt many of them.

The **Ordinance** has some good features: a requirement for clear interest rate disclosure; a "fast track" court system to resolve disputes; and a definition of coercion. Still, it "leaves a lot to be desired," **according to N. Srinivasan**, author of the 2010 microfinance State of the Sector report. I concur:

- Its preamble refers specifically to the need to "[protect] the interests of the SHGs" which "are being exploited by private Micro Finance Institutions." And the provisions only apply to MFI lending to SHGs and SHG members. SHGs, moreover, are defined as ones *that have registered with SERP or its urban counterpart, the Mission for Elimination of Urban Poverty in Municipal Areas (MEUPMA)* (hat tip C.S. Reddy of APMAS). But many SHGs predate these entities and have not registered with them. If women in unregistered SHGs are being driven to suicide by microcredit, that is apparently not a pressing concern for the government of Andhra Pradesh. If women *belonging to no SHG at all* are being driven to suicide by microcredit, that too is apparently not a pressing concern for the government of Andhra Pradesh. What then is the true *intent?* Occam's Razor says: protecting SERP's programs.
- The law includes several provisions that I expect would be unconstitutional in the U.S. and many other countries. For example, it makes it a crime to belong to more than one SHG. Imagine if the government of California jailed people for belonging to more than one book club. It makes it a crime for an MFI to lend to someone with two or more existing loans "irrespective of the source," which could include friends and family. Does the government not realize that **70% of households in rural AP already have three or more loans**, most of those from informal sources? Meanwhile, MFIs must register with the governments of each district in which they operate, and those districts may revoke registrations at any time "after assigning sufficient reasons" even if they are only at the investigating stage. Imagine a California law empowering county governments to immediately shut down supermarkets for "sufficient reasons" without ever defining that phrase. Imagine how, in India, this empowers local officials to demand bribes.
- The law imposes other burdens on MFIs without equivalent demands on SHGs. MFIs, for example, must obtain permission from the district government to lend to SHG members—but not vice versa.
- It contains other strange provisions. It makes it illegal for MFIs to accept collateral even though that would soften the pressure for full repayment. It limits interest to 100% of principal—which seems odd where rates tend to be in the 20s, 30s, and 40s. But as Srinivasan points out this rule could, as it were, make my mortgage illegal since I will pay more interest than principal on it over 30 years.

As Srinivasan says, "The objectives of the ordinance are laudable." But the execution reveals bias, and bias of a particular kind. The law does not merely view SHGs as better. It views MFIs as malevolent. It does not outlaw MFIs but, one wonders, perhaps only because it cannot. The presumption of guilt on the part of MFIs is clear in its draconian requirements.

My bottom line, for now

While the government responded to a real problem, there are real problems in the response. It was hurried because of the media drumbeat (Rajsekhar referred to the TV news several times) and the associated political drumbeat. I believe the government acted in no small part for the best of reasons. Still, India is home to a million small tragedies a day. This is a country where low-level officials routinely steal food coupons meant for the indigent. Solicitousness for the poor does not suffice to explain why microcredit literally came to dominate the government agenda. SERP's **list of alleged suicide cases** (symbolizing a link I **find plausible in principle**) were verified, Rajsekhar said, by "third parties": district revenue agents and certain local non-governmental groups. But causality in suicide cases is delicate, and I don't know enough about these third parties to trust their judgment in such a politicized context.

The main problem in the response, as Vijay Mahajan put it to me, is that the government is an unfair referee. It's a player and a referee. While SERP is not technically part of the government, it is as a matter of political economy an extension of it. SERP felt its interests directly threatened by MFIs.

Clearly self-regulation for microfinance failed miserably in Andhra Pradesh. That calls for the government to step in. But this is not how regulation should be done. Regulations should be written and enforced by disinterested parties and published in draft, with a public comment period. I would tentatively suggest (not knowing enough about India to be sure) that this will contribute to the foreign perception of AP as no longer such a good place to do business: the government can slam the private sector at any time. The Ordinance comes off as assuming that MFIs are devils—companies that act out of pure greed rather than a mix of that with the pursuit of growth and genuine commitment to the poor—and assuming that SHGs and district officials to whom MFIs must now pay obeisance are angels. It's parochial.

So, as is my wont as a child of divorce, I see some symmetry in the tragedy: the government people and the MFI people are both imperfect, acting out of a mix of motives. (Let's not forget that greed—the interest in making new opportunities for bribes—could be playing a role in the political economy on the government side too.) Neither side respects the other.

One could say that the MFIs deserve what they got, maybe even needed it in order to force them to act more responsibly. They blew their chance at self-regulation while exuding disrespect for the government. So they got smacked.

But what's important is not what's fair to MFIs but what helps the poor most. The Ordinance may be better than nothing because it froze a situation that was spinning out of control for many; it may well have saved lives. But it is far from ideal. Despite Rajsekhar's assertions to the contrary, it is not realistic to expect the SHG system, for all the good it does, to meet all the financial needs of the poor. The private sector can help fill that gap. My hope is that this brutal game will ultimately lead the industry to a better equilibrium than before. But mostly it seems that the government wants to get rid of the MFIs, and is pursuing that goal quite efficiently. I believe the SERP is about as committed to serving the poor as is Vikram Akula, founder of SKS; but that does not mean that SERP, any more than he, is acting perfectly in the interests of the poor.

These events should also be cause for introspection at the World Bank, which has financed both sides, but especially the government and SERP (with $1 billion or so). The SERP-administered SHG program may well be doing much good. But World Bank money has also beefed up a political economy hostile to private sector solutions.

Still, the true bottom line is this: credit, the poor, and business-like insistence on regular repayment are a dangerous combination. Pushed too hard, credit can easily become a buzz saw. Change any one those three elements, and it is safer: savings instead of credit (cf. **Gates Foundation**), the well-off instead of the poor, the flexible and somewhat subsidized communality of SHGs instead of the hard-nosed efficiency of MFIs. If microcredit is to safely serve the poor, it must soften its edges. There are many ways to do that. But probably all are harder when growth is rapid. Fast growth in credit to the poor is therefore dangerous, and often unworthy of the label "development."

The Microcredit Attack Documentary
December 5, 2010

I first heard from Danish documentarian **Tom Heinemann** last January. He was probably drawn to me because I had **tweaked Kiva for de facto slight of hand**. He told me he was making a film about microfinance—**the one that premiered last Tuesday evening on Norwegian television.** (An English version is **coming early in 2011**.) I could tell that while we shared a desire to pierce the publicity veils around microfinance, his drive was more purely critical. Basically, it seemed to me that he wanted to get the goods on microfinance. While feeling that the truth about microfinanced is nuanced, I was curious to see what he would come up with.

Over the year, he checked in with me, as I'm sure he did with others in the film, to share his discoveries. He also asked good questions, such as what the interest rate of the Grameen Bank is, which led me to some blogging.

On a Saturday in August, Tom and his wife came to my house to interview me. I appear in the **Norwegian final cut** at 36:40 and 40:25. (Background art credit to **my wife Mai**.)

Overall, Tom seems to have made pretty much the most negative movie he could. As I show just below, the film sensationalizes matters that have more to do with making Muhammad Yunus look bad than whether microcredit is good for the poor; exaggerates the Grameen Bank's interest rates despite my explanations in e-mail to Tom and on this blog; and heavily favors negative voices, depriving viewers of the opportunity to glimpse the complexities of the real world and think for themselves. Talking-head defenders of microcredit do get some airtime. However, as far as I can tell the client voices are all negative. Such voices are important and generally underrepresented, but they are not the whole story. It is easy to find people in Bangladesh who would rather have access to microcredit than not—I know because I met some while **tagging along with Stuart Rutherford for a day in 2008**. As far as I can tell, such microcredit users were not investigated in the course of this investigative journalism on microcredit use. The documentary is therefore designed to give viewers only half the story.

I can see a few potential motives or rationales for the strong negativity:

- *Appropriately counterbalancing the microfinance hype*. I have to say, at this point, it almost seems like the microfinance hype is hyped. The hype is constantly regretted (and it ain't dead yet), but the press coverage has turned negative and the public image may follow. At any rate, I'm open to the Hegelian perspective that the jabs between opposite views are inevitable, even healthy: Muhammad Yunus is the thesis; critics like Tom Heinemann, Thomas Dichter, and **Milford Bateman** are the antithesis; and others, perhaps including me, are the synthesis.
- *Telling the truth*. In other words, if almost everything about microcredit is bad then that's the story a responsible reporter must tell. But that's simply not the case here. Credit is always a source of possibilities, good and bad.
- *Beating up on bad or destructive people and organizations*. This is the negative advertising theory of policy change. You see the other

side as benighted or malign, or at least see yourself as justified in treating them as such. In this case, any attack upon them is in the interests of the poor. The presumption here is, as it were, that God is a Republican. The burden of evidence that one holds a monopoly on the truth ought to be pretty high.

- *Maximizing drama.* Maybe even-handed analysis makes for good blogging (ahem) but it's boring on video. Dramatic tension calls for personification and dichotomization of issues. The medium is the message. That's why this documentary revolves around the character of Yunus.

- *Maximizing attention for the attacker.* Anyone who publishes content seeks attention, so the issue here would be a matter of degree and balance.

By way of making my case that the documentary maxes out on negativity, I'll comment on a few parts:

- All along, I've felt that the most valuable thing Tom has to offer is his footage of women in Bangladesh talking about their troubles with microcredit. Not knowing a word of Bangla or Norwegian, I can't tell what they say in the film, but I can read their tears and long faces. Tom told me that some women he met in Bangladesh said they have contemplated suicide; I expect that made it into the film. At one point, he asks a woman, in English, to show him the house she lost to debt. I think it is worthy to bring such sad stories to life through the powerful medium of video. Anyone who promotes or supports microcredit must recognize that it, like all credit, has a dark side. We don't see it enough.

  That said, I am certain that if Tom had wanted video of people talking about how microcredit had helped them manage life a bit better, he could have shot it. For example, he could have asked the authors of **Portfolios of the Poor** to introduce him to some of their subjects, many of whose stories are told in **Appendix 2** of that book. Those stories are neither of ascent out of poverty nor of descent into indigence, but of people getting by by grasping financial tools within reach. The apparently pure negativity of documentary's client footage is therefore a *choice*—a choice to give viewers only one side of the story. Whether most viewers will realize that, I don't know.

- The talking head footage is dominated by critics, and even more by criticism. I think quotes from middle-of-the-roaders like me and Jonathan Morduch accentuate the negative. Tom cleared three with me: the two negative ones used, and this positive one, which didn't make the final cut: "I do think that we need to give Mohammad Yunus credit for spreading the idea that you can do business with the poor." (I should explain, as I wrote to Tom, that I misspoke in one that he does use: we have essentially no credible evidence that *microcredit* reduces poverty; but we do have one study that shows **microsavings (thus microfinance) reducing poverty**. I feel bad about creating this film editing problem, which has not been solved yet.)

The one ardent defender is **Alex Counts, CEO of the Grameen Foundation**. To be fair, I should note that Yunus refused to be interviewed. But is it just me, or are the shots of Alex less flattering in angle and frame than of the other talking heads? (I did wince at 42:30, when Alex cited the **literature review he commissioned five years ago** as showing that microfinance reduces poverty rather than the **fine, new update** which avoids such claims.)

• A **companion article**, and I assume the film, claim that the Grameen Bank charges 30%/year interest. I told Tom that's wrong. The source appears to be page 61 of **this report**, which Tom sent me, and which contains two errors. First, it assumes that loans repaid in 46 installments are repaid in 46 weeks, which they are not: some weeks no payment is due because of holidays. Extending the repayment period lowers the effective interest rate. Second, and more significantly, the cited figure includes an estimate of *client transaction costs*, such as the rickshaw ride to the weekly meeting. That's interesting, but misleading when cited without explanation.

My sharp measurement of a standard Grameen borrowing pattern, inspired by Tom's queries, **yields a rate of about 24%**. After I blogged that finding, Tom contacted me to share his puzzlement over Grameen Bank transaction logs he had copied. It turned out that the borrowers were **topping up** their loans: having repaid at least half the balance, they borrowed it back again. Explaining this to Tom, I realized that the unusual flexibility of Grameen loans raises average balances without raising interest charges. **Factoring this in** reduces the interest rates to more like 17–20%. And all that is before factoring in Bangladesh's higher inflation rate, which makes 17–20% feel like 13–16% to a Norwegian or American. That is much less than I would pay for an uncollateralized loan from American Express. All the *sturm und drang* about usury in India notwithstanding, microcredit is generally cheap in South Asia. I told Tom, but he stuck with 30%.

- A **companion article**, and perhaps a chunk of the film, sets out to debunk the myth of the "phone ladies," women who began in the late 1990s to take microloans to buy mobile phones and then sell their use by the minute. "The truth is," intones the article in **Google translation**, "that today there is no longer any phone women." But how is this a failure? The truth is that for the Bangladeshi man who **conceived of bringing mobile phones to the masses in the developing world**, Iqbal Quadir, **credit was just a means to the end of connectivity**. When connectivity became so cheap and prevalent as to make phone ladies obsolete, that was success—indeed, given its ripple effects throughout the developing world, one of the most extraordinary development triumphs of our day. As a matter of history, microcredit was a low rung on that ladder to success. Accentuating the negative here looks like mudslinging.
- Likewise, the documentary devotes ~10 of its 60 minutes to documents Tom obtained through a Norwegian Freedom of Information Act request. (I have OCR'd, Google-translated, and archived them **here**.) Most of the documents relate to a previously hidden dispute between the Grameen Bank and the Norwegian government over the former's use of the latter's aid money. For microfinance history geeks like me, this is prime, like Wikileaked State Department cables. But, as I told Tom at the interview, it appears to have no bearing on the important question of how microcredit affects human beings. And even on its own terms, it has been blown way out of proportion.

What is revealed is that in 1996 the Grameen Bank transferred some $100 million in aid receipts from Norway, Sweden, and other donors to a separate, nonprofit entity called Grameen Kalyan—without informing those donors. Grameen Kalyan then lent the money back to the Bank at 2% interest. According to the Bank's **just-released account**, this interest supplied a Social Advancement Fund which was to provide services such as scholarships to Grameen members and employees. A Norwegian official first detected the transaction in a footnote of the Bank's 1996 annual report, which was published in mid-1997. The Norwegian government became alarmed that money it had given to a specific institution for a specific purpose (housing loans) had been transferred to another institution for other purposes without the donor's knowledge. It also pointed out that this gift to Grameen Kalyan reduced the net worth of the Grameen Bank, thus of its shareholder-members. (A good timeline is **here**.)

The Bank's explanations for this strange transaction were and are disturbingly dubious. One rationale **was** and **is** that the Bank gave the money away and borrowed it back because it was afraid that otherwise it would burn a hole in the Bank's pocket. This Bank, entrusted with the serious responsibility of using foreign funds to help the poor, would not entrust itself with the basic function of a bank: holding money safely. Or—more likely—the Bank was and is lying. Another reason given was and is that the deal could reduce Grameen's tax liability. But **according to a Norwegian embassy official**, Yunus first emphasized this rationale, then deemphasized it months later. (And the Bank **disowned** the rationale in a letter to Tom this August.) The dissembling raises suspicions: perhaps the move was nefarious, as **sensational** headlines have **insinuated** in the **last few days**. But lacking evidence to the contrary, I am prepared to believe that the real motive was indeed to set up the social fund, and that the Bank got trapped in rationalizing a contract violation. In the end, the disputants **compromised**: about half the funds (I think) were moved back, after which the Norwegians judged that their interest in the appropriate use of their money was served. On what basis should we second-guess them? [Update: The Norwegian government has, from its point of view, **cleared Grameen of all charges**.]

The episode does shed light on the parting of ways between the Grameen Bank and donors. Yunus has long taken pride in the Bank's independence since the mid-1990s. Whether he is making a virtue of out of an unhappy divorce, or whether the deep cause of the newly exposed dispute was Yunus's growing restiveness under the yoke of the donors, it seems clear that the Bank had developed the confidence to do things its way, on its own. The documents also debunk Milford Bateman's **assertion** that "the rejection of subsidies [for the Grameen Bank] was essentially rooted in changing politics: specifically, the rapid ascendance of the neoliberal political project." There is no sign of Norwegian officials, in their candid moments, planning to neoliberalize the Grameen Bank. Rather, they wanted to subsidize it and have a full say in how their subsidies were used.

Why then make such heavy weather of this dozen-year-old dispute? I suspect the answer lies in the excitement of headlines such as "**Grameen founder Muhammad Yunus in Bangladesh aid probe**"—as distinct from, say, questions of what helps the poor.

Professor Yunus's Opinion
January 15, 2011

The *New York Times* has **published an opinion piece** by Muhammad Yunus on how to keep microcredit on this side of usury:

In the 1970s, when I began working here on what would eventually be called "microcredit," one of my goals was to eliminate the presence of loan sharks who grow rich by preying on the poor. In 1983, I founded Grameen Bank to provide small loans that people, especially poor women, could use to bring themselves out of poverty. At that time, I never imagined that one day microcredit would give rise to its own breed of loan sharks.

But it has.

For close followers of microfinance, Yunus's writing will ring familiar. For the general public, it is a concise statement of his thinking. He makes two concrete points:

- "Commercialization has been a terrible wrong turn for microfinance." Commericalized microfinance is not really microfinance. It is usury, profiteering off the poor. It should stop. Now, as Yunus **clarified in his debate with Vikram Akula** at the Clinton Global Initiative last fall, he is not against *profit* in microfinance, but against *outside ownership* of microfinance institutions—that's what he means by "commercialization." The borrowers should own the lenders. He thus favors cooperative corporate governance, an idea that, like group microfinance itself, **traces back** to the early socialist Robert Owen. The Grameen Bank, of course, is **majority-owned by its borrowers** (page 25).
- Microcreditors should charge no more than 15% above their own cost of funds. Here, the professor valiantly takes on the ancient challenge of defining the just price of credit. Once, the Christian Church, like Islam, deemed any interest unjust. After a thousand years or so, it switched to accepting interest within reasonable bounds. A **papal decision written almost exactly 500 years ago** on how much interest to charge the poor stuck to principles and avoided numbers—wisely, I think.

Overall, I think Yunus makes a good point about the dangers of commercialization as he defines it. Indeed, **events in India** have, to a degree, vindicated him. Although I criticized his line of argument before the Indian implosion (**this**, **this**) and will do so here, I have come to appreciate a contradiction in my own thinking. On the one hand, I have doubted the value of the Grameen Bank's example of cooperative ownership. Can others really be expected to follow it? On the other, I have **blogged in praise of John Bogle** for creating a cooperatively owned financial institution, the **Vanguard**

Group. I trust Vanguard with my money because I know it is not trying to rip me off in order to favor outside investor-owners. Why should microcredit clients think any differently? Moreover, Yunus's distinction resonates historically: all forms of group microcredit popular today descend from the credit *cooperative* movement of 19th-century Germany (which in turn drew inspiration from those English socialists).

So if all the microcreditors could raise all their capital from their clients then, I agree, that is the way to go.

But almost none has—not even the Grameen Bank.

Yunus's achievements should not be slighted. In its pioneer days, the way forward for the Grameen Bank was far tougher and more uncertain than for those that followed. That said, thanks to his pioneering status and his abilities as a salesman, Yunus had help: **a couple hundred million dollars** from the Ford Foundation, the United Nations, Japan, and Western donors. As Vijay Mahajan, the father of commercial microfinance in India, has pointed out, microcreditors today cannot expect the same help, whether because of limited funds among private and public donors or the donors' sense that microcredit has graduated from grants. If microcreditors today want such big chunks of capital from outsiders, they will have to buy it.

In particular, while it is true that Grameen members hold legal claim to 97% of the Grameen Bank's net worth, they **only contributed about $7.5 million** in capital, at 100 taka ($1.40) per member. The Grameen Bank has not shown that microfinance can grow large purely through cooperative ownership.

In fact, as I **wrote last summer**, an irony in Yunus's criticism of for-profit microlenders for going to the capital markets is that Grameen Bank is itself **running low on capital**, by which I mean risk-absorbing, profit sharing funds that banks are required to keep on hand in case of losses. And it is not clear (to me at least) how Grameen will get more. Maybe the government will step in . . .

Also of dubious generalizability is Yunus's 15% spread cap. That limit might work in South Asia, but not very well in the rest of the world. Microcredit is cheaper to do in South Asia because of high population density—meaning that a loan officer can hit more villages in a day, serving more clients—and relative wage equality—which means that the wages of a, say, high-school educated loan officer are not so high compared to the size of the loans the poor can safely manage. That is why Grameen can **charge just 20%**, and why Chuck Waterfield, citing unreleased analayses, could **tell a conference audience** that India's microcredit interest rates are among the lowest in the world. Where workers are more expensive relative to the typical loan size, as in much of Latin America and Africa, they must be paid from higher interest charges (or subsidies, which Yunus eschews). Also, such a rate rule discriminates against creditors aiming to serve the poorest, with particularly little, thus costly, loans; and against small, young creditors that have not yet achieved economies of scale or that are trying to earn extra profits to reinvest in their growth. Adrian Gonzalez of the Microfinance Information Exchange (MIX) **determined** that 75% of microcreditors worldwide are in Yunus's "red zone," charging spreads of more than 15%. This large group makes smaller loans on average, perhaps serving poorer people. And profiteering does not explain the widespread trespass into the red zone: even if profits were zeroed out, it would thin only to 61% of microcreditors.

So there is a kind of stubborn ignorance of facts and reason in this piece that rubs thinkers like me the wrong way—and probably helped make Yunus such an effective doer. On balance, I think it is fair to say that while Yunus has contributed much by being a pioneer, he should be more gracious in recognizing that not everyone can do microcredit the way he did it, let alone the way he says he does it.

Since I share Yunus's diagnosis that commercial microfinance got out of hand in India yet disagree with his prescription, I should offer an alternative. A sensible proposal I heard from two microfinance leaders in India, Mahajan of BASIX and P.N. Vasudevan of Equitas, was for microcreditors, as distinct from governments, to cap their profit rates, as distinct from interest rates. At his office in Hyderabad last November, Mahajan told me that BASIX, which he founded, used to profit at the rate of 2 cents per dollar of assets (2% ROA), where "assets" are dominated by outstanding loans and "return" is interest and other income net of expenses. After competitors started raking in 5% ROA, BASIX inched up to 3% and used the extra profits to grow faster. So a cap of 2–3% might work. A few days before in a Delhi hotel lobby, Vasudevan told me that Equitas publicly limits its ROA, its Return on Equity (ROE), and the ratio in pay between the highest and lowest employees in the company.

Credit is not an ordinary product. It is weighed down by millennia of baggage, for the good reason that it can do real harm. It is like a drug in that it is potentially healthy in small doses, but also potentially addictive. So it stands to reason that sellers of this product must take unusual steps to counteract its special problems of reputation and risk.

Having taken Yunus's piece on its own terms, I want also to view it within its political context. Remarkably, the piece mentions only the controversy in India, not the one swirling around his own head in Bangladesh. I suppose it is not in Yunus's interest to raise awareness about that. But that does not mean his own awareness of the controversy played no role in the writing. Tom Heinemann's documentary was unfair in **only showing the dark side of microcredit**, but he still did a service in shining a light on that dark side. Yunus, by focusing on interest rates, an area of relative strength for Grameen, distracts from the fact that the justness and impact of lending to the poor depend on more than rates. The *amount* of credit matters too, as do the quality of disclosure about program rules, the degree of competition and multiple lending. Even debt at 0% can trap the poor. Focusing on interest rates plays into the Bangladesh government's fixation on that aspect of the credit relationship, as it **sets out to investigate Grameen**, drawing the investigators toward one of the Bank's strengths. In fact, the Grameen Bank is by many accounts a leader in the **flexibility and diversity, cost and transparency**, of its offerings. But none of that, certainly not low interest rates by themselves, guarantees that all is well with the Grameen Bank's clients.

In a final and remarkable parry, Yunus reminds his prime minister, who **recently accused microcreditors** of "sucking blood from the poor in the name of poverty alleviation," that she once **stood side by side** with him and the woman who is now the most powerful diplomat of the most powerful nation, **pledging** to bring microcredit to millions. Prime Minister Hasina's opinion of microcredit may have flipped since 1997, but Secretary Clinton's has not. Perhaps Yunus is signaling to Hasina about how those abroad might take offense if her government goes too far in attacking him . . . or perhaps words published in New York hold little sway over deeds done in Dhaka.

After the Fall, Resignation Edition
May 12, 2011

The news of Yunus's formal resignation is in a sense not news: the highest court in the land **already ruled** that he had to go. But it is also a profoundly sad moment, so much so that I did not want to sully this **transcendent moment** with my perishable thoughts.

But you must be wondering: what next?

I wrote **back in March** about issues facing the Grameen Bank in the post-Yunus era. Those issues haven't gone away. But the situation has, to external appearances, become more grave.

The obvious successor would be Dipal Barua, the **most recently departed** Deputy Managing Director. Barua was born in Jobra, where Yunus made his first loans, and worked under Yunus all those years until early 2010. He was central to the **Grameen II** overhaul. He founded Grameen Shakti, a solar company. The split between Yunus and Barua was evidently bitter, and possibly Barua secretly aided the government in ousting

Yunus. He knows where the skeletons are. On the other hand, recently released **old letters** from another departed deputy, Muzammel Huq, show that in the late 1990s at least, he viewed Barua with scorn; and Huq is now the chairman. So I suppose Huq is the other obvious candidate; and going by Mohsin Rashid's **legal arguments**, it may be Huq who did more to guide the investigative committee.

Of course, we can't assume that the government would be so rational as to appoint someone with years of experience at the Grameen Bank, someone who could bring a mix of continuity, managerial competence, and fresh thinking, thus at least a prayer of saving the Bank as an independent institution. Rumors are flying that Hasina will appoint her sister or **her son**. Whether or not accurate, such rumors lower one's expectations.

Whoever is picked will have far less independence than Yunus. The government appears to be **moving quickly** to amend the law that governs the Grameen Bank, to gain more control. Not surprisingly, the government appears intent on reconstituting the board, so that elected members no longer hold the majority. Those nine women are now the main barrier to government control of the Grameen Bank. I have heard that the government has been pressuring some of them, offering them, shall we say, both carrots and sticks to cajole allegiance. If the women continue to resist, then the government will find it easier to do an end run around them by pushing a new Grameen Bank law through parliament, where it does have a majority.

After **calling for** "tough agitation if Dr Muhammad Yunus is not made chairman," Mohammad Sagirur Rashid Chowdhury, a Grameen Bank employee and spokesperson for its employees' union, was **abducted, tortured, and threatened with death** if the protests were carried out. Before **releasing him at Dhaka University**, the perpetrators told him to remain silent about what they had done to him. He did not. They did not leave calling cards, but they reportedly did not take his watch or wallet, indicating that they were professionals. Four days later, Human Rights Watch **documented** "cases of extrajudicial killings, 'disappearances,' and torture that have taken place in and around Dhaka, after the current Awami League government came to power in January 2009." The force blamed for these atrocities is the government's Rapid Action Battalion. The Awami League, of course, is led by Prime Minister Sheikh Hasina.

The saddest aspect of Yunus's departure is that it says much more about the government of Bangladesh than about microfinance and its leading light.

References

Abbey, Edward. 1977. *The Journey Home.* Plume.

Abrams, Julie, and Damian von Stauffenberg. 2007. "Role Reversal: Are Public Development Institutions Crowding out Private Investment in Microfinance?" MicroRate.

Adams, Dale. 1971. "Agricultural Credit in Latin America: A Critical Review of External Funding Policy." *American Journal of Agricultural Economics* 53 (2): 163–72.

———. 2002. "Filling the Deposit Gap in Microfinance." Paper prepared for the Conference on Commercialization in Microfinance. Park City, Utah, October 12.

———. 2009. "Easing Poverty through Thrift." *Savings and Development* 33 (1): 1–13.

Adams, Dale, Douglas H. Graham, and J. D. Von Pischke, eds. 1984. *Undermining Rural Development with Cheap Credit.* Westview Press.

Akula, Vikram. 2010. *A Fistful of Rice: My Unexpected Quest to End Poverty through Profitability.* Harvard Business Review Press.

Aleem, Ifran. 1990. "Imperfect Information, Screening, and the Costs of Informal Lending: A Study of a Rural Credit Market in Pakistan." *World Bank Economic Review* 4 (3): 329–49.

Altekruse, S. F., and others, eds. 2010. *SEER Cancer Statistics Review, 1975–2007.* National Cancer Institute (seer.cancer.gov/csr/1975_2007).

Anderson, Siwan, and Jean-Marie Baland. 2002. "The Economics of Roscas and Intrahousehold Resource Allocation." *Quarterly Journal of Economics* 117 (3): 963–95.

Angrist, Joshua D., and Jörn-Steffen Pischke. 2010. "The Credibility Revolution in Empirical Economics: How Better Research Design Is Taking the Con out of Econometrics." *Journal of Economic Perspectives* 24 (2): 3–30.

Anscombe, Francis John. 1973. "Graphs in Statistical Analysis." *American Statistician* 27(1): 17–21.

Armendáriz, Beatriz, and Jonathan Morduch. 2010. *The Economics of Microfinance.* 2nd edition. MIT Press.

ASA. 2010. *Annual Report.*

Ashraf, Nava, Dean Karlan, and Wesley Yin. 2006. "Tying Odysseus to the Mast: Evidence From a Commitment Savings Product in the Philippines." *Quarterly Journal of Economics* 121 (2): 635–72.

Bagehot, Walter. 1897. *Lombard Street: A Description of the Money Market.* Charles Scribner's Sons.

Banerjee, Abhijit V., and Esther Duflo. 2007. "The Economic Lives of the Poor." *Journal of Economic Perspectives* 21 (1): 141–67.

———. 2008. "What Is Middle Class about the Middle Classes around the World?" *Journal of Economic Perspectives* 22 (2): 3–28.

———. 2011. *Poor Economics: A Radical Rethinking of the Way to Fight Global Poverty.* PublicAffairs.

Banerjee, Abhijit V. and others. 2009. "The Miracle of Microfinance? Evidence from a Randomized Evaluation." Massachusetts Institute of Technology, Department of Economics.

Barder, Owen. 2005. "Reforming Development Assistance: Lessons from the UK Experience." Working Paper 70. Center for Global Development.

Bateman, Milford. 2010. *Why Doesn't Microfinance Work: The Destructive Rise of Local Neoliberalism.* Zed Books.

Bentham, Jeremy. 1797. "Outline of a Work Entitled Pauper Management Improved." *Annals of Agriculture* 29 (167). Reprinted in *The Works of Jeremy Bentham.* Vol. 8. William Tait, 1843.

Berg, A. Scott. 1978. *Max Perkins: Editor of Genius.* Riverhead Books.

Bernard, Thomas. 1798. "Appendix V." In *Reports of the Society for Bettering the Condition and Increasing the Comforts of the Poor.* Vol. 1.

Bertrand, Marianne, and Adair Morse. 2009. "Information Disclosure, Cognitive Biases and Payday Borrowing." University of Chicago, Booth School of Business.

Bouman, F.J.A. 1979. "The ROSCA: Financial Technology of an Informal Savings and Credit Institution in Developing Countries." *Savings and Development* 3 (4): 253–76.

Bouyer, R.G. 1798. "Extract from an Account of a School of Industry for Sixty Girls, at Bamburgh Castle." In *Reports of the Society for Bettering the Condition and Increasing the Comforts of the Poor.* Vol. 1.

Brabrook, E.W. 1898. *Provident Societies and Industrial Welfare.* Blackie & Son.

Braverman, Avishay, and Luis Guasch. 1986. "Rural Credit Markets and Institutions in Developing Countries: Lessons for Policy Analysis form Practice and Modern Theory." *World Development* 14 (10/11): 1253–67.

Burdon, Rowland. 1798. "Extract from an Account of a Friendly Society at Castle-Eden, in the County of Durham." In *Reports of the Society for Bettering the Condition and Increasing the Comforts of the Poor.* Vol. 1.

Burgess, Robin, and Rohini Pande. "Do Rural Banks Matter? Evidence from the Indian Social Banking Experiment." *American Economic Review* 95 (3): 780–95.

Burki, Hussan-Bano. 2009. *Unraveling the Delinquency Problem (2008/2009) in Punjab-Pakistan.* Islamabad: Pakistan Microfinance Network.

Burra, Neera, Joy Deshmukh-Ranadive, and Ranjani K. Murthy, eds. *Micro-credit, Poverty and Empowerment: Linking the Triad.* Sage Publications.

Calmeadow Foundation. 2005. *Calmeadow at 20.*

————. 2006. *ProFund Internacional, S.A.* (calmeadow.com/ProFund.pdf).

Campion, Anita. 2001. "Client Information Sharing in Bolivia." *Journal of Microfinance* 3 (1): 45–63.

Carruthers, Bruce, Timothy Guinnane, and Yoonseok Lee. 2007. "The Passage of the Uniform Small Loan Law." Paper presented at the annual meeting of the American Sociological Association. New York, August 11.

Cary, Max, and others, eds. 1950. *The Oxford Classical Dictionary.* Clarendon Press.

Caufield, Catherine. 1996. *Masters of Illusion: The World Bank and the Poverty of Nations.* Henry Holt and Company.

CGAP. 2004. "Financial Institutions with a 'Double Bottom Line': Implications for the Future of Microfinance." Occasional Paper 8.

————. 2009a. *Private Transactions Benchmark: Shedding Light on Microfinance Equity Valuation: Past and Present.*

————. 2009b. *Microfinance Dealbook.* MicroCapital.org.

————. 2010a. *CGAP 2010 MIV Survey: Market Data & Peer Group Analysis.*

————. 2010b. *Cross-Border Funding for Microfinance: Results of the CGAP Funding Surveys 2010.*

Chakravarti, J.S. 1920. *Agricultural Insurance: A Practical Scheme Suited to Indian Conditions.* Government Press.

Chambers, William. 1830. *The Book of Scotland.* Robert Buchanan and William Hunter.

Chaudhury, Iftekhar A., and Imran Matin. 2002. "Dimensions and Dynamics of Microfinance Membership Overlap: A Micro Study from Bangladesh." *Small Enterprise Development* 13 (2): 46–55.

Chen, Greg, Stephen Rasmussen, and Xavier Reille. 2010. "Growth and Vulnerabilities in Microfinance." Focus Note 61. CGAP.

Chen, Greg, Stephen Rasmussen, Xavier Reille, and Daniel Rozas. 2010. "Indian Microfinance Goes Public: The SKS Initial Public Offering." Focus Note 65. CGAP.

Chen, Martha Alter. 1983. *A Quiet Revolution: Women in Transition in Rural Bangladesh.* Schenkman.

Cheston, Susy, and Larry Reed. 1999. "Measuring Transformation: Assessing and Improving the Impact of Microcredit." Paper prepared for the Microcredit Summit Meeting of Councils, Abidjan, Côte d'Ivoire, June 24–26.

Chlebowski, Rowan, and others. 2009. "Breast Cancer after Use of Estrogen plus Progestin in Postmenopausal Women." *New England Journal of Medicine* 360 (6): 573–87.

Christen, Robert Peck, Timothy R. Lyman, and Richard Rosenberg. 2003. *Microfinance Consensus Guidelines: Guiding Principles on Regulation and Supervision of Microfinance.* CGAP.

Christen, Bob, and Ignacio Mas. 2009. "It's Time to Address the Microsavings Challenge, Scalably." *Enterprise Development and Microfinance* 20 (4): 274–85.

Churchill, Winston S. 2007. *Liberalism and the Social Problem: A Collection of Early Speeches as a Member of Parliament.* Arc Manor.

Cleveland, Harold van B., and Thomas Huertas, *Citibank, 1812–1970.* Harvard University Press.

Cohen, Edward E. 1992. *Athenian Economy and Society: A Banking Perspective*. Princeton University Press.

Cole, Shawn, and others. 2009. "Barriers to Household Risk Management: Evidence from India." Working Paper 09-116. Harvard Business School.

Coleman, Brett E. 1999. "The Impact of Group Lending in Northeast Thailand." *Journal of Development Economics* 60: 105–41.

———. 2006. "Microfinance in Northeast Thailand: Who Benefits and How Much?" *World Development* 34 (9): 1612–38.

Collins, Daryl, and others. 2009. *Portfolios of the Poor: How the World's Poor Live on $2 a Day*. Princeton University Press.

Commission on Growth and Development. 2008. *The Growth Report: Strategies for Sustained Growth and Inclusive Development*. World Bank.

Commission on Thrift. 2008. *For a New Thrift: Confronting the Debt Culture*. Institute for American Values.

Conger, Lucy, Patricia Inga, and Richard Webb. 2009. *The Mustard Tree: A History of Microfinance in Peru*. Universidad de San Martín de Porres.

Copestake, James. 2002. "Inequality and the Polarizing Impact of Microcredit: Evidence from Zambia's Copperbelt." *Journal of International Development* 14 (6): 743–55

Cull, Robert, Asli Demirgüç-Kunt, and Jonathan Morduch. 2007. "Financial Performance and Outreach: A Global Analysis of Leading Microbanks." *Economic Journal* 117 (517): F107–33.

———. 2009. "Banks and Microbanks." Policy Research Working Paper 5078. World Bank.

Daly, Herman E. 1990. "Sustainable Growth: An Impossibility Theorem." *Journal of the Society for International Development* 3/4 (*1990*): 92–98. Reprinted in Herman E. Daly and Kenneth N. Townsend, eds., *Valuing the Earth: Economics, Ecology, Ethics*, pp. 267–73. MIT Press, 1993.

Danel, Carlos, and Carlos Labarthe. 2008. "A Letter to Our Peers." Compartamos Banco.

Deaton, Angus. 2009. "Instruments of Development: Randomization in the Tropics, and the Search for the Elusive Keys to Economic Development." Text of Keynes Lecture, British Academy, London, October 9, 2008 (princeton.edu/~deaton/downloads/Instruments_of_Development.pdf).

Defoe, Daniel. 1697. "An Essay upon Projects."

Dehejia, Rajeev, Heather Montgomery, and Jonathan Morduch. 2009. "Do Interest Rates Matter? Credit Demand in the Dhaka Slums." Financial Access Initiative.

De Janvry, Alain, Craig McIntosh, and Elisabeth Sadoulet. 2010. "The Supply- and Demand-Side Impacts of Credit Market Information." *Journal of Development Economics* 93 (2): 173–88.

De Mel, Suresh, David McKenzie, and Christopher Woodruff. 2008a. "Returns to Capital in Microenterprises: Evidence from a Field Experiment." *Quarterly Journal of Economics* 123(4): 1329–72.

———. 2008b. "Who Are the Microenterprise Owners? Evidence from Sri Lanka on Tokman v. de Soto." Policy Research Working Paper 4625. World Bank.

Demirgüç-Kunt, Aslı, Thorsten Beck, and Patrick Honohan. 2008. *Finance for All? Policies and Pitfalls in Expanding Access*. World Bank.

Dennett, Laurie. 1998. *A Sense of Security: 150 Years of Prudential*. Granta Editions.

Denton, Frank. 1985. "Data Mining as an Industry." *Review of Economics and Statistics* 67 (1): 124–27.

De Soto, Hernando. 2000. *The Mystery of Capital: Why Capitalism Triumphs in the West and Fails Everywhere Else*. Basic Books.

Dexter, Seymour. 1900. *A Treatise on Co-operative Savings and Loan Associations*. D. Appleton and Company.

Dichter, Thomas. 2007. "A Second Look at Microfinance: The Sequence of Growth and Credit in Economic History." Development Policy Briefing Paper 1. Cato Institute.

Diouf, Wagane. 2010. Testimony before the Subcommittee on International Monetary Policy and Trade, Committee on Financial Services, U.S. House of Representatives. January 27 (j.mp/9RH33L).

Dixon, Mike. 2006. *Rethinking Financial Capability: Lessons from Economic Psychology and Behavioural Finance*. Institute for Public Policy Research.

Dowla, Asif, and Dipal Barua. 2006. *The Poor Always Pay Back: The Grameen II Story*. Kumarian Press.

Duflo, Esther, and others. 2008. "Health Insurance: Opportunities and Challenges." Presentation at the Centre for Microfinance/College of Agricultural Banking Conference on Microfinance. Pune, India, January 18.

Dunham, S. Ann. 2009. *Surviving against the Odds: Village Industry in Indonesia*. Duke University Press.

Dupas, Pascaline, and Jonathan Robinson. 2009. "Savings Constraints and Microenterprise Development: Evidence from a Field Experiment in Kenya." Working Paper 14693. National Bureau of Economic Research.

Easterly, William, Ross Levine, and David Roodman. 2004. "Aid, Policies, and Growth: Comment." *American Economic Review* 94 (3): 774–80.

Eijkman, Frederik, Jake Kendall, and Ignacio Mas. 2010. "Bridges to Cash: The Retail End of M-PESA." Bill & Melinda Gates Foundation and PEP Intermedius.

Feige, Edgar L. 1975. "The Consequences of Journal Editorial Policies and a Suggestion for Revision." *Journal of Political Economy* 83 (6): 1291–96.

Feigenberg, Benjamin, Erica Field, and Rohini Pande. 2010. "Building Social Capital through Microfinance." Working Paper 16018. Cambridge, Mass.: National Bureau of Economic Research.

Fernald, Lia C.H., and others. 2008. "Small Individual Loans and Mental Health: A Randomized Controlled Trial among South African Adults." *BMC Public Health* 8: 409.

Fernandez, Aloysius P. 1985. "An Experiment in Appropriate Sociology." Rural Management Systems Series, Paper 1. MYRADA.

———. 2005. "Self-Help Affinity Groups (SAGS): Their Role in Poverty Reduction and Financial Sector Development." Rural Management Systems Series, Paper 40. MYRADA.

Filene, Edward. 1907. *The Trip Book of 1907: Those Portions Relating to Egypt and India*. Filene Research Institute. j.mp/pGdWUg.

Fisher, Clyde Olin. 1929. "Review of *The Morris Plan of Industrial Banking* by Peter W. Herzog." *American Economic Review* 19 (3): 497–500.

Fishlow, Albert. 1961. "The Trustee Savings Banks, 1817–1861." *Journal of Economic History* 21 (1): 26–40.

Galbraith, John Kenneth. 1993. *A Short History of Financial Euphoria.* Penguin.

Gallagher, Terence. 2006. "Branchless Banking in Brazil." Presentation at "Expanding Financial Services to the Poor: The Role of ITC." International Finance Corporation, Washington, D.C., June 9, 2006.

Garand, Denis. 2005. "VimoSEWA: India." Good and Bad Practices Case Study No. 16. CGAP Working Group on Microinsurance.

Geertz, Clifford. 1962. "The Rotating Credit Association: A 'Middle Rung' in Development." *Economic Development and Cultural Change* 10 (3): 241–63.

Ghatak, Maitreesh. 1999. "Group Lending, Local Information and Peer Selection." *Journal of Development Economics* 60 (1): 27–50.

Ghate, Prabhu. 2007. "Learning from the Andhra Pradesh Crisis." In *What's Wrong with Microfinance?* edited by Thomas Dichter and Malcolm Harper, pp. 163–76. Practical Action Publishing.

Gillingham, Sarah, and Md. Mehrul Islam. 2005a. "The Dynamics of Debt in Southeast Bangladesh." Rural Livelihoods Programme, CARE Bangladesh.

———. 2005b. "Debt and Vulnerability in Northwest Bangladesh. Rural Livelihoods Programme." CARE Bangladesh.

Giné, Xavier, and Dean Karlan. 2008. "Group versus Individual Liability: A Field Experiment in the Philippines." Yale University.

Glasse, Rev. Dr. 1798. "Extract from an Account of the Advantage of a Cottager Keeping a Pig." In *Reports of the Society for Bettering the Condition and Increasing the Comforts of the Poor.* Vol. 1.

Goetz, Anne Mari, and Rina Sen Gupta. 1996. "Who Takes the Credit? Gender, Power, and Control over Loan Use in Rural Credit Programs in Bangladesh." *World Development* 24 (1): 45–63.

Gonzalez, Adrian. 2007. "Efficiency Drivers of Microfinance Institutions (MFIs): The Case of Operating Costs." *MicroBanking Bulletin* 15 (Autumn): 37–42.

———. 2010a. "Analyzing Microcredit Interest Rates: A Review of the Methodology Proposed by Mohammed Yunus." Data Brief 4. Microfinance Information eXchange.

———. 2010b. "Is Microfinance Growing Too Fast?" Data Brief 5. Microfinance Information eXchange.

Goodman, Andy. 2006. *Storytelling as Best Practice*, 3rd ed. A. Goodman.

Gourlay, William R. 1906. "Co-operative Credit in Bengal." *Indian Journal of Agriculture* 1 (3): 216–19.

Government of India, Planning Commission. 2009. *Report of the Expert Group to Review the Methodology for Estimation of Poverty.*

Grameen Bank. 2010. *Audited Financial Statements 2009.*

Guinnane, Timothy W. 1994. "A Failed Institutional Transplant: Raiffeisen's Credit Cooperatives in Ireland, 1894–1914." *Explorations in Economic History* 31: 38–61.

Halcrow, Harold G. 1949. "Actuarial Structures for Crop Insurance." *Journal of Farm Economics* 31 (3): 418–43.

Hamermesh, Daniel S. 2007. "Replication in Economics." *Canadian Journal of Economics* 40(3): 715–33.

Harper, Malcolm. 2007a. "What's Wrong with Groups?" In *What's Wrong with Microfinance?* edited by Thomas Dichter and Malcolm Harper, pp. 35–48. Practical Action Publishing.

———. 2007b. "Microfinance and Farmers: Do They Fit?" In *What's Wrong with Microfinance?* edited by Thomas Dicther and Malcolm Harper, pp. 83–94. Practical Action Publishing.

Harper, Malcolm, and Robert Vogel. 2005. "The Role of Savings as a Form of MFI Funding: Debate." *MicroBanking Bulletin* 11 (August): 5–8.

Hashemi, Syed, Sidney Ruth Schuler, and Ann P. Riley. 1996. "Rural Credit Programs and Women's Empowerment in Bangladesh." *World Development* 24 (4): 635–53.

Hatch, John. 2010. "Who Could Have Predicted?" *Village Bank Notes* 21 (3): 1.

Hazell, Peter. 1992. "The Appropriate Role of Agricultural Insurance in Developing Countries." *Journal of International Development* 4 (6): 567–81.

Hazell, Peter, Carlos Pomareda, and Alberto Valdés. 1986. *Crop Insurance for Agricultural Development: Issues and Experience.* Johns Hopkins University Press.

Heckman, James J., and Sergio Urzua. 2009. "Comparing IV with Structural Models: What Simple IV Can and Cannot Identify." Working Paper 14706. National Bureau of Economic Research.

Herrick, Myron T., and R. Ingalls. 1914. *Rural Credits: Land and Coöperative.* Appleton and Company.

Herzog, Peter W. 1928. *The Morris Plan of Industrial Banking.* A.W. Shaw Company.

Hoffman, Frederick L. 1900. *History of the Prudential Life Insurance Company of America.* Prudential Press.

Hollis, Aidan. 2002. "Women and Microcredit in History: Gender in the Irish Loan Funds." In *Women and Credit: Researching the Past, Refiguring the Future,* edited by Gail Campbell, Beverly Lemire, and Ruth Pearson, pp. 73–89. Berg Press.

Hollis, Aidan, and Arthur Sweetman. 1997. "Complementarity, Competition and Institutional Development: The Irish Loan Funds through Three Centuries." Mimeo.

———. 1998a. "Microcredit: What Can We Learn from the Past?" *World Development* 26 (10): 1875–91.

———. 1998b. "Microcredit in Pre-famine Ireland." *Explorations in Economic History* 35 (4): 347–80.

———. 2001. "The Life-Cycle of a Microfinance Institution: The Irish Loan Funds." *Journal of Economic Behavior and Organization* 46: 291–311.

Honohan, Patrick. 2008. "Cross-country Variation in Household Access to Financial Services." *Journal of Banking and Finance* 32 (11): 2493–2500.

Horne, H. Oliver. 1947. *A History of Savings Banks.* Oxford University Press.

Hughes, Nicholas, and Susie Lonie. 2007. "M-PESA: Mobile Money for the 'Unbanked.'" *Innovations* 2 (1–2): 63–81.

Hulme, David. 2007. "Is Microdebt Good for Poor People? A Note on the Dark Side of Microfinance." In *What's Wrong with Microfinance?* edited by Thomas Dichter and Malcolm Harper, pp. 19–22. Practical Action Publishing.

———. 2008. "The Story of the Grameen Bank: From Subsidised Microcredit to Market-based Microfinance." Working Paper 60. University of Manchester, Brooks World Poverty Institute.

Ito, Sanae. 1999. "The Grameen Bank: Rhetoric and Reality." Ph.D. thesis. University of Sussex.

ITU (International Telecommunication Union). 2011. *The World in 2010: ICT Facts and Figures.*

Jack, William, and Tavneet Suri. 2011. "The Risk Sharing Benefits of Mobile Money." Georgetown University and Massachusetts Institute of Technology.

Jain, Pankaj S. 1996. "Managing Credit for the Rural Poor: Lessons from the Grameen Bank." *World Development* 24 (1): 79–89.

Jain, Pankaj, and Mick Moore. 2003. "What Makes Microcredit Programmes Effective? Fashionable Fallacies and Workable Realities." Working Paper 177. Institute of Development Studies.

Johnson, Doug, and Sushmita Meka. 2010. *Access to Finance in Andhra Pradesh.* IFMR Research-Centre for Micro Finance.

Johnson, Samuel. 1755. *A Dictionary of the English Language.* W. Strahan.

———. 1781. *The Lives of the Most Eminent English Poets.* Vol. 3. S. Johnson.

Johnston, Don, and Jonathan Morduch. 2007. "Microcredit vs. Microsavings: Evidence from Indonesia." Presentation to conference on "Access to Finance." World Bank, Washington, D.C., March 15 (j.mp/bMJECs).

Jordan, Wilbur K. 1959. *Philanthropy in England, 1480–1660: A Study of the Changing Pattern of English Social Aspirations.* Russell Sage Foundation.

———. 1962. *The Charities of Rural England, 1480–1660: The Aspirations and the Achievements of the Rural Society.* Russell Sage Foundation.

Kabeer, Naila. 2001. "Conflicts over Credit: Re-Evaluating the Empowerment Potential of Loans to Women in Rural Bangladesh." *World Development* 29 (1): 63–84.

Kapur, Devesh, John P. Lewis, and Richard Webb. 1997. *The World Bank: Its First Half Century.* Vol. 1. Brookings Institution.

Karim, Lamia. 2008. "Demystifying Micro-Credit: The Grameen Bank, NGOs, and Neoliberalism in Bangladesh." *Cultural Dynamics* 20 (5): 5–29.

Karlan, Dean. 2001. "Microfinance Impact Assessments: The Perils of Using New Members as a Control Group." *Journal of Microfinance* 3 (2): 75–85.

Karlan, Dean, and Jacob Appel. 2011. *More than Good Intentions: How a New Economics Is Helping to Solve Global Poverty.* Dutton.

Karlan, Dean, and Martin Valdivia. 2007. "Teaching Entrepreneurship: Impact of Business Training on Microfinance Clients and Institutions." Working Paper 107. Center for Global Development.

Karlan, Dean, and Jonathan Zinman. 2008a. "Lying about Borrowing." *Journal of the European Economic Association* 6 (2–3): 510–21.

————. 2008b. "Credit Elasticities in Less-Developed Economies: Implications for Microfinance." *American Economic Review* 98 (3): 1040–68.

————. 2009. "Expanding Credit Access: Using Randomized Supply Decisions to Estimate the Impacts in Manila." Yale University and Dartmouth College.

————. 2010. "Expanding Credit Access: Using Randomized Supply Decisions to Estimate the Impacts." *Review of Financial Studies* 23 (1): 433–64.

————. 2011. "Microcredit in Theory and Practice: Using Randomized Credit Scoring for Impact Evaluation." *Science* 332 (6035): 1278–84."

Karlan, Dean, and others. 2010. "Getting to the Top of Mind: How Reminders Increase Saving." Unpublished.

Kashf Foundation. 2008. "Notes to 2007 Financial Statements" (j.mp/dNmPS4).

————. 2009. *Annual Report* (j.mp/hcryEQ).

Kenny, Charles. 2011. *Getting Better: Why Global Development Is Succeeding—And How We Can Improve the World Even More.* Basic Books.

Keyes, Emerson W. 1876. *A History of Savings Banks in the United States from Their Inception in 1816 down to 1874.* Vol. I. Bradford Rhodes.

Khandker, Shahidur R. 1998. *Fighting Poverty with Microcredit: Experience in Bangladesh.* Oxford University Press.

————. 2005. "Microfinance and Poverty: Evidence Using Panel Data from Bangladesh." *World Bank Economic Review* 19 (2): 263–86.

Klein, David R. 1968. "The Introduction, Increase, and Crash of Reindeer on St. Matthew Island." *Journal of Wildlife Management* 32 (2): 350–67.

Klein, David, John Walsh, and Martha Shulski. 2009. "What Killed the Reindeer of Saint Matthew Island?" *Weatherwise* 62 (6): 32–38.

Kneiding, Christoph, and Richard Rosenberg. 2008. "Variations in Microcredit Interest Rates." Brief. Washington, D.C.: CGAP.

Krishnaswamy, Karuna. 2007. "Competition and Multiple Borrowing in the Indian Microfinance Sector." Working Paper. Institute for Financial Management and Research, Centre for Micro Finance.

Lawson, William John. 1850. *The History of Banking.* Richard Bentley.

Leamer, Edward E. 1983. "Let's Take the Con out of Econometrics." *American Economic Review* 73 (1): 31–43.

Levine, Ross. 1997. "Financial Development and Economic Growth: Views and Agenda." *Journal of Economic Literature* 35 (2): 688–726.

Littlefield, Elizabeth, Jonathan Morduch, and Syed Hashemi. 2003. "Is Microfinance an Effective Strategy to Reach the Millennium Development Goals?" Focus Note 24. CGAP.

Maddison, Angus. 2003. *The World Economy: Historical Statistics.* Organization for Economic Cooperation and Development.

Magnoni, Barbara. 2011. "Mission IS-possible: Lessons after a Shake-out in Nicaragua." *MicroCapital Monitor* 6 (2): 3.

Maisch, Felipe Portocarrero, Álvaro Tarazona Soria, and Glenn D. Westley. 2006. "How Should Microfinance Institutions Best Fund Themselves? Sustainable Development Department Best Practices Series." Inter-American Development Bank.

Majumdar, Sumit R., Elizabeth A. Almasi, and Randall S. Stafford. 2004. "Promotion and Prescribing of Hormone Therapy after Report of Harm by the Women's Health Initiative." *Journal of the American Medical Association* 292 (16): 1983–88.

Malthus, Thomas. 1809. *An Essay on the Principle of Population*, Vol. 2, 3rd ed. Roger Chew Weightman.

Manuamorn, Ornsaran Pomme. 2007. "Scaling Up Microinsurance: The Case of Weather Insurance for Smallholders in India." Agriculture and Rural Development Discussion Paper 36. World Bank.

Mas, Ignacio. 2009. "The Economics of Branchless Banking." *Innovations* 4 (2): 57–75.

Mas, Ignacio, and Daniel Radcliffe. 2010. "Mobile Payments Go Viral: M-PESA in Kenya." Bill & Melinda Gates Foundation.

Matin, Imran. 1997a. "Repayment Performance of Grameen Bank Borrowers: The 'Unzipped' State." *Savings and Development* 21 (4): 451–70.

———. 1997b. "The Renegotiation of Joint Liability: Notes from Madhupur." In *Who Needs Credit? Poverty and Finance in Bangladesh*, edited by Geoffrey D. Wood and Iffath A. Sharif, pp. 261–70. Zed Books.

Matin, Imran, and Rabeya Yasmin. 2004. "Managing Scaling Up Challenges of a Program for the Poorest: Case Study of BRAC's IGVGD Program." In *Scaling Up Poverty Reduction: Case Studies in Microfinance*, edited by CGAP and World Bank, pp. 77–94. Washington, D.C.

Maurer, Klaus. 2004. "Bank Rakyat Indonesia: Twenty Years of Large-Scale Microfinance." In *Scaling Up Poverty Reduction: Case Studies in Microfinance*, edited by CGAP and World Bank, pp. 95–106. Washington, D.C.

Mayoux, Linda. 2006. "Women's Empowerment through Sustainable Microfinance: Rethinking 'Best Practice.'" *Development Bulletin* 57 (February): 76–81.

McKenzie, David, and Christopher Woodruff. 2008. "Experimental Evidence on Returns to Capital and Access to Finance in Mexico." *World Bank Economic Review* 22 (3): 457–82.

Menning, Carol Bresnahan. 1993. *Charity and State in Late Renaissance Italy: The Monte di Pietà of Florence*. Cornell University Press.

Meyer, Richard L. 2007. "Measuring the Impact of Microfinance." In *What's Wrong with Microfinance?* edited by Thomas Dichter and Malcolm Harper, pp. 225–40. Practical Action Publishing.

Microfinance Enhancement Facility (2011). "Quarterly Factsheet: December 2010."

Mishra, Pramod Kumar. 1997. *Agricultural Risk, Insurance and Income: A Study of the Impact and Design of India's Comprehensive Crop Insurance Scheme*. Aldershot, U.K.

MIX (Microfinance Information eXchange). 2010. 2009 MFI Benchmarks.

MkNelly, Barbara, and Christopher Dunford. 1998. "Impact of Credit with Education on Mothers and Their Young Children's Nutrition: Lower Pra Rural Bank Credit with Education Program in Ghana." Research Paper No. 4. Freedom from Hunger.

———. 1999. "Impact of Credit with Education on Mothers and Their Young Children's Nutrition: CRECER Credit with Education Program in Bolivia." Research Paper No. 5. Freedom from Hunger.

Mohapatra, Sanket, Dilip Ratha, and Ani Silwal. 2010. "Outlook for Remittance Flows 2011–12." Migration and Development Brief 13. World Bank.

Montgomery, Richard. 1996. "Disciplining or Protecting the Poor? Avoiding the Social Costs of Peer Pressure in Micro-credit Schemes." *Journal of International Development* 8 (2): 289–305.

Moody, J. Carroll, and Gilbert C. Fite. 1971. *The Credit Union Movement: Origins and Development 1850–1970.* University of Nebraska Press.

Morduch, Jonathan. 1995. "Income Smoothing and Consumption Smoothing." *Journal of Economic Perspectives* 9 (3): 103–14.

———. 1998. "Does Microfinance Really Help the Poor? New Evidence from Flagship Programs in Bangladesh." Mimeo (j.mp/bC3Tge).

———. 1999. "The Role of Subsidies in Microfinance: Evidence from the Grameen Bank." *Journal of Development Economics* 60 (1): 229–48.

———. 2000. "The Microfinance Schism." *World Development* 28 (4): 617–29.

———. 2001. "Rainfall Insurance and Vulnerability: Economic Principles and Cautionary Notes." New York University.

———. 2006. "Microinsurance: The Next Revolution?" In *Understanding Poverty*, edited by Abhijit Banerjee, Roland Benabou, and Dilip Mookherjee, pp. 337–56. Oxford University Press.

Morduch, Jonathan, and Barbara Haley. 2002. "Analysis of the Effects of Microfinance on Poverty Reduction." Working Paper 1014. Robert F. Wagner Graduate School of Public Service, New York University.

Murthi, Mamta, Anne-Catherine Guio, and Jean Drèze. 1995. "Mortality, Fertility and Gender Bias in India: A District Level Analysis." *Population and Development Review* 21 (4): 745–82.

Mushinski, David, and Ronnie J. Phillips. 2008. "The Role of Morris Plan Lending Institutions in Expanding Consumer Micro-credit in the United States." In *Entrepreneurship in Emerging Domestic Markets: Barriers & Innovation*, edited by Glenn Yago, James R. Barth, and Betsy Zeidman, pp. 121–40. Milken Institute.

Narayan, Deepa, Lant Pritchett, and Soumya Kapoor. 2009. *Moving Out of Poverty: Success from the Bottom Up.* World Bank.

OED (Operations Evaluation Department), World Bank. 1994. *OED Précis* 60 (February).

Patten, Richard H., and Jay K. Rosengard. 1991. *Progress with Profits: The Development of Rural Banking in Indonesia.* ICS Press.

Patten, Richard H., Jay K. Rosengard, and Don E. Johnston Jr. 2001. "Microfinance Success amidst Macroeconomic Failure: The Experience of Bank Rakyat Indonesia during the East Asian Crisis." *World Development* 29 (6): 1057–69.

Peachey, Stephen, and Alan Roe. 2005. "Access to Finance: Measuring the Contribution of Savings Banks." World Savings Banks Institute.

Persons, W. Frank., and others. 1931. "The Small Loan Business." *American Economic Review* 21 (1): 11–26.

Piesse, Charles. 1841. *Sketch of the Loan Fund System in Ireland.* Alexander Thom.

Pitt, Mark M. 1999. "Reply to Jonathan Morduch's 'Does Microfinance Really Help the Poor? New Evidence from Flagship Programs in Bangladesh.'" Brown University (j.mp/dLNltJ).

Pitt, Mark M. 2011. "Response to Roodman and Morduch's 'The Impact of Microcredit on the Poor in Bangladesh: Revisiting the Evidence.'" Brown University (j.mp/j4x2xV).

Pitt, Mark M., and Shahidur R. Khandker. 1998. "The Impact of Group-Based Credit on Poor Households in Bangladesh: Does the Gender of Participants Matter?" *Journal of Political Economy* 106 (5): 958–96.

Pitt, Mark M., and others. 1999. "Credit Programs for the Poor and Reproductive Behavior in Low Income Countries: Are the Reported Causal Relationships the Result of Heterogeneity Bias?" *Demography* 36 (1): 1–21.

Planet Rating. 2009. *Lift Above Poverty Organization (LAPO), Nigeria.* Paris.

Porteous, David. 2006. "Competition and Microcredit Interest Rates." Focus Note No. 33. CGAP.

Prahalad, C.K. 2006. *The Fortune at the Bottom of the Pyramid: Eradicating Poverty through Profits.* Wharton School Publishing.

ProCredit Holding. 2011. *Annual Report 2010.*

Rahman, Aminur. 1999a. "Micro-credit Initiatives for Equitable and Sustainable Development: Who Pays?" *World Development* 27 (1): 67–82.

———. 1999b. *Women and Microcredit in Rural Bangladesh: Anthropological Study of the Rhetoric and Realities of Grameen Bank Lending.* Westview Press.

Rajagopalan, Shashi. 2005. "Micro-credit and Women's Empowerment: The Lokadrusti Case." In *Micro-credit, Poverty and Empowerment: Linking the Triad,* edited by Neera Burra, Joy Deshmukh-Ranadive, and Ranjani K. Murthy, pp. 245–85. Sage Publications.

Ravallion, Martin. 2009. "Should the Randomistas Rule?" *Economists' Voice* 6 (2): article 6.

Reed, Larry R. 2011. *State of the Microcredit Summit Campaign Report.* Microcredit Summit Campaign.

Reille, Xavier, and others. 2011. "Foreign Capital Investment in Microfinance: Reassessing Financial and Social Return." Focus Note. CGAP.

Reynolds, Paul, and others. 2002. *Global Entrepreneurship Monitor: 2001 Summary Report.* London Business School and Babson College.

Rhyne, Elisabeth. 1994. "A New View of Finance Program Evaluation." In *The New World of Microenterprise Finance: Building Healthy Financial Institutions for the Poor,* edited by María Otero and Elisabeth Rhyne, pp. 105–16. Kumarian Press.

———. 2001. *Mainstreaming Microfinance: How Lending to the Poor Began, Grew, and Came of Age in Bolivia.* Bloomfield, Conn.: Kumarian Press.

———. 2010. Testimony before the Subcommittee on International Monetary Policy and Trade, Committee on Financial Services, U.S. House of Representatives, January 27 (j.mp/coCFIh).

Rhyne, Elisabeth, and Linda S. Rotblatt. 1994. *What Makes Them Tick? Exploring the Anatomy of Major Microenterprise Finance Organizations.* Monograph Series No. 9. Acción International.

Robinson, Marguerite S. 2002. *The Microfinance Revolution: Volume 2: Lessons from Indonesia.* World Bank and Open Society Institute.

Roodman, David. 2007a. "The Anarchy of Numbers: Aid, Development, and Cross-Country Empirics." *World Bank Economic Review* 21 (2): 255–77.

———. 2007b. "Macro Aid Effectiveness Research: A Guide for the Perplexed." Working Paper 135. Center for Global Development.

———. 2009. "A Note on the Theme of Too Many Instruments." *Oxford Bulletin of Economics and Statistics* 71 (1): 135–58.

———. 2011. "Fitting Fully Observed Recursive Mixed-Process Models with cmp." *Stata Journal* 11 (2): 159–206.

Roodman, David, and Jonathan Morduch. 2009. "The Impact of Microcredit on the Poor in Bangladesh: Revisiting the Evidence." Working Paper 174. Center for Global Development.

Roodman, David, and Uzma Qureshi. 2006. "Microfinance as Business." Working Paper 101. Center for Global Development.

Rosenberg, Richard. 2007. "CGAP Reflections on the Compartamos Initial Public Offering: A Case Study on Microfinance Interest Rates and Profits." Focus Note 42. CGAP.

———. 2010. "Does Microcredit Really Help Poor People?" Focus Note 59. CGAP.

Rosenberg, Richard, Adrian Gonzalez, and Sushma Narain. 2009. "The New Money-lenders: Are the Poor Being Exploited by High Microcredit Interest Rates?" Occasional Paper 15. CGAP.

Rossi, Peter H. 1987. "The Iron Law of Evaluation and Other Metallic Rules." *Research in Social Problems and Public Policy* 4: 3–20.

Roth, Jim, Michael J. McCord, and Dominic Liber. 2007. *The Landscape of Microinsurance in the World's 100 Poorest Countries.* Microinsurance Centre.

Rozas, Daniel. 2009. "Throwing in the Towel: Lessons from MFI Liquidations." (j.mp/dlm1tv).

———. 2011. *Weathering the Storm: Hazards, Beacons, and Life Rafts: Case Studies.* Center for Financial Inclusion.

Rozell, Ned. 2003. "When Reindeer Paradise Turned to Purgatory." *Alaska Science Forum,* article 1672.

Rutherford, Stuart. 2004. *Grameen II at the End of 2003: A 'Grounded View' of How Grameen's New Initiative Is Progressing in the Villages.* MicroSave.

———. 2006. *Grameen II: The First Five Years, 2001–2005.* MicroSave.

———. 2008. "Managing Growth of MFIs: ASA Bangladesh—Single-minded Growth." MicroSave.

———. 2009a. *The Poor and Their Money: Microfinance from a Twenty-first Century Consumer's Perspective.* 2nd ed. Practical Action Publishing.

———. 2009b. *The Pledge: ASA, Peasant Politics, and Microfinance in the Development of Bangladesh.* Oxford University Press.

Sanyal, Paromita. 2007. "Credit versus Coalition: Exploring the Influence of Micro-finance Programs on Women's Agency." Paper presented at the annual meeting of the American Sociological Association, New York, Aug 11. allacademic.com/meta/p183905_index.html.

Saulnier, Raymond J. 1940. "Industrial Banking Companies and Their Credit Practices." Studies in Consumer Instalment Financing 4. National Bureau of Economic
Research.

Schumpeter, Joseph A. 1934. *The Theory of Economic Development: An Inquiry into Profits, Capital, Credit, Interest, and the Business Cycle.* Oxford University Press.

———. 1976. *Capital, Socialism, and Democracy.* 5th ed. George Allen & Unwin Ltd.

Schwartz, D., and J. Lellouch. 1967. "Explanatory and Pragmatic Attitudes in Therapeu-
tical Trials." *Journal of Chronic Diseases* 20 (8): 637–48.

Schwarzbach, David. 2006. "Center for Global Development." Presentation at "Using
Smart Cards to 'Bank' the Unbanked and Evaluate Programs." Center for Global
Development, Washington, D.C., June 14. cgdev.org/content/calendar/detail/8069.

Seibel, Hans Dieter. 2005. "Does History Matter? The Old and the New World of
Microfinance in Europe and Asia." Paper presented at "From Moneylenders to
Microfinance: Southeast Asia's Credit Revolution in Institutional, Economic and
Cultural Perspective." Asia Research Institute, National University of Singapore,
October 7–8.

Sen, Amartya. 1999. *Development as Freedom.* Anchor Books.

Shaw, Edward S. 1973. *Financial Deepening in Economic Development.* Oxford University Press.

Sheridan, Thomas. 1787. *The Life of the Rev. Dr. Jonathan Swift, Dean of St. Patrick's,
Dublin.* 2nd ed.

Silva, Alex. 2005. "Investing in Microfinance—Profund's Story." *Small Enterprise Development* 16 (1): 17–29.

Sinha, Frances. 2006. *Self Help Groups in India: A Study of the Lights and Shades.* EDA
Rural Systems Private Ltd. and Andhra Pradesh Mahila Abhivruddhi Society.

———. 2007. "SHGs in India: Numbers Yes, Poverty Outreach and Empowerment,
Partially." In *What's Wrong with Microfinance?* edited by Thomas Dichter and Malcolm Harper, pp. 73–82. Practical Action Publishing.

Skees, Jerry. 2007. "Challenges for Use of Index-Based Weather Insurance in Lower
Income Countries." GlobalAgRisk.

Skees, Jerry, Peter Hazell, and Mario Miranda. 1999. "New Approaches to Crop Yield
Insurance in Developing Countries." EPTD Discussion Paper No. 55. International
Food Policy Research Institute.

Slovic, Paul. 1987. "Perception of Risk." *Science* 236 (4799): 280–85.

Smillie, Ian. 2009. *Freedom from Want: The Remarkable Success Story of BRAC, the Global
Grassroots Organization That's Winning the Fight against Poverty.* Kumarian Press.

Smith, Adam. 1812. *An Inquiry in the Nature and Causes of the Wealth of Nations.* 4th ed.
Volume 1. William Baynes. j.mp/pFDDrI.

Solow, Robert M. 1994. "Perspectives on Growth Theory." *Journal of Economic Perspectives* 8 (1): 45–54.

Srinivasan, N. 2009. *Microfinance India: State of the Sector Report 2009.* Sage.

———. 2010a. *Microfinance India: State of the Sector Report 2010.* Sage.

———. 2010b. "Is the 99% Repayment Rate an Illusion?" *Microfinance Insights* 16:10–12.

Steinwand, Dirk. 2001. *The Alchemy of Microfinance: The Evolution of the Indonesian People's Credit Banks (BPR) from 1895 to 1999 and a Contemporary Analysis.* Verlag für Wissenschaft und Forschung.

Sterling, Theodore D. 1959. "Publication Decisions and Their Possible Effects on Inferences Drawn from Tests of Significance—Or Vice Versa." *Journal of the American Statistical Association* 54 (285): 30–34.

Stiglitz, Joseph. 1990. "Peer Monitoring and Credit Markets." *World Bank Economic Review* 4(3): 351–66.

Sullivan, Nicholas P. 2007. *You Can Hear Me Now: How Microloans and Cell Phones Are Connecting the World's Poor to the Global Economy.* Jossey-Bass.

Swanson, Brad. 2008. "The Role of International Capital Markets in Microfinance." Developing World Markets (dwmarkets.com/media/pdf-international-capital-markets.pdf).

Tanner, Norman P., ed. 1990. *Decrees of the Ecumenical Councils.* Georgetown University Press (papalencyclicals.net/Councils/ecum18.htm).

Tendler, Judith. 1983. "Ventures in the Informal Sector, and How They Worked Out in Brazil." Evaluation Special Study 21. U.S. Agency for International Development.

Tilly, Richard. 1994. "A Short History of the German Banking System." In *Handbook on the History of European Banks*, edited by Manfred Pohl and Sabine Freitag, pp. 299–312. Edward Elgar.

Toaff, Ariel. 2004. "Jews, Franciscans, and the First *Monti di Pietà* in Italy (1462–1500)." In *Friars and Jews in the Middle Ages and Renaissance*, edited by Steven J. McMichael and Susan E. Myers, pp. 239–53. Brill.

Todd, Helen. 1996. *Women at the Center: Grameen Bank Borrowers after One Decade.* University Press Limited.

Townsend, John P. 1878. "Savings Banks." *Journal of Social Science* 9: 44–66.

Tucker, Donald S. 1922. *The Evolution of People's Banks.* Longmans, Green & Co.

Tullock, Gordon. 1959. "Publication Decisions and Tests of Significance—A Comment." *Journal of the American Statistical Association* 54 (287): 593.

Turnell, Sean. 2005. "The Rise and Fall of Cooperative Credit in Colonial Burma." Research Paper 0509. Macquarie University, Department of Economics.

———. 2009. *Fiery Dragons: Banks, Moneylenders and Microfinance in Burma.* Nordic Institute of Asian Studies.

Velasco, Carmen, and Saiko Chiba. 2006. "Expanding Impact: Innovations in Cost-Effectively Integrating Microfinance with Education in Health." Pro Mujer.

Visser, Wayne, and Alastair McIntosh. 1998. "A Short Review of the Historical Critique of Usury." *Accounting, Business & Financial History* 8 (2): 175–89.

Wakefield, Priscilla. 1802. "Extract from an Account of a Female Benefit Club, at Tottenham." In *Reports of the Society for Bettering the Condition and Increasing the Comforts of the Poor.* Vol. 3.

———. 1805. "Extract from an Account of a Charitable Bank at Tottenham for the Savings of the Poor." In *Reports of the Society for Bettering the Condition and Increasing the Comforts of the Poor*, Vol. 4.

Watkins, Calvert. 2000. *The American Heritage Dictionary of Indo-European Roots.* Houghton Mifflin.

Westley, Glenn. 2004. "A Tale of Four Village Banking Programs: Best Practices in Latin America." Inter-American Development Bank.

Westley, Glenn, and Xavier Martin Palomas. 2010. "Is There a Business Case for Small Savers?" Occasional Paper 18. CGAP.

Wilken, Robert Louis. 2003. *The Christians as the Romans Saw Them.* 2nd ed. Yale University Press.

Wilson, Kim. 2010. "Jipange Sasa." In *Financial Promise for the Poor: How Groups Build Microsavings,* edited by Kim Wilson, Malcolm Harper, and Matthew Griffith, pp. 99–107. Kumarian Press.

Wilson, Kim, Malcolm Harper, and Matthew Griffith. 2010. *Financial Promise for the Poor: How Groups Build Microsavings.* Kumarian Press.

Winker, Kevin, and others. 2002. "The Birds of St. Matthew Island, Bering Sea." *Wilson Bulletin* 114 (4): 491–509.

Wolff, Henry W. 1896. *People's Banks: A Record of Social and Economic Success.* 2nd ed. P.S. King & Son.

———. 1898. *Village Banks or Agricultural Credit Societies for Small Occupiers, Village Tradesmen, Etc.: How to Start Them, How to Work Them, What the Rich May Do to Help Them.* 2nd ed. P.S. King & Son.

———. 1927. *Co-operation in India.* 2nd ed. W. Thacker and Company.

World Bank. 2005. *Managing Agricultural Production Risk: Innovations in Developing Countries.*

———. 2011. *World Development Indicators* (publications.worldbank.org/WDI).

World Bank and ING Bank. 2006. *The Role of Postal Networks in Expanding Access to Financial Services,* Vol. 1.

WOCCU (World Council of Credit Unions). 2010. *Statistical Report 2009* (j.mp/ hG39UY).

Wright, Graham, Mosharraf Hossain, and Stuart Rutherford. 1997. "Savings: Flexible Financial Services for the Poor (And Not Just for the Implementing Organization)." In *Who Needs Credit? Poverty and Finance in Bangladesh,* edited by Geoffrey D. Wood and Iffath A. Sharif, pp. 309–49. Zed Books.

Writing Group for the Women's Health Initiative Investigators. 2002. "Risks and Benefits of Estrogen plus Progestin in Healthy Postmenopausal Women: Principal Results from the Women's Health Initiative Randomized Controlled Trial." *Journal of the American Medical Association* 288 (3): 321–33.

Yunus, Muhammad. 2002. "Grameen Bank II: Designed to Open New Possibilities." Grameen Bank (j.mp/au1Rcd).

———. 2004. *Banker to the Poor: Micro-lending and the Battle against World Poverty.* PublicAffairs.

———. 2010. *Building Social Business: The New Kind of Capitalism That Serves Humanity's Most Pressing Needs.* PublicAffairs.

Index

Estrogen study, 154–55
European Fund, 276
Evolutionary perspective. *See* Business
    evolution perspective, microfinance
    institutions

Fedecrédito, El Salvador, 81–82
Feedback problem, information lag,
    243–45, 246–48
Fee fairness, in freedom argument, 178–
    86. *See also* Costs, financial services
Fernandez, Aloysius, 28–29, 85–86
Fernard, Lia, 166–67
Filene, Edward, 59, 60
Financial crisis (2008), 281
Financial services, in Schumpeter's the-
    ory, 226–27
Financial services, purposes: overview,
    15–16; microenterprise expectations,
    24–29; for poor people, 19–24, 29–35;
    for rich people, 16–19. *See also* His-
    tory of microfinance
FINCA (Foundation for International
    Community Assistance), 84, 103, 124,
    140
Findesa, 257–58
First Macro Bank study, Philippines,
    167–69
Fisher, Clyde Olin, 188
A Fistful of Rice (Akula), 128–29
Flat rate interest, 187
Flexibility factor, in freedom argument,
    192–96
Fontela, Delia, 142
Forced savings requirement. *See* Savings
    accounts
Ford Foundation, 79, 233
Foreign aid philosophies, 70–74
For-profit banks, U.S. beginnings, 60–62
For-profit evolution, microfinance insti-
    tutions, 106–09, 232–34
Foundation for International Community
    Assistance (FINCA), 84, 103, 124, 140

France, foreign aid philosophy, 70
Freedom arguments, microfinance
    impact: overview, 11–12, 175–78, 202,
    218–20, 269–70; contract reliability,
    191–92; empowerment quantifica-
    tion studies, 202–04; group dynamics,
    196–97; multiple borrowing problem,
    197–202; pricing fairness, 178–86;
    repayment flexibility, 192–96; trans-
    parency practices, 186–91
Freedom arguments, microfinance
    impact, qualitative studies: debt
    burden stories, 204–07, 210, 212–13;
    group microcredit stories, 209–18;
    individual microcredit stories, 207–09
Freedom from Hunger, 104–05, 106, 151
Friedman, Milton, 97
Friendly societies, 42, 46–47, 48, 51, 58
Frugality banks, 48
FUNDES, 234

Galbraith, John Kenneth, 246
Gates Foundation, 115
Gender patterns: overview, 99–102; in
    borrower classification study, 145–46;
    bundled services, 104–05; in business
    evolution perspective, 122, 126–27;
    Grameen Bank loans, 79; India's
    self-help groups, 87; Ireland's his-
    toric credit system, 37; microfinance
    impact study problems, 161–65; as
    microfinance theme, 126–27; savings
    accounts, 32–33. *See also entries under*
    Freedom arguments; Group-oriented
    financial services
Germany, 48, 50, 53–56, 57, 63, 180
Gesellschaft für Technische Zusammen-
    arbeit (GTZ) agency, 86, 92, 96
Ghate, Prabhu, 194
Gibbons, David, 25, 145–46
Giné, Xavier, 121
Gladstone, William, 50
Glennerster, Rachel, 169–70

The Center for Global Development

The Center for Global Development works to reduce global poverty and inequality through rigorous research and active engagement with the policy community to make the world a more prosperous, just, and safe place for us all. The policies and practices of the rich and the powerful—in rich nations, as well as in the emerging powers, international institutions, and global corporations—have significant impacts on the world's poor people. We aim to improve these policies and practices through research and policy engagement to expand opportunities, reduce inequalities, and improve lives everywhere. By pairing research with action, CGD goes beyond contributing to knowledge about development. We conceive of and advocate for practical policy innovations in areas such as trade, aid, health, education, climate change, labor mobility, private investment, access to finance, and global governance to foster shared prosperity in an increasingly interdependent world.